Keto
Cooking Book
for Beginners

2000 Quick & Easy Keto Recipes and Meal Plans for Beginners
to Start the Ketogenic Diet and Lifestyle

Soledad Bruce

Table of Contents

1   **Introduction**

2   **Fundamentals of Keto Diet**

11   **4-Week Diet Plan**

13   **Chapter 1 Breakfast and Smoothies**

24   **Chapter 2 Snacks and Appetizers**

35   **Chapter 3 Soups, Salad, Stews and Chill**

44   **Chapter 4 Poultry Mains**

57   **Chapter 5 Beef, Pork, and Lambs**

70   **Chapter 6 Fish and Seafood**

87   **Chapter 7 Vegetables and Sides**

95   **Chapter 8 Dessert and Drinks**

105   **Chapter 9 Sauces, Staples, and Dressings**

113   **Conclusion**

114   **Appendix 1 Measurement Conversion Chart**

115   **Appendix 2 Recipes Index**

Introduction

The ketogenic (or keto) diet is a high-fat, moderate protein, and low-carb eating plan. The keto diet has become a popular method for people to lose weight and improve their health. The success of the keto diet is that it trains your body to stop relying on sugar for energy, and it means no more blood sugar spikes causing a rise in insulin levels. Too much sugar in meals may cause poor health and weight loss.

The keto diet demands that you cut down on carbohydrates in your food. This low-carb diet is very simple to adopt, and you don't need to sacrifice your favorite foods. Keto encourages fresh fruits, veggies, lean protein, seeds, nuts, and healthy vegetable oils such as olive oil, avocado oil, etc. There are several ways to help improve health, your body's immune system, and metabolism, and the keto diet is one of these.

Not only can the keto diet promote weight loss, but it also comes with various other health benefits: It lowers cholesterol, manages diabetes, reduces the risk and symptoms of polycystic ovary syndrome, lowers the risk of cardiovascular disease, improves mental clarity and lowers the risk of some cancers.

Come with me, and I will guide you through the ketogenic diet. I'm delighted to be able to show you all the delicious ways to make keto-friendly and low-carb recipes. Making a plan and preparing healthy food is an essential key to success.

Keto works better than any diet, as it causes your body to produce small fuel molecules called ketones. When you eat low-carb foods, your liver produces ketones from fat. These ketones are the fuel source for the whole body and brain. Moreover, the brain is a hungry organ that uses more energy daily and can run on ketones or glucose.

There are various types of the ketogenic diet. SKD (standard ketogenic diet), CKD (cyclical ketogenic diet), and TKD (targeted ketogenic diet). However, only SKD has been studied extensively. Following a ketogenic diet is the most effective way to come into ketosis, helping you to lose weight. Keep reading to find out more!

Fundamentals of Keto Diet

Why Should We Go Keto?

You may have many questions about the keto diet: Can it really help me to lose weight? What are the other benefits? Why should I go keto? What am I allowed to eat on this diet? What foods are forbidden? Here you'll get the answers to all of your questions, so keep reading!

There are many health benefits of this diet. It reduces your appetite, blood sugar and insulin levels, lowers blood pressure, and improves cholesterol levels. This diet encourages you to eat the following foods: Seafood, meat and poultry, eggs, cheese, unsweetened plant-based milk, veggies, nuts, seeds, dark chocolate, berries, olive oil, tea, etc.

The standard ketogenic diet macronutrients requirements are as follows:

Fats	75%
Protein	20%
Carbohydrate	5%

20% calories from protein: Cheese, meat, eggs, etc.

5% calories from carbohydrates: For example, non-starchy veggies and small amounts of leafy veggies.

75% calories from fat: For example, vegetable oil, unprocessed nuts, avocado, olives, and butter

What Is the Keto Diet?

The ketogenic (or keto, for short) diet has gained in popularity around the world. Many people have chosen to adopt this diet in order to lose weight effectively. Many studies show that this type of diet can not only help you to lose weight but also improve your health. If you follow this diet, it will help you to stay healthy and active. It has many health benefits in fighting against epilepsy, diabetes, cancer, and Alzheimer's disease. The keto diet is similar to the Atkins diet and other low-carb diets.

Different Types of the Keto Diet

There are four types of keto diet:

Standard Ketogenic Diet (SKD): The standard keto diet is a low-carb, high-fat, and moderate-protein diet. It contains 10% carbs, 20% protein, and 70% fat.

Targeted Ketogenic Diet (TKD): TKD diet allows you to add carbs during workouts.

Cyclical Ketogenic Diet (CKD): It contains higher carbs, for example, five keto days and two high-carb days weekly.

High-Protein Ketogenic Diet: This diet is similar to SKD but contains more protein. It contains 35% protein 60% fat, and 5% carbs.

What Is Ketosis?

When you restrict the amount of carbohydrates you eat, your body needs to find an alternative fuel source. Once your liver starts preparing your body for the fuel change, the fat from the liver will start producing ketones. Ketosis is a metabolic state in which the human body uses fat for fuel instead of carbs. If you follow the ketogenic diet, it's the most effective way to enter ketosis. It contains a limiting carb intake of around 20 to 50 grams daily and intakes of high amounts of fat from meat,

fish, olives, nuts, oils, eggs, etc.

The chart below provides the carbohydrate contents of commonly eaten foods for reference (fats, poultry, and meats don't contain high amounts of carbs).

Food	Serving size	Carbs (gram)	Calories
Potato	1 big, baked, plain	56	283
Rice	1 cup, white or brown	50	223
Oatmeal	1 cup, dry	49	339
Pinto beans (cooked)	1 cup	45	245
Bagel	1, whole	44	245
Yogurt	1 cup, fruit-flavored, full-fat	42	225
Corn (cooked)	1 cup	41	177
Spaghetti	1 cup	40	221
Pizza	1 slice, cheese	39	290
Apple juice	1 cup	28	113
Sweet potato	1 big	28	118
Orange juice	1 cup	26	112
English muffin	1 whole	25	130
Waffle	1 (7-inch diameter)	25	218
Banana	1 medium	24	105
Apple	1 medium	21	81
Cereal, ready to eat	1 cup	18	103
Pancake	1 (5-inch diameter)	15	90
Milk	1 cup	12	103
Bread	1 slice, white	12	66
Green peas	½ cup	12	63
Strawberries	1 cup	11	45
Cucumber	1 (8-inch diameter)	9	47
Yellow onion	1 medium	8	44
Broccoli	1 stalk	6	51
Zucchini	1 medium	4	33
Carrot	1 medium	4	25
Tomato	1 medium	3	22
White mushrooms	1 cup	2	15
Egg	1 large	0.6	78
Spinach	1 cup	0.4	7

Macronutrients

Carbohydrates, proteins, and fats are called macronutrients or macros. They all provide your body with energy in different ways:

Carbohydrates: Carbs are present in foods such as potatoes, pasta, rice, and bread. These are broken down in the digestive system and release glucose into the blood. Glucose is a source of energy for your body, and it's absorbed rapidly from the digestive tract and transported to the body's cells.

Fats: Fats are a concentrated source of energy, providing the body with more energy per gram than carbohydrates and protein. Fats are slowly digested and need a significant amount of oxygen to convert into ketones that can be burned for energy.

Protein: You need to eat a moderate amount of protein in the keto diet. It's not used for energy except when there is an insufficient supply. If the body is denied glucose, protein is converted into ketones that can be used as fuel for the body.

COOKED MEATS AND PROTEIN (in packets, jars, or cans)	LOW-CARB VEGGIES (in jars or cans)	FATS
Ground beef	Pickles	Olive oil
Chicken	Roasted red bell pepper	Avocado oil
Sardines	Diced tomatoes with green chilies	Ghee
Tuna	Olives	Coconut oil
Nuts and seed butters (almond, peanut, etc.)	Collard greens	Sesame oil
Shrimp	Chipotle peppers	Tallow
Crab meat	Artichoke hearts	Mayonnaise

How Does Ketosis Work?

Standard Diet: Higher Carbohydrate

Step: 1
Eating a higher-carb diet
Step: 2
Glucose levels increase
Step: 3
Pancreas secretes insulin
Step: 4
Insulin allows glucose to enter cells
Step: 5
Energy

Keto Diet: Low-Carb, High Fat

Step: 1
Eating a low-carb diet
Step: 2
Glucose levels drop
Step: 3
Release of stored fatty acids
Step: 4
Fatty acids travel to the liver
Step: 5
Energy – liver produces ketones

There are four major indicators of a body switching into ketosis:

- Energy boost – without carbs, your body now has an excellent fuel source that makes you feel more energetic.
- No more sugar cravings – carbs are highly addictive, and if you eat them daily, you'll keep craving them. Once you cast them out from your diet, you're less likely to want them as much anymore.
- Keto breath – you might detect an odd off-apple scent to your breath. This will only last for a short time, but in the meantime, ensure you're drinking enough water to prevent a dry mouth.
- Testing - to know if your body has entered ketosis, you can use a specialized breath test, urine test strips, or blood analysis.

What to Remember While Following the Keto Diet

To achieve true ketosis and avoid any kind of nutritional deficiencies, visit a nutritionist or a registered dietician before starting the keto diet. It's easy to create an electrolyte imbalance while on the diet plan as you're not permitted to eat many food items from which you get electrolytes, such as vegetables, fruits, and certain grains.

Furthermore, paying attention to the type of fats you consume is critical. As a particular amount of fat is necessary, the keto diet includes all forms of saturated and unsaturated fats. You must try to balance the amount of fat you consume by adding healthier fats. Some healthy sources of fats are olives, fatty fish, nuts, and avocados.

The Length of the Keto Diet

All it needs is 28 days to see a massive transformation. If you want to keep losing weight, you must stick to the diet's principles. You can't walk out and follow your old meal plan. You can easily keep to a low-carb diet as long as you know how to navigate carb-heavy situations like vacations or social gatherings. You just have to eat mindfully.

How to Bring Carbs Back into Your Diet?

Most people who lose weight following a diet regain it within a year. In order to lose weight, it's advised to lower your calorie intake slowly from 2000-1200 calories a day. A gradual and diligent decrease in your calorie intake can help immensely in maintaining weight loss and its associated health benefits, particularly if exercise is the focal point in your weekly regimen.

The Benefits of the Ketogenic Diet

The ketogenic diet can be highly beneficial for your health. From weight loss to longevity, there are advantages that following a ketogenic diet can bring to your life. You will feel healthier, happier, and more energetic.

Weight loss:

On a ketogenic diet, you'll lose weight as the body is forced to generate fewer amounts of glucose, lowering insulin production. When this happens, your kidneys will begin eliminating extra sodium, leading to weight loss.

Loss of appetite:

On a ketogenic diet, you won't feel tired or dull. Once you train your body to run on a low-carb and high-fat diet, you'll experience a drop in appetite and will also feel more energetic. You'll also find that your focus and concentration improve significantly.

Lowered risk of diabetes:

When you cut out the carbs in your diet, your body is forced to lower glucose production, which leads to a lower risk of diabetes.

HDL cholesterol increased and blood pressure lowered:

When you consume a diet including healthy fats, your body will experience a rise in good HDL cholesterol levels, reducing the risk of cardiovascular problems. Cutting out carbs will also reduce your blood pressure, helping to prevent many health problems such as heart disease or stroke.

Improved brain function:

Research shows that replacing carbs with fat as an energy source leads to improved brain function and mental clarity. It's one of the best reasons why you should go keto.

Should I try the keto diet?

As you can see, the ketogenic diet has many health benefits. It helps with weight loss and lowers the risk of diabetes. If you follow the ketogenic diet while also exercising, you'll join the many other people worldwide who have successfully lost weight this way.

If you're beginning the keto diet on your own, you'll need to familiarize yourself with the foods you can and can't eat. As you start to lose weight and learn how to customize your meals, the keto diet plan will become a natural part of your lifestyle, allowing you to maintain your health and weight loss.

The Side Effects of Ketosis

The keto diet has many benefits, but it may come with some side effects. One of the signs of ketosis may include "keto flu," which includes symptoms such as an upset stomach, headache, and fatigue. Other symptoms of ketosis may include:

- Bad breath ("keto breath")
- Constipation
- Insomnia
- Dehydration
- Low bone density (osteopenia) and bone fractures
- High cholesterol (hyperlipidemia)
- Kidney stones

Keto Cooking

Switching the human body from glucose-burning to fat-burning is a huge change. When you're a beginner in the ketogenic diet, it's essential to observe your electrolyte levels, focus on the right foods, and get a lot of rest. Electrolytes are chemicals and nutrients in your body that have vital functions, such as preserving cellular function, stimulating the muscles, regulating your heartbeat, and more. If electrolytes are out of balance, you'll feel tired.

To minimize the side effects, manage your electrolytes in the following ways:

- Firstly, drink plenty of water.
- Add pink Himalayan salt, meat or vegetable broth, or pickle juice to your diet.
- Eat foods rich in potassium but low in sugar, for example, avocado and spinach.

- Get a lot of rest because your body is healing.
- Eat foods rich in magnesium, for example, spinach, fish, nuts, and artichoke.

Drink plenty of water:

If you're following the ketogenic diet, you'll need to drink more water than usual in the early stages. Carbs in your body hold onto water; when you stop eating them, your body will start to release that water, and you'll need to replace it. For example, if you weigh 200 pounds, you must drink at least 100 ounces of water daily.

Find easy ways to get your fats in:

It may seem challenging at first to include so much fat in your daily diet, but there are many ways to make it easier. The easiest way to consume fat is to add healthy oils or butter to your diet.

Get plenty of salt:

In a ketogenic diet, you need to eat food that has plenty of salt in it, such as vegetable or meat broth. I also suggest adding pink Himalayan salt to your meals, as it contains more minerals than table salt, such as iron, copper, magnesium, and potassium.

Kitchen Equipment

You don't need to buy fancy kitchen equipment or appliances to follow the keto diet. However, there are a few essential kitchen items for everyday use that you'll need:

Measuring cups and spoons: For baking recipes, you'll need measuring cups to measure ingredients accurately instead of guessing.

Spatula, slotted spoon, large spoon, whisk, tongs, and rubber scraper: These items are essential for mixing or picking up ingredients and food.

Cutting board: You can accurately and neatly chop, thinly slice, shred, and mince vegetables and meat with a cutting board.

Baking sheet: In many recipes, you'll need a baking sheet for a one-pan meal.

Cheese grater/zester: It's cheaper to grate cheese than to buy pre-shredded. A grater or zester can be used for a variety of recipes, such as desserts or snacks.

Baking pan: Use a baking pan for roasting meat and vegetables.

Knife: You need good quality, sharp chef's knives to cut vegetables and meat quickly and accurately.

Loaf pan: Use loaf pans for baking keto cakes and bread.

Muffin tin: You'll need a standard muffin tin for several of the recipes in this book.

Glass baking dish: These are ideal for baking desserts or making casseroles.

Saucepan: Having a small (2-quart) and a large (4.5-quart) saucepan will allow you to make most recipes.

Colander: A colander is a necessary kitchen item for rinsing vegetables and fruits. You will need a medium-sized colander for your kitchen.

Skillet: I like to use a non-stick skillet as it's easy to clean and works well for keto recipes.

Parchment paper: You'll usually need parchment paper when baking food in the oven.

Mixing bowl: You may find that you'll need at least three mixing bowls while following a recipe.

Blender: A blender is an essential kitchen appliance for making soups, coffee drinks, sauces, pastes, and fresh smoothies. Add fresh ingredients to the blender to create a delicious recipe. If you don't have a blender, you can use a food processor or a pestle and mortar.

Food processor: If you don't have a blender, you can use a food processor.

Mixer: An electric mixer is particularly helpful for preparing desserts. If you don't have one, a whisk will do.

Cooling rack: I transfer a finished dish from the oven to a cooling rack for several of these recipes.

Keto cooking staples:

- Salt
- Freshly ground black pepper
- Ghee (clarified butter, without dairy)
- Olive oil
- Grass-fed butter

Foods Allowed on the Keto Diet

To make things simpler and easier to understand, let's take a look at all the foods that you're allowed to eat while following the keto diet:

All meats

There's no meat restriction on the keto diet. Whether it's poultry, lamb, beef, or seafood, meat of all kinds can be freely eaten as they don't have sugars or extra carbs. This means you can enjoy all types of meat dishes, including shrimp, salmon, chicken, turkey, lamb, beef, crab, and lobster.

Vegetables

Keep in mind that not all vegetables are low in carbs. The following vegetables are permitted while following this diet: cauliflower, broccoli, zucchini, potato, asparagus, eggplant, bell pepper, spinach, pumpkin, lettuce, cucumber, mushroom, corn, green bean, butternut squash, and carrot.

Fruits

You can enjoy the following fruits in abundance: blueberry, strawberry, banana, orange, avocado, apple, pear, lemon, raspberry, etc. You can eat them as they are, in fresh smoothies or fruit desserts.

Cheese

You can eat mozzarella, parmesan, cheddar, goat's cheese, cream, and blue cheese.

Spices/herbs

You can use the following spices and herbs while making dishes: red pepper flakes, chili powder, curry powder, salt, black pepper, cloves, garlic powder, ginger, onion powder, turmeric, cardamom, cinnamon, parsley, basil, lettuce, dill, mint, rosemary, cilantro, oregano, bay leaf, fennel seed, thyme, sage, etc.

Healthy oils

You can use the following oils: olive oil, avocado oil, sunflower oil, canola oil, sesame oil, etc.

Nuts/seeds

Garnish your dishes with the following nuts or seeds: pumpkin seeds, almonds, walnuts, peanuts, pecans, pistachios, and hazelnuts.

Recommended Food Charts

Meats and Seafood

Chicken	Octopus
Crab	Pork (chops, bacon, etc.)
Crawfish	Quail
Duck	Sausage
Fish	Scallops
Goose	Shrimp
Lamb	Veal
Lobster	Venison

Dairy

Blue cheese dressing	Homemade whipped cream
Burrata cheese	Kefalotyri cheese
Cottage cheese	Mozzarella cheese
Cream cheese	Provolone cheese
Eggs	Queso blanco

Greek yogurt (full-fat)	Ranch dressing
Grilling cheese	Ricotta cheese
Halloumi cheese	Unsweetened almond milk
Heavy (whipping) cream	Unsweetened coconut milk

Nuts and seeds

Almonds	Pecans
Brazil nuts	Pine nuts
Chia seeds	Pumpkin seeds
Flaxseeds	Sacha inchi seeds
Hazelnuts	Sesame seeds
Macadamia nuts	Walnuts
Peanuts	

Vegetables and fruits

Alfalfa sprouts	Cucumbers
Asparagus	Garlic (in moderation)
Avocados	Green beans
Bell peppers	Herbs
Blackberries	Jicama
Blueberries	Lemons
Broccoli	Limes
Cabbage	Mushrooms
Carrots (in moderation)	Okra
Cauliflower	Olives
Celery	Onion (in moderation)
Chicory	Pickles
Coconut	Pumpkins
Cranberries	Radish
Raspberries	Strawberries
Salad greens	Tomatoes (in moderation)
Scallions	Zucchini
Spaghetti squash (in moderation)	

Foods Not Allowed on the Diet

Avoiding carbohydrates is the main goal aim of following a ketogenic diet. Other foods to avoid are:

Sugar

Sugar is not keto-friendly, including agave, honey, brown sugar, granulated sugar, maple syrup, etc. Use sugar-free sweeteners and keto sweeteners instead.

Dairy

Not all dairy products can be freely used on a keto diet, and animal milk should be strictly avoided.

Tubers

Tubers are underground-grown vegetables; some are rich in carbs, including yams, sweet potatoes, beets, etc.

Other

Alcohol, condiments containing sugar, legumes, bread, cereals, etc., should also be avoided.

Food-to-Avoid Charts

Meat and meat alternatives

Deli meat (some, not all)	Some sausage	Tofu
Hot dogs	Seitan	

Dairy

	Some sausage	Tofu
Almond milk (sweetened)	Milk	Yogurt (regular)
Coconut milk (sweetened)	Soy milk (regular)	

Nuts and seeds

Cashews	Pistachios
Chestnuts	

Fruits and vegetables

Apples	Chickpeas
Apricot	Corn
Artichokes	Currants
Banana	Dates
Beans (all varieties)	Edamame
Boysenberries	Eggplant
Burdock root	Elderberries
Butternut squash	Gooseberries
Cantaloupe	Grapes
Cherries	Honeydew melon
Huckleberries	Plums
Kiwis	Water chestnuts
Leeks	Prunes
Mangoes	Raisins
Oranges	Sweet potatoes
Parsnips	Taro root
Peaches	Winter squash
Peas	Yams
Pineapples	
Plantains	

Steps to Follow Before Going on the Keto Diet

Are you planning to achieve all your health goals by adopting the ketogenic diet? If yes, then there are certain things that you need to do before starting it.

Do your research:
Reading this cookbook is a part of your research. Memorize what you should and shouldn't be eating. Take a look at the food charts I've created for you and ensure that you follow them. Doing so is an effective way to start your keto diet journey. Remember not to eat high-carb food or drink alcohol while starting your diet. You can also read articles on the ketogenic diet, talk to health experts, ask about people's experiences with this diet, and discuss things with your dietician. This will ensure that you start your diet in the best possible way.

Consult with health experts or dieticians:
It's a good idea to speak with a physician, doctor, or dietician to discuss the keto diet and its suitability for you. You may need to complete a medical checkup before starting the diet, including checking your blood sugar levels, blood pressure, and cholesterol.

Examine your health:
Think about your existing health conditions, and start preparing for your diet accordingly. Remember to also include exercise in your new regime.

Follow the keto diet plan:
The next step is to follow the keto diet plan. In this cookbook, you'll find delicious and satisfying keto diet recipes. These recipes are divided into breakfast, lunch, dinner, desserts, snacks, etc. I've made it easy and fun to follow your new diet.

Get rid of high-carb food:
The last step is to get rid of high-carb food from your kitchen (or anywhere else you have access to it!). Start eliminating carb-rich carbohydrate foods such as sugar, granulated sugar, brown sugar, honey, maple syrup, candies, processed food, bread, flour, desserts, beverages, fast foods, etc.

How to Plan Your Keto Diet?

Meal Planning

Keto meal planning effectively saves money, effort, and time while preparing you for success on a low-carb diet. In your first week, you should notice that any changes have been followed through successfully. You'll feel good about yourself and motivated to continue with your new diet plan. But as time passes, this initial motivation may start to fade. But don't worry; remind yourself of all the benefits following the keto diet will produce.

There are three key components to include while putting together a keto meal plan for the week:

Plan low-carb meals: Select keto recipes for the first week and keep to the recipes strictly.

Start shopping for fresh ingredients: When selecting recipes, list all your ingredients and make one shopping trip.

Batch prepping: Prepare and make meals in large batches, then freeze them to reheat later.

Meal Plan Tips

Cut down on carbs:
When you start following the ketogenic diet, you must cut down on all carb-rich foods. These include honey, maple syrup, bread, alcohol, brown sugar, etc.

Stock up on keto staples:
Keep keto staples, like low-carb sweeteners and low-carb sauces, etc., in your kitchen. Also, make sure you have the following:

- Protein Sources: Seafood, meat, tofu (in moderation), and yogurt.
- Healthy Fats: Avocado, coconut oil, olive oil, nuts, eggs, coconut milk.
- Vegetables: Kale, spinach, broccoli, onions, asparagus, peppers, eggplant.
- Condiments: Keto-friendly mayonnaise, hot sauce, ketchup.

Prepare your grocery list:
After reading this cookbook, prepare your grocery list for one week's meals. You should purchase fresh, good-quality ingredients. Don't deviate from your list!

Store food in containers:
You can store food that you've batch-cooked in plastic containers and either freeze them or put them in the refrigerator.

Don't skip breakfast:
Breakfast is an essential meal, setting you up for the rest of the day. So, please don't skip it.

Sample Meal Plan—Week 1:

DAY	BREAKFAST	LUNCH	DINNER
DAY – 1	Greek yogurt & honey	Pumpkin & apple soup	Cauliflower chowder with quinoa
DAY – 2	Chia pudding & vanilla	Detoxifying salad	Avocado & basil salad
DAY – 3	Veggie breakfast bowl	Gluten-free pasta salad with ginger	Black beans & quinoa burgers
DAY – 4	Fruit granola	Sweet and crispy salad Goodness	Pumpkin and lentil soup
DAY – 5	Blueberry muffin	Chicken salad with cranberry & quinoa	Blackberry salad
DAY – 6	Garlic toast or charred tomatoes with eggs	Red rice in pesto	Squash salad with lemon
DAY – 7	Egg humus with almond	Black rice in coconut	Mushroom steak

Common Keto Abbreviations

Carbs	Carbohydrate
Keto	Ketogenic
DKA	Diabetic ketoacidosis
SKD	Standard ketogenic diet
CKD	Cyclical ketogenic diet
TKD	Targeted ketogenic diet
Macros	Micronutrients

Frequently Asked Questions

How can I calculate my daily carb intake?

Whenever you follow a recipe, look at its contents, and the nutritional values included at the end of the recipe. Calculate the whole day's carbs from this.

Is there any difference between a low-carb and a ketogenic diet?

A low carbohydrate diet is a general term used to describe any diet containing 130 to 150 grams of carbs per day. A ketogenic diet is a form of this general diet plan.

What kind of dairy products are keto-friendly?

Not all dairy products are keto-friendly, as some are rich in carbs. Consult the tables that I've included in this Introduction.

Are peanuts allowed on the keto diet?

Not all legumes are non-ketogenic; peanuts are allowed.

What kinds of fermented food products are allowed on a keto diet?

Products like plain yogurt, kimchi, kombucha, and sauerkraut are all fermented. These are keto friendly.

Is ketosis dangerous for your health?

There is no medical evidence to suggest that ketosis is dangerous.

Can I use sugar on the keto diet?

No, you need to cut out sugar completely on this diet. You can use Swerve, erythritol, and other artificial sweeteners.

4-Week Diet Plan

Week 1

Day 1:
Breakfast: Egg Cups with Sausage-Crust
Lunch:Crunchy Slaw
Snack:Bake Kale Chips
Dinner:Tangy Dill Salmon
Dessert:Coconut Cake

Day 2:
Breakfast: Healthy Cinnamon Granola
Lunch: Turkey Soup
Snack:Dragon Tail Poppahs
Dinner: Keto Crusted Lamb Chops
Dessert:Roasted Nut Clusters

Day 3:
Breakfast: Delicious Scotch Eggs
Lunch: Pesto Pasta
Snack: Taquitos
Dinner: Spiced Curried Lamb
Dessert:Keto Danish

Day 4:
Breakfast:Cheesy Scrambled Eggs with Greens
Lunch: Lasagna Soup
Snack: Avocado Chips
Dinner: Silky Buttered Scallops
Dessert:Pumpkin Pie Cake

Day 5:
Breakfast: Cheesy Fat Bombs
Lunch: Fried Zuck Patties
Snack: Ants On a Log
Dinner: Buttery Snow Crab Legs
Dessert:Simple Cinnamon Pretzels

Day 6:
Breakfast:Deviled Mayo Eggs
Lunch: Zucchini Boats
Snack: Cheese Ball
Dinner: Brownies
Dessert:Berries Mascarpone

Day 7:
Breakfast: Green Citrus Smoothie
Lunch: Radish Potatoes
Snack: Crispy Wings
Dinner: Stuffed Portobello Mushrooms
Dessert:Coffee Cake Bites

Week 2

Day 1:
Breakfast:Spiced Pear Bars
Lunch: Creamed Spinach
Snack: Healthy Peanut Butter Cookies
Dinner: Salmon Burger
Dessert:Sweet Iced Tea

Day 2:
Breakfast: Blue Cheese Omelet
Lunch: Zucchini Fries
Snack:Raspberry Cookies
Dinner: Spicy Creamy Shrimp
Dessert:Fast Fudge

Day 3:
Breakfast: Egg Pizza
Lunch: Smashed Cauliflower
Snack: Healthy Seedy Crackers
Dinner: Grainy Mustard Sauce
Dessert:Creamy Shortbread Cookies

Day 4:
Breakfast: Zucchini Frittata
Lunch: Keto Tater Tots
Snack: Cheesy Broccoli Hot Pockets
Dinner: Delicious Shrimp Stir-Fry
Dessert: Salty Pecan Bark

Day 5:
Breakfast: Mini Breakfast Bagels
Lunch: Cauliflower Rice Balls
Snack: Cheesy Za'atar Pinwheels
Dinner:Nut-stuffed pork chops
Dessert:Tangy Lime Bars

Day 6:
Breakfast:Egg Cups with Jalapeno
Lunch: Burger Bun for One
Snack: Crispy Tortilla Chips
Dinner: Carnitas
Dessert:Candy Almonds

Day 7:
Breakfast: Kale Kiwi Smoothie
Lunch: Parmesan Cauliflower
Snack:Corn Dog
Dinner: Herbed Lamb Racks
Dessert:German Chocolate Cookie

Week 3

Day 1:
Breakfast:Monkey Bread
Lunch: Cheesy Loaded Broccoli
Snack: Egg Salad in Avocados
Dinner: Orange-Herb Pistou
Dessert:Keto Martini

Day 2:
Breakfast: Ham Frittata
Lunch: Savory Zucchini Boats
Snack: Crispy Broccoli Salad
Dinner: Beef and Broccoli Foil Packs
Dessert:Energy Booster Drink

Day 3:
Breakfast:Zucchini Egg Bake
Lunch: Roasted Broccoli Salad
Snack: Sweet Snack
Dinner: Weeknight Chili
Dessert: Chai Latte

Day 4:
Breakfast: Egg Casserole
Lunch: Onion Rings
Snack: Savory Snack
Dinner: Corn Dogs
Dessert:Coconut Nut Cookies

Day 5:
Breakfast: Salmon-Avocado Boats
Lunch: Dinner Rolls
Snack: Savory Cheesy Biscotti
Dinner: Beef and Broccoli Foil Packs
Dessert:Strawberry Cheesecakes

Day 6:
Breakfast: Meatballs with Apple Chutney
Lunch: Flatbread Dippers
Snack: Cheese Crackers
Dinner: Chicken Burgers
Dessert:Nuts Squares

Day 7:
Breakfast: Cheesy Bacon Quiche
Lunch: Pesto Vegetable Skewers
Snack: Healthy Graham Crackers
Dinner: Delicious Jerk Chicken
Dessert:Creamy Coconut Brownies

Week 4

Day 1:
Breakfast:Cheesy Cheddar Soufflés
Lunch: Roasted Salsa
Snack: Pizza Muffin
Dinner: Lettuce-Wrapped Burger
Dessert:Buttery Pecan Ice Cream

Day 2:
Breakfast: Cheesy Keto "Hash Browns"
Lunch: Crispy Eggplant Rounds
Snack: Tasty Pretzel Bites
Dinner:Roasted Whole Chicken with Jicama
Dessert:Chocolate Coconut Torts

Day 3:
Breakfast: Chocolaty Chia Pudding
Lunch: Pan Pizza
Snack: Tropical Macaroons
Dinner: Tropical-Chicken Curry
Dessert:Creamy Coconut Brownies

Day 4:
Breakfast: Traditional Pumpkin Muffins
Lunch: Sweet Pepper Nachos
Snack: Hot Beef Empanadas
Dinner:Roasted Chicken
Dessert:Minty Chocolate Shake

Day 5:
Breakfast: Grain-Free Breakfast Cereal
Lunch: Lemon Caper Cauliflower Steaks
Snack:Chocolate Hazelnut Biscotti
Dinner:Creamy Tangy Chicken
Dessert:Chocolate Almonds   103

Day 6:
Breakfast: Keto Pancakes
Lunch: Cauliflower Rice–Stuffed Peppers
Snack:Chocolate Coated Apricots
Dinner: Mustardy Chicken Drumsticks
Dessert: Creamy Coconut Brownies

Day 7:
Breakfast: Matcha Smoothie
Lunch: Vegetable Burgers
Snack: Herby Mushroom Galettes
Dinner: Crispy Fried Chicken
Dessert:Blueberry Ice Cream

Chapter 1 Breakfast and Smoothies

Healthy Spinach Omelet 14

Cheesy Cheddar Soufflés 14

Egg-Stuffed Meatloaf 14

Zucchini Frittata 14

Bunless Turkey Burgers 14

Egg Cups with Sausage-Crust 14

Mini Breakfast Bagels 14

Traditional Pancake with Keto Twist ... 14

Jalapeño and Bacon Pizza 15

Egg Pizza 15

Cheesy Keto "Hash Browns" 15

Delicious Scotch Eggs 15

Healthy Cinnamon Granola 15

Egg Cups with Jalapeno 15

Chocolaty Chia Pudding 15

Deviled Mayo Eggs 15

Blue Cheese Omelet 16

Cheesy Fat Bombs....................... 16

Cheesy Scrambled Eggs with Greens ... 16

Traditional Pumpkin Muffins 16

Chia Pudding with Mocha and Coconut 16

Keto Pancakes 16

Grain-Free Breakfast Cereal 16

Matcha Smoothie 16

Spiced Pear Bars 17

Delicious Carrot Cake Pudding........... 17

Green Citrus Smoothie 17

Avocado Smoothie....................... 17

Golden Coconut Smoothie 17

Kale Kiwi Smoothie 17

Chocolate Macadamia Smoothie 17

Sausage Gravy with Biscuits.............. 17

Tropical Coconut Smoothie 18

Flaxseed Piña Colada 18

Creamy French Toast..................... 18

Low-Carb Pancakes 18

Egg Cheese Muffin Sandwiches 18

Whey Waffles 18

Monkey Bread 18

Morning Doughnuts 19

Mushroom Quiche....................... 19

Pecan French Toast 19

Sausage Bread Pudding................... 19

Mushroom Cream Crepes 19

Mascarpone Pancakes 20

Italian Breakfast 20

Prosciutto Eggs Benedict 20

Ricotta Sausage Pie 20

Ham Frittata 20

Eggs with Hollandaise Sauce 20

Egg-Stuffed Bell Peppers 21

Spinach Mushroom Quiche 21

Bacon Fritters 21

Chicken with Waffles..................... 21

Zucchini Egg Bake 21

Sausage Stuffed Peppers 21

Eggs with Avocado Salsa 21

Blueberry Cake 21

Meatballs with Apple Chutney 22

Egg Casserole 22

Traditional Spice Muffins 22

Salmon-Avocado Boats 22

Meatballs 22

Cheesy Bacon Quiche 22

Cheddar Breakfast Bake 22

Mexican Breakfast Casserole 22

Avocado Breakfast Tacos 23

Dark Chocolate Matcha................... 23

Healthy Spinach Omelet

Prep time: 5 minutes | Cook time: 12 minutes | Serves: 2

¼ teaspoon salt
4 large eggs
1½ cups chopped fresh spinach leaves
2 tablespoons peeled and chopped

yellow onion
½ cup shredded mild Cheddar cheese
2 tablespoons salted butter, melted

1. In an ungreased 6" round nonstick baking dish, whisk eggs. Stir in spinach, onion, butter, Cheddar, and salt. 2. Place dish into air fryer basket. Set the temperature of air fryer to 320°F/160°C and the timer for 12 minutes. Omelet will be done when browned on the top and firm in the middle. 3. Slice in half and serve warm on two medium plates.
Per Serving: Calories 368; Fat 28g; Sodium 722mg; Carbs 3g; Fiber 1g; Sugar 1g; Protein 20g

Cheesy Cheddar Soufflés

Prep time: 15 minutes | Cook time: 12 minutes | Serves: 4

¼ teaspoon cream of tartar
3 ounces cream cheese, softened
½ cup shredded sharp Cheddar

cheese
3 large eggs, whites, and yolks separated

1. Beat egg whites with ¼ teaspoon cream of tartar until soft peaks form, about 2 minutes. 2. In a separate bowl, beat egg yolks, Cheddar, and cream cheese together until frothy, about 1 minute. Add egg yolk mixture to whites, gently folding until combined. 3. Pour mixture evenly into four 4" ramekins greased with cooking spray—place ramekins into air fryer basket. Set the temperature to 350°F/177°C and the timer for 12 minutes. 4. When done, eggs will be browned on the top and firm in the center. Serve warm.
Per Serving: Calories 183; Fat 14g; Sodium 221mg; Carbs 1g; Fiber 0g; Sugar 1g; Protein 9g

Egg-Stuffed Meatloaf

Prep time: 10 minutes | Cooking time: 35 minutes | Serves: 6

4 hard-boiled eggs, peeled
1 cup baby spinach or kale
1½ pounds ground pork
1 teaspoon smoked paprika
1 teaspoon fennel seeds

½ teaspoon salt
½ teaspoon pepper
½ teaspoon sage
¼ teaspoon cayenne pepper

1. At 400°F/204°C, preheat your oven. 2. Grease a 9x5-inch loaf pan with non-stick spray. 3. In a suitable mixing bowl, mix the ground pork with the spices and mix well with hands. 4. Place a thin layer of pork in the bottom of the prepared pan. 5. Line the baby spinach down the center of this pan and top with the hard-boiled eggs. 6. Place the remaining pork on top and press gently. 7. Bake for almost 35 minutes, or until golden brown. 8. Allow to cool for almost 5–10 minutes. Slice and serve.
Per Serving: Calories 354; Total Fat 31.8g; Sodium 320mg; Total Carbs 9.7g; Fiber 1.7g; Sugars 6.6g; Protein 10.5g

Zucchini Frittata

Prep time: 10 minutes | Cooking time: 25 minutes | Serves: 6

8 large eggs
2 medium zucchinis, sliced
1 red onion, sliced
2 green peppers, sliced
2 cloves garlic, minced

2 tablespoons olive oil
black pepper and sea salt to taste
Optional topping: Pico de Gallo or salsa

1. At 400°F/204°C, preheat your oven. 2. Preheat 1 tablespoon oil in a 9-inch oven-proof pan. Add the onion, zucchini slices, bell pepper, and garlic. Cook for almost 5 minutes, until softened. 3. While the veggies cook, whisk the eggs with the black pepper and salt in a suitable bowl. 4. Add the zucchini mixture to the eggs and mix well. 5. Heat the remaining tablespoon of olive oil in this pan and add the egg mixture. Cook over medium heat for almost 5 minutes. 6. Transfer pan to your oven and bake for almost 20 minutes, until the eggs are set. 7. Remove from oven; allow to cool for almost 10 minutes. Carefully flip onto a serving platter and slice into wedges. 8. Top with Pico de Gallo or salsa, if desired, and serve!
Per Serving: Calories 219; Total Fat 18.8g; Sodium 590mg; Total Carbs 1.7g; Fiber 5.7g; Sugars 2.2g; Protein 4.9g

Bunless Turkey Burgers

Prep time: 5 minutes | Cook time: 15 minutes | Serves: 4

1-pound ground turkey breakfast sausage
¼ teaspoon ground black pepper
¼ cup seeded and chopped green bell pepper

1 medium avocado, peeled, pitted, and sliced
½ teaspoon salt
2 tablespoons mayonnaise

1. Mix sausage with salt, black pepper, bell pepper, and mayonnaise—form the meat into four patties. 2. Place patties into an ungreased air fryer basket. Set the temperature of air fryer to 370°F/188°C and the timer for 15 minutes, turning the cakes halfway through cooking. Burgers will be done when dark brown and have an internal temperature of at least 165°F/74°C. 3. Serve burgers topped with avocado slices on four medium plates.
Per Serving: Calories 276; Fat 17g; Sodium 917mg; Carbs 4g; Fiber 3g; Sugar 0g; Protein 22g

Egg Cups with Sausage-Crust

Prep time: 10 minutes | Cook time: 15 minutes | Serves: 6

¼ teaspoon ground black pepper
6 large eggs
12 ounces ground pork breakfast sausage

½ teaspoon salt
½ teaspoon crushed red pepper flakes

1. Place sausage in six 4" ramekins (about 2 ounces per ramekin) greased with cooking oil. Press sausage down to cover the bottom and about ½" up the sides of ramekins. 2. Crack one egg into each ramekin and sprinkle evenly with salt, black pepper, and red pepper flakes. 3. Place ramekins into the air fryer basket. Set the temperature to 350°F/177°C and the timer for 15 minutes. Egg cups will be done when the sausage is fully cooked to at least 145°F/63°C, and the egg is firm. 4. Serve warm.
Per Serving: Calories 267; Fat 21g; Sodium 679mg; Carbs 1g; Fiber 0g; Sugar 0g; Protein 14g

Mini Breakfast Bagels

Prep time: 5 minutes | Cook time: 10 minutes | Serves: 6

1½ teaspoons baking powder
2 cups shredded mozzarella cheese
3 tablespoons salted butter, divided

2 cups blanched finely ground almond flour
2 large eggs, divided
1 teaspoon apple cider vinegar

1. To make the dough: Mix together the mozzarella cheese, flour, and 1 tablespoon butter and microwave for 90 seconds on high. Form the mixture into a soft ball. Then add the vinegar, 1 egg, and the baking powder and stir until well combined. When dough is cool, divide evenly into six balls. Poke a hole in each rough dough ball with your finger and gently stretch each ball out to be 2" in diameter. 2. In a microwave, melt 2 tablespoons butter for 30 seconds, and cool for 1 minute. Whisk with remaining egg, then brush mixture over each bagel. 3. Prepare the basket with parchment paper and place bagels onto ungreased parchment, working in batches if needed. 4. Set the temperature to 350°F/177°C and the timer for 10 minutes. Halfway through, use tongs to flip bagels for even cooking. 5. Allow bagels to set and cool thoroughly, about 15 minutes, before serving.
Per Serving: Calories 415; Fat 33g; Sodium 447mg; Carbs 10g; Fiber 4g; Sugar 2g; Protein 19g

Traditional Pancake with Keto Twist

Prep time: 5 minutes | Cook time: 30 minutes | Serves: 2

½ teaspoon vanilla extract
1 cup blanched finely ground almond flour
⅓ cup unsweetened almond milk

2 tablespoons granular erythritol
1 large egg
1 tablespoon salted butter, melted

1. In a bowl, mix all ingredients, then pour half the batter into an ungreased 6" round nonstick baking dish. 2. Place dish into air fryer basket. Set the temperature of air fryer to 320°F/160°C for 15 minutes. 3. The pancake will be golden brown on top and firm, and a toothpick inserted in the center will come out clean when done. Repeat with the remaining batter. 4. Slice in half in a dish and serve warm.
Per Serving: Calories 434; Fat 38g; Sodium 111mg; Carbs 23g; Fiber 6g; Sugar 2g; Protein 15g

Jalapeño and Bacon Pizza

Prep time: 5 minutes | Cook time: 10 minutes | Serves: 2

1 cup shredded mozzarella cheese
¼ cup chopped pickled jalapeños
1-ounce cream cheese, broken
into small pieces
4 slices cooked sugar-free bacon,
chopped
¼ teaspoon salt
1 large egg, whisked

1. Place mozzarella in a single layer on the bottom of an ungreased 6" round nonstick baking dish. Scatter cream cheese pieces, bacon, and jalapeños over mozzarella, then pour egg evenly around the baking dish. 2. Sprinkle with salt and place into the air fryer basket. Set the temperature to 330°F/165°C and the timer for 10 minutes. the pizza will be done when the cheese is brown, and the egg is set. 3. Let cool on a large plate for 5 minutes before serving.
Per Serving: Calories 361; Fat 24g; Sodium 1324mg; Carbs 5g; Fiber 0g; Sugar 2g; Protein 26g

Egg Pizza

Prep time: 5 minutes | Cook time: 10 minutes | Serves: 2

1 cup shredded mozzarella cheese
7 slices pepperoni, chopped
1 large egg, whisked
¼ teaspoon dried oregano
¼ teaspoon salt
¼ teaspoon dried parsley
¼ teaspoon garlic powder

1. Place mozzarella in a single layer on the bottom of an ungreased 6" round nonstick baking dish. Scatter pepperoni over cheese, then pour egg evenly around the baking dish. 2. Sprinkle with remaining ingredients and place into air fryer basket. Set the temperature to 330°F/166°C and the timer for 10 minutes. The dish will be done when the cheese is brown and the egg is set. 3. Let cool in dish for 5 minutes before serving.
Per Serving: Calories 241; Fat 15g; Sodium 834mg; Carbs 4g; Fiber 0g; Sugar 1g; Protein 19g

Cheesy Keto "Hash Browns"

Prep time: 30 minutes | Cook time: 24 minutes | Serves: 6

1 large egg
1 (12-ounce) steamer bag
cauliflower, cooked according to
package instructions
½ cup shredded sharp Cheddar
cheese
2 ounces 100% cheese crisps
½ teaspoon salt

1. Let cooked cauliflower cool for 10 minutes. 2. Place cheese crisps into a food processor and pulse on low for 30 seconds until crisps are finely ground. 3. Using a kitchen towel, wash excess moisture from cauliflower and place it into the food processor. 4. Add egg to the food processor and sprinkle with Cheddar and salt. Pulse five times until the mixture is mostly smooth. 5. Prepare the air fryer basket with parchment paper. Separate mixture into six scoops and place three on each piece of ungreased parchment, keeping at least 2" of space between each scoop. Press each into a hash brown shape, about ¼" thick. 6. Place one batch on parchment into the air fryer basket. Set the temperature of air fryer to 375°F/191°C for 12 minutes, turning hash browns halfway through cooking. Hash browns will be golden brown when done. Repeat with the second batch. 7. Allow 5 minutes to cool. Serve warm.
Per Serving: Calories 120; Fat 8g; Sodium 390mg; Carbs 3g; Fiber 1g; Sugar 1g; Protein 8g

Delicious Scotch Eggs

Prep time: 10 minutes | Cook time: 12 minutes | Serves: 8

¼ teaspoon ground black pepper
1 large egg, whisked
½ teaspoon salt
8 large hard-boiled eggs, shells
removed
½ cup blanched finely ground
almond flour
1-pound ground pork breakfast
sausage

1. Mix raw egg with sausage, flour, salt, and pepper. 2. Form ¼ cup of the mixture around 1 hard-boiled egg, thoroughly covering the egg. Repeat with the remaining mixture and hard-boiled eggs. 3. Place eggs into an air fryer basket. Set the temperature to 400°F/205°C and timer for 12 minutes, turning halfway through cooking. Eggs will be done when browned. 4. Let eggs cool for 5 minutes before serving.
Per Serving: Calories 325; Fat 25g; Sodium 630mg; Carbs 2g; Fiber 1g; Sugar 1g; Protein 17g

Healthy Cinnamon Granola

Prep time: 10 minutes | Cook time: 7 minutes | Serves: 6

1 cup unsweetened coconut flakes
2 cups shelled pecans, chopped
1 teaspoon ground cinnamon
2 tablespoons granular erythritol
1 cup slivered almonds

1. In a large bowl, mix all ingredients. Place mixture into an ungreased 6" round nonstick baking dish. 2. Place dish into air fryer basket. Set the temperature of air fryer to 320°F/160°C for 7 minutes, stirring halfway through cooking. 3. Let cool in a dish for 10 minutes before serving. Store in an airtight container at room temperature for up to 5 days.
Per Serving: Calories 445; Fat 42g; Sodium 0mg; Carbs 17g; Fiber 9g; Sugar 3g; Protein 8g

Egg Cups with Jalapeno

Prep time: 10 minutes | Cook time: 14 minutes | Serves: 4

¼ teaspoon garlic powder
4 large eggs
½ teaspoon salt
½ cup shredded sharp Cheddar
cheese
2 ounces cream cheese, softened
¼ teaspoon ground black pepper
¼ cup chopped pickled jalapeños

1. Beat eggs with salt and pepper, then pour evenly into four 4" ramekins greased with cooking spray. 2. Mix jalapeños, cream cheese, garlic powder, and Cheddar in a separate large bowl. Pour ¼ of the mixture into the center of one ramekin. Repeat with the remaining mixture and ramekins. 3. Place ramekins in the air fryer basket. Set the temperature of air fryer to 320°F/160°C for 14 minutes. Eggs will be set when done. Serve warm.
Per Serving: Calories 177; Fat 13g; Sodium 591mg; Carbs 1g; Fiber 0g; Sugar 1g; Protein 11g

Chocolaty Chia Pudding

Prep time: 2 minutes | Cook time: 3 minutes | Serves: 2

½ cup almond flour
1 cup canned coconut milk
2 tablespoons chia seeds
2 tablespoons ground flax seeds
4 tablespoons hemp hearts
Toppings
Toasted almonds
Toasted coconut
¼ tablespoon ground cinnamon
4 scoops chocolate protein
powder
⅔ cup water
¼ tablespoon ground nutmeg

Almond butter

1. Mix the coconut milk with water in a bowl. Combine the chia seeds, protein powder, flax seeds, almond flour, cinnamon, and nutmeg in a separate bowl. 2. Make a well shape in the dry ingredients and pour the milk/water mixture into the dry ingredients while continuously mixing. 3. Repeat until the ingredients are thoroughly mixed together. Cover the bowl and place it in the fridge overnight. 4. Pour the mix in a saucepan and use gentle heat. Bring the mixture to a simmer and frequently stir until it thickens. 5. The thickness should not be too runny but not solid either. This can be to your personal preference. 6. Stir in the hemp hearts just before serving. Divide evenly between two bowls and add your favorite healthy toppings.
Per Serving: Calories 486; Fat 32g; Sodium 256mg; Carbs 20g; Fiber 10g; Sugar 6g; Protein 38g

Deviled Mayo Eggs

Prep time: 10 minutes | Cooking time: 10 minutes | Serves: 4

8 hard-boiled eggs, peeled and
sliced in half
1 tablespoon mayonnaise
1 teaspoon Dijon mustard
1 tablespoon heavy cream
1 tablespoon olive oil
1 clove garlic, minced
1 tablespoon green onion, minced
1 teaspoon lemon juice
2 tablespoons parsley, chopped

1. Gently remove the yolks from the hard-boiled eggs and place in a suitable bowl. Place the egg whites on a serving tray. 2. Add the mayonnaise, mustard, heavy cream, olive oil, garlic, green onion, lemon juice, and parsley. Mash everything until a thick paste forms. Spoon the prepared mixture back into the egg whites. 4. Serve over a bed of salad greens.
Per Serving: Calories 210; Total Fat 13.4g; Sodium 708mg; Total Carbs 3.3g; Fiber 4.3g; Sugars 6.6g; Protein 11.7g

Blue Cheese Omelet

Prep time: 5 minutes | Cook time: 10 minutes | Serves: 4

2 tablespoons hot sauce
4 ounces cream cheese, softened
4 tablespoons blue cheese
6 eggs
2 tablespoons coconut oil
2 tablespoons water
Garnishes: chopped fresh parsley and chives

1. Warm the cream cheese, blue cheese, and hot sauce in a small bowl in the microwave for about 15 seconds. Stir until smooth and combined. 2. Whisk the eggs until frothy. 3. Heat about half a tablespoon coconut oil in a non-stick pan over medium heat. Pour the eggs into the pan. Drop one-quarter of the cream cheese mixture by spoonful over half of the eggs. 4. Once the eggs have firmed up, fold the empty half over the half with filling. Cook on low heat for another minute. 5. Carefully remove from pan, cover with tin foil to keep warm, and repeat with the remaining eggs and filling. Then garnish and serve.
Per Serving: Calories 282; Fat 26g; Sodium 689mg; Carbs 2g; Fiber 0g; Sugar 1g; Protein 12g

Cheesy Fat Bombs

Prep time: 10 minutes plus 45 minutes for refrigerating | Cook time: 0 minutes | Serves: 5

⅓ cup butter, softened
3 large eggs, hard-boiled
¼ cup shredded cheddar cheese
5 slices bacon
Sea salt and pepper to taste
3 tablespoons mayonnaise

1. Preheat the oven to 375°F/191°C. Prepare a baking sheet with parchment paper. Lay the bacon flat and bake for 10–15 minutes until golden brown. Reserve any bacon grease for later use. 2. Peel and quarter the hard-boiled eggs. 3. Add thinly pieced butter to the eggs and mix well. Mash well with a fork. 4. Stir in the shredded cheese, mayonnaise, and any leftover bacon grease—season with salt and pepper. Mix well and place in the refrigerator for about 30–45 minutes until firm. 5. Form 5 balls from the cold egg mixture. 6. Wrap bacon on every ball and store in an airtight container until ready to serve.
Per Serving: Calories 292; Fat 28g; Sodium 689mg; Carbs 2g; Fiber 0g; Sugar 1g; Protein 8g

Cheesy Scrambled Eggs with Greens

Prep time: 5 minutes | Cook time: 10 minutes | Serves: 4

1 cup shredded mozzarella cheese
6 cups kale, baby spinach, or Swiss Chard
2 tablespoons heavy cream
2 tablespoons olive oil
8 large eggs
Sea salt and pepper to taste

1. Crack the eggs into a medium bowl. Add the heavy cream to the eggs and season with salt and pepper. Whisk until well combined. 2. Roughly chop your greens. 3. Heat the olive oil in a pan. Add the baby spinach to the pan. Stir frequently, being careful not to burn. Once the spinach has wilted, reduce heat to low. 4. Add the egg mixture to the spinach and slowly stir until the eggs are almost set. 5. Add the mozzarella cheese and stir until well combined. 6. Once the cheese has melted, divide it onto four plates and serve!
Per Serving: Calories 251; Fat 19g; Sodium 784mg; Carbs 4g; Fiber 2g; Sugar 2g; Protein 16g

Traditional Pumpkin Muffins

Prep time: 10 minutes | Cook time: 30 minutes | Serves: 6

⅔ cup sugar substitute
1½ cups almond flour
1 tablespoon pumpkin pie spice mix
1 teaspoon baking powder
⅔ cup pumpkin puree
4 large eggs

1. Preheat the oven to 300°F/149°C. Prepare a muffin pan with 6 muffin paper liners. 2. Combine the almond flour, pumpkin pie spice, and sugar substitute in a large bowl. Mix well. 3. Add the pumpkin puree and eggs. Beat with an electric mixer until smooth. 4. Evenly divide the batter among the 6 paper liners and bake for 30–40 minutes. 5. Remove from the oven and allow to cool on a wire rack.
Per Serving: Calories 168; Fat 13g; Sodium 623mg; Carbs 9g; Fiber 6g; Sugar 2g; Protein 9g

Chia Pudding with Mocha and Coconut

Prep time: 5 minutes plus 30 minutes for refrigerating | Cook time: 0 minutes | Serves: 4

½ cup coconut cream
2 tablespoons cocoa powder
½ cup chia seeds
4 tablespoons instant coffee
4 tablespoons cacao nibs
1 tablespoon vanilla extract
2 tablespoons sugar substitute
2 cups water

1. Prepare a strong cup of coffee by simmering the instant coffee with 2 cups of water for 15 minutes until the liquid has reduced to about 1 cup. 2. Whisk the cocoa powder, coconut cream, vanilla extract, and sugar substitute into the coffee. 3. Mixing in the chia seeds and cacao nibs. Mix well. 4. Divide into 4 small serving dishes and allow to set for at least 30 minutes. 5. Remove from refrigerator, garnish with a few additional cacao nibs, and serve!
Per Serving: Calories 257; Fat 21g; Sodium 697mg; Carbs 14g; Fiber 11g; Sugar 1g; Protein 7g

Keto Pancakes

Prep time: 10 minutes | Cook time: 5 to 10 minutes | Serves: 4

1 cup almond flour
¼ cup full-fat, plain yogurt
½ cup fresh blueberries
4 large eggs
1 teaspoon cream of tartar
¼ cup coconut oil, melted
½ teaspoon baking soda
1 teaspoon vanilla extract
¼ cup sugar substitute
Additional coconut oil to grease the pan

1. Whisk the eggs until frothy in a bowl. In a separate bowl, mix the almond flour, sugar substitute, baking soda, and cream of tartar until well combined. 2. Stir the vanilla extract and the melted coconut oil into the eggs. 3. Add the dry ingredients to the wet and mix well. 4. Grease a large pan with a teaspoon of coconut oil and spoon 2–3 small pancakes for every serving. 5. Cook on medium for about 5 minutes until the pancake firm up. Flip and cook the other side for about a minute. 6. Cook pancake for about 5 minutes until firm up. Flip and cook the other side for about a minute. Top each serving of pancakes with yogurt and berries. 7. Serve and enjoy!
Per Serving: Calories 368; Fat 33g; Sodium 412mg; Carbs 9g; Fiber 3g; Sugar 2g; Protein 12g

Grain-Free Breakfast Cereal

Prep time: 5 minutes | Cook time: 8 minutes | Serves: 4

4 cups unsweetened almond milk
6 tablespoons butter
1 cup unsweetened, shredded coconut
1 ⅓ cups crushed walnut pieces,
sliced almonds
Blueberries or raisins for topping
Liquid stevia to taste (if desired)
Pinch of salt

1. Preheat the oven to 250°F/121°C. Toast the nuts and shredded coconut (keep separate from each other) until golden brown. 2. In a saucepan over medium heat, melt the butter. 3. Add the toasted nuts and a pinch of salt. Let cook for 1–2 minutes, stirring constantly. Add the toasted coconut and continue stirring. 4. Add the milk and liquid stevia if using. Allow cooking for 5–7 minutes, until heated throughout. 5. Remove from heat, divide into 4 bowls and serve immediately.
Per Serving: Calories 603; Fat 62g; Sodium 697mg; Carbs 10g; Fiber 6g; Sugar 2g; Protein 9g

Matcha Smoothie

Prep time: 10 minutes | Cooking time: 0 minutes | Serves: 1

½ cup canned unsweetened full-fat coconut milk
¼ cup water
1 cup fresh baby spinach leaves
¼ medium avocado, peeled, pitted, and sliced
¾ teaspoon powdered matcha
½ teaspoon fresh lemon juice
⅛ teaspoon sea salt
12 drops liquid stevia
1 cup ice cubes

1. Add the coconut milk, water, spinach, avocado, matcha, lemon juice, salt, and stevia to your high-speed blender and process until smooth. 2. Add the ice cubes and pulse until thick and creamy, tamping down as necessary. 3. Pour into a glass and serve immediately.
Per Serving: Calories 356; Total Fat 35.1g; Sodium 18mg; Total Carbs 2.1g; Fiber 4.6g; Sugars 6.9g; Protein 3.7g

Spiced Pear Bars

Prep time: 5 minutes | Cook time: 22 minutes | Serves: 6

1 large pear, cored and peeled
½ teaspoon nutmeg
¼ teaspoon cloves
¼ cup coconut flour
1 teaspoon cinnamon

3 large eggs
½ teaspoon baking soda
2 tablespoons coconut oil
2 tablespoons maple syrup
¼ teaspoon salt

1. Preheat the oven to 350°F/177°C. Grease an 8x8 baking tray with cooking spray. 2. In a food processor, pulse the pear until pureed. Add the eggs, maple syrup, along with coconut oil. Blend until well combined. 3. Add the salt, baking soda, cinnamon, nutmeg, cloves, and coconut flour. Mix until just combined. 4. Pour the batter into the prepared pan. Sprinkle with additional cinnamon, if desired. 5. Bake for 22–25 minutes until a toothpick test comes out clean. 6. Allow cooling on a wire rack. Cut into 6 squares.
Per Serving: Calories 127; Fat 9g; Sodium 489mg; Carbs 10g; Fiber 1g; Sugar 2g; Protein 4g

Delicious Carrot Cake Pudding

Prep time: 5 minutes | Cook time: 20 minutes | Serves: 4

½ teaspoon nutmeg
2 cups peeled and chopped carrots
½ teaspoon cinnamon
2 tablespoons coconut cream

¼ teaspoon cloves
2 tablespoons almond butter
1 teaspoon vanilla extract
Pinch of sea salt

Garnish: whipped to stiff peaks and/or toasted nuts, heavy cream, optional

1. Cover the carrots in a medium pot with water. Cook the carrots on a medium flame for 10-15 minutes until the fork soft. 2. Drain the water from cooked carrots and put them in a food processor. Add the remaining ingredients in blender and puree until smooth and creamy. 3. Divide into 4 serving dishes, garnish with whipped cream if desired, and enjoy! Sometimes, I like to top with nuts; the nutty flavor complements the pudding.
Per Serving: Calories 108; Fat 7g; Sodium 541mg; Carbs 11g; Fiber 4g; Sugar 3g; Protein 3g

Green Citrus Smoothie

Prep time: 10 minutes | Cooking time: 0 minutes | Serves: 1

⅔ cup canned unsweetened full-fat coconut milk
½ tablespoon milled golden flaxseed
½ teaspoon lemon juice
1 teaspoon lemon zest

1 teaspoon orange zest
¾ teaspoon grated fresh ginger
⅛ teaspoon sea salt
10 drops liquid stevia
1 cup fresh baby spinach leaves
1 cup ice cubes

1. Add the coconut milk, lemon juice, flaxseed, lemon zest, orange zest, ginger, salt, stevia, and spinach to your high-speed blender and process until smooth. 2. Add the ice cubes and pulse until thick and creamy, tamping down as necessary. 3. Pour into a glass and serve immediately.
Per Serving: Calories 482; Total Fat 43.1g; Sodium 255mg; Total Carbs 5.1g; Fiber 1.3g; Sugars 2.9g; Protein 21.4g

Avocado Smoothie

Prep time: 10 minutes | Cooking time: 0 minutes | Serves: 1

⅔ cup canned unsweetened full-fat coconut milk
1 teaspoon lemon juice
1 teaspoon lemon zest
⅛ teaspoon sea salt
10 drops liquid stevia

1 cup chopped kale
¼ medium avocado, peeled, pitted, and sliced
3 sprigs fresh parsley
1 sprig fresh mint
1 cup ice cubes

1. Add the coconut milk, lemon juice, lemon zest, salt, stevia, kale, avocado, parsley, and mint to your high-speed blender and process until smooth. 2. Add the ice cubes and pulse until thick and creamy, tamping down as necessary. 3. Pour into a glass and serve immediately.
Per Serving: Calories 448; Total Fat 31.1g; Sodium 35mg; Total Carbs 2.9g; Fiber 12.8g; Sugars 8.5g; Protein 9g

Golden Coconut Smoothie

Prep time: 10 minutes | Cooking time: 0 minutes | Serves: 1

⅔ cup canned unsweetened full-fat coconut milk
½ tablespoon milled golden flaxseed
¾ teaspoon vanilla extract
¼ teaspoon coconut extract

½ teaspoon ground turmeric
⅛ teaspoon ground black pepper
⅛ teaspoon sea salt
10 drops liquid stevia
1 cup ice cubes

1. Add the coconut milk, flaxseed, vanilla extract, coconut extract, turmeric, black pepper, salt, and stevia to your high-speed blender and process until smooth. 2. Add the ice cubes and pulse until thick and creamy, tamping down as necessary. 3. Pour into a glass and serve immediately.
Per Serving: Calories 180; Total Fat 6.5g; Sodium 92mg; Total Carbs 2g; Fiber 0.8g; Sugars 14.7g; Protein 5.6g

Kale Kiwi Smoothie

Prep time: 10 minutes | Cooking time: 0 minutes | Serves: 1

1 cup chopped kale
½ medium kiwi, peeled and chopped
⅔ cup canned unsweetened full-fat coconut milk

1 teaspoon fresh lemon zest
½ teaspoon fresh lemon juice
⅛ teaspoon sea salt
12 drops liquid stevia
1 cup ice cubes

1. Add the kale, kiwi, coconut milk, lemon zest, lemon juice, salt, and stevia to your high-speed blender and process until smooth. 2. Add the ice cubes and pulse until thick and creamy, tamping down as necessary. 3. Pour into a glass and serve immediately.
Per Serving: Calories 213; Total Fat 13.1g; Sodium 1194mg; Total Carbs 9.3g; Fiber 3.3g; Sugars 4g; Protein 19.4g

Chocolate Macadamia Smoothie

Prep time: 10 minutes | Cooking time: 0 minutes | Serves: 1

1 tablespoon unsalted macadamia nuts
⅔ cup canned unsweetened full-fat coconut milk
1 tablespoon unsweetened cocoa powder

¾ teaspoon vanilla extract
¼ teaspoon coconut extract
⅛ teaspoon sea salt
12 drops liquid stevia
1 cup ice cubes
Pinch flaky sea salt, for garnish

1. Add the macadamia nuts to your high-speed blender and pulse until powdery. 2. Add the coconut milk, cocoa powder, vanilla extract, coconut extract, salt, and stevia to the blender and process until smooth. 3. Add the ice cubes and pulse until thick and creamy, tamping down as necessary. 4. Pour into a glass, sprinkle the flaky sea salt on top, and serve immediately.
Per Serving: Calories 487; Total Fat 45.7g; Sodium 199mg; Total Carbs 0.3g; Fiber 14.5g; Sugars 1.3g; Protein 5.2g

Sausage Gravy with Biscuits

Prep time: 10 minutes | Cooking time: 0 minutes | Serves: 8

½-pound mild Italian turkey sausage
4 ounces cream cheese
½ cup heavy whipping cream
½ cup chicken broth
½ teaspoon garlic powder

½ teaspoon onion powder
¼ teaspoon black pepper
⅛ teaspoon salt
1 batch basic biscuits
1 tablespoon fresh minced parsley, for garnish

1. In a suitable saucepan over medium-high heat, add the sausage. Cook until browned. for almost 5 minutes, using a wooden spoon to break up the meat. 2. Add the cream cheese, cream, chicken broth, garlic powder, onion powder, black pepper, and salt. 3. Turn the heat down to medium and bring to a simmer, whisking to incorporate the cream cheese. 4. Simmer until the sauce is thickened. for almost 5–10 minutes, stirring frequently. 5. Serve each biscuit warm, split open with a ¼ cup sausage gravy spooned inside, topped with fresh parsley.
Per Serving: Calories 222; Total Fat 3.8g; Sodium 193mg; Total Carbs 8.2g; Fiber 7.1g; Sugars 35.5g; Protein 2.3g

Tropical Coconut Smoothie

Prep time: 10 minutes | Cooking time: 0 minutes | Serves: 1

1 tablespoon unsalted macadamia nuts
⅔ cup canned unsweetened full-fat coconut milk
¾ teaspoon vanilla extract
¼ teaspoon coconut extract
⅛ teaspoon sea salt
10 drops liquid stevia
1 cup ice cubes

1. Add the macadamia nuts to your high-speed blender and pulse until powdery. 2. Add the coconut milk, vanilla extract, coconut extract, salt, and stevia to the blender and process until smooth. 3. Add the ice cubes and pulse until thick and creamy, tamping down as necessary. 4. Pour into a glass and serve immediately.
Per Serving: Calories 304; Total Fat 30.9g; Sodium 181mg; Total Carbs 8.2g; Fiber 2g; Sugars 3.9g; Protein 1.4g

Flaxseed Piña Colada

Prep time: 10 minutes | Cooking time: 0 minutes | Serves: 1

¼ cup chopped fresh pineapple
⅔ cup canned unsweetened full-fat coconut milk
1 teaspoon milled golden flaxseed
1 teaspoon vanilla extract
¼ teaspoon coconut extract
⅛ teaspoon sea salt
6 drops liquid stevia
1 cup ice cubes

1. Add the pineapple, coconut milk, flaxseed, vanilla extract, coconut extract, salt, and stevia to your high-speed blender and process until smooth. 2. Add the ice cubes and pulse until thick and creamy, tamping down as necessary. 3. Pour into a glass and serve immediately.
Per Serving: Calories 365; Total Fat 33.6g; Sodium 195mg; Total Carbs 3.6g; Fiber 7g; Sugars 1.8g; Protein 9.7g

Creamy French Toast

Prep time: 10 minutes | Cooking time: 0 minutes | Serves: 2

1 large egg
2 tablespoons heavy cream
1 tablespoon plus 2 teaspoons powdered erythritol
3 drops liquid stevia
½ teaspoon pure vanilla extract
½ teaspoon ground cinnamon
4 slices bread
1 tablespoon coconut oil
4 tablespoons red raspberries

1. In a suitable shallow bowl, lightly beat the egg, cream, 1 tablespoon powdered erythritol, liquid stevia, vanilla, and cinnamon. Dip each slice of bread in the egg mixture, letting it soak in. 2. Heat a suitable nonstick skillet over medium heat. Once hot, add the coconut oil. Once the oil is melted, add the dipped bread slices. 3. Cook until the bread is golden on both sides, for almost 4–5 minutes on the first side and 2–3 minutes on the second side. 4. Sift the remaining 2 teaspoons powdered erythritol on top, sprinkle on the raspberries, and serve.
Per Serving: Calories 282; Total Fat 9.8g; Sodium 162mg; Total Carbs 1.9g; Fiber 5.7g; Sugars 4.3g; Protein 7.8g

Low-Carb Pancakes

Prep time: 10 minutes | Cooking time: 0 minutes | Serves: 2

6 tablespoons almond flour
4 tablespoons golden milled flaxseed
1 tablespoon granulated erythritol
1 teaspoon baking powder
⅛ teaspoon salt
2 large eggs
3 tablespoons half-and-half
1 teaspoon pure vanilla extract
7 drops liquid stevia
4 teaspoons ghee

1. In a suitable bowl, beat the almond flour, flaxseed, granulated erythritol, baking powder, and salt. Beat in the eggs, half-and-half, vanilla, and liquid stevia. Let the batter rest for almost 3 minutes. 2. Preheat a suitable cast-iron skillet over high heat. Once hot, turn the heat down to medium to medium-high. 3. Add the ghee, and use a ¼-cup measure to pour out this pancake batter into the hot skillet. 4. Cook until this pancakes are light golden on both sides, flipping once. for almost 2–3 minutes on the first side and 1–2 minutes on the second side.
Per Serving: Calories 344; Total Fat 17g; Sodium 66mg; Total Carbs 8.9g; Fiber 12.2g; Sugars 27g; Protein 5.6g

Egg Cheese Muffin Sandwiches

Prep time: 10 minutes | Cooking time: 0 minutes | Serves: 4

4 large eggs
1 tablespoon ghee
4 (1-ounce) slices gouda cheese
¾ cup arugula
4 English muffins, split in half and toasted
⅛ teaspoon black pepper

1. In a suitable skillet over medium heat, fry the eggs in the ghee any way you like. Add 1 slice gouda on top of each fried egg. 2. Divide the arugula between four English muffin bottoms, top each with a fried egg, a sprinkle of black pepper, and then the English muffin top. 3. Serve immediately.
Per Serving: Calories 222; Total Fat 13.6g; Sodium 738mg; Total Carbs 2g; Fiber 2g; Sugars 4.4g; Protein 13.7g

Whey Waffles

Prep time: 10 minutes | Cooking time: 0 minutes | Serves: 2

Nonstick spray
6 tablespoons almond flour
4 tablespoons ground flaxseed
1 scoop (26 g) unflavored whey protein powder
1 teaspoon baking powder
1 tablespoon granulated erythritol
8 drops liquid stevia
⅛ teaspoon salt
1 teaspoon pure vanilla extract
3 large eggs
2 tablespoons heavy whipping cream

1. Plug in your waffle iron. Once heated, coat with nonstick spray. 2. In a suitable bowl, beat all the recipe ingredients until well combined, making sure there are no lumps. Alternatively, you can put all the recipe ingredients into your high-speed blender and blend until smooth. 3. Pour half of the batter into the heated and sprayed waffle iron. The waffle is done when it starts to steam. for almost 2 minutes. 4. Carefully remove the waffle and repeat with the remaining waffle batter.
Per Serving: Calories 257; Total Fat 17.9g; Sodium 1062mg; Total Carbs 1.2g; Fiber 0.1g; Sugars 1.2g; Protein 22.2g

Monkey Bread

Prep time: 10 minutes | Cooking time: 50 minutes | Serves: 16

2 teaspoons instant yeast
3 tablespoons warm water
2 cups almond flour
4 tablespoons powdered erythritol
4 teaspoons baking powder
2 teaspoons psyllium husk powder
1 teaspoon ground cinnamon
¼ teaspoon salt
3 cups shredded low-moisture part-skim mozzarella cheese
2 ounces cream cheese
2 large eggs, lightly beaten
2 teaspoons vanilla bean paste
½ teaspoon almond extract
¼ teaspoon stevia glycerite
Coconut oil, for your hands
3 tablespoons unsalted butter, melted
10 tablespoons granulated monk fruit/erythritol blend

1. At 375°F/191°C, preheat your oven. 2. In a suitable bowl, add the yeast and warm water and stir to combine. Keep it aside until foamy. for almost 5–10 minutes. 3. In a suitable bowl, beat the almond flour, powdered erythritol, baking powder, psyllium husk powder, cinnamon, and salt. Keep it aside. 4. In a suitable microwave-safe bowl, add the mozzarella and cream cheese. Microwave for almost 60 seconds and then give it a stir, and continue microwaving in 20-second increments until the cheese is melted. 5. Mix the foamy yeast mixture into the melted cheese until well-mixed. 6. Stir in the beaten eggs, vanilla bean paste, almond extract, and stevia glycerite until well-mixed. 7. Stir in the flour mixture until it forms a dough. 8. Oil your hands with coconut oil, and knead the prepared dough until it comes as a ball. Cover and refrigerate 10 minutes. 9. Divide the prepared dough into sixteen equal pieces and roll each piece into a ball. Roll each ball in melted butter and then in the granulated monk fruit/erythritol blend to coat. 10. Arrange the coated balls of dough in a Bundt cake pan; refrigerate 15 minutes. 11. Bake for 30 minutes uncovered, and then cover the Bundt pan with foil and bake for about 5–10 minutes more. 12. Carefully invert onto a platter while still hot. Serve hot.
Per Serving: Calories 194; Total Fat 10.4g; Sodium 2576mg; Total Carbs 5.2g; Fiber 2.5g; Sugars 1.2g; Protein 21.1g

Morning Doughnuts

Prep time: 15 minutes | Cooking time: 30 minutes | Serves: 6

Doughnuts
Coconut oil spray, for your hands and this pan
1 teaspoon instant yeast
1½ tablespoons warm water
1 cup almond flour
2 tablespoons powdered erythritol
2 teaspoons baking powder
1 teaspoon psyllium husk powder
1½ teaspoons ground cinnamon
⅛ teaspoon salt
1½ cups shredded low-moisture part-skim mozzarella cheese
1 ounce cream cheese
1 large egg, lightly beaten
1 teaspoon vanilla bean paste
¼ teaspoon almond extract
⅛ teaspoon stevia glycerite
3 tablespoons granulated monk fruit/erythritol blend
2 tablespoons unsalted butter, melted
Vanilla glaze
8 tablespoons powdered erythritol
1 tablespoon heavy whipping cream
2 teaspoons water
½ teaspoon pure vanilla extract
Pinch salt
3 drops almond extract

To prepare the doughnuts: 1. At 350°F/177°C, preheat your oven. Spray the inside of a doughnut pan with coconut oil. 2. In a suitable bowl, add the yeast and warm water and stir to combine. Keep it aside until foamy. for almost 5–10 minutes. 3. In a suitable bowl, beat the almond flour, powdered erythritol, baking powder, psyllium husk powder, ½ teaspoon cinnamon, and salt. Keep it aside. 4. In a suitable microwave-safe bowl, add the mozzarella and cream cheese. Microwave for almost 60 seconds and then give it a stir, and continue microwaving in 20-second until the cheese is melted. 5. Mix the foamy yeast mixture into the melted cheese until well-mixed, and then stir in the beaten egg, vanilla bean paste, almond extract, and stevia glycerite until well-mixed. 6. Stir in the flour mixture until it forms a dough. Oil your hands with coconut oil, and knead the prepared dough a couple times until it comes as a ball. Cover the prepared dough with a piece of plastic wrap and let it sit at room temperature for almost 15 minutes. 7. In a shallow bowl, stir the granulated monk fruit/erythritol blend and remaining 1 teaspoon cinnamon to make a cinnamon sugar. 8. Divide the prepared dough into six equal pieces and roll each piece into a ball. Roll a ball in the melted butter, and then roll it in the cinnamon sugar. Poke a mini hole in the center of the ball and shape it into a doughnut shape. Place the prepared doughnut into the prepared doughnut pan. Repeat with the remaining five balls of dough. 9. Bake the prepared doughnuts until golden and a toothpick inserted in the center comes out clean or with just a couple crumbs, for almost 15 minutes. 10. Let the prepared doughnuts cool in this pan 5 minutes before removing.
For the vanilla glaze: 1. In a suitable shallow bowl, stir all the recipe ingredients for the glaze. 2. Dip each doughnut in the glaze, and let the glaze harden before serving.
Per Serving: Calories 123; Total Fat 8.6g; Sodium 762mg; Total Carbs 2.1g; Fiber 0.6g; Sugars 0.7g; Protein 9.8g

Mushroom Quiche

Prep time: 10 minutes | Cooking time: 50 minutes | Serves: 10

1 press-in crust, pressed into a 7" springform pan
2 tablespoons unsalted butter
8 ounces button mushrooms, sliced
5 ounces baby spinach
2 large cloves garlic, minced
¼ cup chopped roasted red bell
pepper
4 large eggs
½ cup heavy whipping cream
½ teaspoon salt
¼ teaspoon black pepper
1 cup shredded sharp white cheddar cheese

1. At 350°F/177°C, preheat your oven. Pre-bake the press-in crust for almost 5 minutes. 2. Add the butter to a suitable, deep skillet over medium heat. Once melted, add the mushrooms and cook until softened, for almost 8–10 minutes, stirring occasionally. 3. Add the spinach and garlic and cook until the spinach is wilted and the liquid is evaporated off, for almost 2–3 minutes, stirring continuously. 4. Turn off the heat, stir in the roasted red bell pepper, and cool slightly. 5. In a suitable bowl, beat the eggs, cream, salt, and black pepper. Stir in the cooled vegetable mixture and the cheddar. 6. Pour the egg mixture into the pre-baked crust. 7. Bake until the quiche is set, for almost 40–50 minutes.
Per Serving: Calories 384; Total Fat 24.7g; Sodium 1130mg; Total Carbs 1.9g; Fiber 2g; Sugars 3.4g; Protein 19.3g

Pecan French Toast

Prep time: 10 minutes | Cooking time: 55 minutes | Serves: 8

1 tablespoon unsalted butter, at room temperature
10 large egg yolks
1½ cups half-and-half
½ cup heavy whipped cream
1/3 cup granulated erythritol
20 drops liquid stevia
1 tablespoon pure vanilla extract
2 teaspoons ground cinnamon
1 teaspoon ground nutmeg
¼ teaspoon salt
4 cups cubed white bread
¼ cup chopped pecans
¼ cup sugar-free maple-flavored syrup (preferably stevia-sweetened maple syrup), for serving

1. Spread the butter on the inside of a 1½-quart casserole dish. 2. In a suitable bowl, beat the egg yolks, half-and-half, cream, granulated erythritol, liquid stevia, vanilla, cinnamon, nutmeg, and salt. Add the bread cubes and toss gently to coat. 3. Pour the prepared mixture into the prepared casserole dish, lightly pushing down the bread so it's mostly submerged in the liquid. Cover this dish with foil and refrigerate overnight. 4. At 375°F/191°C, preheat your oven. Take the casserole dish out of the refrigerator and let it sit at room temperature for almost 20 minutes while your oven is preheating. 5. Bake the casserole (covered with foil) for almost 50 minutes, and then remove the foil, sprinkle the pecans on top, and bake 5 more minutes. 6. Serve warm along with maple-flavored syrup to drizzle on top.
Per Serving: Calories 378; Total Fat 16.2g; Sodium 369mg; Total Carbs 5.8g; Fiber 1.9g; Sugars 15.6g; Protein 7.6g

Sausage Bread Pudding

Prep time: 10 minutes | Cooking time: 1 hour 10 minutes | Serves: 9

6 cornbread muffins
1 pound Italian turkey sausage
2 leeks, white parts only, sliced
2 large cloves garlic, crushed or minced
1 teaspoon minced fresh thyme
7 large eggs
1 cup heavy whipping cream
¼ cup water
1 cup shredded gruyere cheese
¼ teaspoon salt
¼ teaspoon black pepper
Olive oil spray

1. At 350°F/177°C, preheat your oven. Layer a suitable baking tray with parchment paper or a Silpat liner. 2. Cut each cornbread muffin into cubes, spread the cubes out on the prepared baking tray, and bake until golden, for almost 20 minutes. Cool. 3. Heat a suitable skillet over medium-high heat. Once hot, add the sausage, leeks, and garlic and cook until the meat is browned and the liquid is evaporated. for almost 8 minutes, stirring occasionally. Stir in the thyme. Cool. 4. In a suitable bowl, beat the eggs, cream, water, gruyere, salt, and black pepper. Stir in the sausage mixture, and then gently stir in the cornbread cubes. 5. Spray the inside of a 9" × 13" casserole dish with olive oil. Pour the egg mixture into the dish. Cover the dish with foil. 6. Bake (covered) 40 minutes, and then bake (uncovered) 10 minutes more. 7. Let the casserole sit for almost 10–15 minutes before serving. Serve warm.
Per Serving: Calories 383; Total Fat 25.2g; Sodium 184mg; Total Carbs 5g; Fiber 0.9g; Sugars 14.7g; Protein 5.1g

Mushroom Cream Crepes

Prep time: 10 minutes. | Cooking time: 25 minutes. | Serves: 4

1 boneless, skinless chicken breast, cut into ½-inch pieces
1 cup sliced mushrooms
2 cups heavy cream
4 large eggs
1 yellow onion, sliced
4 slices bacon, cooked and chopped
black pepper and sea salt to taste
Olive oil for this pan
Optional garnish: chopped parsley and/or chives

1. Whisk the eggs with about a tablespoon of heavy cream and season with black pepper and salt. 2. Heat a suitable pan over medium heat and add a bit of olive oil to it. 3. Pour approximately ½ cup of the egg mixture to this pan and swirl to evenly coat this pan. 4. Once the eggs have set, flip and cook for almost 1 minute. Transfer to a paper towel and repeat 3 times with the remaining egg mixture. 5. In a suitable pan, sauté the chicken, onions, and mushrooms until the chicken is cooked through. Season with black pepper and salt. 6. Stir in the bacon and the heavy cream. Cook about 4 minutes, until slightly thickened. 7. Divide most the chicken mixture between the 4 egg crepes, fold, and top with the remaining cream. Serve and enjoy!
Per Serving: Calories 302; Total Fat 21.3g; Sodium 354mg; Total Carbs 6g; Fiber 2.3g; Sugars 2.5g; Protein 23.1g

Mascarpone Pancakes

Prep time: 5 minutes | Cooking time: 10 minutes | Serves: 2

6 eggs
1 cup mascarpone cheese
¼ cup ground flaxseeds
¼ cup chia seeds
1½ teaspoons baking powder
½ teaspoon salt

Suggested toppings
Butter
Low-carb syrup
Sour cream
Berries

1. Mix the flaxseeds, chia seeds, baking powder, and salt in a bowl. Add the eggs to the dry ingredients one at a time, whisking well after each egg. 2. Add the mascarpone cheese and whisk until smooth. Alternatively, put all of the ingredients into your high-speed blender to achieve the same results. If you want to sweeten the batter, add about a teaspoon of sugar substitute at this point and mix well. 3. Spray a griddle or nonstick skillet with cooking oil spray and set over medium-high heat. 4. Use a suitable spoon or, preferably, a ladle (this is the perfect size for cooking pancakes) to pour this pancake batter into the skillet once the skillet is hot. 5. Allow this pancake to cook for almost 2 minutes before carefully flipping it over with a spatula. Cook the other side for almost 2 minutes. 6. Set the timing accordingly if you would prefer your pancakes more or less browned.
Per Serving: Calories 117; Total Fat 8.2g; Sodium 354mg; Total Carbs 4.1g; Fiber 1.7g; Sugars 1.1g; Protein 7.3g

Italian Breakfast

Prep time: 15 minutes | Cooking time: 10 minutes | Serves: 2

2 large eggs
3-4 slices prosciutto ham
1 clove garlic, peeled
½ cup arugula

10 cherry tomatoes, halved
Celtic sea salt
Black pepper
4 tablespoons butter

1. Heat 1 tablespoon of butter in a suitable skillet over a medium to high heat. 2. Crack and fry the eggs, preferably sunny-side up, until the edges are golden (usually around 3-4 minutes). Remove from this pan and set to one side for the moment. 3. Next, crush the garlic clove. Add more butter, if needed, then add the garlic to the skillet and sauté until it begins to turn a golden brown. Add a dash of black pepper and salt. 4. Sauté the halved tomatoes for almost 2-3 minutes, turning halfway through.
Per Serving: Calories 233; Total Fat 18.5g; Sodium 97mg; Total Carbs 1.4g; Fiber 1.8g; Sugars 0.2g; Protein 8.3g

Prosciutto Eggs Benedict

Prep time: 10 minutes | Cooking time: 30 minutes | Serves: 4

8 ham or prosciutto slices
8 large eggs
Bun
3 eggs, separated
¼ cup unflavored protein powder
2 tablespoons coconut flour

Hollandaise sauce
3 egg yolks
¼ cup lemon juice
1 tablespoon Dijon mustard
½ cup butter, melted
black pepper and sea salt to taste

To make the buns: 1. At 325°F/163°C, preheat your oven. 2. Separate the eggs (reserve the egg yolks) and whip the egg whites until stiff peaks form. 3. Gently mix in the protein powder and coconut flour. 4. Grease a suitable baking sheet and evenly divide the prepared mixture into 4 mounds, for almost the size of a hamburger bun, onto the sheet. Bake for almost 15–20 minutes or until golden brown. 5. Allow to cool completely before slicing in half lengthwise.
To prepare the hollandaise sauce: 1. Place the reserved egg yolks, lemon juice, and Dijon mustard in the top of a double boiler set over simmering water. Whisk to blend. 2. Whisking constantly, add the melted butter in a slow, steady stream. Cook the sauce, whisking constantly, until thickened. 3. Season with black pepper and salt and remove from heat.
To assemble: 1. Slice a bun in half, plate, and top each half with a slice of ham or prosciutto. 2. Top each half with poached egg and 2-3 tablespoons hollandaise sauce. Serve immediately.
Per Serving: Calories 612 Fat 47g; Sodium 1103mg; Carbs 14.4g; Fiber 1.4g; Sugar 6.6g; Protein 33g

Ricotta Sausage Pie

Prep time: 10 minutes | Cooking time: 35 minutes | Serves: 6

6 cups kale, chopped
1½ cups ricotta cheese
1-pound breakfast sausage
4 eggs
1 cup shredded cheddar cheese

½ yellow onion, diced
3 cloves garlic, minced
2 tablespoons olive oil
black pepper and sea salt to taste

1. At 350°F/177°C, preheat your oven. 2. Heat the olive oil in a suitable skillet and add the onions and garlic. 3. Cook until softened. Add the kale and cook for almost 5 minutes, until wilted. 4. Rub with black pepper and salt and remove from heat. 5. Beat the eggs in a suitable bowl. Add the ricotta and shredded cheddar. 6. Stir in the sautéed kale. 7. Roll out the breakfast sausage and press it into a 9-inch pie pan, making sure to go up the sides of this pan. 8. Pour in the filling and place on a suitable baking sheet to catch any drippings from the sausage. 9. Bake for almost 30–35 minutes, until the eggs are set. 10. Allow to rest for almost 5–10 minutes, slice into 6 pieces and serve!
Per Serving: Calories 158; Total Fat 2.1g; Sodium 90mg; Total Carbs 4.4g; Fiber 7.5g; Sugars 26.1g; Protein 3.1g

Ham Frittata

Prep time: 10 minutes | Cooking time: 30 minutes | Serves: 6

8 ounces diced ham
2 bell peppers, any color, diced
½ red onion, diced
8-10 cherry tomatoes, quartered
½ cup fresh cilantro, chopped
⅔ cup shredded pepper jack cheese

10 large eggs
2 egg whites
½ cup milk
black pepper and sea salt to taste
Optional garnishes: diced green onions, salsa, sour cream

1. At 350°F/177°C, preheat your oven. Grease a 9-inch glass pie pan. 2. Brown the ham in a suitable skillet until golden brown. Remove from pan and keep it aside. 3. Using the same skillet, cook the peppers, onion and cherry tomatoes until softened. 4. In a suitable bowl, beat the eggs, egg whites and milk. 5. Evenly sprinkle the sausage and veggies into the prepared pie pan. Top with the chopped cilantro. Pour the egg mixture on top and season with black pepper and salt. 6. Top with the shredded cheese and bake for almost 25–30 minutes, or until set. 7. Allow to cool for almost 5–10 minutes and slice into 6 servings. 8. Top with optional garnishes and enjoy!
Per Serving: Calories 125; Total Fat 3.2g; Sodium 16mg; Total Carbs 0.4g; Fiber 6.9g; Sugars 11.1g; Protein 5.1g

Eggs with Hollandaise Sauce

Prep time: 10 minutes | Cooking time: 20 minutes | Serves: 4

4 strips of bacon, chopped
2 cups baby spinach or kale
8 large eggs
Optional garnish: fresh basil
Hollandaise sauce

2 egg yolks
¼ cup butter, melted
1 tablespoon lemon juice
¼ teaspoon salt

To prepare the hollandaise sauce: 1. In a high speed blender, blend the egg yolks with the lemon juice and salt. 2. Slowly pour the melted butter into the blender while it's running. Blend for almost 30 seconds, until thickened. 3. Pour into a suitable bowl set over a sauce pan of simmering water to keep warm until ready to use.
For the baked eggs: 1. At 400°F/204°C, preheat your oven. 2. Set the rack in the top third of your oven. 3. Heat a suitable skillet over medium heat. Cook the bacon until crisp. Add the greens and sauté until wilted. 4. Divide the prepared mixture evenly between 4 large ramekins or gratin dishes. 5. Gently crack 2 eggs onto the filling of each ramekin. Place on a suitable baking sheet and into your oven for almost 10–12 minutes, until the white is set, but the yolk is still runny. 6. Drizzle with hollandaise sauce, garnish with fresh basil, if desired, and serve immediately.
Per Serving: Calories 397; Total Fat 37.7g; Sodium 595mg; Total Carbs 5.1g; Fiber 7.3g; Sugars 4.5g; Protein 5.3g

Egg-Stuffed Bell Peppers

Prep time: 10 minutes | Cooking time: 45 minutes | Serves: 4

4 yellow bell peppers, halved lengthwise and seeded
5 large eggs
1 cup shredded cheddar cheese
4 slices bacon, cooked and crumbled
¼ cup heavy cream
¼ cup chopped frozen spinach, thawed
3 green onions, chopped
black pepper and sea salt to taste

1. At 350°F/177°C, preheat your oven. 2. In a suitable bowl, whisk the eggs and heavy cream until frothy. Add the sliced green onions, spinach, half of the shredded cheese and bacon. Mix until well combined and season with black pepper and salt. 3. Place the bell pepper halves in a lightly greased baking dish and divide the egg mixture between the peppers. Sprinkle with the remaining cheese. 4. Cover with foil and bake for almost 45 minutes, until the eggs are set. Serve immediately.
Per Serving: Calories 391; Total Fat 21.2g; Sodium 58mg; Total Carbs 4.6g; Fiber 3.5g; Sugars 24.5g; Protein 13.2g

Spinach Mushroom Quiche

Prep time: 10 minutes | Cooking time: 50 minutes | Serves: 6

1 (10-ounce) box frozen spinach, thawed and drained
2 (4-ounce) cans sliced mushrooms, drained
1 cup shredded mozzarella cheese
⅓ cup grated parmesan cheese
6 large eggs
½ cup heavy cream
½ cup water
½ teaspoon garlic powder
black pepper and sea salt to taste

1. At 350°F/177°C, preheat your oven. Grease a 9-inch pie pan. 2. Evenly spread the thawed and drained spinach into the bottom of the pie pan. Top with the mushroom slices. 3. Whisk the eggs with the heavy cream and water. Mix in the parmesan cheese, garlic powder, salt, and pepper. 4. Pour the egg mixture into this pan. 5. Sprinkle with mozzarella cheese and bake for almost 40–50 minutes, until the center is set and the edges are golden brown. 6. Remove from oven and allow to cool for almost 5–10 minutes. Slice and serve!
Per Serving: Calories 316; Total Fat 18.4g; Sodium 235mg; Total Carbs 7.1g; Fiber 10.6g; Sugars 6.9g; Protein 8.2g

Bacon Fritters

Prep time: 10 minutes | Cooking time: 15 minutes | Serves: 6

⅔ cup cooked and crumbled bacon
1½ cups grated cheddar cheese
1 medium head cauliflower
3 large eggs
3 tablespoons coconut flour
2 cloves garlic, minced
black pepper and sea salt to taste
Coconut oil for this pan

1. Chop the cauliflower into ½-inch pieces and steam for almost 10–15 minutes, until soft. Drain well and mash with a fork or potato masher, pressing to release as much liquid as possible. 2. Transfer the cauliflower to a suitable bowl. Add the eggs, cheese, bacon, garlic, and coconut flour. Season with black pepper and salt and mix well. 3. Heat a suitable skillet over medium heat and add about a tablespoon of coconut oil. 4. Form the cauliflower mixture into flat patties, using about 2–3 tablespoons per patty. 5. Once this pan is hot, add a few of the patties and cook for almost 3–5 minutes, until browned on the bottom. Flip carefully and cook another 3–5 minutes. 6. Transfer the patty to a paper towel-lined plate and repeat with the remaining patties. Serve hot.
Per Serving: Calories 322; Total Fat 21.1g; Sodium 1469mg; Total Carbs 7.5g; Fiber 5.9g; Sugars 10.8g; Protein 8.7g

Chicken with Waffles

Prep time: 10 minutes | Cooking time: 0 minutes | Serves: 4

1 batch oven-fried chicken tenders
1 batch waffles
¼ cup sugar-free maple-flavored
syrup (preferably stevia-sweetened maple syrup), for serving

1. Serve half of each waffle topped with a quarter of the chicken tenders and 1 tablespoon of syrup.
Per Serving: Calories 334; Total Fat 3.4g; Sodium 211mg; Total Carbs 5.9g; Fiber 4.9g; Sugars 21.4g; Protein 11.5g

Zucchini Egg Bake

Prep time: 10 minutes | Cooking time: 25 minutes | Serves: 6

4 small zucchinis, cut into ½-inch thick rounds
6 slices ham or Canadian bacon
½ cup grated asiago cheese
6 large eggs
1 small bunch parsley, chopped
black pepper and sea salt to taste

1. At 350°F/177°C, preheat your oven. Prepare an 8x8 baking dish with non-stick spray. 2. Cut the ham slices in half, then cut each half lengthwise into ¼-inch thick strips. 3. Cook the ham strips in a suitable skillet over medium heat for almost 3 minutes, until golden brown. Add the zucchini and continue to cook for almost 5 minutes, until softened. 4. In a suitable bowl, whisk the eggs until frothy. Season with black pepper and salt. 5. Mix the ham and zucchini into the eggs. Add the chopped parsley and mix until well combined. 6. Pour the prepared mixture into the prepared baking dish. Sprinkle the asiago cheese evenly over the top and bake for almost 20–25 minutes, until the eggs are set. 7. Allow to rest for almost 5 minutes before serving.
Per Serving: Calories 353; Total Fat 21.4g; Sodium 119mg; Total Carbs 3.6g; Fiber 12.6g; Sugars 20.2g; Protein 11.7g

Sausage Stuffed Peppers

Prep time: 10 minutes | Cooking time: 6 hours | Serves: 4

1 pound Italian sausage
4 bell peppers
½ head of cauliflower
1 (8-ounce) can tomato paste
1 small yellow onion, diced
3 garlic cloves, minced
2 teaspoons oregano
black pepper and sea salt to taste

1. Chop the tops off of the bell peppers and discard the seeds. Save the tops. 2. Grate the cauliflower into "rice" with a cheese grater or food processor and transfer to a suitable mixing bowl. 3. Add the minced garlic, oregano, and onion. Mix well to combine. 4. Add the sausage and tomato paste to the cauliflower mixture and mix well with your hands. Season with black pepper and salt. 5. Evenly divide the sausage mixture between the peppers. Cover each pepper with their tops and gently place into your slow cooker. 6. Cook on low for almost 6 hours. Serve and enjoy!
Per Serving: Calories 306; Total Fat 29.6g; Sodium 987mg; Total Carbs 1g; Fiber 4.2g; Sugars 2.9g; Protein 5.8g

Eggs with Avocado Salsa

Prep time: 10 minutes | Cooking time: 30 minutes | Serves: 4

8 large eggs
1 avocado, diced
1 cup cherry tomatoes, quartered
¼ cup red onion, diced
Juice of 1 lime
½ cup cilantro, chopped
½ a jalapeño, minced
¼ cup feta cheese
½ teaspoon sea salt

1.To prepare the avocado salsa: Mix everything except the eggs in a suitable bowl and mix well. Cover and refrigerate until ready to serve. 2. To soft boil the eggs: Fill a suitable saucepan with water and cook to a boil. Reduce its heat to a simmer and add the eggs to the pot. Cook 5 minutes for a runny yolk, or 7 minutes for a soft-set yolk. Remove it from the heat and run the eggs under cold water for almost 1 minute, or until cool enough to peel. 3. Gently peel the eggs and plate with a big scoop of the avocado salsa. Enjoy!
Per Serving: Calories 223; Total Fat 12g; Sodium 845mg; Total Carbs 5.4g; Fiber 3.8g; Sugars 4.8g; Protein 17.4g

Blueberry Cake

Prep time: 10 minutes | Cooking time: 30 minutes | Serves: 6

1 cup fresh or frozen blueberries (or other berry of choice)
4 large eggs, separated
½ cup coconut flour
¼ cup coconut oil
¼ cup sugar substitute
2 teaspoons vanilla extract
¼ teaspoon baking soda
1 teaspoon cream of tartar
Topping
¼ cup coconut sugar
¼ cup coconut oil
2 tablespoons coconut flour
½ teaspoon cinnamon

1. At 350°F/177°C, preheat your oven. Prepare an 8x8 baking pan with non-stick spray. 2. In a suitable bowl, mix the egg whites and cream of tartar. Whisk until stiff peaks form. 3. In another bowl, cream the sugar substitute and coconut oil. Mix in the egg yolks. 4. Slowly stir in the coconut flour, vanilla, and baking soda. Mix until just combined. 5. Gently fold the egg whites into the batter. Pour into the prepared pan. Evenly scatter the blueberries on top. 6. In a suitable bowl, mix the ingredients for the topping. 7. Spread the prepared mixture over the batter. 8. Bake for almost 30 minutes, or until a toothpick inserted comes out clean. 9. Allow to cool to room temperature before cutting into squares.
Per Serving: Calories 348; Total Fat 32.6g; Sodium 595mg; Total Carbs 6.5g; Fiber 8.8g; Sugars 5.5g; Protein 3.4g

Meatballs with Apple Chutney

Prep time: 10 minutes | Cooking time: 30 minutes | Serves: 4

For the meatballs
½ pound lean ground pork
1 teaspoon onion powder
1 teaspoon salt
1 teaspoon garam masala

For the apple chutney
2 medium tart apples (such as granny smith)
¼ cup raisins
2 tablespoons butter
½ teaspoon garam masala
1 tablespoon maple syrup
2 tablespoons water
1 tablespoon apple cider vinegar

1. At 400°F/204°C, preheat your oven. Layer a suitable baking sheet with parchment paper. 2. In a suitable bowl, mix all of the meatball the recipe ingredients. Mix well with hands. 3. Portion into small balls and bake for almost 15–20 minutes, until cooked through.
To prepare the chutney: 1. Mix all of the ingredients into a suitable saucepan over medium heat. 2. Cook to a simmer, cover, and allow to cook for almost 6–8 minutes, stirring occasionally. 3. Mash the chutney with a potato masher or fork until few chunks remain. 4. Top the meatballs with the chutney and enjoy.
Per Serving: Calories 343; Total Fat 26.6g; Sodium 924mg; Total Carbs 1.2g; Fiber 7.1g; Sugars 0.6g; Protein 20.3g

Egg Casserole

Prep time: 10 minutes | Cooking time: 30 minutes | Serves: 6

12 large eggs
1-pound breakfast sausage
1 zucchini, sliced
½ red onion, diced
½ green pepper, diced
1 cup half & half
½ cup shredded cheddar cheese
¼ teaspoon thyme
black pepper and sea salt to taste
Optional garnish: chopped fresh basil leaves

1. At 350°F/177°C, preheat your oven. 2. Prepare an 8x8 baking dish with non-stick spray. In a suitable skillet over medium heat, brown the sausage. 3. Once the sausage is cooked through, add the onions, peppers, and zucchini. 4. Cook until tender. Remove from heat. 5. In a suitable bowl, whisk the eggs until frothy. Season with salt, pepper, and thyme. 6. Add the vegetables to the eggs and pour into the prepared baking dish. Sprinkle evenly with the shredded cheese. 7. Bake for almost 30 minutes, until the eggs are set. 8. Garnish with chopped basil, if desired and serve.
Per Serving: Calories 335; Total Fat 26.5g; Sodium 52mg; Total Carbs 3.4g; Fiber 8.6g; Sugars 2.4g; Protein 16g

Traditional Spice Muffins

Prep time: 5 minutes | Cook time: 15 minutes | Yields: 6 muffins

1 cup blanched finely ground almond flour
2 tablespoons salted butter, melted
1 large egg, whisked
1 teaspoon ground allspice
¼ cup granular erythritol
2 teaspoons baking powder

1. In a large bowl, combine all ingredients. Evenly pour batter into six silicone muffin cups greased with cooking spray. 2. Put the muffin cups in the basket of the air fryer. Set the temperature of air fryer to 320°F/160°C and timer to 15 minutes. When the muffins are ready, they turn golden. 3. Let muffins cool in cups for 15 minutes to avoid crumbling. Serve warm.
Per Serving (1 muffin): Calories 160; Fat 14g; Sodium 123mg; Carbs 20g; Fiber 2g; Sugar 1g; Protein 5g

Salmon-Avocado Boats

Prep time: 10 minutes | Cook time: 0 minutes | Serves: 4

4 ounces wild-caught smoked salmon
2 ripe avocados
2 limes for juice and garnish
Sea salt and pepper to taste
8 cherry tomatoes, halved

1. Marinate the salmon in the juice of one lime for about an hour. 2. Cut the avocados in half lengthwise and remove the seeds. 3. Cut the salmon into strips and place it into the avocado center. 4. Top each avocado half with a lime wedge and several cherry tomato halves. 5. Serve immediately.
Per Serving: Calories 263; Fat 24g; Sodium 987mg; Carbs 4g; Fiber 2g; Sugar 1g; Protein 10g

Meatballs

Prep time: 10 minutes | Cook time: 15 minutes | Serves: 6

½ cup shredded sharp Cheddar cheese
1 pound ground pork breakfast sausage
¼ teaspoon ground black pepper
1 large egg, whisked
½ teaspoon salt
1-ounce cream cheese softened

1. Combine all ingredients in a large bowl—form the mixture into eighteen 1" meatballs. 2. Place meatballs into an air fryer basket. Select the temperature to 400°F/205°C and the timer for 15 minutes, shaking the basket three times during cooking. 3. Meatballs will be browned on the outside and have an internal temperature of at least 145°F/63°C when thoroughly cooked. 4. Serve warm.
Per Serving: Calories 288; Fat 24g; Sodium 742mg; Carbs 1g; Fiber 0g; Sugar 1g; Protein 11g

Cheesy Bacon Quiche

Prep time: 5 minutes | Cook time: 12 minutes | Serves: 2

3 large eggs
2 tablespoons heavy whipping cream
4 slices of cooked sugar-free
bacon, crumbled
½ cup shredded mild Cheddar cheese
¼ teaspoon salt

1. Whisk eggs, cream, and salt until combined. Mix in bacon and Cheddar. 2. Pour mixture evenly into two ungreased 4" ramekins. Place into air fryer basket. Set the temperature of air fryer to 320°F/160°C and the timer for 12 minutes. Quiche will be fluffy and set in the middle when done. 3. Let quiche cool in ramekins for 5 minutes. Serve warm.
Per Serving: Calories 380; Fat 28g; Sodium 971mg; Carbs 2g; Fiber 0g; Sugar 1g; Protein 24g

Cheddar Breakfast Bake

Prep time: 10 minutes | Cooking time: 45 minutes | Serves: 6

1-pound chorizo sausage
1 (8-ounce) can green chilies
1 cup shredded cheddar cheese
1 yellow onion, diced
½ head cauliflower
4 eggs, beaten
½ teaspoon garlic powder
black pepper and sea salt to taste
Optional garnish: sliced green onions

1. At 375°F/191°C, preheat your oven. Grease a 9x13 glass baking dish with olive oil. 2. In a suitable skillet over medium heat, cook the chorizo and onion until golden brown. 3. Add the chilies to this pan and mix well. Transfer to a suitable mixing bowl and allow to cool slightly. 4. Shred the cauliflower into "rice" using a food processor or cheese grater. Add to the bowl. 5. Stir in the beaten eggs and half of the cheese. Season with salt, pepper, and garlic powder. Pour into the prepared dish. Top with the remaining cheese. 6. Bake for almost 45 minutes, until the eggs are set and the cheese is golden brown. 7. Let rest for almost 5 minutes. Top with green onions, if desired. Serve!
Per Serving: Calories 216; Total Fat 20.6g; Sodium 639mg; Total Carbs 8.7g; Fiber 4.3g; Sugars 2.9g; Protein 3.1g

Mexican Breakfast Casserole

Prep time: 10 minutes | Cooking time: 25 minutes | Serves: 6

8 eggs, beaten
½ cup broccoli florets
½ pound bacon
1 yellow onion, diced
1 red bell pepper, diced
8 ounces mushrooms, sliced
1 sweet potato, peeled and diced
2 tablespoons taco seasoning
Garnish: guacamole, salsa, and fresh cilantro

1. Cook the bacon in a suitable skillet until crispy. Keep it aside. Crumble once cooled. 2. In the same skillet, cook the onions until translucent. 3. Transfer the crumbled bacon, onions, sweet potato, bell pepper, mushrooms, broccoli florets and eggs to a slow cooker. Stir to combine. 4. Sprinkle with taco seasoning and mix well. Cook on low for almost 6 hours. 5. Scoop into serving bowls, top with guacamole, salsa, and/or fresh cilantro.
Per Serving: Calories 579; Total Fat 18.3g; Sodium 689mg; Total Carbs 6.7g; Fiber 35.5g; Sugars 11g; Protein 30.2g

Avocado Breakfast Tacos

Prep time: 10 minutes | Cooking time: 15 minutes | Serves: 4

4 eggs
1 (10-ounce) can Rotel tomatoes
1 ripe avocado, sliced

black pepper and sea salt
½ cup fresh cilantro, chopped
4 low-carb tortillas

1. At 400°F/204°C, preheat your oven. Spray a suitable sized, oven-proof skillet with non-stick spray. 2. Pour the tomatoes into the skillet and place over medium heat. 3. Once almost all of the liquid has evaporated from the tomatoes, crack the eggs on top and season with black pepper and salt. 4. Transfer the skillet to your oven and bake for almost 10–12 minutes, until the egg whites are set. 5. Serve each egg alongside sliced avocado and fresh cilantro, with a low-carb tortilla.
Per Serving: Calories 231; Total Fat 21.3g; Sodium 710mg; Total Carbs 7.7g; Fiber 2.5g; Sugars 2.3g; Protein 5g

Dark Chocolate Matcha

Prep time: 5 minutes | Cook time: 0 minutes | Serves: 1

1 teaspoon vanilla extract
¼ teaspoon fresh lemon juice
⅛ teaspoon sea salt
⅔ cup canned unsweetened full-fat coconut milk
1 tablespoon unsweetened cocoa

powder
½ tablespoon milled golden flaxseed
1 cup ice cubes
¾ teaspoon powdered matcha
12 drops liquid stevia

1. Add coconut milk, cocoa powder, flaxseed, matcha, vanilla extract, lemon juice, salt, and stevia to the blender and process until smooth. 2. Add ice cubes and pulsate to thicken and creamy. 3. Pour into a glass and serve immediately.
Per Serving: Calories 359; Fat 35g; Sodium 315mg; Carbs 9g; Fiber 4g; Sugar 1g; Protein 6g

Chapter 2 Snacks and Appetizers

Chicken Meatballs in Buffalo Sauce 25
Tuna Filled Deviled Eggs 25
Egg Salad in Avocados 25
Instant Pot Peanuts 25
Green Chicken Meatballs 25
Hot Jalapeño Poppers 25
Crispy Broccoli Salad 25
Traditional Deviled Eggs 25
Blackened Chicken and Ranch 26
Savory Snack 26
Sweet Snack 26
Almond Crackers with Sesame 26
Healthy Seedy Crackers 26
Cheese Crackers 26
Savory Cheesy Biscotti 26
Healthy Graham Crackers 27
Cheesy Broccoli Hot Pockets 27
Corn Dog 27
Tasty Pretzel Bites 27
Tropical Macaroons 27
Pizza Muffin 28
Cheesy Za'atar Pinwheels 28
Healthy Peanut Butter Cookies 28
Crispy Tortilla Chips 28
Hot Beef Empanadas 28
Herby Mushroom Galettes 29
Chocolate Hazelnut Biscotti 29
Mascarpone Cheesecakes with Strawberry 29
Raspberry Cookies 29
Chocolate Coated Apricots 29
Crispy Wings 29
Jalapeño Chips 30
Radish Chips 30
Avocado Chips 30
Popcorns 30

Taquitos 30
Bake Kale Chips 30
Ants On a Log 30
Cheese Ball 30
Dragon Tail Poppahs 31
Tofu Fries 31
Crackers 31
Creamy Chipped Artichokes 31
Ranch Dorito Crackers 31
Red Pepper Edamame 31
Bacon-Stuffed Mushrooms 31
Bacon-Wrapped Pickles 31
Classy Crudités with Dip 32
Delicious Devil Eggs..................... 32
Bacon Asparagus 32
Cucumber Salsa........................... 32
Buffalo Chicken Thighs................... 32
Traditional El Presidente Guac 32
Hot Chili-Garlic Wings 32
Cheesy Hangover Homies 32
Steak Bites with Pepper Sauce 33
Bacon and Cheese Stuffed Jalapeños ... 33
Loaded Chayote Fries 33
Tropical Shrimp Dippers 33
Zucchini Chips 33
Parmesan Zucchini Fries 33
Cheesy Buffalo Chicken Quesadillas ... 34
Pretzel Bites with Sauce 34
Cheeseburgers 34
Stuffed Mushrooms with Burrata 34
Traditional Spinach-Artichoke Dip 34

Chicken Meatballs in Buffalo Sauce

Prep time: 4 minutes | Cook time: 10 minutes | Serves: 4

1-pound ground chicken	¼ teaspoon garlic powder
½ cup almond flour	1 cup water
2 tablespoons cream cheese	2 tablespoons butter, melted
1 packet dry ranch dressing mix	⅓ cup hot sauce
½ teaspoon salt	¼ cup crumbled feta cheese
¼ teaspoon pepper	¼ cup sliced green onion

1. Mix ground chicken, almond flour, cream cheese, ranch, salt, pepper, and garlic powder in a large bowl. Roll mixture into 16 balls. 2. Place meatballs on steam rack and add 1 cup water to Instant Pot. Click lid closed. Select the Meat button of pot and set the time for 10 minutes. 3. Combine butter and hot sauce. When timer beeps, remove meatballs and place in clean large bowl. Toss in hot sauce mixture. 4. Top with sprinkled feta and green onions to serve.
Per Serving: Calories 367; Fat 24.9g; Sodium 1131mg; Carbs 8.6g; Fiber 1.8g; Sugar 1.3g; Protein 25g

Tuna Filled Deviled Eggs

Prep time: 11 minutes | Cook time: 8 minutes | Serves: 3

1 cup water	1 celery stalk, diced finely
6 eggs	¼ teaspoon Dijon mustard
1 (5-ounce) can tuna, drained	¼ teaspoon chopped fresh dill
4 tablespoons mayo	¼ teaspoon salt
1 teaspoon lemon juice	⅛ teaspoon garlic powder

1. Add water to Instant Pot. Place a steam rack or steamer basket inside the pot. Carefully put eggs into the steamer basket. Click lid closed. Select the Egg button and adjust the time for 8 minutes. 2. Add remaining ingredients to medium bowl and mix. 3. When timer beeps, quick-release the steam and remove eggs. Place in bowl of cool water for 10 minutes, then remove shells. 4. Cut eggs in half and remove hard-boiled yolks, setting whites aside. Place yolks in a food processor and pulse until smooth, or mash with fork. 5. Add yolks to bowl with tuna and mayo, mixing until smooth. Spoon mixture into egg-white halves. Serve chilled.
Per Serving: Calories 303; Fat 22.4g; Sodium 558mg; Carbs 1.5g; Fiber 0.2g; Sugar 0.7g; Protein 20.2g

Egg Salad in Avocados

Prep time: 11 minutes | Cook time: 8 minutes | Serves: 2

1 cup water	½ teaspoon chili powder
6 eggs	¼ teaspoon salt
1 avocado	2 tablespoons mayo
2 tablespoons lime juice	2 tablespoons chopped cilantro

1. Pour water into Instant Pot. Place eggs on steam rack or in steamer basket inside pot. 2. Click lid closed. Select the Egg button and set the time for 8 minutes. While egg is cooking, cut avocado in half and scoop out flesh. Blend until smooth paste. 3. Transfer avocado to a medium bowl and add lime juice, chili powder, salt, mayo, and cilantro. 4. When timer beeps, carefully remove eggs and place in bowl of cold water for 5 minutes. 5. Peel eggs and chop into bite-sized pieces. Fold chopped eggs into avocado mixture. Serve chilled.
Per Serving: Calories 426; Fat 32.6g; Sodium 615mg; Carbs 8.7g; Fiber 5g; Sugar 1.2g; Protein 20.5g

Instant Pot Peanuts

Prep time: 4 minutes | Cook time: 60 minutes | Serves: 4

2 pounds raw green peanuts in shell	1 cup water
	¼ cup salt

1. Add all ingredients to Instant Pot. Peanuts will float, so place a steam rack or a steamer basket upside down on top of peanuts. 2. Select the Manual setting of the pot and adjust the time for 60 minutes. 3. When the timer beeps, allow a 20-minute natural release and quick-release the remaining pressure.
Per Serving: Calories 200; Fat 13.2g; Sodium 473mg; Carbs 13.4g; Fiber 5.5g; Sugar 1.6g; Protein 8.5g

Green Chicken Meatballs

Prep time: 5 minutes | Cook time: 15 minutes | Serves: 6

1-pound ground chicken	1 teaspoon salt
½ cup frozen spinach	¼ teaspoon pepper
1 egg	¼ teaspoon garlic powder
½ cup shredded pepper jack cheese	¼ teaspoon dried parsley
1 ounce cream cheese	1 cup water
	2 tablespoons coconut oil

1. Mix all ingredients except water and coconut oil in a large mixing bowl. Roll into 12 balls. 2. Pour water into Instant Pot and place steamer rack in bottom. Place meatballs on rack Click lid closed. 3. Select the Manual setting of the pot and adjust the time for 10 minutes. When timer beeps, allow a 5-minute natural release. Quick-release the remaining pressure. 4. Remove rack with meatballs and set aside. Pour out water and replace the inner pot. 5. Press the Sauté button and add coconut oil to Instant Pot. Once oil is heated, add meatballs until browned and crispy.
Per Serving: Calories 216; Fat 14.9g; Sodium 528mg; Carbs 1.2g; Fiber 0.4g; Sugar 0.3g; Protein 17.3g

Hot Jalapeño Poppers

Prep time: 11 minutes | Cook time: 3 minutes | Serves: 4

6 jalapeños, with seeds and membrane removed	cheese
4 ounces cream cheese	1 cup water
¼ cup shredded sharp cheddar	¼ cup cooked crumbled bacon

1. Cut the processed jalapeños lengthwise and then set them aside. 2. Mix cream cheese and cheddar in a small bowl. Spoon into emptied jalapeños. Pour water into Instant Pot and place steamer basket in the bottom. 3. Place stuffed jalapeños on the steamer rack. Click lid closed. Select the Manual setting of the pot and adjust the time 3 minutes. 4. When the timer beeps, quick-release the pressure. Serve topped with crumbled bacon.
Per Serving: Calories 185; Fat 14.3g; Sodium 342mg; Carbs 2.8g; Fiber 0.6g; Sugar 1.8g; Protein 7.5g

Crispy Broccoli Salad

Prep time: 11 minutes | Cook time: 10 minutes | Serves: 4

6 slices bacon	3 tablespoons Thai chili sauce
4 cups fresh broccoli, chopped	2 tablespoons pumpkin seeds
¼ cup mayo	

1. Press the Sauté button and add bacon to Instant Pot. Cook bacon until crisp. 2. Remove bacon when cooked and move on a paper towel until cool. Add broccoli into the bacon grease and stir-fry for 3 minutes until just beginning to soften. 3. Press the Cancel button. Remove the cooked broccoli and place it in a large bowl to set aside. 4. In a small bowl, mix mayo and chili sauce. Add sauce mixture to a large bowl. Crumble bacon over the bowl and toss. 5. Sprinkle the pumpkin seeds on top to serve. Serve warm or cold.
Per Serving: Calories 319; Fat 26.2g; Sodium 463mg; Carbs 10.7g; Fiber 0.4g; Sugar 5.0g; Protein 7.9g

Traditional Deviled Eggs

Prep time: 16 minutes | Cook time: 8 minutes | Serves: 3

6 eggs	⅛ teaspoon pepper
1 cup water	½ teaspoon yellow mustard
¼ cup mayo	¼ teaspoon paprika
½ teaspoon salt	

1. Place eggs on a steamer basket and add to the Instant Pot. Pour water into a pot and close the lid. Select the Egg button and set the time for 8 minutes. 2. When the timer beeps, quick-release the pressure and remove steamer basket. Place eggs in cold water and peel when cooled. Slice eggs in half lengthwise. 3. Remove yolks and set egg whites aside. Place yolks, mayo, salt, pepper, and mustard in a food processor and blend until smooth. 4. Place filling into egg whites. Sprinkle with paprika and refrigerate at least 30 minutes or until chilled.
Per Serving: Calories 268; Fat 22.1g; Sodium 650mg; Carbs 1g; Fiber 0.1g; Sugar 0.5g; Protein 12.8g

Blackened Chicken and Ranch

Prep time: 4 minutes | Cook time: 15 minutes | Serves: 1

2 ounces boneless, skinless chicken breast, cubed
¼ teaspoon dried thyme
¼ teaspoon paprika
¼ teaspoon pepper
¼ teaspoon garlic powder
3 tablespoons coconut oil
½ cup ranch dressing
2 tablespoons hot sauce

1. Toss chicken pieces in seasonings. Press the Sauté button and add coconut oil to Instant Pot. Sear chicken until dark golden brown and thoroughly cooked. 2. To make sauce, remove chicken from Instant Pot and press the Cancel button. Pour ranch and hot sauce into Instant Pot. 3. Use wooden spoon to scrape any seasoning from bottom of pot. Heat on Keep Warm for 5 minutes. 4. Pour into a small bowl for serving. Serve chicken bites warm with dipping sauce.
Per Serving: Calories 228; Fat 21.4g; Sodium 135mg; Carbs 1g; Fiber 0.3g; Sugar 0.2g; Protein 6.8g

Savory Snack

Prep time: 4 minutes | Cook time: 120 minutes | Serves: 8

2 cups whole almonds
2 cups pork rinds
½ cup pecans
4 tablespoons butter
1 teaspoon chili powder
½ teaspoon garlic powder
⅛ teaspoon cayenne

1. Place all ingredients into Instant Pot, place slow cooker lid on pot, and press the Slow Cook button. 2. Slow cook for 2 hours, stirring occasionally.
Per Serving: Calories 321; Fat 27.8g; Sodium 75mg; Carbs 8.9g; Fiber 5g; Sugar 1.8g; Protein 10g

Sweet Snack

Prep time: 4 minutes | Cook time: 120 minutes | Serves: 8

2 cups pork rinds
1 cup pecans
½ cup almonds
½ cup flaked unsweetened coconut
4 tablespoons butter
½ cup powdered erythritol
2 egg whites
½ teaspoon cinnamon
2 teaspoons vanilla extract
¼ cup low-carb chocolate chips

1. Break pork rinds into bite-sized pieces and place into Instant Pot. Press the Sauté button and add pecans, almonds, coconut flakes, and butter. Cook for 2–4 minutes until butter is completely melted. Press the Cancel button. 2. In a medium bowl, whip erythritol, egg whites, cinnamon, and vanilla until soft peaks form. Slowly add to Instant Pot. Gently fold mixture into ingredients already in pot. 3. Place slow cooker lid on pot and press the Slow Cook button. Adjust time for 2 hours. Stir every 20–30 minutes. 4. When mixture is dry and crunchy, place on a parchment-lined baking sheet to cool. 5. Once cooled fully, sprinkle with chocolate chips and store in sealed container.
Per Serving: Calories 274; Fat 23.9g; Sodium 80mg; Carbs 18.5g; Fiber 3.4g; Sugar 1.3g; Protein 6.4g

Almond Crackers with Sesame

Prep time: 4 minutes | Cook time: 20 minutes | Serves: 8

8 tablespoons unsalted butter, softened slightly
2 large egg whites
½ teaspoon salt
¼ teaspoon black pepper
2¼ cups almond flour
2 tablespoons sesame seeds

1. Preheat the oven to 350°F/175°C. 2. Beat the butter, egg whites, salt, and black pepper in a large bowl together. 3. Stir in the sesame seeds and almond flour. 4. Roll the dough between paper to a rectangle about the size of a half sheet pan (18" × 13"). 5. Peel off the top piece of the paper and place the crackers onto a half sheet pan. Peel off the top paper and use a ruler with a knife or pizza cutter to score the dough into crackers (to get forty-eight crackers, make six cuts lengthwise and eight cuts across). 6. Bake until golden, for about 18–24 minutes, rotating the tray once halfway through. 7. Cool completely, and then break up the crackers where the dough was scored.
Per Serving: Calories 229; Fat 28g; Sodium 172mg; Carbs 7g; Fiber 4g; Sugar 1g; Protein 8g

Healthy Seedy Crackers

Prep time: 11 minutes | Cook time: 30 minutes | Serves: 4

1 teaspoon extra-virgin olive oil, and more
½ cup golden flaxseed meal
½ cup raw sunflower seeds
1 tablespoon sesame seeds
1 large egg, lightly beaten
½ teaspoon salt

1. Line a sheet of parchment paper over a baking sheet and drizzle on 1 teaspoon olive oil. 2. Add the remaining olive oil, flaxseed meal, sunflower seeds, sesame seeds, the egg, and salt to a suitable bowl and toss them together until well combined. 3. Oil your hands, then press the dough onto the prepared baking tray into an 8" circle. 4. Bake the crackers for 15 minutes, then carefully flip the slab over and bake for an additional 15 minutes. 5. Let the cracker disk cool completely in the oven with the door ajar. 6. Once cooled, break into 1"–2" crackers (you'll get about sixteen crackers). 7. Serve crackers, or store them in an airtight container at room temperature for up to two weeks.
Per Serving: Calories 199; Fat 16g; Sodium 313mg; Carbs 9g; Fiber 6g; Sugar 1g; Protein 8g

Cheese Crackers

Prep time: 11 minutes | Cook time: 60 minutes | Serves: 8

4 tablespoons unsalted butter, softened slightly
1 large egg white
¼ teaspoon salt
1 cup plus 2 tablespoons almond
flour
1 teaspoon minced fresh thyme
1 cup shredded sharp white Cheddar cheese

1. Preheat the oven to 300°F/150°C. 2. Beat the egg white, butter, and salt together in a large bowl. 3. Stir in the almond flour, thyme, and then the Cheddar cheese until well incorporated. 4. Roll the dough between two pieces of parchment paper to a rectangle about 11" long by 9" wide. 5. Peel off the top paper and place the crackers (still on the bottom piece of parchment paper) onto an 18" x 13" half sheet pan. 6. Use a ruler with a knife or pizza cutter to score the dough into crackers (you should get around thirty-two crackers). 7. Bake until golden, for about 45–55 minutes, rotating the tray once halfway through. 8. Cool completely, and then break up the crackers where the dough was scored. 9. Keep them in an airproof container at room temperature for up to two weeks.
Per Serving: Calories 200; Fat 18g; Sodium 178mg; Carbs 4g; Fiber 2g; Sugar 1g; Protein 7g

Savory Cheesy Biscotti

Prep time: 11 minutes | Cook time: 15 minutes | Serves: 5

⅔ cup almond flour
2 tablespoons golden flaxseed meal
2 tablespoons freshly grated Parmesan cheese
1 tablespoon coconut flour
1 teaspoon garlic powder
1 teaspoon dried Italian herb
seasoning
¾ teaspoon baking powder
¼ teaspoon salt
⅛ teaspoon black pepper
2 tablespoons extra-virgin olive oil
2 large eggs

1. Preheat the oven to 350°F/175°C. Prepare a baking sheet with parchment paper. 2. Whisk together the almond flour, flaxseed meal, Parmesan, coconut flour, garlic powder, Italian herb seasoning, baking powder, salt, and black pepper. 3. Whisk in the olive oil with the eggs. Let the batter sit for 3 minutes to thicken slightly. Pour and spread the batter to a rectangle about 8"–9" long by 4"–5" wide. Bake the biscotti for 10 minutes, and then remove from oven. 4. Turn the oven down to 300°F/150°C. Cool the loaf for 10 minutes, then use a serrated knife to slice the loaf on a slight diagonal into ½"-thick slices. 5. Arrange the biscotti on the baking tray and bake until golden, about 35 minutes, flipping the biscotti over once halfway through. 6. Cool the biscotti in the oven.
Per Serving: Calories 194; Fat 17g; Sodium 243mg; Carbs 6g; Fiber 3g; Sugar 1g; Protein 7g

Healthy Graham Crackers

Prep time: 11 minutes | Cook time: 20 minutes | Serves: 8

8 tablespoons unsalted butter, softened slightly
2 large egg whites
1½ teaspoons blackstrap molasses
1 teaspoon pure vanilla extract
14 drops of liquid stevia
2¼ cups almond flour
4 tablespoons granulated erythritol
2 teaspoons ground cinnamon
½ teaspoon salt
⅛ teaspoon baking soda

1. Preheat the oven to 325°F/160°C. Beat the butter, egg whites, blackstrap molasses, vanilla, and liquid stevia in a bowl. Stir in the almond flour, granulated erythritol, cinnamon, salt, and baking soda. 2. Roll the dough between two parchment paper to a rectangle about the size of a half sheet pan (18" × 13"). Peel off the top paper and place the crackers (still on the bottom piece of parchment paper) onto a half sheet pan. 3. Score the dough into crackers. 4. Bake the crackers until golden, for about 20 minutes, rotating the tray once halfway through. Cool completely, then break up the crackers where the dough was scored.
Per Serving: Calories 293; Fat 27g; Sodium 192mg; Carbs 14g; Fiber 4g; Sugar 2g; Protein 8g

Cheesy Broccoli Hot Pockets

Prep time: 16 minutes | Cook time: 25 minutes | Serves: 12

Broccoli Cheddar Filling:
1½ cups chopped broccoli
1 tablespoon unsalted butter
1 large clove garlic, minced
3 ounces cream cheese
¼ cup heavy whipping cream
½ teaspoon Dijon mustard
¼ teaspoon onion powder
¼ teaspoon hot sauce
⅛ teaspoon salt
⅛ teaspoon black pepper
1 cup shredded yellow Cheddar cheese

Hot Pocket Crust:
3 cups shredded low-moisture part-skim mozzarella cheese
2 ounces cream cheese
2 large eggs
1 teaspoon apple cider vinegar
3 drops of liquid stevia
2 cups almond flour
2 teaspoons baking powder
Avocado oil, for your hands
1 large egg
1 tablespoon water

For the Broccoli Cheddar Filling: 1. Steam the broccoli for 2 minutes and drain well. Set aside. 2. In a small saucepan over low heat, heat the butter and cook the garlic for 30 seconds. Add the cream cheese, cream, Dijon, onion powder, hot sauce, salt, and black pepper, whisking until smooth. 3. Once smooth, whisk in the Cheddar a handful at a time. Stir the broccoli in the sauce.
For the Hot Pocket Crust: 1. Add the cream cheese and mozzarella cheese to a suitable microwave-safe bowl and melt in a microwave. Microwave the mixture for 60 seconds, then stir, and microwave again in 20-second increments until the cheese is thoroughly melted and combined when stirred. Whisk together the eggs, vinegar, and liquid stevia in a small bowl. 2. In a bowl, whisk the almond flour and baking powder. 3. Stir the egg mix in the melted cheese until combined, and then stir in the almond flour and mix until the dough forms. 4. Oil your hands and knead the dough until it comes together as a ball. Divide the dough into equal portions, forming each into a ball. 5. Roll each ball between two pieces of parchment paper to a rectangle 12" long by 9" wide. 6. Cut each dough ball once lengthwise down the middle, and three times crosswise, so you end up with twelve rectangles of dough (six from each dough ball), each 6" long by 3" wide.
To Assemble and Bake: 1. Preheat the oven to 375°F/190°C. Line two large baking trays with Silpat liners or parchment paper. 2. Spoon 4 tablespoons chilled Broccoli Cheddar Filling onto each of six rectangles, spreading it in an even layer but leaving a ¼" border along the outside. 3. To seal each pastry, carefully pick up one rectangle of dough that doesn't have filling and place it on top of a pastry with filling. Lightly press down the edges to seal, and then use a fork to crimp. Continue this way until all six pastries are formed. 4. Carefully arrange the pastries on the prepared baking trays. 5. In a bowl, mix the egg with water, and lightly brush the egg wash on top of each pastry. 6. Bake the pastries for about 18 to 20 minutes, or until the pastries are golden, rotating the trays once halfway through. Serve warm.
Per Serving: Calories 317; Fat 26g; Sodium 407mg; Carbs 8g; Fiber 2g; Sugar 2g; Protein 16g

Corn Dog

Prep time: 11 minutes | Cook time: 20 minutes | Serves: 8

Avocado oil spray
1 cup almond flour
2 tablespoons coconut flour
1½ teaspoons baking powder
¼ teaspoon salt
¼ teaspoon garlic powder
¼ teaspoon onion powder
⅛ teaspoon black pepper
2 large eggs
¼ cup water
¼ cup heavy cream
6 tablespoons butter, unsalted, melted
4 organic uncured beef hot dogs

1. Preheat the oven to 350°F/175°C. Lightly spray twenty-four wells of a mini muffin tray with avocado oil. 2. Whisk together the almond flour, coconut flour, baking powder, salt, garlic powder, onion powder, and black pepper. 3. Whisk together the eggs, water, cream, and butter. 4. Stir the wet ingredients and dry ingredients, and let the batter rest for 3 minutes. 5. Divide the formed batter into the mini muffin wells with a spoon. 6. Cut each hot dog into six pieces and place one in the center of each muffin well. 7. Bake until the corn dog bites are golden along the outside, about 20 minutes. 8. Let the bites cool for 10 minutes in the pan before removing.
Per Serving: Calories 243; Fat 23g; Sodium 336mg; Carbs 5g; Fiber 2g; Sugar 1g; Protein 8g

Tasty Pretzel Bites

Prep time: 16 minutes | Cook time: 15 minutes | Serves: 8

1 teaspoon instant yeast
2 tablespoons warm water
1 cup almond flour
1 teaspoon psyllium husk powder
1 teaspoon baking powder
1½ cups shredded low-moisture part-skim mozzarella cheese
1 ounce cream cheese
1 large egg, lightly beaten
Avocado oil, for your hands
1 tablespoon unsalted butter, melted
½ teaspoon coarse kosher salt

1. Preheat the oven to 425°F/220°C. 2. Arrange the lined baking sheet with parchment paper. 3. Add the yeast and warm water in a small bowl and stir to combine. Set aside until foamy, for about 5–10 minutes. 4. Whisk the almond flour, psyllium husk powder, and baking powder. Whisk the almond flour, psyllium husk powder, and baking powder in a medium bowl. Set aside. 5. In a microwave-safe bowl, melt the mozzarella with cream cheese. Microwave for 60 seconds, then stir it and continue microwaving in 20-second increments until the cheese is fully melted and combined when stirred. Mix the foamy yeast mixture into the melted cheese until combined, and then stir in the beaten egg until combined. 6. Add in the almond flour mixture until it forms a dough. 7. Knead the dough with oily hands until it comes together as a ball. 8. Divide the pretzels dough into four equal pieces. 9. Roll each dough ball into a log about 4" long and cut each log into four bites, so you end up with sixteen edges total. 10. Arrange the bites on the lined baking sheet and bake until golden, for about 10 minutes. 11. Brush the pretzel bite with melted butter and sprinkle on a little kosher salt. Cool slightly before serving.
Per Serving: Calories 180; Fat 14g; Sodium 332mg; Carbs 5g; Fiber 2g; Sugar 1g; Protein 9g

Tropical Macaroons

Prep time: 11 minutes | Cook time: 25 minutes | Serves: 2

½ cup shredded coconut
½ cup ground almonds
1 large egg white
¼ cup sugar substitute
1 ounce sugar-free chocolate chips
2 tablespoons butter
Salt, to taste

1. Preheat oven to 350°F/175°C. 2. Sprinkle the coconut and almonds evenly on a lined baking dish. 3. Toast for 3-5 minutes until fragrant and golden brown. 4. Beat the eggs white with an electric mixer. Gradually add sugar substitute until stiff peaks form, mix in the toasted coconut, almonds, and salt. 5. Shape the mixture into desire-sized balls and arrange them on the lined baking dish. 6. Bake the balls in the oven for 15-18 minutes until their tops are golden brown. 7. Melt the butter and chocolate chips in the microwave. 8. Once the nutty macaroons are done, remove from the oven and let them cool for 5 minutes. 9. Drizzle the macaroons with chocolate and enjoy.
Per Serving: Calories 102; Fat 8g; Sodium 235mg; Carbs 5g; Fiber 1g; Sugar 1g; Protein 1g

Pizza Muffin

Prep time: 16 minutes | Cook time: 20 minutes | Serves: 6

Avocado oil spray
1 cup almond flour
2 tablespoons coconut flour
1½ teaspoons baking powder
½ teaspoon salt
¼ teaspoon black pepper
¼ teaspoon onion powder
2 large eggs
¼ cup water
¼ cup heavy whipping cream
4 tablespoons unsalted butter,
melted
1 teaspoon apple cider vinegar
5 drops of liquid stevia
2 tablespoons no-sugar-added pizza sauce
¼ cup finely chopped pepperoni
6 tablespoons shredded mozzarella cheese
1½ teaspoons dried Italian herb seasoning

1. Preheat the oven to 350°F/175°C. Lightly spray twenty-four wells of a mini muffin tray with avocado oil. 2. Whisk together the almond flour, coconut flour, baking powder, salt, black pepper, and onion powder in a large bowl. 3. Whisk together the eggs, water, cream, butter, vinegar, and liquid stevia in a medium bowl. 4. Mix all wet and dry ingredients, and let the batter rest for 3 minutes. 5. Spoon the cake batter into the prepared mini muffin wells. 6. Top each muffin with ¼ teaspoon pizza sauce. Add the pepperoni to the sauce, and then top each with ¾ teaspoon mozzarella. Sprinkle the Italian herb seasoning on top. 7. Bake until the pizza muffin bites are golden along the outside, for about 15–20 minutes. 8. Let the bites cool for 10 minutes in the muffin tray before removing.
Per Serving: Calories 295; Fat 27g; Sodium 466mg; Carbs 7g; Fiber 3g; Sugar 1g; Protein 10g

Cheesy Za'atar Pinwheels

Prep time: 16 minutes | Cook time: 25 minutes | Serves: 8

1 tablespoon unsalted butter
2 small onions, peeled and diced
1 teaspoon instant yeast
2 tablespoons warm water
1 cup almond flour
1 teaspoon psyllium husk powder
1 teaspoon baking powder
1½ cups shredded low-moisture
part-skim mozzarella cheese
1 ounce cream cheese
1 large egg, lightly beaten
Olive oil, avocado oil, or ghee, for your hands
4 ounces crumbled goat cheese
2 tablespoons za'atar

1. Preheat the oven to 375°F/190°C. Prepare a baking tray with parchment paper. 2. In a skillet heat the butter and add the onion and cook until softened, for about 5 minutes. Cool slightly. 3. Add the yeast and warm water in a small bowl and stir to combine. Set aside until foamy, for about 5–10 minutes. 4. Whisk the almond flour, psyllium husk powder, and baking powder and set aside. 5. In a large bowl, add the mozzarella and cream cheese. Microwave for 60 seconds, mix and continue microwaving in 20-second increments until fully melted. 6. Stir the yeast mixture in melted cheese along with beaten egg. Add in the almond flour mixture until it forms a dough. 7. Oil your hands and knead the dough until it comes together as a ball. 8. Roll the keto dough to a rectangle shape about 12" long by 9" wide. 9. Spread the onion out on top of the dough, leaving a border of about ¼" along the outside. Sprinkle the goat cheese on top, and then sprinkle on the za'atar. 10. Use the parchment paper to help roll up the dough into a log. Freeze the log for 5 minutes, and then cut the log crosswise into eight equal pieces. 11. Spread the rolls out evenly on the prepared baking tray. 12. Bake until golden, for about 24–26 minutes. 13. Cool slightly before serving.
Per Serving: Calories 242; Fat 19g; Sodium 241mg; Carbs 7g; Fiber 2g; Sugar 2g; Protein 13g

Healthy Peanut Butter Cookies

Prep time: 11 minutes | Cook time: 15 minutes | Serves: 2

1 cup peanut butter
½ cup almond flour
½ cup sugar substitute
2 eggs
1 teaspoon vanilla extract
¼ teaspoon salt

1. Preheat oven to 350°F/175°C. 2. Line a baking sheet with nonstick cooking spray. 3. Place the peanut butter, eggs, almond flour, sugar substitute, salt, and vanilla extract in a bowl and mix well with a beater to form a smooth dough. 4. Divide the dough into 12 servings and shape them into small balls and arrange on the prepared baking sheet. 5. Using a fork, make crisscross marks on the cookies and bake in the oven for 16-18 minutes until golden brown.
Per Serving: Calories 96; Fat 5g; Sodium 451mg; Carbs 6g; Fiber 1g; Sugar 1g; Protein 4g

Crispy Tortilla Chips

Prep time: 4 minutes| Cook time: 5 minutes| Serves: 6

1½ cups shredded low-moisture part-skim mozzarella cheese
½ cup almond flour
1 tablespoon golden flaxseed meal
¼ teaspoon salt
⅛ teaspoon black pepper

1. Preheat the oven to 375°F/190°C. 2. Prepare two large baking sheets with parchment liners. In a bowl, add the mozzarella. Microwave for 60 seconds, mix, and continue microwaving in 15-second increments until the cheese is fully melted and you can stir it together with a fork. 3. Mix the almond flour, flaxseed meal, salt, and black pepper in a melted cheese. Knead it in a dough. 4. Divide the dough into two parts. Then spread the dough out onto the prepared baking sheets until each is a rectangle about 8" × 10". Cut each into square- or triangle chips. 5. Then lay the tortilla chips out on the baking sheets. 6. Bake the chips until golden brown on both sides, for about 10–15 minutes, flipping the chips once halfway through. 7. For overnight chips, bake them on a large baking sheet for 5 minutes at 350°F/175°C to re-crisp them.
Per Serving: Calories 143; Fat 11g; Sodium 289mg; Carbs 4g; Fiber 1g; Sugar 1g; Protein 9g

Hot Beef Empanadas

Prep time: 16 minutes | Cook time: 18 minutes | Serves: 10

Spiced Beef Filling:
1 pound 85% lean ground beef
1 medium onion, peeled and chopped
4 large cloves garlic, minced
½ cup water
1 tablespoon good-quality red wine vinegar
1 tablespoon tomato paste
1 teaspoon dried oregano
1 teaspoon dried thyme
1 teaspoon salt
½ teaspoon black pepper
½ teaspoon cumin
½ teaspoon sweet paprika
Pinch cayenne pepper
3 drops of liquid stevia
3 tablespoons pimiento-stuffed green olives, halved
Empanada Crust:
4½ cups shredded low-moisture part-skim mozzarella cheese
3 ounces cream cheese
3 large eggs
1½ teaspoons apple cider vinegar
9 drops of liquid stevia
3 cups almond flour
3 teaspoons baking powder
Other:
Avocado oil, for your hands
1 large egg
1 tablespoon water

For the Spiced Beef Filling: 1. Heat a large skillet over medium-high heat. Once hot, add the beef and onion. Cook until browned, to break up the meat. 2. Add the garlic and cook 30 seconds more, stirring constantly. 3. Stir in the water, red wine vinegar, tomato paste, oregano, thyme, salt, black pepper, cumin, sweet paprika, cayenne pepper, and liquid stevia. 4. Cover the skillet, boil the heat down to simmer, and cook for 20 minutes, stirring occasionally. If the sauce needs additional thickening, cook it uncovered for a few minutes, stirring frequently, until it reaches your desired consistency. 5. Stir in the olives.
For the Empanada Crust: 1. Add the mozzarella and cream cheese in a large microwave-safe bowl, then stir it, and continue heating in 20-second increments until fully melted. 2. Whisk together the eggs, apple cider vinegar, and liquid stevia in a small bowl. In a bowl, whisk the almond flour with baking powder. 3. Combine the egg mixture into the melted cheese, and then add in the almond flour mixture and knead into dough. 4. Knead the dough until it comes as a ball with oily hands. Divide the dough into three equal portions. 5. Roll dough to a circle about 11" in diameter. Use a 3" biscuit cutter to stamp out the dough into circles, gathering and re-rolling the dough as necessary (you should get thirty-eight to forty dough circles).
To Assemble and Bake: 1. Preheat the oven to 375°F/190°C temp setting. Line two large baking trays with Silpat liners or parchment paper. 2. Place 2 teaspoons Spiced Beef Filling in the center of each dough circle and gently fold the dough over onto itself to close up the filling, pressing the seam together. 3. Arrange the empanadas on the prepared baking sheets about ½" apart and use a fork to crimp the seam. 4. In a bowl, mix the egg with water, and lightly brush the egg wash on top of each pastry. 5. Bake until the empanadas are golden, about 15–18 minutes, rotating the trays once halfway through. Serve warm.
Per Serving: Calories 491; Fat 37g; Sodium 815mg; Carbs 13g; Fiber 4g; Sugar 3g; Protein 31g

Herby Mushroom Galettes

Prep time: 16 minutes | Cook time: 20 minutes | Serves: 6

Mushroom and Thyme Filling:
1½ tablespoons unsalted butter
6 ounces button mushrooms, sliced
1 large clove garlic, minced
1 teaspoon minced fresh thyme
Pinch salt
Pinch black pepper
½ cup shredded white Cheddar cheese
Galette Crust:

½ teaspoon beef gelatin
1 tablespoon boiling water
½ teaspoon apple cider vinegar
3 drops of liquid stevia
1 large egg white
1½ cups almond flour
¼ teaspoon salt
2 tablespoons chilled unsalted butter, diced
1 large egg
1 tablespoon water

For the Mushroom and Thyme Filling: 1. Preheat a large skillet over medium heat. Add the butter and the mushrooms and cook until softened, stirring occasionally, for about 8–10 minutes. 2. Cook the garlic, thyme, salt, and black pepper for 1 minute more along with mushrooms, stirring constantly. Cool on room temperature. 3. Stir the Cheddar into the mushroom mixture and refrigerate to chill, for about 15 minutes.
For the Galette Crust: 1. Add the beef gelatin and boiling water in a small bowl, stir to dissolve, and cool a few minutes until lukewarm. Whisk in the vinegar, liquid stevia, and egg white. 2. Whisk the almond flour and salt. 3. Mix the egg white mixture into the dry ingredients, and then crumble in the butter until it forms a crumbly dough. 4. Wrap in plastic paper and refrigerate until well chilled for 2 hours.
To Assemble and Bake: 1. Preheat the oven to 350°F/175°C. Line a baking tray. 2. Divide the dough into six equal pieces. Roll each dough into a ball, and then roll the balls out between two sheets of parchment paper into a circle about 4"–5" in diameter. 3. Use a thin metal spatula or pastry scraper to transfer the dough circles to the prepared baking tray, arranging them so they don't touch. 4. Divide the mushroom filling between the six dough circles, putting the filling in the center of each. 5. Gently use a thin metal spatula to fold the outer part of the dough circle up partway over the filling, molding the dough so it's smooth. 6. If the dough cracks a bit, you can gently mold and pinch it together. If the dough is very hard to work with, pop everything into the freezer to chill for 5 minutes. 7. Once all the galettes are formed, transfer the baking tray to the freezer to chill for 5 minutes. 8. Lightly brush the crust with egg wash. Bake until the galettes are golden, about 20 minutes. 9. Serve hot, warm, or at room temperature.
Per Serving: Calories 280; Fat 25g; Sodium 289mg; Carbs 8g; Fiber 3g; Sugar 2g; Protein 11g

Chocolate Hazelnut Biscotti

Prep time: 16 minutes | Cook time: 30 minutes | Serves: 12

⅔ cup almond flour
5 tablespoons granulated monk fruit/erythritol blend
2 tablespoons golden flaxseed meal
1 tablespoon coconut flour
¾ teaspoon baking powder
¼ teaspoon salt
3 tablespoons unsalted butter,

melted
15 drops of liquid stevia
2 large eggs
¾ teaspoon pure vanilla extract
¼ teaspoon pure almond extract
½ cup chopped hazelnuts
⅓ cup stevia-sweetened chocolate chips

1. Preheat the oven to 300°F/150°C. Prepare a baking tray with parchment paper. 2. Whisk together the almond flour, granulated monk fruit/erythritol blend, flaxseed meal, coconut flour, baking powder, and salt in a medium bowl. 3. Mix the melted butter, liquid stevia, eggs, vanilla, and almond extract in a separate medium bowl. Stir the butter mixture into the almond flour mixture. 4. Place a piece of plastic wrap directly on top of the dough and chill in the freezer for 8 minutes. 5. Stir in the hazelnuts and chocolate chips. 6. Spread the batter on the lined baking tray and spread it to a rectangle about 8"–9" long by 4"–5" wide. Cool for 15 minutes. 7. Cut into ½"-thick slices, and place them back on the baking tray. 8. Bake the slices for another 30 minutes, flipping them over once halfway through. 9. Leave the biscotti inside with the oven door closed until they're golden, for about 5 minutes. 10. Let the biscotti cool to room temperature before serving.
Per Serving: Calories 135; Fat 12g; Sodium 87mg; Carbs 12g; Fiber 3g; Sugar 1g; Protein 4g

Mascarpone Cheesecakes with Strawberry

Prep time: 11 minutes | Cook time: 0 minutes | Serves: 2

4 ounces mascarpone
7 strawberries
¼ cup almond flour
3 tablespoons butter, melted

½ cup sugar substitute
¼ cup crème Fraiche
1 teaspoon vanilla extract

1. To prepare the crust, combine the melted butter, almond flour, and about ⅔ of the sugar substitute in a bowl and mix well. 2. Divide the mixture evenly into 2 serving bowls, lightly pressing with your hands. 3. To prepare the filling, puree the strawberries in a food processor, leaving 2 strawberries to the side for garnish. 4. Add the remaining sugar substitute, vanilla extract, mascarpone, and crème Fraiche to the food processor. Blend until it reaches a smooth consistency. 5. Spoon the mixture over the crusts and allow it to chill in the refrigerator for at least 1 hour. 6. Slice the remaining strawberries and arrange on each bowl. Serve and enjoy.
Per Serving: Calories 442; Fat 31g; Sodium 412mg; Carbs 8g; Fiber 2g; Sugar 3g; Protein 17g

Raspberry Cookies

Prep time: 11 minutes | Cook time: 12 minutes | Serves: 2

1 tablespoon coconut flour
1 cup almond butter
1 egg
½ teaspoon vanilla extract

⅔ cup sugar substitute
3-4 tablespoons raspberry jam, no-sugar-added
¼ teaspoon baking powder

1. Preheat oven to 350°F/175°C. 2. Using an electric mixer, beat the egg together with the almond butter and sugar substitute. Add the coconut flour, baking powder, and vanilla extract. Mix well to form a smooth dough. 3. Make small balls of mixture and arrange on a baking sheet lined with parchment paper. 4. Make a slight indentation on the top each of the cookies with your thumb or the back of a spoon. Fill with about ½ teaspoon of the jam. 5. Bake the balls in the oven for 10-12 minutes until the cookies are golden brown around the edges.
Per Serving: Calories 173; Fat 15g; Sodium 235mg; Carbs 6g; Fiber 3g; Sugar 2g; Protein 6g

Chocolate Coated Apricots

Prep time: 16 minutes | Cook time: 15 minutes | Serves: 2

½ cup bittersweet chocolate chips
36 dried apricots

½ cup shredded coconut

1. Melt the chocolate chips in the microwave. Stir the chocolate and continue microwaving in 30-second intervals until melted. 2. Coat half of each apricot with the melted chocolate and arrange on a baking sheet lined with parchment. Sprinkle the apricots with the shredded coconut. 3. Serve chilled.
Per Serving: Calories 349; Fat 1g; Sodium 236mg; Carbs 4g; Fiber 1g; Sugar 2g; Protein 0g

Crispy Wings

Prep time: 15 minutes | Cook time: 60 minutes | Serves: 4

1-pound chicken wing sections
2 large eggs, beaten
¼ cup heavy whipping cream
2 ounces ground pork rinds

⅛ teaspoon chili powder
¼ teaspoon salt
⅛ teaspoon ground black pepper

1. Preheat oven to 375°F/190°C. Prepare a baking sheet with parchment paper. 2. Mix all ingredients except wings and pork rinds in a large bowl. Stir in wings until coated. 3. Spread pork rinds on a large plate. Shake excess batter off wing sections and dredge both sides in rinds. 4. Evenly space wings on the prepared baking sheet so they are not touching. Bake for 60 minutes, gently flipping halfway through. Serve warm.
Per Serving: Calories 328; Fat 22g; Sodium 355mg; Carbs 0g; Fiber 0g; Sugar 0g; Protein 29g

Jalapeño Chips

Prep time: 10 minutes | Cook time: 13 minutes | Serves: 6

1½ cups shredded Parmesan
cheese
6 strips no-sugar-added bacon,
cooked and crumbled

1½ cups shredded Cheddar cheese
2 medium jalapeños, thinly sliced
in rings

1. Preheat oven to 380°F/195°C. Prepare a baking sheet with parchment paper. 2. Put 1-tablespoon-sized mounds of Parmesan on the baking sheet, 1" apart, until all Parmesan is distributed. 3. Top each with an equal amount of Cheddar and press down to form compact circles no more than 2" across. 4. Place a jalapeño ring centered on top of each circle. Cover evenly with bacon bits. 5. Bake for 10–13 minutes until firm and starting to brown. Serve warm.
Per Serving: Calories 252; Fat 17g; Sodium 714mg; Carbs 2g; Fiber 0g; Sugar 0g; Protein 18g

Radish Chips

Prep time: 10 minutes | Cook time: 13 minutes | Serves: 1

⅛ teaspoon salt
⅛ teaspoon ground black pepper
1 cup thinly sliced (⅛" thick)
radishes
½ teaspoon garlic powder

1 teaspoon finely chopped fresh
parsley
1 tablespoon olive oil
1 tablespoon white vinegar

1. Add all ingredients except parsley in a medium bowl and stir until all radish slices are coated with seasonings. 2. Place in an air fryer and cook at 380°F/195°C for 12–13 minutes. Shake the basket to turn chips halfway through. 3. Cool slightly, sprinkle with parsley, and serve.
Per Serving: Calories 145; Fat 13g; Sodium 335mg; Carbs 5g; Fiber 2g; Sugar 2g; Protein 1g

Avocado Chips

Prep time: 10 minutes | Cook time: 24 minutes | Serves: 4

2 medium avocados, peeled,
pitted, and mashed
1½ cups shredded Swiss cheese
⅛ teaspoon ground black pepper
½ teaspoon paprika

2 teaspoons 100% lemon juice
½ teaspoon garlic powder
½ teaspoon Italian seasoning
⅛ teaspoon salt

1. Preheat oven to 350°F/175°C. Prepare a baking sheet with parchment paper. 2. In a bowl, stir all ingredients except paprika. Scoop teaspoon-sized mounds of the mixture onto the prepared baking sheet, spaced out at least ½" to prevent touching after they are flattened. 3. Spray the back of a serving spoon with nonstick cooking spray and press it into the mounds to flatten each into an irregular shape. Sprinkle "chips" with even amounts of paprika. 4. Bake for 21–24 minutes until crispy and starting to brown. 5. Remove from oven, distribute into four small bowls, and serve immediately.
Per Serving: Calories 269; Fat 20g; Sodium 106mg; Carbs 9g; Fiber 5g; Sugar 1g; Protein 12g

Popcorns

Prep time: 5 minutes | Cook time: 40 minutes | Serves: 4

1 head cauliflower, cut it bite-
sized florets
1 tablespoon butter-flavored salt,

divided
¼ cup butter-flavored coconut oil,
melted

1. Add cauliflower to a large bowl and top with oil and ½ tablespoon butter-flavored salt. Stir to coat. 2. Add ¼ of the florets to an air fryer crisper tray, spaced out as much as possible. Cook for 10 minutes at 400°F/200°C, shaking the basket halfway through. 3. Repeat the process until all "popcorn" is cooked. 4. Top with remaining butter-flavored salt. Serve warm.
Per Serving: Calories 182; Fat 14g; Sodium 1806mg; Carbs 10g; Fiber 4g; Sugar 4g; Protein 4g

Taquitos

Prep time: 15 minutes | Cook time: 11 minutes | Serves: 4

4 (1-ounce) deli slices Cheddar
cheese
¼ teaspoon garlic powder
⅛ teaspoon ground black pepper
1 large black olive, sliced
2 ounces full-fat cream cheese,

softened
1 (5-ounce) can white meat
chicken, drained and shredded
2 tablespoons finely chopped
green onion, divided

1. Preheat oven to 360°F/180°C. Prepare a baking sheet by lining parchment paper. 2. Place cheese slices on the baking sheet. 3. Bake the cheese for 8–10 minutes until edges start to brown. 4. Microwave cream cheese along with chicken, garlic powder, 1 tablespoon green onion, and pepper for 1 minute. 5. Mix well until blend. 6. Place equal amounts of chicken mixture on each cheese square. 7. Roll the cheese slice like a little burrito and make tiny taquitos. Then garnish the taquitos with sliced olive. 8. Place rolls onto a plate, sprinkle with the remaining tablespoon green onion, and serve warm.
Per Serving: Calories 193; Fat 13g; Sodium 406mg; Carbs 1g; Fiber 0g; Sugar 1g; Protein 14 g

Bake Kale Chips

Prep time: 10 minutes | Cook time: 20 minutes | Serves: 8

2 tablespoons olive oil
¼ teaspoon garlic powder
¼ teaspoon Italian seasoning
¼ teaspoon salt

⅛ teaspoon ground black pepper
2 medium bunches kale, stems
and ribs removed
¼ cup grated Parmesan cheese

1. Chop the kale into bite-size pieces. 2. Preheat oven to 300°F/150°C. Prepare a baking sheet with parchment paper. 3. In a bowl, whisk all ingredients except kale and Parmesan. Place the chopped kale in a large bowl and top with seasoning mixture. Toss until all leaves are coated. 4. Evenly spread the kale on the baking pan and cook for 10 minutes. Turn leaves and bake for another 10 minutes until crispy. 5. Let cool slightly, sprinkle evenly with cheese, and serve.
Per Serving: Calories 46; Fat 4g; Sodium 131mg; Carbs 1g; Fiber 0g; Sugar 0g; Protein 1g

Ants On a Log

Prep time: 10 minutes | Cook time: 0 minutes | Serves: 4

2 (5-ounce) cans tuna packed in
oil, drained
4 medium stalks celery, cut into
3"–4" sections

¼ cup sliced black olives
¼ cup full-fat mayonnaise
1 tablespoon 100% lemon juice
¼ teaspoon salt

1. Stir to combine all ingredients except celery and olives in a medium bowl. 2. Evenly spread tuna mixture on celery, filling the grooves of each stalk. 3. Place several olive slices in a line along with the tuna mixture on each stalk. Serve immediately.
Per Serving: Calories 222; Fat 16g; Sodium 590mg; Carbs 3g; Fiber 1g; Sugar 1g; Protein 16g

Cheese Ball

**Prep time: 10 minutes plus 1 hour for chilling
| Cook time: 0 minutes | Serves: 8**

8 ounces full-fat cream cheese,
softened
1 cup shredded Italian cheese
blend
½ teaspoon garlic powder
½ teaspoon salt

⅛ teaspoon ground black pepper
½ cup no-sugar-added bacon bits
½ cup finely chopped green
onion, divided
¼ cup sun-dried tomatoes, diced

1. In a large mixing bowl, add cheeses, ¼ cup green onion, tomatoes, garlic powder, salt, and pepper and mix until smooth. 2. Spread the cling film on the counter and scoop out the cheese mixture into a mound on top. Form the plastic wrap around the mixture and shape into a ball. 3. Let cool in refrigerator for 1 hour. Set aside the remaining ingredients. 4. Before serving, spread bacon and remaining green onion on parchment paper. Roll the unwrapped ball on the mixture until evenly coated. 5. Serve on a fancy holiday plate.
Per Serving: Calories 181; Fat 14g; Sodium 513mg; Carbs 3g; Fiber 0g; Sugar 1g; Protein 9g

Dragon Tail Poppahs

Prep time: 15 minutes | Cook time: 19 minutes | Serves: 8

8 (2") jalapeños, halved, seeded, and deveined
1 (1-ounce) package ranch powder seasoning mix

½ cup shredded Cheddar cheese
4 ounces full-fat cream cheese, softened
¼ cup full-fat mayonnaise

1. Preheat oven to 375°F/190°C. Prepare a baking sheet with parchment paper. 2. In a medium microwave-safe bowl, microwave peppers with ¼ cup water for 3 minutes to soften. Drain and let cool. 3. Line up peppers on baking sheet, cut-side up. 4. Add cream cheese, mayonnaise, ranch powder, and shredded cheese in a separate medium microwave-safe bowl. Microwave for 30 seconds and stir. Microwave another 15 seconds and stir. 5. Carefully scoop mixture into sandwich-sized bag. 6. Using makeshift pastry bag, fill jalapeño halves evenly with mixture. 7. Bake for 15 minutes until peppers are fully softened and cheese is golden brown.
Per Serving: Calories 153; Fat 12g; Sodium 173mg; Carbs 2g; Fiber 1g; Sugar 1g; Protein 7g

Tofu Fries

Prep time: 25 minutes | Cook time: 20 minutes | Serves: 4

1 (12-ounce) package extra-firm tofu
⅛ teaspoon salt, divided
⅛ teaspoon black pepper, divided

2 tablespoons sesame oil
⅛ teaspoon creole seasoning, divided

1. Wrap tofu in a paper towel for 20 minutes to remove excess water. 2. Once water has drained out, cut it into the small cubes. Heat oil over medium heat in a cooking pan. 3. In a bowl, mix salt, pepper, and creole seasoning. Sprinkle one-third of spice mixture evenly into pan and add tofu evenly. 4. Sprinkle one-third of spices on top and let fry for 5 minutes on each side, flipping three times (for the four sides), browning all four sides. 5. Dust tofu with remaining spice mixture. 6. Remove from heat. Enjoy while hot!
Per Serving: Calories 119; Fat 10g; Sodium 126mg; Carbs 1g; Fiber 1g; Sugar 1g; Protein 7g

Crackers

Prep time: 15 minutes | Cook time: 40 minutes | Serves: 10

1 cup blanched almond flour
2 tablespoons psyllium husk powder
2 tablespoons chia seeds
2 tablespoons hemp hearts
2 tablespoons flaxseed meal
2 tablespoons shelled pumpkin

seeds
2 tablespoons Everything and More seasoning
½ tablespoon salt
1½ cups water
1 squirt liquid stevia

1. Preheat oven to 350°F/175°C. 2. In a mixing bowl, combine dry ingredients. Add water and liquid stevia and mix until a thick dough is formed. 3. Place dough between two pieces of parchment paper and roll out to desired cracker thickness. 4. Remove top of parchment sheet and use a pizza cutter to cut dough into desired cracker shapes. 5. While cracker shapes are still on bottom piece of parchment paper, put on a baking sheet and into oven. 6. Bake for 30–40 minutes until centers of the crackers are hard. 7. Let cool for 5 minutes, then serve.
Per Serving: Calories 111; Fat 6g; Sodium 541mg; Carbs 7g; Fiber 2g; Sugar 1g; Protein 5g

Creamy Chipped Artichokes

Prep time: 5 minutes | Cook time: 35 minutes | Serves: 4

½ teaspoon salt, divided
½ cup full-fat mayonnaise

2 large artichokes, trimmed
2 tablespoons lemon juice

1. In a large pot, prepare 1" water with ¼ teaspoon salt. 2. Put artichokes in a steamer basket inside the pot, stem-side up, and cover pot. When boiling starts, lower heat and leave untouched for 25 minutes. 3. Test to see if done by pulling off outer leaf using tongs. If it doesn't come off easily, add additional water to pot and steam for 5–10 more minutes. Let cool. 4. Serve with dip, combining lemon juice, mayonnaise, and remaining salt.
Per Serving: Calories 219; Fat 20g; Sodium 497mg; Carbs 8g; Fiber 5g; Sugar 1g; Protein 2g

Ranch Dorito Crackers

Prep time: 15 minutes | Cook time: 37 minutes | Serves: 7

2 cups riced cauliflower, uncooked
⅛ teaspoon salt
⅛ teaspoon black pepper

1½ cups grated Parmesan cheese
2 teaspoons ranch seasoning powder

1. Preheat oven to 375°F/190°C. 2. In a medium microwave-safe bowl, microwave riced cauliflower for 1 minute. Stir and microwave for 1 more minute. 3. Let cool and scoop cauliflower onto a clean dish towel. Squeeze out excess water. 4. Return to bowl and add Parmesan, ranch seasoning, salt, and pepper. Mix thoroughly until a moist dough is formed. 5. Place the dough on parchment paper. Then place the second piece of parchment paper on top of the dough. Use a rolling pin to flatten the dough to the thickness of a Dorito. 6. After the dough is rolled to the desired thickness, remove the top parchment sheet and cut it into triangle shapes roughly the size of Doritos. 7. Place the parchment paper with crackers to a baking sheet. Leave enough space between each cracker to cook evenly and won't stick to nearby crackers during baking. 8. Bake for 25–35 minutes until golden brown. 9. Let cool and serve.
Per Serving: Calories 98; Fat 5g; Sodium 510mg; Carbs 5g; Fiber 1g; Sugar 1g; Protein 7g

Red Pepper Edamame

Prep time: 18 minutes | Cook time: 1 minutes | Serves: 4

2 cups frozen raw edamame in the shell
2 cloves garlic, peeled and minced

1 tablespoon peanut oil
⅛ teaspoon salt
½ teaspoon red pepper flakes

1. In a medium microwave-safe bowl with ½ cup water, microwave edamame for 4–5 minutes. 2. In a medium saucepan over medium heat, add peanut oil. Add minced garlic and salt. Stir 3–5 minutes to soften the garlic. 3. Add edamame and stir 2–3 minutes until well heated and coated. Turn off heat and cover saucepan to steam edamame for 5 additional minutes. 4. Add red pepper flakes and toss well to coat evenly. Serve immediately for best results.
Per Serving: Calories 131; Fat 7g; Sodium 87mg; Carbs 9g; Fiber 6g; Sugar 1g; Protein 10g

Bacon-Stuffed Mushrooms

Prep time: 15 minutes | Cook time: 23 minutes | Serves: 4

12 large whole mushrooms, approximately 2" wide
2 tablespoons unsalted butter
1 medium green onion, finely chopped
1 teaspoon paprika
⅛ teaspoon salt

⅛ teaspoon black pepper
8 ounces cooked no-sugar-added bacon, crumbled
7 ounces full-fat cream cheese, softened
½ cup full-fat mayonnaise

1. Preheat oven to 400°F/200°C. Prepare a baking sheet with parchment paper. 2. Remove mushroom stems from caps, being very careful not to break edges of cap, and scrape out the black gills if the mushroom is mature enough for the gills to be visible. Chop the trimmed stem pieces finely. 3. In a frying pan, fry mushroom trimmings with butter for 3 minutes until soft over medium heat. Place caps on baking sheet, rounded-side down. 4. In a medium bowl, combine fried mushroom trimmings with the remaining ingredients. Scoop the mixture evenly into the caps. 5. Bake for 20 minutes until filling bubbles and turns golden brown.
Per Serving: Calories 690; Fat 59g; Sodium 1387mg; Carbs 6g; Fiber 1g; Sugar 3g; Protein 25g

Bacon-Wrapped Pickles

Prep time: 5 minutes | Cook time: 20 minutes | Serves: 4

6 strips uncooked no-sugar-added bacon, cut in half lengthwise

3 large pickles
¼ cup ranch dressing

1. Preheat oven to 425°F/220°C. Prepare a baking sheet with foil. 2. Quarter each pickle lengthwise (yielding twelve spears). 3. Wrap each pickles with a strip of bacon. Place on a baking sheet. Bake for 20 minutes or until crispy, flipping at the midpoint. 4. Serve your crispy bacon-wrapped pickles while still hot with a side of the ranch dipping sauce.
Per Serving: Calories 96; Fat 6g; Sodium 1117mg; Carbs 3g; Fiber 1g; Sugar 1g; Protein 6g

Classy Crudités with Dip

Prep time: 15 minutes | Cook time: 0 minutes | Serves: 8

Vegetables

1 cup green beans, trimmed
2 cups broccoli florets
2 cups cauliflower florets
1 cup whole cherry tomatoes

1 bunch asparagus, trimmed
1 green bell pepper, seeded and
chopped

Sour Cream Dip

2 cups full-fat sour cream
½ teaspoon garlic powder
⅛ teaspoon salt
⅛ teaspoon black pepper

3 tablespoons dry chives
1 tablespoon lemon juice
½ cup dried parsley

1. Cut vegetables into bite-sized uniform pieces. Arrange in like groups around the outside edge of a large serving platter, leaving room in the middle for dip. 2. Make dip by combining dip ingredients in a medium-sized decorative bowl and mixing well. 3. Place dip bowl in the center of platter and serve.
Per Serving: Calories 146; Fat 10g; Sodium 88mg; Carbs 9g; Fiber 3g; Sugar 5g; Protein 4g

Delicious Devil Eggs

Prep time: 10 minutes | Cook time: 9 minutes | Serves: 6

6 large eggs
3 tablespoons full-fat mayonnaise
⅛ teaspoon salt
⅛ teaspoon black pepper

⅛ teaspoon ground cayenne
⅛ teaspoon paprika
1 teaspoon plain white vinegar
1 teaspoon spicy mustard

1. Hard-boil eggs using a steamer basket in the Instant Pot on high pressure for 9 minutes. Release pressure and remove eggs. 2. Peel eggs and slice in half lengthwise—place yolks in a medium bowl. Mash and mix yolks with mayonnaise, vinegar, mustard, salt, and black pepper. 3. Scrape the mixture into a sandwich-sized plastic bag and snip off one corner, making a hole about the width of a pencil. Use a makeshift pastry bag to fill egg white halves with yolk mixture. 4. Garnish Devilish Eggs with cayenne and paprika (mostly for color) and serve.
Per Serving: Calories 125; Fat 9g; Sodium 164mg; Carbs 1g; Fiber 0g; Sugar 1g; Protein 6g

Bacon Asparagus

Prep time: 20 minutes | Cook time: 25 minutes | Serves: 6

6 strips no-sugar-added bacon,
uncooked
24 asparagus spears

2 tablespoons olive oil
⅛ teaspoon salt

1. Line up asparagus and cut entire bunch at the "snapping" point, making all of your stalk's uniform in length. 2. On a microwave-safe plate, microwave asparagus for 2 minutes to soften. Let cool for 5 minutes. 3. Lay strip of bacon on a cutting board at a 45-degree angle. Lay four asparagus spears centered on bacon in an "up and down" position. 4. Pick up bacon and asparagus where they meet and wrap two ends of bacon around the asparagus in opposite. 5. Wrap bacon tightly and secure, pinning bacon to asparagus at ends with toothpicks. Don't worry if bacon doesn't cover entire spears. 6. Grease asparagus with olive oil and sprinkle with salt. Heat a medium nonstick pan over medium heat. Cook asparagus/bacon for 3–5 minutes per side while turning to cook thoroughly. Continue flipping until bacon is brown and crispy.
Per Serving: Calories 106; Fat 8g; Sodium 243mg; Carbs 3g; Fiber 1g; Sugar 1g; Protein 5g

Cucumber Salsa

Prep time: 10 minutes | Cook time: 0 minutes | Serves: 8

2 medium cucumbers
2 medium tomatoes
1 clove garlic, peeled and minced
2 tablespoons lime juice
4 medium jalapeño peppers,
deveined, seeded, and finely
chopped

½ medium red onion, peeled and
chopped
2 teaspoons dried parsley
2 teaspoons finely chopped
cilantro
½ teaspoon salt

1. Finely chop or pulse cucumbers and tomatoes separately in a food processor to desired consistency. 2. Add to a mixing bowl along with rest of the ingredients and mix thoroughly. Serve.
Per Serving: Calories 23; Fat 0g; Sodium 149mg; Carbs 6g; Fiber 1g; Sugar 3g; Protein 1g

Buffalo Chicken Thighs

Prep time: 15 minutes | Cook time: 30 minutes | Serves: 10

2 (4.2-ounce) chicken breasts
from cooked rotisserie chicken
1 (8-ounce) package full-fat
cream cheese, softened
½ cup finely chopped green onion
¼ cup buffalo wing sauce
1 teaspoon garlic powder
½ pound no-sugar-added bacon,

cooked and crumbled
2 cups shredded whole milk
mozzarella cheese
1 cup shredded Cheddar cheese
1 (1-ounce) package ranch
powder seasoning mix
1 cup full-fat mayonnaise
1 cup full-fat sour cream

1. Preheat oven to 350°F/175°C. Grease a 2-quart (8" × 8") baking dish. 2. In a small bowl, finely shred chicken. In the baking dish, combine chicken with remaining ingredients, except bacon, to mix well. 3. Bake for 25–30 minutes; stop when bubbling and browned on top. 4. Top with the crumbled bacon. Serve immediately.
Per Serving: Calories 538; Fat 43g; Sodium 1236mg; Carbs 5g; Fiber 0g; Sugar 2g; Protein 25g

Traditional El Presidente Guac

Prep time: 10 minutes | Cook time: 0 minutes | Serves: 4

2 large avocados, peeled and
pitted
1 tablespoon garlic powder
1 tablespoon onion powder
⅛ teaspoon salt

⅛ teaspoon chili powder
4 tablespoons finely chopped
cilantro
1 Roma tomato, finely chopped
4 teaspoons lime juice

1. In a medium bowl, mash avocados and combine with dry spices. 2. Add cilantro, tomato, and lime juice and mix again. Serve.
Per Serving: Calories 131; Fat 9g; Sodium 83mg; Carbs 10g; Fiber 5g; Sugar 1g; Protein 2g

Hot Chili-Garlic Wings

Prep time: 15 minutes | Cook time: 60 minutes | Serves: 4

3 tablespoons Thai chili-garlic
sauce
12 chicken wings, separated at the
joint
½ teaspoon salt
½ teaspoon freshly ground black

pepper
2 tablespoons avocado oil
2 teaspoons onion powder
1 garlic clove, minced
2 scallions, for garnish

1. Preheat the oven to 375°F/190°C. Set aside a rimmed baking sheet lined with parchment paper or aluminum foil. 2. Combine the chili-garlic sauce, oil, onion powder, and garlic in a resealable bag. Add the wings to the bag, seal, and shake until well coated. 3. Arrange the wings on the baking sheet in a single layer and sprinkle with the salt and pepper. 4. Bake for 1 hour until crispy and fully cooked, turning once halfway through. Remove from the oven and serve garnished with the sliced scallions.
Per Serving: Calories 685; Fat 49g; Sodium 645mg; Carbs 2g; Fiber 1g; Sugar 0g; Protein 56g

Cheesy Hangover Homies

Prep time: 10 minutes | Cook time: 15 minutes | Serves: 2

1 tablespoon avocado oil
1 large turnip, peeled and diced
1 tablespoon minced onion
4 large eggs, lightly beaten
¼ cup sour cream
¼ cup shredded cheddar cheese

½ avocado, peeled, pitted, and
sliced
Pinch salt
Pinch freshly ground black pepper
1 scallion, both green and white
parts, chopped

1. In a pan, heat the oil over medium-high flame. Add the turnip and onion and cook, stirring frequently, until tender, for 12 to 15 minutes. 2. Meanwhile, warm a nonstick pan over medium heat. Pour in the eggs and pull them from side to side with a spatula as they cook to form soft curds. Evenly divide the cooked eggs between two plates. 3. When the turnip mixture is done, add it to the eggs, dividing evenly. 4. Mix the sour cream and cheddar in a small bowl, then add to the eggs and turnips. 5. Divide the avocado between the plates and season with salt and pepper. Garnish with the scallion. Serve immediately.
Per Serving: Calories 439; Fat 34g; Sodium 457mg; Carbs 15g; Fiber 6g; Sugar 7g; Protein 19g

Steak Bites with Pepper Sauce

Prep time: 15 minutes | Cook time: 5 minutes | Serves: 4

For the steak
1-pound sirloin steak, cut into 1-inch cubes
2 tablespoons unsalted butter, divided
¼ teaspoon salt
¼ teaspoon freshly ground black pepper
For the sauce
12-ounce jar roasted red bell peppers, drained
½ cup extra-virgin olive oil
2 tablespoons freshly squeezed lemon juice
1 garlic clove, peeled
½ teaspoon dried basil
¼ teaspoon salt
¼ teaspoon freshly ground black pepper

To make the steak: 1. Season the steak cubes with the salt and pepper. 2. In a large pan, melt 1 tablespoon of butter over medium-high heat. Once the butter begins to brown, working in batches, add the steak to the pan in a single layer. Cook without stirring or flipping for 30 to 45 seconds, then flip the pieces over with a spatula and cook for 30 to 45 seconds. This will brown the outside but keep the inside medium-rare. 3. Transfer to the plate and repeat the process with the remaining butter and steak cubes.
To make the sauce: 1. In a blender, puree the roasted peppers, oil, lemon juice, garlic, basil, salt, and pepper until smooth. 2. Transfer the sauce to four small bowls for dipping. Serve immediately with the steak bites.
Per Serving: Calories 528; Fat 46g; Sodium 866mg; Carbs 5g; Fiber 1g; Sugar 3g; Protein 23g

Bacon and Cheese Stuffed Jalapeños

Prep time: 15 minutes | Cook time: 15 minutes | Serves: 12

6 bacon slices
8 ounces cream cheese, at room temperature
½ cup crumbled blue cheese
1 teaspoon onion powder
1 teaspoon garlic powder
Pinch salt
Pinch freshly ground black pepper
12 jalapeño peppers, halved lengthwise and seeded

1. Preheat the oven to 400°F/200°C. Set aside a rimmed baking sheet lined with parchment paper or aluminum foil. 2. In a pan, cook the bacon over medium-high heat until the fat renders, for about 10 minutes. Transfer to a lined plate with paper towels to cool, then crumble. 3. Transfer to a lined plate with paper towels; mix the bacon, cream cheese, blue cheese, garlic, onion powder, salt, and pepper. 4. Fill the hollow of each jalapeño half with the bacon and cheese mixture and arrange cut-side up on the baking sheet. Bake for 15 minutes, rotating the sheet halfway through. 5. Serve hot.
Per Serving: Calories 75; Fat 7g; Sodium 874mg; Carbs 1g; Fiber 0g; Sugar 1g; Protein 3g

Loaded Chayote Fries

Prep time: 10 minutes | Cook time: 30 minutes | Serves: 4

4 bacon slices
4 chayote squash
1 tablespoon avocado oil, extra-virgin
½ teaspoon salt
⅛ teaspoon freshly ground black pepper
½ cup shredded cheddar cheese
4 scallions, sliced

1. Preheat the oven to 425°F/220°C. Set aside a rimmed baking sheet lined with parchment paper or aluminum foil. 2. In a pan, cook the bacon over medium-high heat until the fat renders, about 10 minutes. Transfer to a lined plate with paper towels to cool, then crumble. 3. Peel off the skin from the chayote squash. Rinse the sticky coating from the peeled squash. Spiralize the chayote into curly shapes. Or, if you don't have a spiralizer, cut the squash into ¼-inch-thick fry-style wedges. Discard any remnants of the center seeds. Toss the chayote with the oil, salt, and pepper then spread on the baking sheet in a single layer. 4. Roast for 15 minutes for curly fries or 20 minutes for wedges, or until tender and browned. 5. Remove the chayote fries from the oven and set the temperature to broil. Sprinkle the cheddar evenly over the top and return to the oven. Broil the fries for 1 - 2 minutes until the cheese melted. 6. Sprinkle the bacon and scallions over the top. Serve immediately.
Per Serving: Calories 175; Fat 12g; Sodium 421mg; Carbs 11g; Fiber 4g; Sugar 4g; Protein 8g

Tropical Shrimp Dippers

Prep time: 15 minutes | Cook time: 15 minutes | Serves: 6

For the shrimp
Coconut oil cooking spray
½ cup coconut flour
1 teaspoon freshly ground black pepper
2 large eggs
½ cup unsweetened coconut flakes
⅓ cup crushed pork rinds
30 large shrimp, peeled and
deveined, tails left on
For the sauce
½ cup unsweetened peanut butter or almond butter
½ cup tamari or coconut aminos
¼ cup water
1 tablespoon red curry paste
1 teaspoon Thai chili-garlic sauce (optional)

To make the shrimp: 1. Preheat the oven to 425°F/220°C. Mist a rimmed baking sheet with coconut oil and set aside. 2. Prepare three shallow bowls for dredging: Combine the coconut flour and pepper in the first bowl. 3. In the second bowl, beat the eggs. In the third bowl, mix the coconut flakes and crushed pork rinds. Line the bowls up in the same order, with the prepped baking sheet at the end. 4. Dip each shrimp into the flour mixture, the egg, and the coconut flake mixture. 5. Place the coated shrimp on the baking sheet. Continue until all the shrimp are dredged, then mist the tops of the shrimp with coconut oil. 6. Bake the shrimp for 10 minutes, then flip and continue baking for 5 to 6 minutes, until the shrimp are fully cooked.
To make the sauce: 1. In a bowl, stir the peanut butter, tamari, water, curry paste, and chili-garlic sauce (if using) until smooth. 2. Transfer to a group serving bowl or individually portioned dishes. 3. Serve the shrimp with the dipping sauce.
Per Serving: Calories 317; Fat 17g; Sodium 376mg; Carbs 13g; Fiber 7g; Sugar 4g; Protein 28g

Zucchini Chips

Prep time: 20 minutes plus 2 hours to marinate | Cook time: 120 minutes | Serves: 4

2 large zucchinis, thinly sliced crosswise
½ cup apple cider vinegar
1 tablespoon extra-virgin olive oil
1 teaspoon sea salt

1. Place the sliced zucchini in a shallow glass dish and cover with the vinegar. Let it marinate in the refrigerator for 2 hours or overnight. 2. Once marinated, lay out sheets of paper towel and place the drained zucchini on them in a single layer. Cover with additional paper towels and set a weighted baking sheet on top to remove excess moisture. 3. Preheat the oven to 235°F/115°C. Prepare two rimmed baking trays by lining them with parchment paper and lightly brushing each with some oil. 4. Arrange the zucchini slices closely on the baking sheets but in a single layer. Grease the rest of the oil and sprinkle with the salt. 5. Bake for 2 hours, without flipping, until crisp and golden. If some zucchini slices cook faster than others, remove the crisp slices and allow the damp ones to bake longer. 6. Transfer the finished zucchini to cool the pans to fresh, dry paper towels. Serve.
Per Serving: Calories 64; Fat 4g; Sodium 475mg; Carbs 5g; Fiber 2g; Sugar 3g; Protein 2g

Parmesan Zucchini Fries

Prep time: 10 minutes | Cooking time: 10 minutes | Serves: 8

2 medium zucchini, ends removed, quartered lengthwise, and sliced into 3"-long fries
½ teaspoon salt
⅓ cup heavy whipping cream
½ cup blanched finely ground almond flour
¾ cup grated parmesan cheese
1 teaspoon Italian seasoning

1. Sprinkle zucchini with salt and wrap in a kitchen towel to draw out excess moisture. 2. Let sit 2 hours. 3. Pour cream into a suitable bowl. In a separate suitable bowl, beat flour, parmesan, and Italian seasoning. 4. Place each zucchini fry into cream, then gently shake off excess. 5. Press each fry into dry mixture, coating each side, then place into ungreased air fryer basket. 6. Set the temperature to 400°F/200°C and set the timer for almost 10 minutes, turning fries halfway through cooking. Fries will be golden and crispy when done. 7. Place on clean parchment sheet to cool 5 minutes before serving.
Per serving: Calories: 112; Total fat 9.2g; Sodium 344mg; Total Carbs 3.4g; Fiber 1g; Sugars 0.6g; Protein 4.8g

Cheesy Buffalo Chicken Quesadillas

Prep time: 15 minutes | Cook time: 35 minutes | Serves: 4

For the tortillas
2 large eggs
10½ tablespoons unsweetened coconut milk beverage or unsweetened almond milk, divided
For the filling
2 tablespoons extra-virgin olive oil
1 large boneless, skinless chicken

8 teaspoons coconut flour
1 teaspoon unflavored gelatin powder or psyllium husk powder
Extra-virgin olive oil, for greasing the pan

breast
1 cup shredded cheddar cheese
¼ cup Buffalo hot sauce

To make the tortillas: 1. In a large bowl, whisk the eggs, 6½ tablespoons of coconut milk, and the coconut flour until the batter is smooth. 2. In a bowl, combine the remaining coconut milk and gelatin powder and let sit for 5 minutes. 3. Whisk the gelatin mixture until smooth, without clumps, then pour into the coconut flour batter and whisk to combine. 4. The batter should be a liquid, pourable consistency. If it's too thick, add additional coconut milk, 1 tablespoon at a time, until the batter is thin enough to pour and easily spread over the pan. 5. Lightly coat a medium nonstick pan with oil and warm over medium heat. Pour one-quarter of the batter (about ¼ cup) into the hot pan and swirl to distribute the mixture and coat the bottom of the pan as you would when making omelets or crepes. 6. Cover and cook for 2 minutes. Flip the tortilla, cover, and cook for an additional 2 minutes. Transfer to a clean plate. 7. Repeat to make a total of 4 tortillas.
To make the filling: 1. In a large pan, heat the oil over medium-high heat. Add the chicken breast and cook for 4 to 5 minutes per side, turning once, until no longer pink. 2. Remove from the heat. When cool enough, shred or dice. Combine the cooked chicken, cheddar, and Buffalo hot sauce in a large bowl. 3. Set the nonstick pan over medium-low heat. Lay one of the tortillas in the pan. Spread one-quarter of the chicken mixture (about ½ cup) on half of the tortilla, then fold the other side over the top. 4. Cover and cook for 1 minute, then flip, cover, and cook for another minute, or until the cheese has melted. Remove from the heat. Repeat the steps for all four quesadillas. 5. Cut into triangle wedges and serve immediately.
Per Serving: Calories 267; Fat 17g; Sodium 666mg; Carbs 9g; Fiber 2g; Sugar 2g; Protein 20g

Pretzel Bites with Sauce

Prep time: 25 minutes | Cook time: 10 minutes | Serves: 6

For the pretzels
1 tablespoon warm water
1 teaspoon active dry yeast
½ cup almond flour
1 large egg
1 cup shredded low-moisture
For the cheese sauce
1 tablespoon unsalted butter
¼ cup heavy cream
¼ cup shredded cheddar cheese
½ teaspoon mustard powder

mozzarella cheese
2 tablespoons cream cheese
1 tablespoon unsalted butter, melted
¼ teaspoon coarse salt

¼ teaspoon freshly ground black pepper
⅛ teaspoon fine salt

To make the pretzels: 1. Preheat the oven to 400°F/200°C. Prepare a rimmed baking tray by lining it with parchment paper or a silicone baking mat and set aside. 2. In a bowl, mix the water with the yeast and let rest for 5 to 10 minutes, until the yeast rehydrates. Add the almond flour and egg and whisk to combine. 3. In a microwave-safe bowl, microwave the mozzarella and cream cheese in 30-second intervals, stirring with a fork, until the cheese is soft, pliable, and fully melted. 4. Transfer the melted cheese to the bowl with the yeast mixture and use a fork to mix until thoroughly combined. 5. Divide the dough into four equal portions. Spread sheet of parchment paper on the work surface. 6. Wet your hands with warm water and roll one dough portion into a long rope about 1 inch in diameter. 7. Cut the dough into 1-inch lengths and place them on the baking sheet. Repeat with the remaining dough. 8. Brush the dough pieces with the melted butter and sprinkle with the salt. Bake for 10 to 12 minutes, until golden brown.
To make the cheese sauce: 1. In a saucepan, melt the butter. Whisk cream in and bring the butter cream mix to boil, and then remove from the heat. 2. Stir in the cheddar, mustard powder, pepper, and salt until smooth and thoroughly combined. Transfer to a serving dish. 3. Serve the pretzel bites with the cheese sauce for dipping.
Per Serving: Calories 221; Fat 19g; Sodium 478mg; Carbs 4g; Fiber 1g; Sugar 1g; Protein 9g

Cheeseburgers

Prep time: 15 minutes | Cook time: 20 minutes | Serves: 4

For the buns
6 egg whites, large size
½ teaspoon baking powder
½ teaspoon xanthan gum
1 (30-gram) scoop unsweetened unflavored whey protein powder
1 teaspoon ground flaxseed
¼ teaspoon sesame seeds
For the burgers
1 pound ground beef

¼ teaspoon salt
¼ teaspoon freshly ground black pepper
1 tablespoon unsalted butter
4 cheddar cheese slices
For assembly
1 tablespoon mayonnaise
1 tablespoon yellow mustard
1 dill pickle, sliced

1. Preheat the oven to 350°F/175°C. Prepare a rimmed baking tray with parchment paper or a silicone baking mat and set aside. 2. To make the buns: In a bowl, beat the egg whites, baking powder, and xanthan gum on medium for 7 to 8 minutes, until stiff peaks form. 3. Mix the protein powder and ground flaxseed together in a small bowl, then gently fold into the egg white mixture. 4. Scoop four separate mounds of the mixture onto the baking sheet. Sprinkle the sesame seeds over the top. 5. Bake them for 15-20 minutes until golden brown. Remove from the oven to cool, then slice the rolls in half horizontally.
6. To make the burgers: Combine the ground beef, salt, and pepper in a large bowl. Divide the meat into four portions and form into 1-inch-thick patties with the palms of your hand or a burger press. 7. In a pan, melt the butter. Place the patties in the hot pan without crowding them. Cook patties for 3 to 4 minutes, then flip and top with the cheddar slices. Cook again 3 to 4 minutes, until the burgers reach your preferred doneness. 8. To assemble: Dress the buns with a thin layer of mayonnaise and mustard. 9. Place the cheesy patties on the bottom half of the buns and top with pickle slices. 10. Top with the buns and serve immediately.
Per Serving: Calories 508; Fat 38g; Sodium 478mg; Carbs 3g; Fiber 0g; Sugar 1g; Protein 36g

Stuffed Mushrooms with Burrata

Prep time: 15 minutes | Cook time: 15 minutes | Serves: 10

20 cremini mushroom caps, cleaned
1 tablespoon extra-virgin olive oil
¼ cup chopped arugula, divided
6 ounces fresh burrata cheese or fresh mozzarella, at room

temperature, cut or torn into 20 even-size chunks
5 cherry tomatoes, quartered
¼ teaspoon flaky sea salt
¼ teaspoon freshly ground black pepper

1. Preheat the oven to 425°F/220°C. Prepare a rimmed baking tray by lining it with parchment paper or aluminum foil. 2. Tossing the mushroom caps in the oil on the prepared baking sheet and place them gill-side up. Distribute half of the arugula evenly among the mushrooms. 3. Place a burrata chunk in each cap, followed by a cherry tomato quarter. Sprinkle the salt, pepper, and remaining arugula over the tops of the stuffed mushrooms. 4. Bake the mushrooms for 15 to 20 minutes, until the mushrooms are tender. Transfer to a platter and serve immediately.
Per Serving: Calories 73; Fat 5g; Sodium 74mg; Carbs 2g; Fiber 1g; Sugar 1g; Protein 5g

Traditional Spinach-Artichoke Dip

Prep time: 10 minutes | Cook time: 15 minutes | Serves: 6

1 tablespoon extra-virgin olive oil
¼ medium onion, diced
1 package frozen spinach, thawed and drained
1 can artichoke hearts
1 garlic clove, minced
8 ounces cream cheese, at room

temperature
¼ cup grated Parmesan cheese
1 cup Greek yogurt
¼ cup mayonnaise
Pinch salt
Pinch freshly ground black pepper

1. In a pan, heat the oil and cook the onion until translucent, about 10 minutes. Add the spinach, artichokes, and garlic and sauté for 3 to 5 minutes, until the spinach and artichokes are tender. 2. Lower the heat and add in the cream cheese and Parmesan until melted. Eliminate from the heat and stir in the yogurt and mayonnaise until thoroughly combined—season with salt and pepper. 3. Serve as a dip or a spread.
Per Serving: Calories 341; Fat 31g; Sodium 847mg; Carbs 10g; Fiber 4g; Sugar 3g; Protein 8g

Chapter 3 Soups, Salad, Stews and Chill

Crunchy Slaw 36

"Potato" Soup 36

Cheddar Cheesy Soup 36

Delicious Sausage-Sauerkraut Soup 36

Cheesy Bacon Keto Soup 36

Turkey Soup 36

Chicken and nacho Soup 36

Bacon It Up Chicken Soup 36

Pollo Soup 37

Lasagna Soup 37

Sausage Soup................................... 37

Cilantro & Lime Soup 37

Herby Cucumber Soup 37

Amazing Cheeseburger Soup 37

Healthy Jambalaya Soup 37

Regular Beef Stew........................... 37

Chicken Stew with Coconut Cream 38

Asian Vegetable Stew 38

Meat with Vegetable Stew 38

Spicy Cilantro Soup 38

Spicy Chipotle Chicken Chili 38

Texas Chili...................................... 38

Zesty Chicken Soup 38

Shellfish Stock 38

Italian Soup 39

Jalapeno & Lime in Shrimp Soup 39

Buffalo Chicken Soup 39

Cheesy Bacon Soup 39

Chicken Cheese Soup 39

Beef Veggie Broth 39

Chicken Veggie Broth 39

Garlic Chicken Soup 39

Leftover Bone Broth 40

Greek Egg Soup............................... 40

Chicken Zucchini Noodle Soup 40

Regular Italian Beef Soup 40

Easy Jalapeño Popper Soup 40

Red Chili 40

Creamy Tuscan Soup........................ 40

Cabbage Roll Soup 41

Lobster Bisque 41

Balsamic Beef Stew 41

Chicken Cordon Bleu Soup 41

Chicken and Cauliflower Rice Soup 41

Broccoli Cheddar Soup 41

Mac & Cheese Stew 41

Turkey, Onion & Sage Stew 41

Chicken Bacon Chowder 42

White Chicken Chili 42

Creamy Enchilada Soup 42

Loaded Taco Soup 42

Spicy Bacon Cheeseburger Soup 42

Hamburger Beef Stew 42

Autumn Harvest Stew 42

Herbed Broccoli Stew 43

Creamy Mixed Vegetable Stew 43

Asparagus & Mushroom Nutmeg Stew... 43

Balsamic Tofu Stew 43

Quick Cream of Asparagus Soup 43

Pumpkin Kale Vegetarian Stew 43

No Bean Chili 43

Turmeric Stew 43

Creamy Mushroom Soup 43

Crunchy Slaw

Prep time: 10 minutes | Cook time: 0 minutes | Serves: 5

1 (16-ounce) bag coleslaw mix	1 tablespoon 0g net carbs
⅓ cup full-fat mayonnaise	sweetener
1 tablespoon apple cider vinegar	¼ teaspoon salt
1 teaspoon 100% lemon juice	⅛ teaspoon ground black pepper

1. In a large bowl, add coleslaw mix. 2. In a bowl, mix all ingredients. Stir to mix thoroughly. Stir to mix thoroughly. 3. Using a spatula, add dressing to the coleslaw mix. Stir to combine. 4. Cover and put in refrigerator until ready to serve. Serve chilled.
Per Serving: Calories 124; Fat 11g; Sodium 225mg; Carbs 7g; Fiber 2g; Sugar 3g; Protein 1g

"Potato" Soup

Prep time: 5 minutes | Cook time: 25 minutes | Serves: 6

1 (12-ounce) bag frozen cauliflower pieces, broken into bite-sized florets	1 tablespoon minced garlic
	4 cups chicken broth
	½ cup full-fat cream cheese
2 tablespoons unsalted butter	2 (3.7-gram) chicken-flavored
1 cup finely chopped radishes	bouillon cubes
1 cup sliced zucchini	⅛ teaspoon ground black pepper
½ cup chopped green onions, divided	2 cups shredded cheddar cheese
	¼ cup cooked bacon bits

1. In a large microwave-safe dish, add cauliflower. Cover the bowl and microwave on high 4–5 minutes until tender. 2. While cauliflower cooks melt butter in a large soup pot over medium heat. Add radishes, zucchini, ¼ cup onion, and garlic. Sauté for 3–4 minutes until softened. 3. Add cauliflower, broth, cream cheese, bouillon, and pepper to soup pot. Bring covered pot to a boil, then simmer on low heat for 20 minutes while stirring. 4. Using an immersion blender, pulse soup ingredients 1–2 minutes to desired consistency. 5. Add cheddar to soup and fold in. 6. Pour into six small bowls and top with equal amounts bacon bits and remaining green onion. Serve immediately.
Per Serving: Calories 310; Fat 22g; Sodium 1354mg; Carbs 7g; Fiber 2g; Sugar 4g; Protein 15g

Cheddar Cheesy Soup

Prep time: 15 minutes | Cook time: 6 hours | Serves: 6

1 tablespoon butter	8 ounces cream cheese, cubed
5 cups chicken broth	2 cups shredded cheddar cheese
1 cup coconut milk	Salt, for seasoning
2 celery stalks, chopped	Freshly ground black pepper, for
1 carrot, chopped	seasoning
½ sweet onion, chopped	1 tablespoon chopped fresh thyme
Pinch cayenne pepper	for garnish

1. Lightly grease the slow cooker with the butter. 2. Place the broth, coconut milk, celery, carrot, onion, and cayenne pepper in the insert. 3. Cover it and cook on low temperature setting for 6 hours. 4. Stir in the cream cheese and cheddar, then season with salt and pepper. 5. Serve topped with thyme.
Per Serving: Calories 406; Fat 36g; Sodium 88mg; Carbs 7g; Fiber 1g; Sugar 2g; Protein 15g

Delicious Sausage-Sauerkraut Soup

Prep time: 15 minutes | Cook time: 6 hours | Serves: 6

1 tablespoon extra-virgin olive oil	2 teaspoons minced garlic
6 cups beef broth	2 tablespoons butter
1 pound organic sausage, cooked and sliced	1 tablespoon hot mustard
	½ teaspoon caraway seeds
2 cups sauerkraut	½ cup sour cream
2 celery stalks, chopped	2 tablespoons chopped fresh
1 sweet onion, chopped	parsley for garnish

1. Lightly oil the slow cooker with olive oil. 2. Place the broth, sausage, sauerkraut, celery, onion, garlic, butter, mustard, and caraway seeds in the insert. 3. Cover it and cook on low temp setting for 6 hours. 4. Stir in the sour cream. 5. Serve topped with the parsley.
Per Serving: Calories 332; Fat 28g; Sodium 69mg; Carbs 6g; Fiber 2g; Sugar 2g; Protein 15g

Cheesy Bacon Keto Soup

Prep time: 15 minutes | Cook time: 6 hours | Serves: 6

1 tablespoon extra-virgin olive oil	2 cups chopped cauliflower
4 cups chicken broth	1 sweet onion, chopped
2 cups coconut milk	3 teaspoons minced garlic
2 cups chopped cooked chicken	½ cup cream cheese, cubed
1 cup chopped cooked bacon	2 cups shredded cheddar cheese

1. Lightly oil the slow cooker with olive oil. 2. Place the broth, coconut milk, chicken, bacon, cauliflower, onion, and garlic in the insert. 3. Cover it and cook on low temp setting for 6 hours. 4. Stir in the cream cheese and Cheddar, and serve.
Per Serving: Calories 540; Fat 44g; Sodium 120mg; Carbs 6g; Fiber 1g; Sugar 2g; Protein 35g

Turkey Soup

Prep time: 20 minutes | Cook time: 7 to 8 hours | Serves: 8

1 tablespoon extra-virgin olive oil	2 teaspoons chopped fresh thyme
4 cups chicken broth	1 cup cream cheese, diced
½ pound skinless turkey breast, cut into ½-inch chunks	2 cups heavy (whipping) cream
	1 cup green beans, chopped into
2 celery stalks, chopped	1-inch bites
1 carrot, diced	Salt, for seasoning
1 sweet onion, chopped	Freshly ground black pepper, for
2 teaspoons minced garlic	seasoning

1. Lightly oil the slow cooker with olive oil. 2. Place the broth, turkey, celery, carrot, onion, garlic, and thyme in the insert. 3. Cover it and cook on low temperature setting for 7 to 8 hours. 4. Stir in the cream cheese, heavy cream, and green beans. 5. Season with salt and pepper, and serve.
Per Serving: Calories 415; Fat 35g; Sodium 231mg; Carbs 5g; Fiber 2g; Sugar 2g; Protein 20g

Chicken and nacho Soup

Prep time: 15 minutes | Cook time: 6 hours | Serves: 8

3 tablespoons extra-virgin olive oil, divided	4 cups chicken broth
	2 cups coconut milk
1 pound ground chicken	1 tomato, diced
1 sweet onion, diced	1 jalapeño pepper, chopped
1 red bell pepper, chopped	2 cups shredded cheddar cheese
2 teaspoons minced garlic	½ cup sour cream, for garnish
2 tablespoons taco seasoning	scallion, chopped, for garnish

1. Lightly grease the slow cooker with 1 tablespoon of olive oil. 2. In a pan, heat the remaining 2 tablespoons of the olive oil. Add the chicken and sauté until it is cooked through about 6 minutes. 3. Add the onion, red bell pepper, garlic, taco seasoning, and sauté for 3 minutes. 4. Transfer the chicken mixture to the insert, and stir in the broth, coconut milk, tomato, and jalapeño pepper. 5. Cover it and cook on low temp setting for 6 hours. 6. Stir in the cheese. Serve topped with sour cream and scallion.
Per Serving: Calories 434; Fat 35g; Sodium 189mg; Carbs 7g; Fiber 2g; Sugar 3g; Protein 22g

Bacon It Up Chicken Soup

Prep time: 15 minutes | Cook time: 8 hours | Serves: 8

1 tablespoon extra-virgin olive oil	2 teaspoons minced garlic
6 cups chicken broth	1½ cups heavy (whipping) cream
3 cups cooked chicken, chopped	1 cup cream cheese
1 sweet onion, chopped	1 cup cooked chopped bacon
2 celery stalks, chopped	1 tablespoon chopped fresh
1 carrot, diced	parsley, for garnish

1. Lightly oil the slow cooker with olive oil. 2. Add the broth, chicken, onion, celery, carrot, and garlic. Cover it and cook on low temperature setting for 8 hours. 3. Stir in the heavy cream, cream cheese, and bacon. 4. Serve topped with the parsley.
Per Serving: Calories 488; Fat 37g; Sodium 156mg; Carbs 10g; Fiber 1g; Sugar 1g; Protein 27g

Pollo Soup

Prep time: 10 minutes | Cook time: 20 minutes | Serves: 4

1 pound boneless, skinless
chicken thighs, sliced
1 (10-ounce) can no-sugar-added
diced tomatoes and green chiles
2 cups chicken broth
2 tablespoons unsalted butter
¼ cup chopped green onion
2 teaspoons minced garlic
½ tablespoon onion powder
1 teaspoon chili powder
½ teaspoon ground cumin
½ tablespoon paprika
½ medium jalapeño pepper,
seeded, deveined, and diced
½ teaspoon salt
1 medium avocado, peeled, pitted,
and sliced
1 tablespoon chopped fresh
cilantro

1. In Instant Pot, combine all ingredients except avocado and cilantro. Stir to mix. 2. Put on lid and close pressure release. Cook on High Pressure for 20 minutes. Carefully quick-release pressure and remove cover. Stir to mix well. 3. Serve warm, top with avocado slices and a sprinkle of cilantro.
Per Serving: Calories 317; Fat 18g; Sodium 1060mg; Carbs 9g; Fiber 4g; Sugar 3g; Protein 25g

Lasagna Soup

Prep time: 20 minutes | Cook time: 6 hours | Serves: 6

3 tablespoons extra-virgin olive
oil, divided
1 pound ground beef
½ sweet onion, chopped
2 teaspoons minced garlic
4 cups beef broth
1 (28-ounce) can diced tomatoes,
undrained
1 zucchini, diced
1½ tablespoons dried basil
2 teaspoons dried oregano
4 ounces cream cheese
1 cup shredded mozzarella

1. Lightly grease the slow cooker with 1 tablespoon of olive oil. 2. In a large pan over medium-high heat, heat the remaining 2 tablespoons of the olive oil. Add the ground beef and sauté until it is cooked through about 6 minutes. 3. Sauté the onion and garlic for an additional 3 minutes. 4. Transfer the meat mixture to the insert. Stir in the broth, tomatoes, zucchini, basil, and oregano. 5. Cover it and cook on low temperature setting for 6 hours. Stir in the cream cheese and mozzarella and serve.
Per Serving: Calories 472; Fat 36g; Sodium 111mg; Carbs 9g; Fiber 3g; Sugar 3g; Protein 30g

Sausage Soup

Prep time: 15 minutes | Cook time: 6 hours | Serves: 6

3 tablespoons olive oil, divided
1½ pounds sausage, without
casing
6 cups chicken broth
2 celery stalks, chopped
1 carrot, diced
1 leek, thoroughly cleaned and
chopped
2 teaspoons minced garlic
2 cups chopped kale
1 tablespoon chopped fresh
parsley, for garnish

1. Lightly grease the slow cooker with 1 tablespoon of olive oil. 2. In a large pan over medium-high heat, heat the remaining 2 tablespoons of the olive oil. Add the sausage and sauté until it is cooked through for about 7 minutes. 3. Transfer the sausage to the insert, and stir in the broth, celery, carrot, leek, and garlic. 4. Cover it and cook on low temperature setting for 6 hours. 5. Stir in the kale. Serve topped with the parsley.
Per Serving: Calories 383; Fat 31g; Sodium 171mg; Carbs 5g; Fiber 1g; Sugar 2g; Protein 21g

Cilantro & Lime Soup

Prep time: 15 minutes plus 1 hour for chilling | Cook time: 0 minutes | Serves: 6

4 cups vegetable broth
1 cup heavy cream
2 ripe avocados, pitted and sliced
½ cup freshly chopped cilantro
2 tablespoons freshly squeezed
lime juice
½ teaspoon sea salt

1. Add all the ingredients in a blender. 2. Blend until smooth. 3. Chill for 1 hour before serving.
Per Serving: Calories 232; Fat 21g; Sodium 689mg; Carbs 7g; Fiber 5g; Sugar 3g; Protein 5g

Herby Cucumber Soup

Prep time: 16 minutes plus 1 hour chilling time | Cook time: 0 minutes | Serves: 6

4 cups chicken broth
1 cup heavy cream
2 cucumbers, sliced
1 teaspoon freshly chopped
rosemary
1 teaspoon freshly chopped thyme
1 pinch of salt & black pepper, to
taste

1. Blend all the ingredients and chill for at least 1 hour before serving.
Per Serving: Calories 111; Fat 9g; Sodium 632mg; Carbs 5g; Fiber 1g; Sugar 1g; Protein 4g

Amazing Cheeseburger Soup

Prep time: 15 minutes | Cook time: 6 hours | Serves: 8

3 tablespoons olive oil, divided
1 pound ground beef
1 sweet onion, chopped
2 teaspoons minced garlic
6 cups beef broth
1 (28-ounce) can diced tomatoes
2 celery stalks, chopped
1 carrot, chopped
1 cup heavy (whipping) cream
2 cups shredded cheddar cheese
½ teaspoon freshly ground black
pepper
1 scallion, white and green parts,
chopped, for garnish

1. Lightly grease the slow cooker with 1 tablespoon of olive oil. 2. In a large pan over medium-high heat, heat the remaining 2 tablespoons of the olive oil. Add the ground beef and sauté until it is cooked through about 6 minutes. 3. Sauté the onion and garlic for an additional 3 minutes. 4. Transfer the beef mixture to the insert, and stir in the broth, tomatoes, celery, and carrot. 5. Cover it and cook on low temperature setting for 6 hours. 6. Stir in the heavy cream, cheese, and pepper. Serve hot, top with the scallion.
Per Serving: Calories 413; Fat 32g; Sodium 101mg; Carbs 8g; Fiber 2g; Sugar 3g; Protein 26g

Healthy Jambalaya Soup

Prep time: 15 minutes | Cook time: 6 to 7 hours | Serves: 8

1 tablespoon extra-virgin olive oil
6 cups chicken broth
1 (28-ounce) can diced tomatoes
1 pound spicy organic sausage, sliced
1 cup chopped cooked chicken
1 red bell pepper, chopped
½ sweet onion, chopped
1 jalapeño pepper, chopped
2 teaspoons minced garlic
3 tablespoons Cajun seasoning
½ pound medium shrimp, peeled,
deveined, and chopped
½ cup sour cream, for garnish
1 avocado, diced, for garnish
2 tablespoons chopped cilantro,
for garnish

1. Lightly oil the slow cooker with olive oil. 2. Add the broth, tomatoes, sausage, chicken, red bell pepper, onion, jalapeño pepper, garlic, and Cajun seasoning. 3. Cover it and cook on low temperature setting for 6 to 7 hours. 4. Stir in the shrimp and leave on low for 30 minutes, or until the shrimp are cooked through. 5. Serve topped with avocado, sour cream, and cilantro.
Per Serving: Calories 400; Fat 31g; Sodium 1783mg; Carbs 9g; Fiber 4g; Sugar 1g; Protein 24g

Regular Beef Stew

Prep time: 15 minutes | Cook time: 8 hours | Serves: 6

3 tablespoons extra-virgin olive
oil, divided
1 (2-pound) beef chuck roast, cut
into 1-inch chunks
½ teaspoon salt
¼ teaspoon freshly ground black
pepper
2 cups beef broth
1 cup diced tomatoes
¼ cup apple cider vinegar
1½ cups cubed pumpkin, cut into
1-inch chunks
½ sweet onion, chopped
2 teaspoons minced garlic
1 teaspoon dried thyme
1 tablespoon chopped fresh
parsley, for garnish

1. Lightly grease the slow cooker with 1 tablespoon of olive oil. 2. Lightly season the beef chucks with salt and pepper. 3. In a pan heat 2 tablespoons of the olive oil. Add the meat and brown on all sides for about 7 minutes. 4. Transfer the beef to the insert and stir in the broth, tomatoes, apple cider vinegar, pumpkin, onion, garlic, and thyme. 5. Cover it and cook on low temperature setting heat for about 8 hours until the beef is very tender. 6. Serve topped with the parsley.
Per Serving: Calories 461; Fat 24g; Sodium 100mg; Carbs 10g; Fiber 3g; Sugar 2g; Protein 32g

Chicken Stew with Coconut Cream

Prep time: 20 minutes | Cook time: 6 hours | Serves: 6

3 tablespoons extra-virgin olive oil, divided
1 pound boneless chicken thighs, diced into 1½-inch pieces
½ sweet onion, chopped
2 teaspoons minced garlic
2 cups chicken broth
2 celery stalks, diced
1 carrot, diced
1 teaspoon dried thyme
1 cup shredded kale
1 cup coconut cream
Salt, for seasoning
Freshly ground black pepper, for seasoning

1. Lightly grease the slow cooker with 1 tablespoon of olive oil. 2. In a large pan over medium-high heat, heat the remaining 2 tablespoons of the olive oil. Add the chicken and sauté until it is just cooked through about 7 minutes. 3. Sauté the onion and garlic for an additional 3 minutes. Sauté the onion and garlic for an additional 3 minutes. Transfer the chicken mixture to the insert, and stir in the broth, celery, carrot, and thyme. 4. Cover it and cook on low temperature setting for 6 hours. 5. Stir in the kale and coconut cream. 6. Sprinkle salt and pepper, and serve warm.
Per Serving: Calories 276; Fat 22g; Sodium 0mg; Carbs 4g; Fiber 2g; Sugar 1g; Protein 17g

Asian Vegetable Stew

Prep time: 15 minutes | Cook time: 7 to 8 hours | Serves: 6

1 tablespoon extra-virgin olive oil
4 cups coconut milk
1 cup diced pumpkin
1 cup cauliflower florets
1 red bell pepper, diced
1 zucchini, diced
1 sweet onion, chopped
2 teaspoons grated fresh ginger
2 teaspoons minced garlic
1 tablespoon curry powder
2 cups shredded spinach
1 avocado, diced, for garnish

1. Lightly oil the slow cooker with olive oil. 2. Add the coconut milk, pumpkin, cauliflower, bell pepper, zucchini, onion, ginger, garlic, and curry powder. 3. Cover it and cook on low temperature setting for 7 to 8 hours. Stir in the spinach. 4. Garnish each bowl with a spoonful of avocado and serve.
Per Serving: Calories 502; Fat 44g; Sodium 235mg; Carbs 19g; Fiber 10g; Sugar 6g; Protein 7g

Meat with Vegetable Stew

Prep time: 20 minutes | Cook time: 7 to 8 hours | Serves: 6

3 tablespoons extra-virgin olive oil, divided
1 pound turkey breast, boneless, cut into 1-inch pieces
1 leek, thoroughly cleaned and sliced
2 teaspoons minced garlic
2 cups chicken broth
1 cup coconut milk
2 celery stalks, chopped
2 cups diced pumpkin
1 carrot, diced
2 teaspoons chopped thyme
Salt, for seasoning
Freshly ground black pepper, for seasoning
1 scallion, chopped, for garnish

1. Grease the slow cooker with olive oil. In a pan, heat the remaining 2 tablespoons of the olive oil. Add the turkey and sauté until browned, about 5 minutes. 2. Add the leek and garlic and sauté for an additional 3 minutes. 3. Transfer the turkey mixture to the insert and stir in the broth, coconut milk, celery, pumpkin, carrot, and thyme. Cover it and cook on low temperature setting for 7 to 8 hours. 4. Season with salt and pepper. Serve topped with the scallion.
Per Serving: Calories 356; Fat 27g; Sodium 580mg; Carbs 11g; Fiber 4g; Sugar 2g; Protein 21g

Spicy Cilantro Soup

Prep time: 10 minutes | Cook time: 4 hours | Serves: 6

6 cups chicken broth
3 boneless, skinless chicken breasts
Juice from 1 lime
1 yellow onion, chopped
2 cloves garlic, chopped
1 jalapeno pepper, seeded and sliced
1 handful fresh cilantro
Salt & black pepper, to taste

1. Add all the ingredients excluding the cilantro, salt, and black pepper to the base of a slow cooker. 2. Cook on high setting for 4 hours. Add the cilantro and season with salt and black pepper. 3. Shred the chicken and served.
Per Serving: Calories 108; Fat 3g; Sodium 689mg; Carbs 4g; Fiber 1g; Sugar 2g; Protein 16g

Spicy Chipotle Chicken Chili

Prep time: 20 minutes | Cook time: 7 to 8 hours | Serves: 6

3 tablespoons extra-virgin olive oil, divided
1 pound ground chicken
½ sweet onion, chopped
2 teaspoons minced garlic
1 (28-ounce) can diced tomatoes
1 cup chicken broth
1 cup diced pumpkin
1 green bell pepper, diced
3 tablespoons chili powder
1 teaspoon chipotle chili powder
1 cup sour cream, for garnish
1 cup shredded cheddar cheese, for garnish

1. Lightly grease the slow cooker with 1 tablespoon of olive oil. 2. In a large pan over medium-high heat, heat the remaining 2 tablespoons of the olive oil. Add the chicken and sauté until it is cooked through about 6 minutes. Sauté the onion and garlic for an additional 3 minutes. 3. Transfer the chicken mixture to the insert and stir in the tomatoes, broth, pumpkin, bell pepper, chili powder, and chipotle chili powder. 4. Cover it and cook on low temperature setting for 7 to 8 hours. 5. Serve topped with sour cream and cheese.
Per Serving: Calories 390; Fat 30g; Sodium 102mg; Carbs 14g; Fiber 5g; Sugar 3g; Protein 22g

Texas Chili

Prep time: 20 minutes | Cook time: 7 to 8 hours | Serves: 4

¼ cup extra-virgin olive oil
1½ pounds beef sirloin, cut into 1-inch chunks
1 sweet onion, chopped
2 green bell peppers, chopped
1 jalapeño pepper, seeded, finely chopped
2 teaspoons minced garlic
1 (28-ounce) can diced tomatoes
1 cup beef broth
3 tablespoons chili powder
½ teaspoon ground cumin
¼ teaspoon ground coriander
1 cup sour cream, for garnish
1 avocado, diced, for garnish
1 tablespoon cilantro, chopped, for garnish

1. Lightly grease the slow cooker with 1 tablespoon of olive oil. 2. In a large pan over medium-high heat, heat the remaining 2 tablespoons of the olive oil. Add the beef and sauté until it is cooked through about 8 minutes. 3. Add the onion, bell peppers, jalapeño pepper, garlic, and sauté for 4 minutes. 4. Transfer the beef mixture to the insert and stir in the tomatoes, broth, chili powder, cumin, and coriander. 5. Cover it and cook on low temperature setting for 7 to 8 hours. 6. Serve topped with the sour cream, avocado, and cilantro.
Per Serving: Calories 752; Fat 50g; Sodium 826mg; Carbs 34g; Fiber 11g; Sugar 13g; Protein 45g

Zesty Chicken Soup

Prep time: 10 minutes | Cook time: 4 hours | Serves: 6

6 cups chicken broth
3 boneless, skinless chicken breasts
Juice from 1 lemon
1 yellow onion, chopped
2 cloves garlic, chopped
1 teaspoon cayenne pepper
1 teaspoon dried thyme
1 handful of fresh parsley, minced
Salt & black pepper, to taste

1. Add all the ingredients excluding the salt, black pepper, and parsley to the base of a slow cooker instead of the parsley and cook on high for 4 hours. 2. Add the parsley and spiced with salt and black pepper. Shred the chicken and served.
Per Serving: Calories 108; Fat 3g; Sodium 365mg; Carbs 4g; Fiber 1g; Sugar 2g; Protein 16g

Shellfish Stock

Prep time: 10 minutes | Cooking time: 120 minutes | Serves: 6

4 cups shellfish shells
6 cups water
1 medium onion, peeled and chopped
2 tablespoons apple cider vinegar
2 bay leaves
2 celery stalks, chopped

1. Add all the recipe ingredients to Instant Pot. Turn the pot's lid to close. Hit the manual button and adjust time for almost 120 minutes. 2. Allow a 30-minute natural release, then quick-release the remaining pressure. 3. When pressure valve drops, strain stock and store in sealed containers in fridge for almost 1–2 days or freeze.
Per Serving: Calories 328; Total Fat 25.9g; Sodium 9mg; Total Carbs 4.5g; Fiber 9.8g; Sugars 12.6g; Protein 5.3g

Italian Soup

Prep time: 10 minutes | Cook time: 4 hours | Serves: 6

6 cups chicken broth
3 boneless, skinless chicken breasts
1 cup canned diced tomatoes
1 yellow onion, chopped
2 cloves garlic, chopped

1 cup shredded mozzarella cheese
1 jalapeno pepper, seeded and sliced
1 teaspoon dried thyme
1 teaspoon dried oregano
Salt & black pepper to taste

1. Add all the ingredients excluding the salt and black pepper to the base of a slow cooker instead of the cheese and cook on high for 4 hours. 2. Stir in the cheese and season with salt and black pepper. 3. Shred the chicken and served.
Per Serving: Calories 125; Fat 4g; Sodium 74mg; Carbs 5g; Fiber 1g; Sugar 1g; Protein 17g

Jalapeno & Lime in Shrimp Soup

Prep time: 10 minutes | Cook time: 35 minutes | Serves: 6

4 cups chicken broth
Juice from 1 lime
1 pound peeled, deveined shrimp
1 yellow onion, chopped
1 shallot, chopped
3 cloves garlic, chopped

1 jalapeno pepper, seeded and sliced
Salt & black pepper, to taste
1 tablespoon coconut oil for cooking

1. Heat the coconut oil in a stockpot. Add the shrimp, onion, shallot, and garlic and cook until the shrimp are pink. 2. Add the remaining ingredients instead of the salt and black pepper, and bring to a boil. 3. Simmer on low for 30 minutes. 4. Spice with salt and black pepper, and serve.
Per Serving: Calories 153; Fat 5g; Sodium 69mg; Carbs 6g; Fiber 1g; Sugar 2g; Protein 21g

Buffalo Chicken Soup

Prep time: 10 minutes | Cooking time: 25 minutes | Serves: 4

2 tablespoons diced onion
2 tablespoons butter
3 cups store-bought chicken broth
2 (6-ounce) boneless, skinless chicken breasts, cubed
1 teaspoon salt
¼ teaspoon garlic powder

¼ teaspoon pepper
2 celery stalks, chopped
½ cup hot sauce
4 ounces cream cheese
½ cup shredded cheddar cheese
¼ teaspoon xanthan gum

1. Hit the sauté button on the Instant Pot and add onion and butter to Instant Pot. Sauté 2–3 minutes until onions begin to soften. Hit the cancel button. 2. Add broth and chicken to Instant Pot. Sprinkle salt, garlic powder, and pepper on chicken. 3. Add celery and hot sauce and place cream cheese on top of chicken. Turn the pot's lid to close. 4. Hit the manual button and adjust time for almost 25 minutes. When the pot beeps, quick-release the pressure and stir in cheddar and xanthan gum. 5. Serve warm.
Per Serving: Calories 270; Total Fat 8.4g; Sodium 1761mg; Total Carbs 5.7g; Fiber 13.3g; Sugars 24.1g; Protein 14.8g

Cheesy Bacon Soup

Prep time: 15 minutes | Cook time: 40 minutes | Serves: 6

1 pound of lean ground beef
6 slices uncured bacon
6 cups beef broth
1 cup heavy cream
1 cup shredded cheddar cheese
1 yellow onion, chopped
1 teaspoon garlic powder

½ teaspoon onion powder
½ teaspoon cumin
½ teaspoon paprika
½ cup sour cream, for serving
1 tablespoon coconut oil, for cooking

1. Add the coconut oil to a pan and cook the bacon. 2. Chop the cooked crispy bacon into small chunks. 3. Add the ground beef to the pan with the bacon fat and cook until well browned and cooked. 4. Add the onions and cook it for another 2 to 3 minutes. 5. In a stockpot, add all the ingredients instead of the bacon, heavy cream, sour cream, and cheese to a stockpot and stir—cook for 25 minutes. 6. Warm the heavy cream, and then add the warmed cream and cheese and serve with the bacon and a dollop of sour cream.
Per Serving: Calories 498; Fat 34g; Sodium 145mg; Carbs 5g; Fiber 1g; Sugar 1g; Protein 41g

Chicken Cheese Soup

Prep time: 20 minutes | Cook time: 33 to 40 minutes | Serves: 6

2 boneless, skinless chicken breasts
2 cups chicken broth
2 cups water
1 cup whipped cream cheese
½ cup shredded cheddar cheese
1 yellow onion, chopped

2 cloves garlic, chopped
1 teaspoon chili powder
½ teaspoon cumin
½ teaspoon salt
¼ teaspoon black pepper
1 tablespoon coconut oil, for cooking

1. Heat a ½ tablespoon coconut oil in a pan. Sear the chicken breasts until cooked through. Set aside. 2. Sauté the garlic and onion to a large stockpot with the remaining 1 tablespoon of the coconut oil until translucent over low to medium heat. 3. Add this chicken broth and water. 4. On low heat whisk in the cream cheese and keep whisking until combined. 5. Add the spices and boil. Cut the chicken into bite-sized pieces and add to the stockpot. Simmer on low heat for 30 to 35 minutes. 6. Stir in the cheddar cheese and serve.
Per Serving: Calories 157; Fat 7g; Sodium 463mg; Carbs 5g; Fiber 1g; Sugar 1g; Protein 17g

Beef Veggie Broth

Prep time: 10 minutes | Cooking time: 120 minutes | Serves: 6

2 pounds beef bones
2 celery stalks, chopped
2 medium halved carrots
1 medium onion, peeled and

halved
2 bay leaves
2 sprigs fresh thyme
6 cups water

1. Add all the recipe ingredients to Instant Pot. Turn the pot's lid to close. 2. Hit the manual button and adjust time for almost 120 minutes. 3. When the pot beeps, allow a full natural release. When pressure valve drops, remove large pieces of vegetables. 4. Pour broth through fine-mesh strainer and store in closed containers in fridge or freezer.
Per Serving: Calories 52; Total Fat 2.1g; Sodium 766mg; Total Carbs 1.8g; Fiber 0.3g; Sugars 0.9g; Protein 6.3g

Chicken Veggie Broth

Prep time: 10 minutes | Cooking time: 120 minutes | Serves: 6

2 pounds chicken bones
2 celery stalks, chopped
2 medium halved carrots
1 medium onion, peeled and

halved
2 bay leaves
2 sprigs fresh thyme
6 cups water

1. Add all the recipe ingredients to Instant Pot. Turn the pot's lid to close. Hit the manual button and adjust time for almost 120 minutes. 2. When the pot beeps, allow a full natural release. When pressure valve drops, remove large pieces of vegetables. 3. Pour broth through fine-mesh strainer and store in closed containers in fridge or freezer.
Per Serving: Calories 367; Total Fat 28.6g; Sodium 663mg; Total Carbs 8.5g; Fiber 4.8g; Sugars 1.1g; Protein 22.7g

Garlic Chicken Soup

Prep time: 10 minutes | Cooking time: 20 minutes | Serves: 6

10 roasted garlic cloves
½ medium onion, diced
4 tablespoons butter
4 cups chicken broth
½ teaspoon salt
¼ teaspoon pepper

1 teaspoon thyme
1 pound boneless, skinless chicken thighs, cubed
½ cup heavy cream
2 ounces cream cheese

1. In suitable bowl, mash roasted garlic into paste. 2. Hit the sauté button on the Instant Pot and add garlic, onion, and butter to Instant Pot. Sauté for almost 2–3 minutes until onion begins to soften. Hit the cancel button. 3. Add chicken broth, salt, pepper, thyme, and chicken to Instant Pot. Turn the pot's lid to close. Hit the manual button and adjust time for almost 20 minutes. 4. When the pot beeps, quick-release the pressure. Stir in heavy cream and cream cheese until smooth. 5. Serve warm.
Per Serving: Calories 291; Total Fat 10.8g; Sodium 2153mg; Total Carbs 2.1g; Fiber 1.6g; Sugars 5.6g; Protein 37g

Leftover Bone Broth

Prep time: 10 minutes | Cooking time: 3 hours | Serves: 6

2–3 pounds leftover chicken bones
3 tablespoons coconut oil
2 medium halved carrots
2 celery stalks, chopped

2 tablespoons apple cider vinegar
1 medium onion, large dice
2 whole cloves garlic
2 bay leaves
8 cups water

1. Hit the sauté button on the Instant Pot and add meat bones and coconut oil to Instant Pot. Sauté for almost 5 minutes. Hit the cancel button. 2. Add remaining ingredients to pot and hit the soup button. Hit the adjust button to set heat to more. Set time for almost 3 hours. 3. When the pot beeps, allow a 20-minute natural release. Quick-release the remaining pressure. 4. Strain liquid and store in sealed jars in fridge up to 5 days.
Per Serving: Calories 311; Total Fat 15.9g; Sodium 610mg; Total Carbs 4.4g; Fiber 9.7g; Sugars 6g; Protein 10.6g

Greek Egg Soup

Prep time: 10 minutes | Cooking time: 15 minutes | Serves: 4

4 cups store-bought chicken broth
4 eggs, separated

1 lemon

1. Hit the sauté button. Add chicken broth to Instant Pot to warm. 2. In two suitable bowls, separate egg yolks and egg whites. Beat egg yolks and stir into broth. Hit the cancel button so Instant Pot switches to stay warm mode. 3. Using whisk or hand mixer, whisk egg whites until they form soft peaks. Add into Instant Pot. 4. Squeeze in juice from lemon. Foam may stay at the top of soup initially, but with continued occasional stirring, will dissipate by the end of cooking.
Per Serving: Calories 354; Total Fat 19.2g; Sodium 318mg; Total Carbs 0.3g; Fiber 3.5g; Sugars 5g; Protein 26.3g

Chicken Zucchini Noodle Soup

Prep time: 10 minutes | Cooking time: 20 minutes | Serves: 6

3 stalks celery, diced
2 tablespoons diced pickled jalapeño
1 cup bok choy, sliced into strips
½ cup fresh spinach
3 zucchinis, spiralized
1 tablespoon coconut oil
¼ cup button mushrooms, diced

¼ medium onion, diced
2 cups cooked diced chicken
3 cups store-bought chicken broth
1 bay leaf
1 teaspoon salt
½ teaspoon garlic powder
⅛ teaspoon cayenne pepper

1. Place celery, jalapeño, bok choy, and spinach into suitable bowl. Spiralize zucchini; keep it aside in a separate suitable bowl. (the zucchini will not go in the pot during the pressure cooking.) 2. Hit the sauté button on the Instant Pot and add the coconut oil to Instant Pot. Once the oil is hot, add mushrooms and onion. 3. Sauté for almost 4–6 minutes until onion is translucent and fragrant. Add celery, jalapeños, bok choy, and spinach to Instant Pot. Cook for additional 4 minutes. Hit the cancel button. 4. Add cooked diced chicken, broth, bay leaf, and seasoning to Instant Pot. Turn the pot's lid to close. Hit the soup button and set time for almost 20 minutes. 5. When the pot beeps, allow a 10-minute natural release, and quick-release the remaining pressure. 6. Add spiralized zucchini on keep warm mode and cook for additional 10 minutes or until tender. Serve warm.
Per Serving: Calories 568; Total Fat 20.8g; Sodium 1493mg; Total Carbs 1.8g; Fiber 3.8g; Sugars 10.2g; Protein 75.8g

Regular Italian Beef Soup

Prep time: 10 minutes | Cook time: 4 hours | Serves: 6

1 pound lean ground beef
1 cup beef broth
1 cup heavy cream
½ cup shredded mozzarella cheese

½ cup diced tomatoes
1 yellow onion, chopped
2 cloves garlic, chopped
1 tablespoon Italian seasoning
Salt & pepper to taste

1. Put in all the ingredients to a slow cooker excluding the heavy cream and mozzarella cheese—cook on high for 4 hours. 2. Warm the heavy cream, and then add the warmed cream and cheese to the soup. Stir well and serve.
Per Serving: Calories 241; Fat 14g; Sodium 111mg; Carbs 4g; Fiber 1g; Sugar 1.6g; Protein 25g

Easy Jalapeño Popper Soup

Prep time: 10 minutes | Cooking time: 25 minutes | Serves: 4

2 tablespoons butter
½ medium diced onion
¼ cup sliced pickled jalapeños
¼ cup cooked crumbled bacon
2 cups chicken broth
2 cups cooked diced chicken
4 ounces cream cheese

1 teaspoon salt
½ teaspoon pepper
¼ teaspoon garlic powder
⅓ cup heavy cream
1 cup shredded sharp cheddar cheese

1. Hit the sauté button. Add butter, onion, and sliced jalapeños to Instant Pot. Sauté for almost 5 minutes, until onions are translucent. Add bacon and hit the cancel button. 2. Add broth, cooked chicken, cream cheese, salt, pepper, and garlic to Instant Pot. Turn the pot's lid to close. Hit the soup button and adjust time for almost 20 minutes. 3. When the pot beeps, quick-release the steam. Stir in heavy cream and cheddar. Continue stirring until cheese is fully melted. Serve warm.
Per Serving: Calories 137; Total Fat 7.1g; Sodium 1067mg; Total Carbs 6.2g; Fiber 3.8g; Sugars 4.7g; Protein 3.1g

Red Chili

Prep time: 10 minutes | Cooking time: 35 minutes | Serves: 6

4 slices bacon
½ pound 85% lean ground beef
½ pound 84% lean ground pork
1 green pepper, diced
½ medium onion, diced
2 cups beef broth
1 (14.5-ounce) can diced tomatoes

1 (6-ounce) can tomato paste
1 tablespoon chili powder
2 teaspoons salt
½ teaspoon pepper
⅛ teaspoon cayenne
¼ teaspoon xanthan gum

1. Hit the sauté button on the Instant Pot and cook bacon. Remove bacon, crumble, and keep it aside. In bacon grease, brown beef and pork until fully cooked. Add green pepper and onion to Instant Pot and allow to soften for almost 1 minute. 2. Hit the cancel button and add remaining ingredients except xanthan gum to pot. Turn the pot's lid to close. Hit the soup button and adjust time for almost 30 minutes. Allow a 10-minute natural release and then quick-release the remaining pressure. 3. Stir in cooked bacon and xanthan gum then allow to thicken for almost 10 minutes. Serve warm with favorite chili toppings. 4. For thicker chili, remove lid when timer goes off and hit the sauté button. Add xanthan gum and reduce chili, stirring frequently, until desired thickness. 5. Top with additional diced onions or other toppings.
Per Serving: Calories 285; Total Fat 7.5g; Sodium 1367mg; Total Carbs 5.6g; Fiber 9.6g; Sugars 18.2g; Protein 4.4g

Creamy Tuscan Soup

Prep time: 10 minutes | Cooking time: 17 minutes | Serves: 4

4 slices bacon
1 pound ground Italian sausage
4 tablespoons butter
½ medium onion, diced
2 cloves garlic, finely minced
3 cups store-bought chicken broth

4 ounces cream cheese
2 cups kale, chopped
½ cup heavy cream
1 teaspoon salt
½ teaspoon pepper

1. Hit the sauté button on the Instant Pot and fry bacon until crispy. Remove bacon and chop into pieces, then keep it aside. 2. Add Italian sausage to Instant Pot and sauté until no pink remains. Add butter and onion to Instant Pot. 3. Sauté until onions are translucent. Add garlic and sauté for almost 30 seconds. Hit the cancel button. 4. Add broth and cream cheese to pot. Turn the pot's lid to close. Hit the soup button and adjust time for almost 7 minutes. 5. When the pot beeps, quick-release the pressure and add remaining ingredients to pot. 6. Leave Instant Pot on keep warm setting and allow to cook additional 10 minutes, stirring occasionally until kale is wilted. Serve warm.
Per Serving: Calories 122; Total Fat 10.1g; Sodium 143mg; Total Carbs 4.9g; Fiber 1.2g; Sugars 1.1g; Protein 3.6g

Cabbage Roll Soup

Prep time: 10 minutes | Cooking time: 8 minutes | Serves: 4

½ pound 84% lean ground pork	½ cup diced tomatoes
½ pound 85% lean ground beef	2 cups chicken broth
½ medium onion, diced	1 teaspoon salt
½ medium head of cabbage, sliced	½ teaspoon thyme
2 tablespoons tomato paste	½ teaspoon garlic powder
	¼ teaspoon pepper

1. Hit the sauté button on the Instant Pot and add beef and pork to Instant Pot. Brown meat until no pink remains. Add onion and continue cooking until onions are fragrant and soft. Hit the cancel button. 2. Add remaining ingredients to Instant Pot. Hit the manual button and adjust time for almost 8 minutes. 3. When the pot beeps, allow a 15-minute natural release and then quick-release the remaining pressure. Serve warm.

Per Serving: Calories 194; Total Fat 10.9g; Sodium 292mg; Total Carbs 1.7g; Fiber 6.4g; Sugars 9g; Protein 6.4g

Lobster Bisque

Prep time: 10 minutes | Cooking time: 10 minutes | Serves: 4

4 tablespoons butter	¼ teaspoon paprika
½ medium onion, diced	⅛ teaspoon cayenne
1 clove garlic, finely minced	2 tablespoons tomato paste
1 pound cooked lump lobster meat	1 cup store-bought seafood stock
½ teaspoon salt	1 cup store-bought chicken broth
¼ teaspoon pepper	½ cup heavy cream
	½ teaspoon xanthan gum

1. Hit the sauté button on the Instant Pot and add butter and onions to Instant Pot. Sauté for almost 2–3 minutes until onions begin to soften. Add garlic and sauté 30 seconds. Hit the cancel button. 2. Add lobster, seasonings, tomato paste, and broths. Hit the manual button and adjust time for almost 7 minutes. 3. When the pot beeps, quick-release the pressure. Stir in heavy cream and xanthan gum. Allow a few minutes to thicken. 4. Serve warm.

Per Serving: Calories 171; Total Fat 10g; Sodium 2629mg; Total Carbs 8.6g; Fiber 2.6g; Sugars 13.8g; Protein 4.3g

Balsamic Beef Stew

Prep time: 10 minutes | Cooking time: 6 hours | Serves: 6

1 pound sirloin steak, cubed	1 cup beef broth
1 red onion, sliced	¼ cup parsley, freshly chopped
3 cloves garlic, chopped	1 teaspoon salt
2 carrots, chopped	¼ teaspoon black pepper
¼ cup balsamic vinegar	¼ cup sour cream, for serving

1. Add the sirloin steak to the base of a slow cooker and cook for almost 10 minutes. 2. Add in the remaining ingredients and cook on low for almost 6 hours. 3. Serve with a dollop of sour cream per serving.

Per Serving: Calories 164; Total Fat 1.8g; Sodium 469mg; Total Carbs 9.2g; Fiber 12.6g; Sugars 8.2g; Protein 14g

Chicken Cordon Bleu Soup

Prep time: 10 minutes | Cooking time: 15 minutes | Serves: 6

2 (6-ounce) boneless, skinless chicken breasts, cubed	½ teaspoon pepper
4 cups chicken broth	½ teaspoon garlic powder
½ cup cubed ham	½ cup heavy cream
8 ounces cream cheese	2 cups grated Swiss cheese
1 teaspoon salt	2 teaspoons Dijon mustard

1. Place all the recipe ingredients except heavy cream, cream cheese, and mustard into Instant Pot. Turn the pot's lid to close. 2. Hit the soup button and adjust time for almost 15 minutes. When the pot beeps, quick-release the pressure. 3. Stir in heavy cream, cheese, and mustard. Serve warm.

Per Serving: Calories 136; Total Fat 14.3g; Sodium 9mg; Total Carbs 3.5g; Fiber 0g; Sugars 0g; Protein 0.3g

Chicken and Cauliflower Rice Soup

Prep time: 10 minutes | Cooking time: 20 minutes | Serves: 4

4 tablespoons butter	¼ teaspoon dried parsley
¼ cup diced onion	1 bay leaf
2 stalks celery, chopped	2 cups chicken broth
½ cup fresh spinach	2 cups diced cooked chicken
½ teaspoon salt	¾ cup uncooked cauliflower rice
¼ teaspoon pepper	½ teaspoon xanthan gum
¼ teaspoon dried thyme	

1. Hit the sauté button on the Instant Pot and add butter to Instant Pot. Add onions and sauté until translucent. Place celery and spinach into Instant Pot and sauté for almost 2–3 minutes until spinach is wilted. Hit the cancel button. 2. Sprinkle seasoning into Instant Pot and add bay leaf, broth, and cooked chicken. Turn the pot's lid to close. Hit the soup button and adjust time for almost 10 minutes. 3. When the pot beeps, quick-release the pressure and stir in cauliflower rice. Leave Instant Pot on keep warm setting to finish cooking cauliflower rice additional 10 minutes. 4. Serve warm.

Per Serving: Calories 139; Total Fat 11.9g; Sodium 60mg; Total Carbs 5.4g; Fiber 3.1g; Sugars 1g; Protein 5g

Broccoli Cheddar Soup

Prep time: 10 minutes | Cooking time: 10 minutes | Serves: 4

2 tablespoons butter	1 cup broccoli, chopped
⅛ cup onion, diced	1 tablespoon cream cheese, softened
½ teaspoon garlic powder	¼ cup heavy cream
½ teaspoon salt	1 cup shredded cheddar cheese
¼ teaspoon pepper	
2 cups chicken broth	

1. Hit the sauté button on the Instant Pot and add butter to Instant Pot. Add onion and sauté until translucent. Hit the cancel button and add garlic powder, salt, pepper, broth, and broccoli to pot. 2. Turn the pot's lid to close. Hit the soup button and set time for almost 5 minutes. 3. When the pot beeps, stir in heavy cream, cream cheese, and cheddar.

Per Serving: Calories 666; Total Fat 3.5g; Sodium 198mg; Total Carbs 8.5g; Fiber 44.1g; Sugars 15.4g; Protein 39g

Mac & Cheese Stew

Prep time: 10 minutes| Cooking time: 4 hours| Serves: 6

1 pound lean ground beef	2 cups shredded cheddar cheese
1 cup butternut squash, cubed	1 cup broccoli florets, chopped
1 yellow onion, chopped	1 teaspoon dried thyme
3 cloves garlic, chopped	Salt & black pepper, to taste

1. Add all the recipe ingredients minus the salt and black pepper to the base of a slow cooker and cook on high for almost 4 hours. 2. Season with salt and black pepper and serve.

Per Serving: Calories 529; Total Fat 7.7g; Sodium 743mg; Total Carbs 1g; Fiber 19g; Sugars 9.5g; Protein 28g

Turkey, Onion & Sage Stew

Prep time: 10 minutes | Cooking time: 4 hours | Serves: 6

1 pound ground turkey	3 cups fresh spinach
1 yellow onion, chopped	2 teaspoons dried sage
3 cloves garlic, chopped	1 teaspoon dried oregano
2 cups shredded mozzarella cheese	Salt & black pepper, to taste
	Water

1. Add all the recipe ingredients minus the salt and black pepper to the base of a slow cooker and cover with about ¼ cup of water. Cook on high for almost 4 hours. 2. Season with salt and black pepper and serve.

Per Serving: Calories 300; Total Fat 4.3g; Sodium 1377mg; Total Carbs 5.2g; Fiber 7.7g; Sugars 6.2g; Protein 21.6g

Chicken Bacon Chowder

Prep time: 10 minutes | Cooking time: 20 minutes | Serves: 6

½ pound bacon	½ cup button mushrooms, sliced
1 teaspoon salt	½ medium onion, diced
½ teaspoon pepper	1 cup broccoli florets
½ teaspoon garlic powder	½ cup cauliflower florets
¼ teaspoon dried thyme	4 ounces cream cheese
3 (6 ounces) boneless, skinless	3 cups store-bought chicken broth
chicken breasts	½ cup heavy cream

1. Hit the sauté button on the Instant Pot and then hit the adjust button to lower heat to less. Add bacon to Instant Pot and fry for a few minutes until fat begins to render, working in multiple batches if necessary. Hit the cancel button. 2. Hit the sauté button on the Instant Pot and then hit the adjust button to set heat to normal. Continue frying bacon until fully cooked and crispy. 3. Remove from pot and keep it aside. Sprinkle salt, pepper, garlic powder, and thyme over chicken breasts. Sear each side of the chicken for almost 3–5 minutes or until dark and golden. 4. Hit the cancel button. Add mushrooms, onion, broccoli, cauliflower, cream cheese, and broth to pot with chicken. 5. Turn the pot's lid to close. Hit the manual button and adjust time for almost 12 minutes. 6. When the pot beeps, quick-release the pressure. Remove chicken and shred or dice; add to pot. Crumble cooked bacon and stir into pot with heavy cream. 7. Serve warm.
Per Serving: Calories 176; Total Fat 9.6g; Sodium 122mg; Total Carbs 5.7g; Fiber 4.5g; Sugars 3.8g; Protein 7.8g

White Chicken Chili

Prep time: 10 minutes | Cooking time: 20 minutes | Serves: 6

4 tablespoons butter	broth
¼ cup chopped onions	1 pound boneless, skinless
1 (4-ounce) can green chilies,	chicken breasts, cubed
drained	1 teaspoon salt
2 cloves garlic, minced	¼ teaspoon pepper
1 green pepper, chopped	4 ounces cream cheese
1½ cups store-bought chicken	¼ cup heavy cream

1. Hit the sauté button on the Instant Pot and place butter and onions into Instant Pot. Sauté until onions are fragrant and translucent. Add chilies, garlic, and green pepper. Sauté for almost 3 minutes, stirring frequently. 2. Hit the cancel button and add broth, chicken, seasoning, and cream cheese to pot. Hit the manual button and adjust time for almost 30 minutes. 3. When the pot beeps allow a 10-minute natural release and quick-release the remaining pressure. Stir in heavy cream. 4. Top it with avocado!
Per Serving: Calories 110; Total Fat 4.3g; Sodium 81mg; Total Carbs 6.4g; Fiber 5.4g; Sugars 6.1g; Protein 3.8g

Creamy Enchilada Soup

Prep time: 10 minutes | Cooking time: 40 minutes | Serves: 6

2 (6-ounce) boneless, skinless	2 cups chicken broth
chicken breasts	⅛ cup pickled jalapeños
½ tablespoon chili powder	4 ounces cream cheese
½ teaspoon salt	1 cup uncooked cauliflower rice
½ teaspoon garlic powder	1 avocado, diced
¼ teaspoon pepper	1 cup shredded mild cheddar
½ cup red enchilada sauce	cheese
½ medium onion, diced	½ cup sour cream
1 (4-ounce) can green chilies	

1. Sprinkle seasoning over chicken breasts and keep it aside. Pour enchilada sauce into Instant Pot and place chicken on top. 2. Add onion, chilies, broth, and jalapeños to the pot, then place cream cheese on top of chicken breasts. Turn the pot's lid to close. Adjust time for almost 25 minutes. 3. When the pot beeps, quick-release the pressure and shred chicken with forks. 4. Mix soup and add cauliflower rice, with pot on keep warm setting. Replace lid and let pot sit for almost 15 minutes, still on keep warm. 5. This will cook cauliflower rice. Serve with avocado, cheddar, and sour cream.
Per Serving: Calories 236; Total Fat 8.1g; Sodium 14mg; Total Carbs 2.1g; Fiber 6.3g; Sugars 0.8g; Protein 2.3g

Loaded Taco Soup

Prep time: 10 minutes | Cooking time: 10 minutes | Serves: 4

1 pound 85% lean ground beef	3 cups beef broth
½ medium onion, diced	⅓ cup heavy cream
1 (7-ounce) can diced tomatoes	¼ teaspoon xanthan gum
and chilies	1 avocado, diced
1 teaspoon salt	½ cup sour cream
1 tablespoon chili powder	1 cup shredded cheddar cheese
2 teaspoons cumin	¼ cup chopped cilantro

1. Hit the sauté button on the Instant Pot and brown ground beef in Instant Pot. When halfway done, add onion. Once beef is completely cooked, add diced tomatoes with chilies, seasoning, and broth. 2. Turn the pot's lid to close. Hit the soup button and adjust time for almost 10 minutes. 3. When the pot beeps, quick-release the pressure. Stir in cream and xanthan gum. 4. Serve warm and top with diced avocado, sour cream, cheddar, and cilantro.
Per Serving: Calories 110; Total Fat 3.4g; Sodium 1446mg; Total Carbs 3.9g; Fiber 5.4g; Sugars 3.8g; Protein 8.2g

Spicy Bacon Cheeseburger Soup

Prep time: 10 minutes | Cooking time: 15 minutes | Serves: 6

1 pound 85% lean ground beef	1 teaspoon salt
½ medium onion, sliced	½ teaspoon pepper
½ (14.5-ounce) can fire-roasted	½ teaspoon garlic powder
tomatoes	2 teaspoons Worcestershire sauce
3 cups beef broth	4 ounces cream cheese
¼ cup cooked crumbled bacon	1 cup sharp cheddar cheese
1 tablespoon chopped pickled	1 pickle spear, diced
jalapeños	

1. Hit the sauté button on the Instant Pot and add ground beef. Brown beef halfway and add onion. Continue cooking beef until no pink remains. 2. Hit the cancel button. Add tomatoes, broth, bacon, jalapeños, salt, pepper, garlic powder, and Worcestershire sauce, and stir. Place cream cheese on top in middle. 3. Turn the pot's lid to close. Hit the soup button and adjust time for almost 15 minutes. 4. When the pot beeps, quick-release the pressure. 5. Top with diced pickles. Feel free to add additional cheese and bacon.
Per Serving: Calories 120; Total Fat 2.3g; Sodium 2mg; Total Carbs 4.1g; Fiber 2.3g; Sugars 10g; Protein 3.6g

Hamburger Beef Stew

Prep time: 10 minutes | Cooking time: 4 hours | Serves: 6

1 pound lean ground beef	1 yellow onion, chopped
¼ cup beef broth	2 cups shredded cheddar cheese
½ cup tomato paste	1 teaspoon Italian seasoning
½ cup canned diced tomatoes	Salt & black pepper, to taste

1. Add all the recipe ingredients minus the salt and black pepper to the base of a slow cooker and cook on high for almost 4 hours. 2. Season with salt and black pepper and serve.
Per Serving: Calories 557; Total Fat 10g; Sodium 2706mg; Total Carbs 7.6g; Fiber 17.8g; Sugars 5.6g; Protein 29.2g

Autumn Harvest Stew

Prep time: 10 minutes | Cooking time: 4 hours | Serves: 6

1 pound beef chuck, cubed	3 cloves garlic, chopped
¼ cup beef broth	1 cup kale, chopped
¼ cup balsamic vinegar	1 teaspoon dried thyme
1 cup butternut squash, cubed	1 teaspoon dried oregano
1 carrot, chopped	1 teaspoon dried sage
1 yellow onion, chopped	Salt & black pepper, to taste

1. Add all the recipe ingredients minus the salt and black pepper to the base of a slow cooker and cook on high for almost 4 hours. 2. Season with salt and black pepper and serve.
Per Serving: Calories 425; Total Fat 8.8g; Sodium 284mg; Total Carbs 8.6g; Fiber 15.2g; Sugars 3.1g; Protein 20.6g

Herbed Broccoli Stew

Prep time: 10 minutes | Cooking time: 4 hours | Serves: 6

6 cups vegetable broth
1 cup full-fat coconut milk
2 cups broccoli florets
1 cup canned diced tomatoes (no sugar added)
1 yellow onion, chopped

2 cloves garlic, chopped
1 teaspoon dried sage
1 teaspoon dried oregano
1 teaspoon dried rosemary
Salt & black pepper, to taste

1. Add all the recipe ingredients minus the salt, black pepper, and coconut milk to a slow cooker and cook on high for almost 4 hours. 2. Stir in the coconut milk and season with salt and black pepper.
Per Serving: Calories 390; Total Fat 15.3g; Sodium 1086mg; Total Carbs 5g; Fiber 17.3g; Sugars 6.6g; Protein 18.2g

Creamy Mixed Vegetable Stew

Prep time: 10 minutes | Cooking time: 4 hours | Serves: 6

4 cups vegetable broth
1 cup heavy cream
1 cup shredded parmesan cheese
1 cup broccoli florets, chopped

1 cup canned diced tomatoes
1 yellow onion, chopped
Salt & black pepper, to taste

1. Add all the recipe ingredients minus the heavy cream, salt and black pepper to the base of a slow cooker. Cook on high for almost 4 hours. 2. Once cooked, warm the cream, and then stir into the stew. 3. Season with salt and black pepper and serve.
Per Serving: Calories 562; Total Fat 2.1g; Sodium 238mg; Total Carbs 1.8g; Fiber 19g; Sugars 5.3g; Protein 28.6g

Asparagus & Mushroom Nutmeg Stew

Prep time: 10 minutes | Cooking time: 4 hours | Serves: 6

6 cups vegetable broth
1 cup heavy cream
1 cup asparagus, chopped
1 cup cremini mushrooms

2 cloves garlic, chopped
1 yellow onion, chopped
½ teaspoon nutmeg
Salt & black pepper, to taste

1. Add all the recipe ingredients minus the heavy cream, salt, and black pepper to a slow cooker and cook on high for almost 4 hours. 2. Once cooked, warm the heavy cream, and then stir into the stew. 3. Season with salt and black pepper and serve.
Per Serving: Calories 276; Total Fat 11.8g; Sodium 888mg; Total Carbs 3.1g; Fiber 6.2g; Sugars 2.6g; Protein 14.4g

Balsamic Tofu Stew

Prep time: 10 minutes | Cooking time: 20 minutes | Serves: 4

2 cups vegetable broth
¼ cup balsamic vinegar
1½ cups firm tofu, cubed
1 green bell pepper, seeded and chopped

1 yellow onion, chopped
1 teaspoon garlic powder
1 tablespoon coconut oil, for cooking
Salt & black pepper, to taste

1. Add the coconut oil to a suitable skillet over medium heat and sauté the tofu, bell pepper, and onion for almost 10 minutes. 2. Add the vegetable broth, balsamic and garlic powder and bring to a simmer. 3. Cook for 10 minutes more or until the stew begins to thicken. 4. Season with salt and black pepper and serve.
Per Serving: Calories 589; Total Fat 22.7g; Sodium 266mg; Total Carbs 6.5g; Fiber 23.9g; Sugars 5.1g; Protein 25.5g

Quick Cream of Asparagus Soup

Prep time: 10 minutes | Cooking time: 30 minutes | Serves: 4

4 cups vegetable broth
1 cup heavy cream
1 bunch asparagus, chopped into

1-inch pieces
2 cloves garlic, chopped
1 pinch of sea salt

1. Add all the recipe ingredients to a stockpot over medium heat minus the heavy cream and cook to a boil. 2. Reduce its heat to a simmer and cook for almost 30 minutes. 3. Warm the heavy cream, and then stir into the soup. 4. Use an immersion blender and blend until smooth.
Per Serving: Calories 353; Total Fat 28.2g; Sodium 472mg; Total Carbs 4.9g; Fiber 9.9g; Sugars 1.2g; Protein 14.6g

Pumpkin Kale Vegetarian Stew

Prep time: 10 minutes | Cooking time: 40 minutes | Serves: 6

4 cups vegetable broth
1 cup pumpkin, cubed
2 carrots, chopped
1 yellow onion, chopped

2 cloves garlic, chopped
1 cup kale, chopped
Salt & black pepper, to taste

1. Add all the recipe ingredients minus the salt and black pepper to a stockpot and cook to a boil. Reduce its heat to a simmer and cook for almost 40 minutes. 2. Season with salt and black pepper and serve.
Per Serving: Calories 100; Total Fat 1.1g; Sodium 741mg; Total Carbs 9.4g; Fiber 5.2g; Sugars 6.2g; Protein 4.3g

No Bean Chili

Prep time: 10 minutes | Cooking time: 40 minutes | Serves: 6

4 cups vegetable broth
4 ounces tomato paste
¼ cup balsamic vinegar
1 yellow onion, chopped
1 green bell pepper, seeded and

chopped
2 cloves garlic, chopped
2 teaspoons chili powder
Salt & black pepper, to taste

1. Add all the recipe ingredients minus the salt and black pepper to a stockpot and cook to a boil. Reduce its heat to a simmer and cook for almost 40 minutes. 2. Season with salt and black pepper and serve.
Per Serving: Calories 300; Total Fat 4g; Sodium 429mg; Total Carbs 6.8g; Fiber 22.7g; Sugars 11.3g; Protein 19.7g

Turmeric Stew

Prep time: 10 minutes | Cooking time: 40 minutes | Serves: 6

4 cups vegetable broth
1 cauliflower head, cut into florets
1 cup full-fat coconut milk
2 cloves garlic, chopped
1 yellow onion, chopped

2 teaspoons ground turmeric
1 teaspoon ground cinnamon
1 teaspoon dried oregano
Salt & black pepper, to taste

1. Add all the recipe ingredients minus the salt, black pepper, and coconut milk to a stockpot and cook to a boil. 2. Reduce its heat to a simmer and cook for almost 40 minutes. 3. Stir in the coconut milk. 4. Season with salt and black pepper and serve.
Per Serving: Calories 460; Total Fat 10.1g; Sodium 332mg; Total Carbs 3.9g; Fiber 20.3g; Sugars 14.5g; Protein 21.7g

Creamy Mushroom Soup

Prep time: 10 minutes | Cooking time: 10 minutes | Serves: 4

1 pound sliced button mushrooms
3 tablespoons butter
2 tablespoons diced onion
2 cloves garlic, minced
2 cups chicken broth

½ teaspoon salt
¼ teaspoon pepper
½ cup heavy cream
¼ teaspoon xanthan gum

1. Hit the sauté button on the Instant Pot and then hit the adjust button to set heat to less. Add mushrooms, butter, and onion to pot. Sauté for almost 5–8 minutes or until onions and mushrooms begin to brown. Add garlic and sauté until fragrant. Hit the cancel button. 2. Add broth, salt, and pepper. Turn the pot's lid to close. Hit the manual button and adjust time for almost 3 minutes. 3. When the pot beeps, quick-release the pressure. Stir in heavy cream and xanthan gum. 4. Allow a few minutes to thicken and serve warm.
Per Serving: Calories 330; Total Fat 29.1g; Sodium 348mg; Total Carbs 2.6g; Fiber 1.6g; Sugars 0g; Protein 7.7g

Chapter 4 Poultry Mains

Garlicky Dill Wings 45
Delicious Chicken Fajita Poppers 45
Pesto Chicken Pizzas...................... 45
Cheesy Stuffed Chicken 45
Tangy Fried Chicken 45
Herby Chicken Thighs 45
Spiced Wings............................. 45
Spicy Chicken with Pork Rind 45
Delicious Chipotle Drumsticks 46
Garlicky Parmesan Drumsticks............ 46
Nut Crusted Chicken Tenders 46
Alfredo Chicken 46
Butter Chicken 46
Chicken Cordon Bleu 46
Cheese Filled Chicken Nuggets 46
Cajun-Crusted Chicken Bites 46
Buffalo Chicken Meatballs 47
Spicy Chipotle Aioli Wings 47
Spicy Jerk Chicken Kebabs 47
Golden Chicken Thighs.................... 47
Chicken Ginger 47
Mustard Wings 47
Spicy Blackened Chicken Tenders 47
Chicken Curry with Bamboo Shoots...... 47
Moroccan Chicken with Vegetable Tagine 48
Arabic Chicken Shawarma 48
Balsamic Chicken with Vegetables 48
Crispy Wrapped Chicken 48
Green Chili Chicken Skewers 48
Chicken Zucchini "Pasta" 48
Lemon-Rosemary Chicken 48
Chicken Fajita Stuffed Peppers 49
Barbecued Chicken with Bacon 49
Carne Asada Bowls 49
Crispy Chicken Thighs with Veggies ... 49
Cheesy Chicken Tenderloin Packets 49
Avocado Chicken Thigh Chili 49
Creamy Chicken and Spinach Bake 49
Tangy Chicken Zoodle Bowls 50
Spaghetti Chicken Bowls 50
Traditional Chicken Teriyaki.............. 50
Chicken in Lettuce Cups 50
Creamy Chicken with Mushrooms 50

Spinach Stuffed Chicken Thighs 50
Tandoori Chicken Vegetable Skewers ... 51
Classical Kung Pao Chicken 51
Chicken Tenders 51
Cheesy Chicken Nuggets 51
Harissa Chicken with Yogurt 51
Indian Chicken Tikka Masala 51
Greek Chicken 52
Feta Stuffed Chicken Thighs 52
Lemon Chicken and Veggies Stir-Fry ... 52
Braised Chicken Thighs 52
Sesame Chicken Thighs 52
Chicken Mole with Black Pepper 52
Spicy Paprika Chicken 52
Tropical Chicken 53
Delicious Turkey Meatloaf 53
Cheesy Turkey Rissoles.................. 53
Crispy Bacon-Mushroom Chicken 53
Chicken Breasts with Mushrooms........ 53
Spice -Infused Turkey Breast 53
Crispy Chicken Thighs 53
Regular Buffalo Chicken 54
Traditional Hungarian Chicken 54
Creamy Tangy Chicken 54
Hot Chicken Wings 54
Tropical-Chicken Curry................... 54
Roasted Chicken 54
Smoked Paprika Drumsticks 54
Chicken Burgers 55
Delicious Jerk Chicken 55
Chicken Cacciatore with Mushroom...... 55
Lettuce-Wrapped Burger 55
"Roasted" Duck 55
Turkey Ragout with Pumpkin 55
Bacon Ranch Cheesy Chicken Breasts ... 55
Mustardy Chicken Drumsticks 56
Traditional Jamaican Jerk Chicken 56
Roasted Whole Chicken with Jicama ... 56
Roasted Chicken Thighs And Zucchini In
Wine 56
Chicken Thighs with Tangy Lemon Sauce 56
Crispy Fried Chicken.................... 56

Garlicky Dill Wings

Prep time: 5 minutes | Cook time: 25 minutes | Serves: 4

2 pounds bone-in chicken wings, separated at joints
½ teaspoon salt
½ teaspoon ground black pepper
½ teaspoon onion powder
½ teaspoon garlic powder
1 teaspoon dried dill

1. Toss wings with salt, pepper, onion powder, garlic powder, and dill until evenly coated. Place wings into an ungreased air fryer basket in a single layer. 2. Adjust the temperature setting to 400°F/200°C and timer for 25 minutes, shaking the basket every 7 minutes during cooking. 3. Wings should be golden brown when done. Serve warm.
Per Serving: Calories 319; Fat 22g; Sodium 430mg; Carbs 1g; Fiber 0g; Sugar 0g; Protein 29g

Delicious Chicken Fajita Poppers

Prep time: 11 minutes | Cook time: 20 minutes | Serves: 6

1-pound ground chicken thighs
½ green bell pepper, finely chopped
¼ medium yellow onion, peeled and finely chopped
½ cup shredded pepper jack cheese
1 (1-ounce) packet gluten-free fajita seasoning

1. In a large bowl, combine all ingredients. Form mixture into eighteen 2" balls and place in a single layer into the ungreased air fryer basket. 2. Adjust the temperature setting to 350°F/175°C and timer for 20 minutes. 3. Carefully use tongs to turn poppers halfway through cooking. 4. When 5 minutes remain on a timer, increase the temperature to 400°F/200°C to give the poppers a dark golden-brown color. Shake the basket once more when 2 minutes remain on a timer. 5. Serve warm.
Per Serving: Calories 164; Fat 8g; Sodium 397mg; Carbs 5g; Fiber 0g; Sugar 0g; Protein 16g

Pesto Chicken Pizzas

Prep time: 11 minutes | Cook time: 12 minutes | Serves: 4

1-pound ground chicken thighs
¼ teaspoon salt
⅛ teaspoon ground black pepper
¼ cup basil pesto
1 cup shredded mozzarella cheese
4 grape tomatoes, sliced

1. Cut four parchment paper pieces to fit into your air fryer basket. 2. Put ground chicken in a bowl and spice with salt and pepper. Divide the mixture into four equal parts. 3. With wet hands, press each section into a 6" circle onto a piece of ungreased parchment. Place each chicken crust into the air fryer basket. 4. Adjust the temperature setting to 350°F/175°C and timer for 10 minutes, turning halfway for even cooking. 5. When the timer beeps, spread 1 tablespoon pesto across the top of each crust, then sprinkle with ¼ cup mozzarella and top with 1 sliced tomato. Continue cooking at 350°F/175°C for 2 minutes. 6. The cheese will be melted and brown when done. Serve warm.
Per Serving: Calories 318; Fat 19g; Sodium 546mg; Carbs 4g; Fiber 0g; Sugar 2g; Protein 28g

Cheesy Stuffed Chicken

Prep time: 16 minutes | Cook time: 20 minutes | Serves: 4

2 ounces cream cheese, softened
1 cup chopped fresh broccoli, steamed
½ cup shredded sharp Cheddar cheese
4 (6-ounce) boneless, skinless chicken breasts
2 tablespoons mayonnaise
¼ teaspoon salt
¼ teaspoon garlic powder
⅛ teaspoon ground black pepper

1. In a medium bowl, combine cream cheese, broccoli, and Cheddar. Cut a 4" pocket into each chicken breast. Evenly divide the mixture between chicken breasts; stuff the pocket of each chicken breast with the mixture. 2. Spread ¼ tablespoon mayonnaise per side of each chicken breast, then sprinkle both sides of the breasts with salt, garlic powder, and pepper. 3. Place stuffed chicken breasts into the ungreased air fryer basket so that the open seams face up. Adjust the temperature setting to 350°F/175°C and timer for 20 minutes, turning the chicken halfway through cooking. When done, the chicken will be golden and have an internal temperature of at least 165°F/75°C. Serve warm.
Per Serving: Calories 364; Fat 16g; Sodium 415mg; Carbs 3g; Fiber 1g; Sugar 1g; Protein 43g

Tangy Fried Chicken

Prep time: 1 hour 15 minutes | Cook time: 20 minutes | Serves: 4

4 (4-ounce) boneless, skinless chicken thighs
⅓ cup dill pickle juice
1 large egg
2 ounces plain pork rinds, crushed
½ teaspoon salt
¼ teaspoon ground black pepper

1. Place chicken thighs in a large sealable bowl or bag and pour pickle juice over them. Place sealed bowl or bag into refrigerator and allow to marinate at least 1 hour up to overnight. 2. In a small bowl, whisk egg. Place pork rinds in a separate medium bowl. 3. Remove chicken thighs from marinade. Shake off excess pickle juice and pat thighs dry with a paper towel. Sprinkle with salt and pepper. 4. Dip each thigh into the egg and gently shake off excess. Press into pork rinds to coat each side. 5. Place thighs into an ungreased air fryer basket. Adjust the temperature setting to 400°F/200°C and timer for 20 minutes. 6. When chicken thighs are done, they will be golden and crispy on the outside with an internal temperature of at least 165°F/75°C. Serve warm.
Per Serving: Calories 344; Fat 16g; Sodium 711mg; Carbs 0g; Fiber 0g; Sugar 0g; Protein 44g

Herby Chicken Thighs

Prep time: 11 minutes | Cook time: 25 minutes | Serves: 4

4 (4-ounce) bone-in, skin-on chicken thighs
½ teaspoon salt
½ teaspoon garlic powder
2 teaspoons chili powder
1 teaspoon paprika
1 teaspoon ground cumin
1 small lime, halved

1. Pat dry chicken spice with salt, garlic powder, chili powder, paprika, and cumin. 2. Squeeze juice from ½ lime over thighs. Place thighs into an ungreased air fryer basket. Adjust the temperature setting to 380°F/195°C and timer for 25 minutes, turning the thighs halfway through cooking. 3. Thighs will be crispy and browned with an internal temperature of at least 165°F/75°C when done. 4. Transfer thighs to a large serving plate and drizzle with remaining lime juice. Serve warm.
Per Serving: Calories 255; Fat 10g; Sodium 475mg; Carbs 2g; Fiber 1g; Sugar 0g; Protein 34g

Spiced Wings

Prep time: 5 minutes | Cook time: 25 minutes | Serves: 4

2 pounds bone-in chicken wings, separated at joints
1 teaspoon salt
½ teaspoon ground black pepper

1. Sprinkle wings with salt and pepper, then place them into the ungreased air fryer basket in a single layer. 2. Adjust the temperature setting to 400°F/200°C and the timer for 25 minutes, shaking the basket every 7 minutes during cooking. Wings should be golden brown when done. Wings should Serve warm.
Per Serving: Calories 316; Fat 22g; Sodium 720mg; Carbs 0g; Fiber 0g; Sugar 0g; Protein 29g

Spicy Chicken with Pork Rind

Prep time: 40 minutes | Cook time: 20 minutes | Serves: 4

¼ cup buffalo sauce
4 (4-ounce) boneless, skinless chicken breasts
½ teaspoon paprika
½ teaspoon garlic powder
¼ teaspoon ground black pepper
2 ounces plain pork rinds, finely crushed

1. Pour buffalo sauce into a large sealable bowl or bag. Add chicken and toss to coat. Place sealed bowl or bag into refrigerator and let marinate at least 30 minutes up to overnight. 2. Remove chicken from marinade but do not shake excess sauce off the chicken. Sprinkle both sides of the thighs with paprika, garlic powder, and pepper. 3. Place pork rinds into a large bowl and press each chicken breast into pork rinds to coat evenly on both sides. 4. Place chicken into an ungreased air fryer basket. Adjust the temp setting to 400°F/200°C and timer for 20 minutes, turning the chicken halfway through cooking. 5. The chicken will be golden and have an internal temperature of at least 165°F/75°C when done. Serve warm.
Per Serving: Calories 185; Fat 7g; Sodium 731mg; Carbs 1g; Fiber 0g; Sugar 0g; Protein 27g

Delicious Chipotle Drumsticks

Prep time: 5 minutes | Cook time: 25 minutes | Serves: 4

1 tablespoon tomato paste
½ teaspoon chipotle powder
¼ teaspoon apple cider vinegar
¼ teaspoon garlic powder

8 chicken drumsticks
½ teaspoon salt
⅛ teaspoon ground black pepper

1. In a small bowl, combine tomato paste, chipotle powder, vinegar, and garlic powder. 2. Sprinkle drumsticks with salt and pepper, then place into a large bowl and pour in tomato paste mixture. Toss or stir to evenly coat all drumsticks in the mixture. 3. Place drumsticks into an ungreased air fryer basket. Adjust the temperature setting to 400°F/200°C and timer for 25 minutes, turning drumsticks halfway through cooking. 4. Drumsticks will be dark red with an internal temperature of at least 165°F/75°C when done. Serve warm.
Per Serving: Calories 432; Fat 22g; Sodium 623mg; Carbs 1g; Fiber 0g; Sugar 0g; Protein 48g

Garlicky Parmesan Drumsticks

Prep time: 5 minutes | Cook time: 25 minutes | Serves: 4

8 (4-ounce) chicken drumsticks
½ teaspoon salt
⅛ teaspoon ground black pepper
½ teaspoon garlic powder

2 tablespoons salted butter, melted
½ cup grated Parmesan cheese
1 tablespoon dried parsley

1. Spice drumsticks with salt, pepper, and garlic powder. 2. Place drumsticks into an ungreased air fryer basket. 3. Adjust the temperature setting to 400°F/200°C and timer for 25 minutes, turning halfway through cooking. Drumsticks will be golden when done. 4. Transfer drumsticks to a large serving dish. Pour butter over drumsticks, and sprinkle with Parmesan and parsley. Serve warm.
Per Serving: Calories 533; Fat 30g; Sodium 845mg; Carbs 3g; Fiber 0g; Sugar 0g; Protein 52g

Nut Crusted Chicken Tenders

Prep time: 11 minutes | Cook time: 12 minutes | Serves: 4

2 tablespoons mayonnaise
1 teaspoon Dijon mustard
1-pound boneless, skinless chicken tenders

½ teaspoon salt
¼ teaspoon ground black pepper
½ cup chopped roasted pecans, finely ground

1. In a bowl, whisk the mayonnaise with mustard until combined. Brush mixture onto chicken tenders on both sides, then sprinkle tenders with salt and pepper. 2. Place pecans in a medium bowl and press each tender into pecans to coat each side. 3. Place tenders into the ungreased air fryer basket in a single layer, Adjust the temperature setting to 375°F/190°C and timer for 12 minutes, turning tenders halfway through cooking. Tenders will be golden brown and have an internal temperature of at least 165°F/75°C when done. Serve warm.
Per Serving: Calories 237; Fat 15g; Sodium 469mg; Carbs 2g; Fiber 1g; Sugar 1g; Protein 22g

Alfredo Chicken

Prep time: 11 minutes | Cook time: 20 minutes | Serves: 4

4 (6-ounce) boneless, skinless chicken breasts
4 teaspoons coconut oil
½ teaspoon salt
¼ teaspoon ground black pepper
4 strips cooked sugar-free bacon,

broken into 24 pieces
½ cup Alfredo sauce
1 cup shredded mozzarella cheese
¼ teaspoon crushed red pepper flakes

1. Cut six horizontal slits in the top of each chicken breast. Drizzle with coconut oil and sprinkle with salt and black pepper. Place into an ungreased 6" round nonstick baking dish. 2. Place 1 bacon piece in each slit in chicken breasts. Pour Alfredo sauce over chicken and sprinkle with mozzarella and red pepper flakes. 3. Place dish into the air fryer basket. Adjust the temperature setting to 370°F/185°C and timer for 20 minutes. 4. The chicken will be cooked when the internal temperature is at least 165°F/75°C and the cheese is browned. Serve warm.
Per Serving: Calories 396; Fat 17g; Sodium 921mg; Carbs 3g; Fiber 0g; Sugar 1g; Protein 49g

Butter Chicken

Prep time: 11 minutes | Cook time: 65 minutes | Serves: 6

1 (4-pound) whole chicken
2 tablespoons salted butter, softened
1 teaspoon dried thyme

½ teaspoon garlic powder
1 teaspoon salt
½ teaspoon ground black pepper
6 slices sugar-free bacon

1. Pat dry chicken with a paper towel. Rub with butter on all sides of chicken. 2. Spiced with thyme, garlic powder, salt, and pepper over the chicken. 3. Place chicken into the ungreased air fryer basket, breast side up. 4. Lay bacon over chicken and secure with toothpicks. 5. Adjust the temperature setting to 350°F/175°C and timer for 65 minutes, halfway through cooking, remove and set aside bacon and flip the chicken over. 6. The chicken will be done when the skin is golden and crispy. Serve warm with bacon.
Per Serving: Calories 416; Fat 26g; Sodium 666mg; Carbs 0g; Fiber 0g; Sugar 0g; Protein 36g

Chicken Cordon Bleu

Prep time: 16 minutes | Cook time: 25 minutes | Serves: 4

4 (6-ounce) boneless, skinless chicken breasts
4 (1-ounce) slices Swiss cheese
4 (1-ounce) slices no-sugar-added

ham
¼ cup Dijon mustard
½ teaspoon salt
¼ teaspoon ground black pepper

1. Cut a 5"-long slit in the side of each chicken breast. Place Swiss cheese and ham inside each slit. 2. Brush chicken with mustard, then sprinkles with salt and pepper on both sides. 3. Place chicken into the ungreased air fryer basket. Adjust the temperature setting to 375°F/175°C and timer for 25 minutes, turning chicken halfway through cooking. 4. Chicken will be golden brown when done. Serve warm.
Per Serving: Calories 388; Fat 14g; Sodium 1154mg; Carbs 3g; Fiber 0g; Sugar 0g; Protein 53g

Cheese Filled Chicken Nuggets

Prep time: 11 minutes | Cook time: 15 minutes | Serves: 4

1-pound ground chicken thighs
½ cup shredded mozzarella cheese
1 large egg, whisked

½ teaspoon salt
¼ teaspoon dried oregano
¼ teaspoon garlic powder

1. In a large bowl, combine all ingredients. Form mixture into twenty nugget shapes, about 2 tablespoons each. 2. Place nuggets into an ungreased air fryer basket. Adjust the temperature setting to 375°F/175°C and timer for 15 minutes, turning nuggets halfway through cooking. 3. Cool for 5 minutes before serving.
Per Serving: Calories 222; Fat 12g; Sodium 472mg; Carbs 1g; Fiber 0g; Sugar 0g; Protein 25g

Cajun-Crusted Chicken Bites

Prep time: 11 minutes | Cook time: 12 minutes | Serves: 4

1-pound boneless, skinless chicken breasts, cut into 1" cubes
½ cup heavy whipping cream
½ teaspoon salt
¼ teaspoon ground black pepper

1-ounce plain pork rinds, finely crushed
¼ cup unflavored whey protein powder
½ teaspoon Cajun seasoning

1. Place chicken in a bowl with cream. Stir to coat. Sprinkle with salt and pepper. 2. In a separate large bowl, combine pork rinds, protein powder, and Cajun seasoning. Remove chicken from cream, shaking off any excess, and toss in dry mix until fully coated. 3. Place bites into an ungreased air fryer basket. Adjust the temperature setting to 400°F/200°C and timer for 12 minutes, shaking the basket twice during cooking. 4. Bites will be done when golden brown and have an internal temperature of at least 165°F/75°C. Serve warm.
Per Serving: Calories 285; Fat 16g; Sodium 497mg; Carbs 1g; Fiber 0g; Sugar 1g; Protein 34g

Buffalo Chicken Meatballs

Prep time: 5 minutes | Cook time: 15 minutes | Serves: 4

1-pound ground chicken thighs
1 large egg, whisked
½ cup hot sauce, divided
½ cup crumbled blue cheese

2 tablespoons dry ranch seasoning
¼ teaspoon salt
¼ teaspoon ground black pepper

1. Combine ground chicken, egg, ¼ cup hot sauce, blue cheese, ranch seasoning, salt, and pepper. 2. Divide the mixture into eight equal sections of about ¼ cup each and form each section into a ball. Place meatballs into an ungreased air fryer basket. 3. Adjust the temperature setting to 370°F/185°C and timer for 15 minutes. Meatballs will be done when golden and have an internal temperature of at least 165°F/75°C. 4. Transfer meatballs to a large serving dish and toss with the remaining hot sauce. Serve warm.
Per Serving: Calories 254; Fat 14g; Sodium 1749mg; Carbs 4g; Fiber 0g; Sugar 0g; Protein 25g

Spicy Chipotle Aioli Wings

Prep time: 5 minutes | Cook time: 25 minutes | Serves: 6

2 pounds bone-in chicken wings
½ teaspoon salt
¼ teaspoon ground black pepper

2 tablespoons mayonnaise
2 teaspoons chipotle powder
2 tablespoons lemon juice

1. In a bowl, toss wings in salt and pepper, then place the ungreased air fryer basket. Adjust the temperature setting to 400°F/200°C and timer for 25 minutes, shaking the basket twice while cooking. 2. Wings will be done when golden and have an internal temperature of at least 165°F/75°C. 3. Whisk together mayonnaise, chipotle powder, and lemon juice in a small bowl. Place cooked wings into a large serving bowl and drizzle with aioli. 4. Toss to coat. Serve warm.
Per Serving: Calories 243; Fat 18g; Sodium 368mg; Carbs 0g; Fiber 0g; Sugar 0g; Protein 19g

Spicy Jerk Chicken Kebabs

Prep time: 11 minutes | Cook time: 14 minutes | Serves: 4

8 ounces chicken thighs, boneless, skinless, cut into 1" cubes
2 tablespoons jerk seasoning
2 tablespoons coconut oil
½ red bell pepper, cut into 1"

pieces and seeds removed
¼ red onion, peeled, cut into 1" pieces
½ teaspoon salt

1. Place chicken in a medium bowl and sprinkle with jerk seasoning and coconut oil. Toss to coat on all sides. 2. Using eight 6" skewers, build skewers by alternating chicken, pepper, and onion pieces, about three repetitions per skewer. 3. Sprinkle salt over skewers and place into an ungreased air fryer basket. Adjust the temperature setting to 370°F/175°C and timer for 14 minutes, turning skewers halfway through cooking. 4. The chicken will be golden and have an internal temperature of at least 165°F/75°C when done. Serve warm.
Per Serving: Calories 138; Fat 7g; Sodium 550mg; Carbs 2g; Fiber 0g; Sugar 1g; Protein 10g

Golden Chicken Thighs

Prep time: 5 minutes | Cook time: 25 minutes | Serves: 4

4 (4-ounce) boneless, skin-on chicken thighs
2 tablespoons coconut oil, melted
½ teaspoon ground turmeric

½ teaspoon salt
½ teaspoon garlic powder
½ teaspoon ground ginger
¼ teaspoon ground black pepper

1. In a bowl, place chicken thighs and drizzle with coconut oil. Sprinkle with remaining ingredients and toss to coat both sides of thighs. 2. Place thighs skin side up into an ungreased air fryer basket. Adjust the temperature setting to 400°F/200°C and timer for 25 minutes. After 10 minutes, turn thighs. 3. When 5 minutes remains, flip thighs once more. Chicken will be golden brown and the internal temperature is at least 165°F/75°C. 4. Serve warm.
Per Serving: Calories 306; Fat 17g; Sodium 435mg; Carbs 1g; Fiber 0g; Sugar 0g; Protein 34g

Chicken Ginger

Prep time: 30 minutes | Cook time: 12 minutes | Serves: 4

1-pound boneless, skinless chicken thighs, cut into 1" pieces
¼ cup soy sauce
2 cloves garlic, peeled and finely

minced
1 tablespoon minced ginger
¼ teaspoon salt

1. Place all ingredients in a large sealable bowl or bag. Place the sealed bowl or bag into refrigerator and let marinate for at least 30 minutes up to overnight. 2. Remove chicken from marinade and place into an ungreased air fryer basket. Adjust the temperature setting to 375°F/175°C and timer for 12 minutes, shaking the basket twice during cooking. 3. The chicken will be golden and have an internal temperature of at least 165°F/75°C when done. Serve warm.
Per Serving: Calories 140; Fat 6g; Sodium 184mg; Carbs 0g; Fiber 0g; Sugar 0g; Protein 20g

Mustard Wings

Prep time: 5 minutes | Cook time: 25 minutes | Serves: 4

1-pound bone-in chicken wings, separated at joints
¼ cup yellow mustard

½ teaspoon salt
¼ teaspoon ground black pepper

1. In a bowl, place wings and toss with mustard to fully coat. Sprinkle with salt and pepper. 2. Place wings into an ungreased air fryer basket. Adjust the temperature setting to 400°F/200°C and timer for 25 minutes, shaking the basket three times during cooking. Wings will be done when browned and cooked to an internal temperature of at least 165°F/75°C. Serve warm.
Per Serving: Calories 182; Fat 12g; Sodium 538mg; Carbs 1g; Fiber 1g; Sugar 0g; Protein 16g

Spicy Blackened Chicken Tenders

Prep time: 5 minutes | Cook time: 12 minutes | Serves: 4

1-pound boneless, skinless chicken tenders
2 tablespoons coconut oil, melted
1 teaspoon paprika
½ teaspoon chili powder

½ teaspoon salt
¼ teaspoon ground black pepper
¼ teaspoon garlic powder
¼ teaspoon cayenne pepper

1. In a bowl, toss chicken tenders in coconut oil. Sprinkle each side of chicken tenders with paprika, chili powder, salt, black pepper, garlic powder, and cayenne pepper. 2. Place tenders into ungreased air fryer basket. Adjust the temperature setting to 375°F/190°C and timer for 12 minutes. Tenders will be dark brown and have an internal temperature of at least 165°F/75°C when done. Serve warm.
Per Serving: Calories 156; Fat 7g; Sodium 404mg; Carbs 1g; Fiber 0g; Sugar 0g; Protein 21g

Chicken Curry with Bamboo Shoots

Prep time: 11 minutes | Cook time: 25 minutes | Serves: 4

¼ cup coconut oil
¼ cup diced onion
1 cup bamboo shoots
1-pound boneless chicken thighs, diced
1 teaspoon minced fresh ginger
1 tablespoon curry powder

1 tablespoon paprika
1¼ cups coconut milk
¼ cup heavy (whipping) cream
¼ teaspoon salt
⅛ teaspoon freshly ground black pepper

1. In a pan heat the coconut oil for about 1 minute. Add the onion, bamboo shoots, and chicken meat. Cook for 5 minutes. 2. Stir in the ginger, curry powder, and paprika. Add the coconut milk and heavy cream. 3. Reduce the heat to medium-low. Simmer for about 15 minutes. Season with salt and pepper. Serve over cauliflower "rice" or zucchini noodles.
Per Serving: Calories 582; Fat 52g; Sodium 1036mg; Carbs 9g; Fiber 4g; Sugar 1g; Protein 24g

Moroccan Chicken with Vegetable Tagine

Prep time: 11 minutes | Cook time: 60 minutes | Serves: 6

½ cup extra-virgin olive oil, divided
1½ pounds chicken thighs, boneless and skinless, cut into 1-inch chunks
1½ teaspoons salt, divided
½ teaspoon freshly ground black pepper
1 small red onion, chopped
1 red bell pepper, chunks

1 cup water
2 medium tomatoes, chopped or 1½ cups diced canned tomatoes
2 medium zucchinis, sliced into ¼-inch-thick half moons
1 cup pitted halved olives
¼ cup chopped fresh cilantro or flat-leaf Italian parsley
Riced cauliflower or sautéed spinach, for serving

1. In a Dutch oven, heat ¼ cup olive oil over medium-high heat. Spice the chicken with salt and pepper and sauté until just browned on all sides, 6 to 8 minutes. Add the onions, peppers, and sauté until wilted for another 6 to 8 minutes. Add the chopped tomatoes and water, bring to a boil, and reduce the heat to low. 2. Cover and simmer. Cook the meat until tender, for 30 to 45 minutes on low. Add the remaining ¼ cup olive oil, zucchini, olives, and cilantro, stirring to combine. 3. Continue cooking over low heat until the zucchini is tender, for about 10 minutes. Serve warm over riced cauliflower or atop a bed of sautéed spinach.
Per Serving: Calories 358; Fat 25g; Sodium 896mg; Carbs 8g; Fiber 3g; Sugar 2g; Protein 25g

Arabic Chicken Shawarma

Prep time: 5 minutes | Cook time: 30 minutes | Serves: 6

1½ pounds boneless, skinless chicken breast
1-pound skinless chicken thighs
5 tablespoons olive oil, divided
2 teaspoons paprika
1 teaspoon allspice
¾ teaspoon ground turmeric
¼ teaspoon garlic powder

¼ teaspoon ground cinnamon
Pinch cayenne pepper
Salt
Freshly ground black pepper
Leafy greens, for serving
Cooked cauliflower rice, for serving

1. Put the chicken breast and thighs in a large resealable plastic bag and add 4 tablespoons of the olive oil, paprika, allspice, turmeric, garlic powder, cinnamon, cayenne, salt, and pepper, seal, and shake to make sure the chicken is evenly coated. 2. Let marinate in the refrigerator for at least 2 hours or up to 24 hours. 3. Preheat the oven to 400°F/200°C temperature setting. 4. Line a 9-by-13-inch dish with aluminum foil. 5. Place the marinated chicken in the baking dish, ensuring the pieces don't touch. 6. Bake the chicken, flipping at least once, until no longer pink inside, 15 to 20 minutes. 7. Slice the cooked chicken into thin strips. 8. Heat the oil, cook the chicken strips for 5 to 7 minutes, or until crispy. If desired, serve on a bed of leafy greens with some cauliflower rice.
Per Serving: Calories 410; Fat 30g; Sodium 963mg; Carbs 0g; Fiber 0g; Sugar 0g; Protein 35g

Balsamic Chicken with Vegetables

Prep time: 5 minutes | Cook time: 15 minutes | Serves: 1

1 teaspoon balsamic vinegar
2 tablespoons avocado oil, divided
1 teaspoon Dijon mustard
1 garlic clove, minced

Pinch red pepper flakes
2 boneless chicken thighs
4 asparagus spears, woody ends removed
4 cherry tomatoes, halved

1. In a small bowl, combine the vinegar, 1 tablespoon of oil, the mustard, garlic, and red pepper flakes. Whisk until fully combined, and set aside. 2. In a skillet, add the 1 tablespoon of oil. Thoroughly season the chicken thighs with salt and freshly ground black pepper, and add them to the skillet, searing each side for 3 minutes or until golden. 3. Remove the chicken from the skillet, and set it on a plate. Next, add the asparagus and tomatoes to the same skillet, season with more salt and pepper to taste, and cook for about 5 minutes, until the asparagus is bright green and the tomatoes are slightly wilted. 4. Make space for chicken by moving veggies on the side and add chicken in the skillet. Pour the balsamic mixture to the chicken and vegetables. 5. Toss everything together, and cook for about 5 minutes more, until the chicken is fully cooked and the vinaigrette has thickened.
Per Serving: Calories 650; Fat 54g; Sodium 863mg; Carbs 8g; Fiber 5g; Sugar 2g; Protein 33g

Crispy Wrapped Chicken

Prep time: 5 minutes | Cook time: 25 minutes | Serves: 1

2 garlic cloves, minced
1 tablespoon avocado oil

2 boneless chicken thighs
4 bacon slices

1. Preheat the oven to 400°F/200°C temperature setting and line a baking sheet with parchment paper. Mix the garlic and oil in a bowl. Coat the chicken thighs in the garlic mixture, and wrap each thigh in 2 slices of bacon. 2. Bake the chicken for about 25 minutes, flipping the pieces halfway through until the bacon is crisp.
Per Serving: Calories 887; Fat 71g; Sodium 874mg; Carbs 3g; Fiber 0g; Sugar 0g; Protein 59g

Green Chili Chicken Skewers

Prep time: 16 minutes | Cook time: 10 minutes | Serves: 4

1 cup fresh cilantro leaves, chopped
2 tablespoons olive oil
¼ cup red chili paste
2 tablespoons soy sauce
2 garlic cloves, minced
1 teaspoon onion powder
1 teaspoon minced fresh ginger

¼ teaspoon freshly ground black pepper
1-pound boneless chicken thighs, cut into 1-inch cubes
1 onion, roughly chopped
2 red bell peppers, roughly chopped

1. Preheat the oven to broil setting. 2. In a bowl, mix the cilantro, olive oil, red chili paste, soy sauce, garlic, onion powder, ginger, and black pepper. 3. Add the thigh meat. Toss to coat. Refrigerate for 15 minutes to marinate. Skewer the marinated chicken cubes, with the onions and peppers. 4. Place a foil-lined baking sheet on the low oven rack. 5. Lay the chicken skewers on the middle rack and cook for 3 minutes. 6. Turn the skewers after every 3 minutes for 2 times. 7. Remove from oven when done.
Per Serving: Calories 355; Fat 25g; Sodium 647mg; Carbs 11g; Fiber 2g; Sugar 0.6g; Protein 22g

Chicken Zucchini "Pasta"

Prep time: 11 minutes | Cook time: 15 minutes | Serves: 1

1 tablespoon butter or ghee
2 boneless chicken thighs, cubed
¼ medium white onion, diced
2 garlic cloves, minced
½ zucchini, peeled into thin

ribbons or spiralized
1 teaspoon avocado oil
¼ cup basil pesto
4 cherry tomatoes, halved

1. In a skillet, melt butter. Add the chicken and onion, and cook for several minutes until the chicken begins to brown. In a pan add the garlic and cook for another 2 to 3 minutes, until the chicken is cooked. Turn the heat down to low. 2. In a medium bowl, coat the zucchini in the oil. 3. Add the zucchini in it and cook for 1 minute, stirring occasionally. 4. Transfer the mixture to a medium bowl, and toss with the pesto and tomatoes.
Per Serving: Calories 875; Fat 74g; Sodium 1066mg; Carbs 15g; Fiber 8g; Sugar 1g; Protein 37g

Lemon-Rosemary Chicken

Prep time: 22 minutes | Cook time: 45 minutes | Serves: 8

½ cup extra-virgin olive oil, divided
1 (3- to 4-pound) roasting chicken, spatchcocked
8 garlic cloves, roughly chopped
2 to 4 tablespoons chopped fresh

rosemary
2 teaspoons salt, divided
1 teaspoon freshly ground black pepper, divided
2 lemons, thinly sliced

1. Preheat the oven to 425°F/220°C. Pour oil in the bottom of a 9-by-13-inch baking dish and swirl to coat the bottom. Place the chicken in the baking dish. 2. Loosen the skin. 3. In a bowl, combine ¼ cup olive oil, garlic, rosemary, 1 teaspoon salt, and ½ teaspoon pepper and whisk. Rub the garlic-herb oil evenly under each breast and thigh's skin. 4. Add the lemon slices evenly to the same areas. Whisk the remaining 2 tablespoons olive oil, 1 teaspoon salt, and ½ teaspoon pepper and rub over the outside of the chicken. 5. Roast in the oven, uncovered, for 45 minutes, or until cooked through and golden brown. Let it rest 5 minutes before carving.
Per Serving: Calories 435; Fat 34g; Sodium 678mg; Carbs 2g; Fiber 0g; Sugar 1g; Protein 28g

Chicken Fajita Stuffed Peppers

Prep time: 11 minutes | Cook time: 50 minutes | Serves: 6

½ cup butter, divided
1-pound boneless chicken thighs
½ cup chopped onion
1½ cups cauliflower rice
¼ cup chopped scallions
½ cup chicken broth
2 teaspoons chili powder
1 teaspoon paprika
1 teaspoon salt

½ teaspoon cumin
½ teaspoon garlic powder
¼ teaspoon dried oregano
¼ teaspoon cayenne pepper
6 bell peppers, tops removed and seeded
1 cup shredded Mexican cheese blend

1. Preheat the oven to 350°F/175°C. In a large pan heat 6 tablespoons of butter. Sear the chicken for 3 to 4 minutes on each side. 2. Lower the heat and cook further for 10 to 12 minutes. Set cooked chicken aside to cool. 3. Shred the chicken into small pieces. Set aside. 4. In a pan melt the remaining butter. 5. Cook the onion until translucent for 3-4 minutes. 6. Add the cauliflower "rice," shredded chicken, scallions, chicken broth, chili powder, paprika, salt, cumin, garlic powder, dried oregano, and cayenne pepper in the cooked onions. 7. Cut the thin piece of the top of the pepper and deseeded it like a pocket. 8. Fill bell pepper with the chicken mixture. Top evenly with the Mexican cheese blend. Place the pepper on the sheet in the oven—bake for about 30 minutes, or until the cheese browns.
Per Serving: Calories 419; Fat 28g; Sodium 699mg; Carbs 12g; Fiber 4g; Sugar 2g; Protein 28g

Barbecued Chicken with Bacon

Prep time: 16 minutes | Cook time: 15 minutes | Serves: 8

8 (6-ounce) skinless and boneless chicken breasts
½ cup brown erythritol blend
½ cup soy sauce
3 tablespoons olive oil

1 teaspoon garlic powder
½ teaspoon freshly ground black pepper
16 bacon slices

1. Preheat the grill to medium-high heat. Soak 16 toothpicks in water. 2. Place a chicken breast between two large pieces of plastic wrap and use a rolling pin or mallet to pound to ¼-inch thickness. 3. Repeat with the remaining chicken breasts. Mix the brown sweetener, soy sauce, olive oil, garlic powder, and pepper in a small bowl. 4. Rub or brush half of the mixture onto both sides of the breasts. Roll up a chicken breast and wrap with two slices of bacon, end to end, secured with toothpicks. 5. Brush more of the soy sauce mixture on the bacon, and repeat with the remaining breasts. Place the chicken on the grill, seam-side down, and grill for 6 to 8 minutes on each side, or until cooked through.
Per Serving: Calories 487; Fat 28g; Sodium 669mg; Carbs 14g; Fiber 0g; Sugar 0g; Protein 54g

Carne Asada Bowls

Prep time: 11 minutes | Cook time: 25 minutes | Serves: 4

¼ cup extra-virgin olive oil, divided
2 tablespoons low-sodium soy sauce
2 tablespoons lime juice
½ cup minced fresh cilantro
2 garlic cloves, minced
1 teaspoon ground cumin
1 teaspoon smoked paprika

¼ teaspoon cayenne pepper
1-pound boneless, skinless chicken thighs
1 small head cauliflower, riced
1 tablespoon coconut oil
1 avocado, pitted, peeled, and sliced
½ cup sour cream
4 radishes, thinly sliced

1. Preheat the oven to 350°F/175°C. Mix 3 tablespoons of olive oil, soy sauce, lime juice, cilantro, garlic, cumin, paprika, and cayenne in a small baking dish. 2. Coat the chicken thoroughly in the mixture. Bake for 25 minutes until cooked through. Use a fork to shred the chicken. 3. Heat the oil and stir-fry the cauliflower for 5 minutes, until just heated through. Divide the cauliflower rice among the serving dishes. Place equal portions of the cooked chicken and some pan juices over the rice. 4. Top each serving with a quarter of avocado, sour cream, and radish slices.
Per Serving: Calories 422; Fat 31g; Sodium 1101mg; Carbs 9g; Fiber 5g; Sugar 3g; Protein 28g

Crispy Chicken Thighs with Veggies

Prep time: 5 minutes | Cook time: 35 minutes | Serves: 4

4 large bone-in, skin-on chicken thighs (6 ounces each)
Salt
Freshly ground black pepper
3 tablespoons olive oil

1-pound radishes, halved
1 (8-ounce) container white mushrooms, sliced
Chopped fresh parsley, for garnish

1. Preheat the oven to 375°F/190°C. Season the chicken with salt and pepper. In an oven-safe pot, heat the oil. Cooking in batches if needed, place the chicken in the skillet, skin-side down. Cook for 10 minutes until the skin is golden brown and crispy. 2. Remove the chicken and set it aside. Add the radishes and mushrooms to the skillet. Cook, frequently stirring, for 5 minutes. 3. Return the chicken to the skillet, place it in the oven, and roast for 15 minutes, or the juices run clear from a cut into the thickest part of the thigh. Garnish with the parsley and serve.
Per Serving: Calories 433; Fat 34g; Sodium 769mg; Carbs 6g; Fiber 2g; Sugar 0g; Protein 26g

Cheesy Chicken Tenderloin Packets

Prep time: 11 minutes | Cook time: 20 minutes | Serves: 4

2 pounds chicken tenderloins
14 ounces broccoli, cut into florets (about 2 small heads)
8 ounces radishes, halved
¼ cup (2 ounces) unsalted butter

¼ cup grated Parmesan cheese
Salt
Freshly ground black pepper
¼ cup olive oil

1. Preheat the oven to 400°F/200°C. Cut four 12-inch squares of aluminum foil. 2. Divide the chicken, broccoli, and radishes evenly among the foil squares. Add 1 tablespoon each of butter and Parmesan to each packet. 3. Season well with salt and pepper. With foil make bowls and add 1 tablespoon of oil to each packet and seal the top by pinching the foil together. 4. Put the packets on a baking sheet to bake for 20 minutes, or the juices run clear.
Per Serving: Calories 537; Fat 33g; Sodium 674mg; Carbs 9g; Fiber 4g; Sugar 1g; Protein 51g

Avocado Chicken Thigh Chili

Prep time: 16 minutes | Cook time: 40 minutes | Serves: 4

3 tablespoons olive oil, divided
1-pound boneless, skinless chicken thighs, diced
1 onion, chopped
2 jalapeño peppers, minced
1 tablespoon minced garlic
2 cups diced raw or frozen pumpkin

1 cup low-sodium chicken stock
1 cup canned coconut milk
3 tablespoons no-salt-added tomato paste
3 tablespoons chili powder
Juice of 1 lime
1 avocado, diced

1. In a pan heat oil and sauté the chicken until just cooked through, for 10 to 12 minutes. Transfer the chicken to a plate. 2. Add the remaining olive oil and sauté the onion, jalapeños, and garlic until softened for about 5 minutes. 3. Stir in the cooked chicken, pumpkin, chicken stock, coconut milk, tomato paste, chili powder, and lime juice. 4. Boil it than simmer the chicken and vegetables until tender, for about 20 minutes. Serve topped with avocado.
Per Serving: Calories 461; Fat 36g; Sodium 589mg; Carbs 18g; Fiber 7g; Sugar 2g; Protein 20g

Creamy Chicken and Spinach Bake

Prep time: 10 minutes | Cooking time: 30 minutes | Serves: 4

Nonstick cooking spray
1 pound boneless, skinless chicken breasts, cubed
10 ounces baby spinach
8 ounces cream cheese, at room temperature

¾ cup shredded mozzarella cheese
¼ cup sour cream
2 teaspoons minced garlic
Salt
Black pepper

1. At 400°F/200°C, preheat your oven. 2. Grease a 9-by-13-inch baking dish with cooking spray. Spread out the chicken in the dish. 3. Layer the spinach over the top, keeping it as flat as possible. 4. In a suitable bowl, mix the cream cheese, ¼ cup of mozzarella, the sour cream, and garlic. Season with black pepper and salt. Spoon the prepared mixture on top of the spinach. 5. Cover with foil sheet and bake for almost 20 minutes. 6. Remove from your oven, uncover, and top with the remaining ½ cup of mozzarella. 7. Bake for another 10 to 15 minutes, until the chicken has reached an internal temperature of 165°F/75°C.
Per Serving: Calories 476, Fat 27.6g, Sodium 992mg, Carbs 4.5g, Fiber 4g, Sugars 4.3g; Protein 16.8g

Tangy Chicken Zoodle Bowls

Prep time: 22 minutes | Cook time: 7 to 10 minutes | Serves: 4

2 medium zucchinis, spiralized
Sea salt
Freshly ground black pepper
¼ cup extra-virgin olive oil, divided
1-pound boneless chicken thighs, cut into 1-inch pieces
½ cup roughly chopped fresh basil
1-pint grape tomatoes, halved
1 garlic clove, minced
8 ounces fresh mozzarella, cut into ½-inch pieces

1. Place the zucchini noodles into a colander and season very generously with salt. 2. Place the colander into the sink and let the zucchini sweat for 20 minutes. 3. Rinse the zucchini with fresh water and wring as much moisture as possible from the noodles, trying not to break them. 4. Heat a large skillet over high heat. Spice the chicken with salt and pepper. On the hot skillet, add 2 tablespoons of olive oil. Cook for 5-7 minutes until cooked through. Transfer to a large serving dish. In the same skillet, sauté the zucchini noodles for 2 to 3 minutes, or until hot but not browned. 5. Transfer the cooked zucchini to the serving dish along with the basil, tomatoes, garlic, and fresh mozzarella. Give everything a good toss, drizzle with the remaining olive oil, and season with salt and pepper.
Per Serving: Calories 456; Fat 31g; Sodium 775mg; Carbs 6g; Fiber 1g; Sugar 0.8g; Protein 37g

Spaghetti Chicken Bowls

Prep time: 11 minutes | Cook time: 30 minutes | Serves: 4

1 small spaghetti squash
2 tablespoons canola oil, divided
1½ pounds chicken thighs, boneless, skinless, cut into 2-inch pieces
Sea salt
Freshly ground black pepper
1 teaspoon minced ginger
1 teaspoon minced garlic
Pinch red pepper flakes
2 tablespoons toasted sesame oil
¼ cup low-sodium soy sauce
Juice of 1 lime
¼ cup roasted cashews

1. Preheat the oven to 375°F/190°C. Slice the spaghetti squash into 1-inch-thick rings, and scoop out the strings and seeds. 2. Place the squash rings onto a rimmed baking sheet and brush with 1 tablespoon of the canola oil. Roast for 30 minutes, until tender. 3. Heat oil in a skillet. Season the chicken with salt and pepper. Sear the chicken in the pan, and cook for 5 to 7 minutes until it is well browned and cooked through. 4. Add the ginger with garlic, and red pepper flakes and cook for 30 seconds. Remove the pan from the heat. 5. When the spaghetti squash rings are cool enough to handle, use a fork to shred the flesh into long, thin strands. 6. Divide the squash among the serving bowls, and top with equal portions of the cooked chicken. 7. Whisk the sesame oil, soy sauce, and lime juice in a small measuring cup. Pour the sauce over the spaghetti squash bowls and top with the roasted cashews.
Per Serving: Calories 440; Fat 25g; Sodium 1020mg; Carbs 13g; Fiber 2g; Sugar 1g; Protein 40g

Traditional Chicken Teriyaki

Prep time: 5 minutes | Cook time: 35 minutes | Serves: 4

2 pounds chicken breasts and thighs, boneless, skin-on
2 tablespoons olive oil
⅓ cup erythritol
¼ cup tamari
1 teaspoon freshly squeezed lemon juice
½ teaspoon garlic powder
¼ teaspoon ground ginger
⅓ cup water
2 tablespoons psyllium husk powder
Cooked cauliflower rice, for serving

1. In a resealable bag, put the chicken and add the olive oil, erythritol, tamari, lemon juice, garlic, ginger, water, and psyllium husk powder, seal, and shake to make sure the chicken is evenly coated. 2. Marinate the chicken in bag for 1 hour or up to 24 hours. When there is 15 to 20 minutes of marinating left, preheat the oven to 400°F/200°C and prepare the baking dish with aluminum foil lining. 3. Remove the chicken from the marinade (discard the marinade) and place in the baking dish, making sure the pieces don't touch. 4. Roast the marinated chicken for about 30 minutes, flipping halfway through, until cooked rough—an internal temperature of 165°F/75°C. Serve with cauliflower rice and/or cucumber salad, if desired.
Per Serving: Calories 452; Fat 32g; Sodium 932mg; Carbs 1g; Fiber 0g; Sugar 0g; Protein 40g

Chicken in Lettuce Cups

Prep time: 11 minutes | Cook time: 10 minutes | Serves: 4

2 tablespoons toasted sesame oil
2 tablespoons canola oil
1-pound boneless, skinless chicken thighs, finely diced
8 ounces button mushrooms, finely diced
2 teaspoons minced ginger, divided
2 teaspoons minced garlic, divided
Sea salt
Freshly ground black pepper
3 tablespoons low-sodium soy sauce, divided
Juice of 1 lime
⅓ cup natural peanut butter
Pinch red pepper flakes
8 to 12 butter lettuce leaves
¼ cup roughly chopped roasted peanuts
¼ cup grated carrot
1 scallion, thinly sliced

1. Heat the sesame oil along with canola oil over medium-high heat. Add the chicken, mushrooms, and sauté until cooked and well-browned, for about 10 minutes. Add 1 teaspoon of ginger and garlic and cook for another 30 seconds. Stir in 1 tablespoon of soy sauce. 2. Remove the pan from the heat. Season with salt and pepper. Meanwhile, combine the remaining 1 teaspoon of ginger, 1 teaspoon of garlic, 2 tablespoons of soy sauce, peanut butter, lime juice, and red pepper flakes in a small jar. 3. Cover tightly with a lid and shake vigorously. Thin with 3 tablespoons of water until it reaches the desired consistency. 4. Add a spoonful of the chicken mushroom mixture into each lettuce cup. Top with a pinch of peanuts, carrot, and scallion. Serve with the mixed sauce.
Per Serving: Calories 490; Fat 34g; Sodium 951mg; Carbs 12g; Fiber 3g; Sugar 1g; Protein 35g

Creamy Chicken with Mushrooms

Prep time: 11 minutes | Cook time: 20 minutes | Serves: 4

2 tablespoons canola oil
8 boneless, skinless chicken thighs
Sea salt
Freshly ground black pepper
1 shallot, minced
8 ounces mushrooms, sliced
¼ cup port wine
½ cup heavy (whipping) cream

1. Heat the oil over medium-high heat in a skillet. Dry the chicken and spice generously with salt and pepper. 2. Sear the chicken until well browned and cooked to an internal temperature of 165°F/75°C, for about 8 minutes. Transfer them to a dish. Add the shallot and mushrooms to the pan and cook for 10 minutes, until the mushrooms are browned and most moisture has evaporated from the pan. 3. Add the port wine and cook until reduced to just a couple of tablespoons, for about 2 minutes. Stir the heavy cream in and bring to the barest simmer. Return the chicken thighs to the pan, basting with the cream sauce. Season with salt and pepper.
Per Serving: Calories 389; Fat 24g; Sodium 855mg; Carbs 6g; Fiber 1g; Sugar 0g; Protein 30g

Spinach Stuffed Chicken Thighs

Prep time: 16 minutes| Cook time: 35 minutes| Serves: 4

5 bacon slices
2 tablespoons butter
1½ cups spinach
1 teaspoon minced garlic
¾ cup cream cheese, at room temperature
1-pound boneless chicken thighs
¼ cup shredded Swiss cheese, divided
¼ teaspoon salt
¼ teaspoon freshly ground black pepper

1. Preheat the oven to 425°F/220°C. 2. Bake the bacon slices about ½ inch apart for 10 to 15 minutes, or until crispy. Set aside to cool. 3. Melt the butter and cook the spinach and garlic in a cooking pan for 2 minutes until wilts. 4. Remove the spinach from the skillet. Set aside. Chop the cooled bacon into small pieces. Mix the cream cheese, sautéed spinach, and chopped bacon in a large bowl. 5. Spread the meat open on the flat surface. 6. Place the cream cheese mixture on each piece of chicken. 7. Top each with the Swiss cheese. Close the thighs and secure with toothpicks. Spice with the salt and pepper. 8. Place the chicken pockets in a baking dish. Bake for about 18 minutes.
Per Serving: Calories 527; Fat 44g; Sodium 766mg; Carbs 2g; Fiber 0g; Sugar 0g; Protein 29g

Tandoori Chicken Vegetable Skewers

Prep time: 11 minutes | Cook time: 15 minutes | Serves: 4

½ cup yogurt
2 tablespoons lemon juice
1 tablespoon minced garlic
1 teaspoon ground turmeric
1 teaspoon ground coriander
1 teaspoon ground cumin
1 teaspoon garam masala
¼ teaspoon cayenne pepper
1½ pounds chicken thighs, cut into
2-inch pieces, boneless, skinless
2 tablespoons canola oil
1 green bell pepper, seeds and ribs

removed, cut into 2-inch pieces
1 yellow bell pepper, seeds and ribs removed, cut into 2-inch pieces
1 red onion
Sea salt
Freshly ground black pepper
2 tablespoons white wine vinegar
¼ cup extra virgin olive oil
4 cups arugula
1 cup grape tomatoes, halved
1 tablespoon sesame seeds

1. Preheat grill pan to medium-high. Whisk the yogurt, lemon juice, garlic, turmeric, coriander, cumin, garam masala, and cayenne pepper in a large glass bowl. 2. Add the chicken thighs to the yogurt mixture and toss to coat. Allow the chicken to marinate for at least 15 minutes. 3. Slice the onion reserving two parts for the salad. Thread the chicken, green and yellow peppers, and red onion onto bamboo or wooden skewers. 4. Brush the vegetables with the canola oil. Season them generously with salt and pepper. 5. Grill the skewers for about 15 minutes total, turning the skewers as you go so the chicken and vegetables are gently browned on all sides. 6. Meanwhile, whisk the white wine vinegar and olive oil in a large mixing bowl. Slice the remaining red onion into thin pieces and toss with the arugula and tomatoes in the vinaigrette. 7. Divide the salad and grilled chicken skewers among the serving plates, and sprinkle each with an equal portion of the sesame seeds.
Per Serving: Calories 463; Fat 30g; Sodium 995mg; Carbs 8g; Fiber 1g; Sugar 0.8g; Protein 39g

Classical Kung Pao Chicken

Prep time: 5 minutes | Cook time: 15 minutes | Serves: 4

½ teaspoon ground Sichuan peppercorns
2 tablespoons soy sauce,
2 tablespoons balsamic vinegar
1 tablespoon rice wine
1 teaspoon toasted sesame oil
3 tablespoons canola oil
1½ pounds chicken thighs, boneless, skinless, cut into 2-inch

pieces Sea salt
Freshly ground black pepper
1 red bell pepper, chopped in 1-inch chunks
4 scallions, thinly sliced
1 teaspoon minced garlic
1 teaspoon minced ginger
¼ teaspoon red pepper flakes
½ cup peanuts

1. Whisk the Sichuan pepper, soy sauce, vinegar, rice wine or sherry, and sesame oil in a small bowl. 2. Heat the oil. Season the chicken with salt and pepper. 3. Sauté the chicken in the hot oil until just cooked to an internal temperature of 165°F/75°C, for about 10 minutes. 4. Transfer the chicken to a separate dish. Cook the bell pepper and scallions in the same skillet for 3 minutes, or until crisp-tender. 5. Add the scallions, garlic, ginger, and red pepper flakes to the skillet and cook for 30 seconds, just until fragrant. 6. Return the cooked chicken and any accumulated juices to the pan and add the Sichuan pepper sauce. 7. Cook for 1 minute to allow the flavors to come together. Garnish each portion with a quarter of the peanuts.
Per Serving: Calories 451; Fat 27g; Sodium 852mg; Carbs 10g; Fiber 3g; Sugar 0g; Protein 42g

Chicken Tenders

Prep time: 16 minutes | Cook time: 20 minutes | Serves: 4

2 large eggs
½ cup pork rinds, ground
½ cup shredded Parmesan cheese
1 teaspoon garlic powder
1 teaspoon onion powder

¼ teaspoon salt
⅛ teaspoon freshly ground black pepper
1-pound boneless chicken thighs, halved

1. Preheat the oven to 400°F/200°C temperature setting. 2. Line a baking sheet with parchment lining. 3. In a bowl, beat the eggs. 4. In another bowl, combine the pork rinds with Parmesan cheese, garlic powder, onion powder, salt, and pepper. 5. Take thigh and dredge in the egg wash, then coat in the rind mixture. Place the "breaded" thigh on the baking sheet. 6. Repeat with the all the thigh halves. 7. Bake the breaded thighs for 18-20 minutes until golden brown.
Per Serving: Calories 489; Fat 33g; Sodium 906mg; Carbs 2g; Fiber 0g; Sugar 0g; Protein 46g

Cheesy Chicken Nuggets

Prep time: 16 minutes | Cook time: 30 minutes | Serves: 4

Nonstick cooking spray
1-pound ground chicken
1 large beaten egg
¼ cup almond flour
½ teaspoon sea salt
¼ teaspoon onion powder
⅛ teaspoon freshly ground black

pepper
¾ cup finely crushed pork rinds
3 tablespoons Parmesan cheese
¾ teaspoon dried oregano
½ teaspoon garlic powder
½ teaspoon paprika

1. Preheat the oven to 350°F/175°C. 2. Prepare a baking sheet with parchment lining and spray with cooking spray. 3. Mix the chicken, egg, flour, salt, onion powder, and pepper in a large bowl until well combined. 4. In a bowl, combine the pork rinds, Parmesan, oregano, garlic powder, and paprika. Scoop the chicken mixture 1 tablespoon at a time and form into your chosen shape. 5. Completely coat in the pork rind mixture and place on the prepared baking sheet. Bake for 15 minutes, flip, and bake for an additional 15 minutes until golden. 6. Serve immediately.
Per Serving: Calories 275; Fat 17g; Sodium 974mg; Carbs 3g; Fiber 1g; Sugar 1g; Protein 28g

Harissa Chicken with Yogurt

Prep time: 11 minutes | Cook time: 60 minutes | Serves: 4

½ cup extra-virgin olive oil, divided
2 tablespoons harissa
1½ teaspoons salt, divided
½ teaspoon ground cumin
4 skin-on, bone-in chicken thighs
1-pound Brussels sprouts, ends trimmed and halved

½ cup plain Greek yogurt
1 garlic clove, finely minced
Zest and juice of 1 lemon
½ cup chopped mint leaves, for serving
½ cup chopped cilantro leaves, for serving

1. Preheat the oven to 425°F/220°C. In a small bowl, whisk 6 tablespoons olive oil, the harissa, 1 teaspoon salt, and cumin. 2. In a bowl, put the chicken and drizzle half of the harissa mixture over top. Toss to combine well. Place spiced chicken on the prepared baking sheet and roast for 20 minutes. 3. While the chicken roasts, place the Brussels sprouts in a large bowl and drizzle with the remaining harissa mixture. 4. Toss to combine well. Roast chicken for 20 minutes, remove from the oven and add the Brussels sprouts to the baking sheet in a single layer around the chicken. 5. Return to the oven and continue roasting until the chicken is cooked and the Brussels sprouts are golden and crispy, another 20 to 25 minutes. 6. In a bowl, combine the yogurt along with the remaining 2 tablespoons of olive oil, garlic, lemon zest and juice, and the remaining ½ teaspoon salt and whisk. 7. Remove the chicken and veggies from the oven and cool for 10 minutes. Drizzle with yogurt sauce and sprinkle with mint and cilantro. Toss to combine and serve warm.
Per Serving: Calories 607; Fat 52g; Sodium 741mg; Carbs 13g; Fiber 5g; Sugar 2g; Protein 25g

Indian Chicken Tikka Masala

Prep time: 11 minutes | Cook time: 20 minutes | Serves: 4

1 tablespoon olive oil
1½ pounds boneless, skinless chicken thighs, diced
1 cup tomato sauce
1 tablespoon onion powder
2 teaspoons minced garlic
2 teaspoons garam masala

1 teaspoon ground cumin
1 teaspoon paprika
½ teaspoon ground turmeric
Salt
2 tablespoons heavy (whipping) cream

1. Set a suitable pot over medium heat and then add oil. Add the chicken and cook for about 10 minutes, or until the outsides are browned. 2. Transfer the chicken from the skillet into a pressure cooker bowl. Add the tomato sauce, onion powder, garlic, garam masala, cumin, paprika, turmeric, and ½ teaspoon salt. 3. Stir well. Lock the pressure cooker lid with the steam vent set to Sealing. Select high pressure and timer for 10 minutes. 4. After cooking, quick release the pressure. Open the lid and stir the heavy cream and spice with salt to taste. Serve warm.
Per Serving: Calories 459; Fat 35g; Sodium 687mg; Carbs 7g; Fiber 2g; Sugar 0g; Protein 29g

Greek Chicken

Prep time: 11 minutes | Cook time: 15 minutes | Serves: 4

½ cup extra-virgin olive oil
¼ cup dry white wine
6 garlic cloves, finely minced
Zest and juice of 1 lemon
1 tablespoon dried oregano
1 teaspoon dried rosemary
½ teaspoons salt

½ teaspoon freshly ground black pepper
1-pound boneless, skinless chicken thighs, cut into 1½-inch chunks
1 cup tzatziki or Greek yogurt, for serving

1. In a bowl, mix the oil with white wine, garlic, lemon zest and juice, oregano, rosemary, salt, and pepper and whisk well. 2. Marinade the chicken and toss well to coat. Cover to marinate in the refrigerator for at least 1 hour, or up to 24 hours. 3. In a bowl, submerge wooden skewers in water and soak for at least 30 minutes before using. 4. Heat the grill and thread the marinated chicken on the skewers, reserving the marinade. 5. Grill until cooked through, occasionally so that the chicken cooks evenly for 5 to 8 minutes. Remove and keep warm. 6. Boil the reserved sauce in a saucepan. Reduce the heat. Simmer for 3 to 5 minutes. Serve chicken skewers drizzled with hot marinade, adding more olive oil if desired, and tzatziki.
Per Serving: Calories 677; Fat 61g; Sodium 822mg; Carbs 8g; Fiber 0g; Sugar 0g; Protein 26g

Feta Stuffed Chicken Thighs

Prep time: 16 minutes | Cook time: 20 minutes | Serves: 4

1 cup crumbled feta cheese
¼ cup shredded Swiss cheese
1 teaspoon minced garlic
1 tablespoon olive oil
¼ cup olives, chopped

1-pound boneless chicken thighs
¼ teaspoon salt
¼ teaspoon freshly ground black pepper

1. Preheat the oven to 425°F/200°C. Mix the feta cheese, Swiss cheese, garlic, olive oil, and olives in a large bowl. 2. Spread the meat on the flat surface. 3. Place the feta mixture on each piece of chicken. 4. Close the thighs. Secure with toothpicks. Season with the salt and pepper. Place the chicken pockets in a baking dish. 5. Bake the chicken pockets for about 18 minutes or when the internal temperature reaches 165°F/75°C.
Per Serving: Calories 407; Fat 31g; Sodium 770mg; Carbs 3g; Fiber 0g; Sugar 0g; Protein 27g

Lemon Chicken and Veggies Stir-Fry

Prep time: 5 minutes | Cook time: 25 minutes | Serves: 4

2 tablespoons olive oil
1½ pounds chicken breasts, skinless, cut into 1-inch cubes
1-pound asparagus, ends trimmed, cut into 2-inch pieces

¼ cup chicken broth
2 tablespoons soy sauce
Juice of 1 lemon
Salt
Freshly ground black pepper

1. Heat oil and add the chicken. Cook, frequently stirring, for 10 minutes or until browned all over. Add the asparagus and cook, frequently stirring, for another 5 minutes. Add the broth and soy sauce and mix well. 2. Cook for 10 minutes until the asparagus is tender but still crisp. Stir the lemon juice in and spice with salt and pepper.
Per Serving: Calories 293; Fat 11g; Sodium 856mg; Carbs 6g; Fiber 3g; Sugar 0g; Protein 41g

Braised Chicken Thighs

Prep time: 15 minutes | Cook time: 7 to 8 hours | Serves: 4

¼ cup extra-virgin olive oil, divided
1½ pounds boneless chicken thighs
1 teaspoon paprika
salt, for seasoning
freshly ground black pepper, for

seasoning
1 sweet onion, chopped
4 garlic cloves, thinly sliced
½ cup chicken broth
2 tablespoons freshly squeezed lemon juice
½ cup Greek yogurt

1. Lightly grease the slow cooker with 1 tablespoon of olive oil. 2. Season the thighs with paprika, salt, and pepper. 3. Heat the remaining olive oil. Sear the chicken for 5 minutes, turning once. Transfer the chicken to the insert and add the onion, garlic, broth, and lemon juice. 4. Cover it and cook on low temperature setting for 7 to 8 hours. 5. Stir in the yogurt and serve.
Per Serving: Calories 434; Fat 36g; Sodium 1080mg; Carbs 5g; Fiber 1g; Sugar 1g; Protein 22g

Sesame Chicken Thighs

Prep time: 5 minutes | Cook time: 20 minutes | Serves: 4

4 chicken thighs, bone-in, skin-on
¼ teaspoon salt
¼ teaspoon ground black pepper
2 tablespoons soy sauce
2 tablespoons maple syrup

1 tablespoon sesame oil
1 teaspoon garlic, minced
1 teaspoon red wine vinegar
½ teaspoon red pepper flakes, crushed

1. Season the chicken with salt and pepper. Set aside. In a bowl combine the soy sauce along with maple syrup, sesame oil, garlic, vinegar, and red pepper flakes and mix well. 2. Reserve about one-quarter of the marinade for sauce. 3. Add the chicken to the bowl, skin-side up. Submerge in the marinade. 4. Refrigerate for at least 15 minutes. 5. Preheat the oven to broil setting. 6. Place the marinated thighs skin-side down in the baking dish. 7. Place the dish in the oven, about 6 inches from the broiler. Broil the chicken for 5-6 minutes with the oven door slightly ajar. 8. After that turn the chicken skin side up and broil for 2 minutes. 9. Place the dish in the oven on the bottom rack while the chicken is skin-side down. 10. Broil the smoky chicken for another 6 to 8 minutes with door close. Baste it with the reserved sauce and broil it for 2 minutes. Remove from oven when done.
Per Serving: Calories 360; Fat 26g; Sodium 663mg; Carbs 2g; Fiber 0g; Sugar 0g; Protein 27g

Chicken Mole with Black Pepper

Prep time: 15 minutes | Cook time: 7 to 8 hours | Serves: 6

3 tablespoons ghee, divided
2 pounds boneless chicken thighs and breasts
Salt, for seasoning
Freshly ground black pepper, for seasoning
1 sweet onion, chopped
1 tablespoon minced garlic
1 (28-ounce) can diced tomatoes
4 dried chili peppers, soaked in

water for 2 hours and chopped
3 ounces dark chocolate, chopped
¼ cup natural peanut butter
1½ teaspoons ground cumin
¾ teaspoon ground cinnamon
½ teaspoon chili powder
½ cup coconut cream
2 tablespoons chopped cilantro, for garnish

1. Lightly grease the slow cooker with 1 tablespoon of ghee. 2. In a large pan over medium-high heat, heat the remaining 2 tablespoons of the ghee. 3. Lightly spiced the chicken with salt and pepper, add to the pan, and sear for about 5 minutes. 4. Sauté the onion and garlic for an additional 3 minutes. 5. Transfer the chicken, onion, and garlic to the slow cooker, and stir in the tomatoes, chiles, chocolate, peanut butter, cumin, cinnamon, and chili powder. 6. Cover it and cook on low temperature setting for 7 to 8 hours. 7. Stir in the coconut cream, and serve hot, topped with the cilantro.
Per Serving: Calories 501; Fat 28g; Sodium 310mg; Carbs 22.5g; Fiber 6g; Sugar 11g; Protein 41g

Spicy Paprika Chicken

Prep time: 10 minutes | Cook time: 25 minutes | Serves: 4

4 (4-ounce) chicken breasts, skin-on
Sea salt
Freshly ground black pepper
1 tablespoon olive oil
½ cup chopped sweet onion

½ cup heavy (whipping) cream
2 teaspoons smoked paprika
½ cup sour cream
2 tablespoons chopped fresh parsley

1. Lightly spiced the chicken with salt and pepper. Place a large pan over medium-high heat and add the olive oil. 2. Sear the chicken on both sides until almost cooked through, about 15 minutes. Remove the chicken to a plate. 3. Sauté the onion to the pan until tender, about 4 minutes. Stir in the cream and paprika and bring the liquid to a simmer. 4. Return the chicken with accumulated juices to the pan and simmer the chicken for 5 minutes until thoroughly cooked. 5. Stir in the sour cream and remove the pan from the heat. 6. Serve topped with the parsley.
Per Serving: Calories 389; Fat 30g; Sodium 475mg; Carbs 4g; Fiber 0g; Sugar 0g; Protein 25g

Tropical Chicken

Prep time: 15 minutes | Cook time: 25 minutes | Serves: 4

2 tablespoons olive oil
4 (4-ounce) chicken breasts, cut into 2-inch chunks
½ cup chopped sweet onion
1 cup coconut milk

1 tablespoon curry powder
1 teaspoon ground cumin
1 teaspoon ground coriander
¼ cup chopped fresh cilantro

1. In a pan heat olive oil over medium-high heat. Sauté the chicken until almost cooked through, for about 10 minutes. 2. Add the onion and sauté for an additional 3 minutes. 3. Whisk together the coconut milk, curry powder, cumin, and coriander in a medium bowl. 4. Pour the sauce into the cooking pan with the cooked chicken and boil the liquid. Simmer on low heat until the chicken is tender and the sauce has thickened for about 10 minutes. 5. Serve the chicken with the sauce, top with cilantro.
Per Serving: Calories 382; Fat 31g; Sodium 632mg; Carbs 5g; Fiber 1g; Sugar 2g; Protein 23g

Delicious Turkey Meatloaf

Prep time: 10 minutes | Cook time: 35 minutes | Serves: 6

1 tablespoon olive oil
½ sweet onion, chopped
1½ pounds ground turkey
⅓ cup heavy (whipping) cream
¼ cup freshly grated Parmesan

cheese
1 tablespoon chopped fresh parsley
Pinch sea salt
Pinch freshly ground black pepper

1. Heat the oven to 450°F/230°C. 2. Heat the olive oil over medium heat. Sauté the onion until it is tender, about 4 minutes. 3. Transfer the cooked onion to a bowl and add the turkey, heavy cream, Parmesan cheese, parsley, salt, and pepper. 4. Stir until the ingredients are combined and held together. Press the mixture into a loaf pan. Bake until cooked through, about 30 minutes. 5. Rest the meatloaf for 10 minutes and serve.
Per Serving: Calories 216; Fat 19g; Sodium 774mg; Carbs 1g; Fiber 0g; Sugar 0g; Protein 19g

Cheesy Turkey Rissoles

Prep time: 10 minutes | Cook time: 25 minutes | Serves: 4

1 pound ground turkey
1 scallion, finely chopped
1 teaspoon minced garlic
Pinch sea salt

Pinch freshly ground black pepper
1 cup ground almonds
2 tablespoons olive oil

1. Preheat the oven to 350°F/175°C. Arrange a baking sheet with aluminum foil and set it aside. 2. In a medium bowl, mix the turkey, scallion, garlic, salt, and pepper until well combined. 3. Shape the turkey mixture into 8 patties and flatten them out. 4. Place the ground almonds in a shallow bowl and dredge the turkey patties in the ground almonds to coat. 5. Heat olive oil over medium heat. Sear the turkey patties on both sides, about 10 minutes in total. 6. Transfer the browned patties to the baking sheet and bake them until cooked through, flipping them once, for about 15 minutes.
Per Serving: Calories 440; Fat 34g; Sodium 965mg; Carbs 7g; Fiber 4g; Sugar 3g; Protein 27g

Crispy Bacon-Mushroom Chicken

Prep time: 15 minutes | Cook time: 7 to 8 hours | Serves: 8

3 tablespoons coconut oil, divided
¼ pound bacon, diced
2 pounds chicken (breasts, thighs, drumsticks)
2 cups quartered button mushrooms

1 sweet onion, diced
1 tablespoon minced garlic
½ cup chicken broth
2 teaspoons chopped thyme
1 cup coconut cream

1. Lightly grease the slow cooker with 1 tablespoon of coconut oil. 2. In a large pan over medium-high heat, heat the remaining 2 tablespoons of coconut oil and cook the bacon till crispy. Transfer the bacon to a plate and set it aside. 3. Sear the chicken to the pan with the bacon fat for 5 minutes, turning once. 4. Transfer the chicken and bacon to the insert and add the mushrooms, onion, garlic, broth, and thyme. 5. Cover it and cook on low temperature setting for 7 to 8 hours. 6. Stir in the coconut cream and serve.
Per Serving: Calories 406; Fat 34g; Sodium 870mg; Carbs 5g; Fiber 2g; Sugar 1g; Protein 22g

Chicken Breasts with Mushrooms

Prep time: 30 minutes | Cook time: 30 minutes | Serves: 4

1 tablespoon butter
¼ cup chopped sweet onion
½ cup goat cheese, at room temperature
¼ cup Kalamata olives, chopped
¼ cup chopped roasted red pepper

2 tablespoons chopped fresh basil
4 (5-ounce) chicken breasts, skin-on
2 tablespoons extra-virgin olive oil

1. Preheat the oven to 400°F/200°C. 2. Melt the butter. Sauté the onion in butter until tender in a small pan over medium heat. In a medium bowl transfer the onion and add the cheese, olives, red pepper, and basil. Stir until well blended, then refrigerate for about 30 minutes. 3. Cut horizontal pockets into each chicken breast, and stuff them evenly with the filling. Secure the two sides of each breast with toothpicks. 4. Place a large ovenproof pan over medium-high heat and add the olive oil. 5. Sear the chicken on both sides, about 10 minutes in total. 6. Place the pan in the oven and roast until the chicken is just cooked through, about 15 minutes. Remove the toothpicks and serve.
Per Serving: Calories 389; Fat 30g; Sodium 724mg; Carbs 3g; Fiber 0g; Sugar 0g; Protein 25g

Spice -Infused Turkey Breast

Prep time: 15 minutes | Cook time: 7 to 8 hours | Serves: 6

3 tablespoons extra-virgin olive oil, divided
1½ pounds boneless turkey breasts
Salt, for seasoning
Freshly ground black pepper, for seasoning
1 cup coconut milk

2 teaspoons minced garlic
2 teaspoons dried thyme
1 teaspoon dried oregano
1 avocado, peeled, pitted, and chopped
1 tomato, diced
½ jalapeño pepper, diced
1 tablespoon chopped cilantro

1. Lightly grease the slow cooker with 1 tablespoon of olive oil. 2. In a large pan over medium-high heat, heat the remaining 2 tablespoons of the olive oil. 3. Lightly spice the turkey with salt and pepper. Add the turkey to the pan and sear for about 7 minutes, turning once. 4. Transfer the turkey to the insert and add the coconut milk, garlic, thyme, and oregano. 5. Cover it and cook on low temperature setting for 7 to 8 hours. 6. Stir together the avocado, tomato, jalapeño pepper, and cilantro in a small bowl. 7. Serve the turkey topped with avocado salsa.
Per Serving: Calories 347; Fat 27g; Sodium 701mg; Carbs 5g; Fiber 3g; Sugar 2g; Protein 25g

Crispy Chicken Thighs

Prep time: 10 minutes | Cook time: 50 minutes | Serves: 4

Coconut or olive oil, for greasing
¼ teaspoon paprika
¼ teaspoon onion powder
¼ teaspoon garlic powder
⅛ teaspoon dried oregano
⅛ teaspoon dried basil
⅛ teaspoon dried thyme
⅛ teaspoon dried rosemary
⅛ teaspoon dried parsley

⅛ teaspoon cayenne pepper
4 skin-on, bone-in chicken thighs
1 yellow onion, quartered
8 garlic cloves, peeled and left whole
¼ cup extra-virgin olive oil
1 tablespoon freshly squeezed lemon juice

1. Preheat the oven to 350ºF/175ºC. Grease a cast iron pan with oil. 2. Stir the paprika, onion powder, garlic powder, oregano, basil, thyme, rosemary, parsley, and cayenne in a large bowl. Add the chicken and toss to coat. 3. Place the chicken in the prepared pan, skin-side up along with the quartered onion, and sprinkle the whole garlic in the pan, preferably to touch the bottom. 4. Drizzle the oil along with lemon juice over the chicken. Cook in the oven for 30 to 40 minutes until cooked through. 5. Baste the breasts with fluid from the bottom of the pan. Turn on the broil setting and broil it for 5-10 minutes, watching closely, until the skin has crisped up to your liking. 6. Remove from the oven, break apart the onion, and enjoy the chicken with the onions and caramelized garlic cloves alongside your favorite vegetable.
Per Serving: Calories 392; Fat 32g; Sodium 766mg; Carbs 6g; Fiber 1g; Sugar 1g; Protein 20g

Regular Buffalo Chicken

Prep time: 10 minutes | Cook time: 6 hours | Serves: 4

3 tablespoons olive oil, divided
1 pound boneless chicken breasts
1 cup hot sauce
½ sweet onion, finely chopped
⅓ cup coconut oil, melted

¼ cup water
1 teaspoon minced garlic
2 tablespoons chopped fresh parsley, for garnish

1. Lightly grease the slow cooker with 1 tablespoon of olive oil. 2. In a large pan over medium-high heat, heat the remaining 2 tablespoons of the olive oil. Sear the chicken for 5 minutes, turning once. Transfer the chicken to the insert and arrange in one layer on the bottom. 3. Whisk together the hot sauce, onion, coconut oil, water, and garlic in a small bowl. Pour the mixture over the chicken. 4. Cover it and cook on low temperature setting for 6 hours. 5. Serve topped with the parsley.
Per Serving: Calories 473; Fat 39g; Sodium 535mg; Carbs 8g; Fiber 2g; Sugar 4.7g; Protein 25g

Traditional Hungarian Chicken

Prep time: 10 minutes | Cook time: 7 to 8 hours | Serves: 4

1 tablespoon extra-virgin olive oil
2 pounds boneless chicken thighs
½ cup chicken broth
Juice and zest of 1 lemon
2 teaspoons minced garlic

2 teaspoons paprika
¼ teaspoon salt
1 cup sour cream
1 tablespoon chopped parsley, for garnish

1. Lightly oil the slow cooker with olive oil. 2. Place the chicken thighs in the insert. 3. Stir together the broth, lemon juice and zest, garlic, paprika, and salt in a small bowl. Pour the broth mixture over the chicken. 4. Cover it and cook on low temperature setting for 7 to 8 hours. 5. Turn off the heat and stir in the sour cream. 6. Serve topped with the parsley.
Per Serving: Calories 404; Fat 32g; Sodium 121mg; Carbs 4g; Fiber 0g; Sugar 0g; Protein 23g

Creamy Tangy Chicken

Prep time: 10 minutes | Cook time: 7 to 8 hours | Serves: 6

3 tablespoons extra-virgin olive oil
2 tablespoons butter
1½ pounds boneless chicken thighs
½ sweet onion, diced
2 teaspoons minced garlic
2 teaspoons dried oregano

½ teaspoon salt
⅛ teaspoon pepper, depending on taste
1½ cups chicken broth
Juice and zest of 1 lemon
1 tablespoon Dijon mustard
1 cup heavy (whipping) cream

1. Lightly grease the slow cooker with 1 tablespoon of olive oil. 2. Heat the remaining 2 tablespoons of the olive oil and the butter in a large pan over medium-high heat. Sear the chicken for 5 minutes, turning once. Transfer the chicken to the insert and add the onion, garlic, oregano, salt, and pepper. 3. Whisk together the broth, lemon juice, zest, and mustard in a small bowl. Pour the mixture over the chicken. 4. Cover it and cook on low temperature setting for 7 to 8 hours. 5. Remove from the heat, stir in the heavy cream, and serve.
Per Serving: Calories 558; Fat 44g; Sodium 1416mg; Carbs 20g; Fiber 0g; Sugar 2g; Protein 22g

Hot Chicken Wings

Prep time: 15 minutes | Cook time: 6 hours | Serves: 8

1 (12-ounce) bottle hot pepper sauce
¾ cup melted grass-fed butter
1 tablespoon dried oregano

2 teaspoons garlic powder
1 teaspoon onion powder
3 pounds chicken wing sections

1. In a bowl mix hot sauce, butter, oregano, garlic powder, and onion powder until blended. 2. Add the pat dry chicken wings and toss to coat well in sauce. Pour the mixture into a slow cooker. 3. Cover it and cook on low temperature setting for 6 hours. Serve.
Per Serving: Calories 375; Fat 23g; Sodium 1283mg; Carbs 1.6g; Fiber 0g; Sugar 0g; Protein 38g

Tropical-Chicken Curry

Prep time: 15 minutes | Cook time: 7 to 8 hours | Serves: 6

3 tablespoons extra-virgin olive oil, divided
1½ pounds boneless chicken breasts
½ sweet onion, chopped
1 cup quartered baby bok choy
1 red bell pepper, diced
2 cups coconut milk
2 tablespoons almond butter

1 tablespoon red Thai curry paste
1 tablespoon coconut aminos
2 teaspoons grated fresh ginger
Pinch red pepper flakes
¼ cup chopped peanuts, for garnish
2 tablespoons chopped cilantro, for garnish

1. Lightly grease the slow cooker with 1 tablespoon of olive oil. 2. In a large pan over medium-high heat, heat the remaining 2 tablespoons of the olive oil. Add the chicken and sear for about 7 minutes. 3. Transfer the chicken to the slow cooker and add the onion, baby bok choy, and bell pepper. 4. In a bowl whisk the coconut milk, almond butter, curry paste, coconut aminos, ginger, and red pepper flakes, until well blended. 5. Pour the coconut sauce over the cooked chicken and vegetables, and mix to coat. Cover it and cook on low temperature setting for 7 to 8 hours. 6. Serve topped with peanuts and cilantro.
Per Serving: Calories 543; Fat 42g; Sodium 1001mg; Carbs 10g; Fiber 5g; Sugar 2g; Protein 35g

Roasted Chicken

Prep time: 15 minutes | Cook time: 7 to 8 hours | Serves: 8

¼ cup extra-virgin olive oil, divided
1 (3-pound) whole chicken, washed and patted dry
Salt, for seasoning
Freshly ground black pepper, for

seasoning
1 lemon, quartered
6 thyme sprigs
4 garlic cloves, crushed
3 bay leaves
1 sweet onion, quartered

1. Lightly grease the slow cooker with 1 tablespoon of olive oil. 2. Rub the remaining olive oil all over the chicken and season with salt and pepper. Stuff the lemon quarters, thyme, garlic, and bay leaves into the chicken cavity. 3. Spread the onion quarters on the bottom of the slow cooker and place the chicken on top so it does not touch the base of the insert. 4. Cover it and cook on low temp setting for 7 to 8 hours, or until the internal temperature reaches 165°F/75°C on an instant-read thermometer. 5. Serve warm.
Per Serving: Calories 427; Fat 34g; Sodium 689mg; Carbs 2g; Fiber 0g; Sugar 0g; Protein 29g

Smoked Paprika Drumsticks

Prep time: 5 minutes | Cook time: 45 minutes | Serves: 6

Oil or cooking spray, for greasing
1 tablespoon smoked paprika
1 tablespoon garlic powder
1 tablespoon onion powder
1 teaspoon baking powder
1 teaspoon sea salt

½ teaspoon freshly ground black pepper
¼ teaspoon cayenne pepper
2 tablespoons nutritional yeast
6 chicken drumsticks, patted dry
2 tablespoons butter, melted

1. Preheat the oven to 300ºF/150ºC. Prepare a baking sheet by lining aluminum foil. 2. Place the rack on the sheet and grease it with oil. 3. In a resealable plastic bag, add the paprika powder, garlic powder, onion powder, baking powder, salt, pepper, cayenne, and nutritional yeast and shake well until well combined. 4. Add the chicken drumsticks to the spiced mix bag and shake well until coated. 5. Place the drumsticks on rack and cook for 20-25 minutes. 6. After 25 minutes, raise the oven to 400ºF/200ºC temperature setting. 7. Grease the drumsticks with the melted butter and bake for an additional 20 minutes or until crispy.
Per Serving: Calories 200; Fat 12g; Sodium 985mg; Carbs 3g; Fiber 1g; Sugar 1g; Protein 20g

Chicken Burgers

Prep time: 10 minutes | Cook time: 25 minutes | Serves: 6

1-pound ground chicken
8 bacon slices, chopped
¼ cup ground almonds
1 teaspoon chopped fresh basil
¼ teaspoon sea salt

Pinch freshly ground black pepper
2 tablespoons coconut oil
4 large lettuce leaves
1 avocado, peeled, pitted, and sliced

1. Preheat the oven to 350°F/175°C. 2. Add the chicken, bacon, ground almonds, basil, salt, and pepper in a medium bowl and combined until well mixed. Form the mixture into 6 equal patties. 3. Place a pan and add the coconut oil over medium heat. Pan sear the chicken patties until brown on both sides, about 6 minutes. 4. Place the browned patties on the baking sheet and bake until thoroughly cooked through about 15 minutes. 5. Serve on the lettuce leaves, topped with the avocado slices.
Per Serving: Calories 374; Fat 33g; Sodium 421mg; Carbs 3g; Fiber 2g; Sugar 1g; Protein 18g

Delicious Jerk Chicken

Prep time: 15 minutes | Cook time: 7 to 8 hours | Serves: 6

½ cup extra-virgin olive oil, divided
2 pounds boneless chicken (breast and thighs)
1 sweet onion, quartered
4 garlic cloves
2 scallions, coarsely chopped
2 habanero chiles, stemmed and seeded

2 tablespoons granulated erythritol
1 tablespoon grated fresh ginger
2 teaspoons allspice
1 teaspoon dried thyme
½ teaspoon cardamom
½ teaspoon salt
2 tablespoons chopped cilantro, for garnish

1. Lightly grease the slow cooker with 1 tablespoon of olive oil. 2. Arrange the chicken pieces in the bottom of the insert. 3. In a blender, pulse the remaining olive oil, onion, garlic, scallions, chiles, erythritol, ginger, allspice, thyme, cardamom, and salt until a thick, uniform sauce forms. 4. Pour the sauce over the chicken, turning the pieces to coat. 5. Cover it and cook on low temperature setting for 7 to 8 hours. 6. Serve topped with cilantro.
Per Serving: Calories 457; Fat 30g; Sodium 464mg; Carbs 9g; Fiber 1g; Sugar 4g; Protein 37g

Chicken Cacciatore with Mushroom

Prep time: 15 minutes | Cook time: 8 hours | Serves: 6

3 tablespoons extra-virgin olive oil, divided
2 pounds boneless chicken thighs
Salt, for seasoning
Freshly ground black pepper, for seasoning
1 (14-ounce) can stewed tomatoes
2 cups chicken broth

1 cup quartered button mushrooms
½ sweet onion, chopped
1 tablespoon minced garlic
1 tablespoon dried oregano
1 teaspoon dried basil
Pinch red pepper flakes

1. Lightly grease the slow cooker with 1 tablespoon of olive oil. 2. Lightly season the chicken thighs with salt and pepper. 3. Heat remaining olive oil in a pan over medium heat and add the chicken thighs and sear for about 8 minutes, turning once. 4. Transfer the chicken to the pot and add the tomatoes, broth, mushrooms, onion, garlic, oregano, basil, and red pepper flakes. 5. Cover it and cook on low temperature setting for 8 hours. Serve warm.
Per Serving: Calories 425; Fat 32g; Sodium 128mg; Carbs 8g; Fiber 1g; Sugar 4g; Protein 27g

Lettuce-Wrapped Burger

Prep time: 5 minutes | Cook time: 10 minutes | Serves: 1

1 tablespoon avocado oil
6 ounces ground chicken
1 avocado, pitted, peeled, and sliced

4 Bibb lettuce leaves
salt, to taste
black pepper, freshly ground

1. In a pan, heat the oil. Form the ground chicken into a patty and season with salt and freshly ground black pepper. 2. Add the chicken patty to the pan and cook until it is nicely browned and no longer pink in the center about 3 to 5 minutes on each side. 3. Top the patty with the sliced avocado, and wrap it in the lettuce leaves.
Per Serving: Calories 682; Fat 54g; Sodium 698mg; Carbs 16g; Fiber 12g; Sugar 5g; Protein 33g

"Roasted" Duck

Prep time: 15 minutes | Cook time: 7 to 8 hours | Serves: 8

3 tablespoons extra-virgin olive oil, divided
1 (2½-pound) whole duck, giblets removed
Salt, for seasoning
Freshly ground black pepper, for seasoning

4 garlic cloves, crushed
6 thyme sprigs, chopped
1 cinnamon stick, broken into several pieces
1 sweet onion, coarsely chopped
¼ cup chicken broth

1. Lightly grease the slow cooker with 1 tablespoon of olive oil. 2. Rub the remaining 2 tablespoons of olive oil all over the duck and season with salt and pepper—stuff the garlic, thyme, and cinnamon into the duck's cavity. 3. Spread the onion quarters on the bottom of the slow cooker and place the duck on top so it does not touch the base of the insert, and pour in the broth. 4. Cover it and cook on low temp setting for 7 to 8 hours, or until the internal temperature reaches 180°F/80°C on an instant-read thermometer. 5. Serve warm.
Per Serving: Calories 364; Fat 28g; Sodium 752mg; Carbs 2g; Fiber 1g; Sugar 0g; Protein 29g

Turkey Ragout with Pumpkin

Prep time: 15 minutes | Cook time: 8 hours | Serves: 6

1 tablespoon extra-virgin olive oil
1 pound boneless turkey thighs, cut into 1½-inch chunks
3 cups cubed pumpkin, cut into 1-inch chunks
1 red bell pepper, diced
½ sweet onion, cut in half and sliced
1 tablespoon minced garlic

1½ cups chicken broth
1½ cups coconut milk
2 teaspoons chopped fresh thyme
½ cup coconut cream
Salt, for seasoning
Freshly ground black pepper, for seasoning
12 slices cooked bacon, chopped, for garnish

1. Lightly oil the slow cooker with olive oil. 2. Add the turkey, pumpkin, red bell pepper, onion, garlic, broth, coconut milk, and thyme. 3. Cover it and cook on low temperature setting for 8 hours. 4. Stir in the coconut cream and season with salt and pepper. 5. Serve topped with the bacon.
Per Serving: Calories 418; Fat 34g; Sodium 665mg; Carbs 6g; Fiber 1g; Sugar 1g; Protein 25g

Bacon Ranch Cheesy Chicken Breasts

Prep time: 10 minutes | Cooking time: 55 minutes | Serves: 4

Cooking spray for the baking dish
3 tablespoons olive oil
4 boneless chicken breasts
½ teaspoon salt
¼ teaspoon black pepper, freshly ground
1 tablespoon garlic powder
8 bacon slices sliced into ½-inch pieces

¼ cup butter
¼ cup ranch dressing, or purchased bottled dressing
½ cup shredded cheddar cheese
½ cup shredded mozzarella cheese
½ cup grated parmesan cheese
½ teaspoon dried parsley

1. At 350°F/175°C, preheat your oven and prepare a baking dish with cooking spray. 2. In a suitable skillet over medium-high heat, heat the olive oil for almost 1 minute. 3. Season the chicken breasts with the salt, pepper, and garlic powder. Add them to the skillet. Sear each breast for almost 5 minutes per side. 4. Place the chicken into the prepared dish. 5. Spread 1 tablespoon of butter and 1 tablespoon of ranch dressing over each breast. 6. Top the chicken with the bacon, covering each breast completely. 7. Place the dish in the preheated oven. Bake for almost 30 minutes. 8. Remove from your oven. Sprinkle equal amounts of the cheddar, mozzarella, and parmesan cheeses over the bacon-topped breasts. 9. Season with the dried parsley. Return the dish to your oven. 10. Bake for another 10 to 12 minutes, or until the cheese melts.
Per serving: Calories: 314; Total fat 13.3g; Sodium 194mg; Total Carbs 4.9g; Fiber 6.8g; Sugars 16g; Protein 26g

Mustardy Chicken Drumsticks

Prep time: 15 minutes | Cook time: 20 minutes | Serves: 4

1½ pounds chicken drumsticks
¼ teaspoon salt
¼ teaspoon freshly ground black pepper
2 tablespoons butter
3 tablespoons finely chopped shallots
2 fresh thyme sprigs
1 tablespoon balsamic vinegar
¼ cup dry white wine
1 teaspoon Worcestershire sauce
½ cup chicken broth
2 teaspoons tomato paste
½ cup heavy (whipping) cream
1 tablespoon Dijon mustard
2 tablespoons finely chopped fresh parsley

1. Season the drumsticks with salt and pepper. Set aside. In a large pan melt the butter, and cook the drumsticks for 6-7 minutes, until browned. 2. Transfer the cooked drumsticks to a serving dish. Keep warm. Add the shallots with thyme to the same pan and cook for 1 minutes until tender. 3. Add the vinegar, and Worcestershire sauce and white wine. Bring the wine mixture to a boil. Stir the chicken broth in the wine mix. Return the mixture to a boil. 4. Add the tomato paste. Stir to combine well with the wine mix and cook for 5-6 minutes, until the mixture reduces. 5. Add the heavy cream in the sauce and boil it. 6. Whisk the mustard in the wine sauce. Pour the delicious sauce over the drumsticks. Serve topped with the chopped parsley and enjoy.
Per Serving: Calories 420; Fat 21g; Sodium 654mg; Carbs 3g; Fiber 0g; Sugar 0g; Protein 48g

Traditional Jamaican Jerk Chicken

Prep time: 10 minutes plus 4 hours to marinate | Cook time: 60 minutes | Serves: 4

1 onion, finely chopped
½ cup finely chopped scallions
3 tablespoons soy sauce
1 tablespoon apple cider vinegar
1 tablespoon olive oil
2 teaspoons chopped fresh thyme
2 teaspoons Splenda, or another sugar substitute
1 teaspoon liquid smoke
1 teaspoon salt
1 teaspoon allspice
1 teaspoon cayenne pepper
1 teaspoon freshly ground black pepper
½ teaspoon nutmeg
½ teaspoon cinnamon
1 whole chicken, quartered

1. In a bowl, mix the onion, scallion, soy sauce, cider vinegar, olive oil, thyme, Splenda, liquid smoke, salt, allspice, cayenne pepper, black pepper, nutmeg, and cinnamon. 2. Place the chicken pieces in a baking dish, skin-side down. Pour the marinade over it. Place the marinate covered, in the refrigerator, for at least 4 hours. 3. Preheat the oven to 425°F/220°C. Cook for 30 minutes. Remove the baking dish from the oven. 4. Turn the chicken skin-side up. Return the pan to the oven—cook for 20 to 30 minutes more, or until the internal temperature reaches 165°F/75°C.
Per Serving: Calories 557; Fat 36g; Sodium 965mg; Carbs 4g; Fiber 1g; Sugar 1g; Protein 43g

Roasted Whole Chicken with Jicama

Prep time: 15 minutes | Cook time: 60 minutes | Serves: 4

1 shallot, minced
2 fresh thyme sprigs, chopped
2 fresh rosemary sprigs, chopped
2 garlic cloves, minced
2 fresh sage sprigs, chopped
2 tablespoons chopped fresh parsley
1 (5-pound) chicken
¼ cup olive oil
1 cup roughly chopped jicama
½ teaspoon salt
¼ teaspoon freshly ground black pepper

1. Preheat the oven to 425°F/220°C. Add the shallot, thyme, rosemary, and garlic to a food processor or blender—pulse to chop. 2. Add the sage and parsley. Pulse lightly until mixed. On a flat surface, place the chicken breast side up. Carefully separate the skin, creating a pocket of the meat. 3. Stuff the herb mixture in equal amount under the skin of the chicken. Place the herb stuffed chicken in a baking dish. 4. Grease the herbed chicken with olive oil. 5. Place the dish in the preheated oven—bake for 15 minutes. 6. Spread the jicama all around the chicken, and spiced with salt and pepper. Return back the pan to the oven. Lower the heat to 375°F/190°C. Cook the chicken again for 1 hour. Remove the chicken from the oven. 7. Rest for 15 minutes before serving.
Per Serving: Calories 604; Fat 49g; Sodium 632mg; Carbs 3g; Fiber 2g; Sugar 1g; Protein 39g

Roasted Chicken Thighs And Zucchini In Wine

Prep time: 10 minutes | Cook time: 30 minutes | Serves: 4

2 tablespoons coconut oil
8 bone-in, skin-on chicken thighs
Sea salt
Freshly ground black pepper
2 zucchinis, halved lengthwise,
cut into 1-inch pieces
1 teaspoon minced fresh thyme
½ cup dry red wine
3 tablespoons cold butter, cut into pieces

1. Preheat the oven to 400°F/200°C. 2. Melt the coconut oil in the ovenproof pan over medium heat. 3. Pat dry the chicken thighs with paper towels. Season generously with salt and pepper. 4. Place the chicken skin-side down in the ovenproof pan, and cook for 5 to 7 minutes, until a crispy skin develops. Flip the chicken, and add the zucchini and thyme to the pan. 5. Transfer the pan to the oven and bake for 20 minutes, or until the chicken is cooked through. 6. Transfer the chicken and zucchini to individual serving plates. Using pot holders, return the pan to the stove top. 7. Pour the red wine into the pan and simmer over medium heat until reduced by half, about 5 minutes. 8. Remove the pan from the heat. Whisk butter in 1 tablespoon at a time. The sauce will become thick and glossy. Drizzle the sauce around the chicken and zucchini.
Per Serving: Calories 490; Fat 34g; Sodium 698mg; Carbs 5g; Fiber 1g; Sugar 1g; Protein 36g

Chicken Thighs with Tangy Lemon Sauce

Prep time: 15 minutes | Cook time: 20 minutes | Serves: 4

1 tablespoon butter
1 tablespoon minced shallots
1 cup sour cream
2 tablespoons freshly squeezed lemon juice
½ teaspoon salt, divided
¼ teaspoon freshly ground black pepper, divided
1 pound bone-in chicken thighs

1. Preheat the oven to 425°F/220°C. Melt the butter in a cooking pan. 2. Add the shallots—cook for 3-4 minutes, or until tender. 3. Lower the heat and add the sour cream, lemon juice, ¼ teaspoon of salt, and ⅛ teaspoon of pepper. Mix well to combine. 4. Refrigerate until ready to serve—Season the chicken with the remaining ¼ teaspoon of salt and ⅛ teaspoon of pepper. Place the chicken into a 9-inch-square baking dish. 5. Bake for about 18 minutes or it reaches 165°F/75°C. Place the chicken, spooning an equal amount of lemon cream sauce on each thigh.
Per Serving: Calories 393; Fat 32g; Sodium 698mg; Carbs 3g; Fiber 0g; Sugar 1g; Protein 22g

Crispy Fried Chicken

Prep time: 15 minutes | Cook time: 45 minutes | Serves: 8

3 cups lard, coconut oil, or avocado oil, for frying
8 chicken thighs, bone-in, skin-on (about 3 pounds)
2 teaspoons salt, divided
1½ cups whey protein isolate, unflavored
1 teaspoon garlic powder
1 teaspoon freshly ground black pepper
1 teaspoon baking powder
1 teaspoon baking soda
½ cup buttermilk
½ cup almond milk
3 large eggs

1. Preheat your oven to 325°F/165°C, and put a cooling rack on a baking sheet. Place a large pan on the stove, and fill it with the lard or oil. 2. Spice the chicken thighs with 1 teaspoon of salt. Put two shallow bowls on the counter beside the stove. 3. Combine the whey protein, garlic powder, remaining teaspoon of salt, and pepper in one bowl, and mix well. In the other bowl, combine the baking powder and baking soda, and mix. 4. Add the buttermilk, almond milk, and eggs. Whisk well with a fork. 5. Heat the oil to 350°F/175°C. Dredge one of the thighs in the whey protein mixture, then dredge the chicken thigh in the egg mixture, coat well, and then back to the whey protein mixture until fully coated. 6. Pick up the thigh and carefully lay in the hot oil. When the edges around the thigh are golden brown, use tongs to turn the thigh over and cook for 2 or 3 minutes, until golden brown. 7. Transfer the thigh onto the cooling rack on the baking sheet. One at a time, repeat coating and frying with each thigh, and then place the baking sheet in the oven for 15 to 20 minutes. Remove from the oven and serve.
Per Serving: Calories 418; Fat 24g; Sodium 874mg; Carbs 2g; Fiber 0g; Sugar 0g; Protein 49g

Chapter 5 Beef, Pork, and Lambs

Flank Steak with Chimichurri 58

Delicious Flank Steak with
Orange-Herb Pistou 58

Cabbage Rolls 58

Hanger Steak with Herb Cream Sauce ... 58

Delicious Mediterranean Meatloaf 58

Steak with Broccoli Noodles.............. 58

Cheesy Southwestern Meat Loaf 59

Shepherd's Pie 59

Beef and Broccoli Foil Packs 59

Slow Cooker Herb-and-Garlic Short Rib Stew 59

Corn Dogs 59

Weeknight Chili............................ 60

Steak with Blue Cheese Butter 60

Cheese-Stuffed Steak Burgers 60

Slow Cooker Swedish Meatballs 60

Mozzarella-Stuffed Meatloaf.............. 60

Marinated Steak Kebabs 60

Bacon and Blue Cheese Burgers 61

Blackened Steak Nuggets 61

Spinach and Provolone Steak Rolls 61

Spicy Brisket 61

Marinated Rib Eye......................... 61

Roast Beef 61

Mexican-Style Shredded Beef 61

London Broil 61

Buttery Pot Roast 62

Creamy Mushroom Pot Roast 62

Broiled Lamb Chops with Mint Gremolata and
Pan-Fried Zucchini 62

Quick Bratwurst 62

Sausage Stuffing with Veggies 62

Rosemary Mint Marinated Lamb Chops 62

Cheesy Bacon Stuffed Pork Chops 63

Parmesan Pork Chops 63

Crispy Pork 63

Pork Ribs 63

Crispy Baked Pork Chops with Veggie Gravy 63

Wrapped Pork Tenderloin 63

Lamb Sausage 63

Sweet and Spicy Ribs 64

Delicious Pork Meatballs 64

Spiced Pork Loin 64

Tangy Pulled Pork 64

Pork Chops in Mushroom Gravy 64

Cabbage Egg Roll 64

Chipotle Pork Chops 64

Dijon Pork Chops 65

Roasted Pork Loin with
Grainy Mustard Sauce 65

Herb-Crusted Lamb Chops 65

Herb-Braised Pork Chops 65

Rack of Lamb with Kalamata Tapenade 65

Italian-Spiced Pork Tenderloin 65

Nut-stuffed pork chops 66

Lamb Dogs with Tzatziki 66

Pork-and-Sauerkraut Casserole 66

Cranberry Pork Roast 66

Pancetta-And-Brie–Stuffed Pork Tenderloin66

Carnitas 66

Chops with Kalamata Tapenade 67

Herbed Lamb Racks 67

Lamb Leg with Red Pesto 67

Shepherd's Pie with Cauliflower Mash ... 67

Rosemary Lamb Chops 67

Tender Lamb Roast 67

Lamb-Vegetable............................ 68

Lamb Kebabs with Mint Pesto 68

Lamb Shanks with Mushrooms........... 68

Spiced Curried Lamb...................... 68

Herbed Lamb Chops 68

Keto Crusted Lamb Chops 68

Tunisian Lamb Ragout 68

Sweet-and-Sour Pork Chops 69

Cheese-Stuffed Tenderloin 69

Lemon Pork 69

Flank Steak with Chimichurri

Prep time: 15 minutes | Cook time: 12 minutes | Serves: 4

½ cup olive oil
½ cup finely chopped kale
2 tablespoons finely chopped fresh parsley
2 tablespoons freshly squeezed lime juice
1 tablespoon minced garlic

1 tablespoon finely chopped chili pepper
½ teaspoon salt, plus more for seasoning
½ teaspoon black pepper, plus more for seasoning
1 pound flank steak

1. Stir the olive oil, kale, parsley, lime juice, garlic, chili pepper, salt, and pepper in a medium bowl until well combined. Set aside. Preheat the barbecue to medium-high heat. 2. Lightly spiced the steak with salt and pepper. Grill the steak 5 to 6 minutes per side for medium-rare. 3. If you do not have a barbecue, preheat the oven to broil and broil the steak until it is the desired doneness, 5 to 6 minutes per side for medium-rare. 4. Let the steak rest for 10 minutes before slicing it thinly across the grain. Serve with the chimichurri.
Per Serving: Calories 426; Fat 35g; Sodium 896mg; Carbs 2g; Fiber 0g; Sugar 0g; Protein 25g

Delicious Flank Steak with Orange-Herb Pistou

Prep time: 10 minutes | Cook time: 20 minutes | Serves: 4

1 pound flank steak
½ cup extra-virgin olive oil, divided
2 teaspoons salt, divided
1 teaspoon freshly ground black pepper, divided
½ cup chopped fresh flat-leaf

Italian parsley
¼ cup chopped fresh mint leaves
2 garlic cloves, roughly chopped
Zest and juice of 1 orange
1 teaspoon red pepper flakes
1 tablespoon red wine vinegar

1. Heat the grill to medium-high heat or, if using an oven, preheat to 400°F/200°C. 2. Rub the steak with 2 tablespoons of olive oil and sprinkle with 1 teaspoon salt and ½ teaspoon pepper. 3. In a blender, combine the parsley, mint, garlic, orange zest, and juice, remaining 1 teaspoon salt, red pepper flakes and remaining ½ teaspoon pepper. 4. Pulse until finely chopped. With the processor running, stream in the red wine vinegar and remaining 6 tablespoons of olive oil until well combined. This pistou will be more oil-based than traditional basil pesto. 5. Cook the steak on the grill, for 6 to 8 minutes per side. Remove from the grill and allow to rest for 10 minutes on a cutting board. 6. If cooking in the oven, heat cast iron. Add the steak and brown for 1 to 2 minutes per side until browned. 7. Place the cast iron pan to the oven and cook for 10 to 12 minutes, or until the steak reaches your desired temperature. To serve, slice the steak and drizzle with the pistou.
Per Serving: Calories 441; Fat 36g; Sodium 986mg; Carbs 3g; Fiber 0g; Sugar 1g; Protein 25g

Cabbage Rolls

Prep time: 15 minutes | Cook time: 7-8 hours | Serves: 4

3 tablespoons extra-virgin olive oil, divided
1 pound ground beef
1 sweet onion, chopped
2 cups finely chopped cauliflower
2 teaspoons minced garlic
1 teaspoon dried thyme

¼ teaspoon salt
¼ teaspoon freshly ground black pepper
4 cups shredded cabbage
2 cups marinara sauce
½ cup cream cheese

1. Lightly grease the slow cooker with 1 tablespoon of olive oil. 2. Press the ground beef along the bottom of the insert. 3. Heat 2 tablespoons of olive oil. Add the onion, cauliflower, garlic, thyme, salt, and pepper, and sauté until the onion is softened about 3 minutes. 4. Add the cabbage and sauté for an additional 5 minutes. 5. Transfer the cabbage mixture to the insert, pour the marinara sauce over the cabbage, and top with the cream cheese. Cover it and cook on low temperature setting for 7 to 8 hours. 6. Stir before serving.
Per Serving: Calories 547; Fat 42g; Sodium 133mg; Carbs 6g; Fiber 4g; Sugar 2g; Protein 34g

Hanger Steak with Herb Cream Sauce

Prep time: 5 minutes | Cook time: 1 hour | Serves: 4

1 head garlic
1 pint heavy (whipping) cream
2 to 4 fresh herb sprigs (e.g., tarragon, rosemary)
2 teaspoons salt, divided

1½ pounds hanger steak
1 teaspoon freshly ground black pepper
2 tablespoons olive oil
2 tablespoons unsalted butter

1. Separate the garlic cloves and crush them with a knife. 2. In a small saucepan, combine the garlic, cream, herbs, and 1 teaspoon salt. Simmer on low heat, uncovered for about 1 hour, stirring occasionally. Strain to remove the herbs and garlic. While the sauce is simmering, allow the steak to come to room temperature. 3. Cook the steak when the cream sauce is almost ready. Heat a heavy pan over medium-high heat. Spiced the steak with the pepper and the remaining 1 teaspoon of salt. Pour the oil into the hot pan, then add the steak. 4. Cook it for 4 minutes without lifting or moving it. Turn the steak and add the butter to the pan. 5. Cook the steak for 4 minutes while continuously spooning the melted butter over the top. Transfer to a plate when a thermometer reads 125°F/50°C (for medium-rare) in the thickest part of the steak. 6. Cover and allow steak to rest for 8 to 10 minutes. Thinly slice the steak against the grain. Spoon the cream sauce over the sliced steak.
Per Serving: Calories 884; Fat 80g; Sodium 1564mg; Carbs 5g; Fiber 0g; Sugar 0g; Protein 37g

Delicious Mediterranean Meatloaf

Prep time: 15 minutes | Cook time: 7 to 8 hours | Serves: 8

3 tablespoons extra-virgin olive oil, divided
½ sweet onion, chopped
2 teaspoons minced garlic
1 pound ground beef
1 pound ground pork
½ cup almond flour
½ cup heavy (whipping) cream

2 eggs
2 teaspoons dried oregano
1 teaspoon dried basil
¼ teaspoon salt
¼ teaspoon freshly ground black pepper
¾ cup tomato purée
1 cup goat cheese

1. Lightly grease the slow cooker with 1 tablespoon of olive oil. 2. In a medium pan over medium-high heat, heat the remaining 2 tablespoons of olive oil. Sauté garlic and onion until softened about 3 minutes. 3. In a large bowl, mix the onion mixture, beef, pork, almond flour, heavy cream, eggs, oregano, basil, salt, and pepper until well combined. 4. Transfer the meat mixture to the insert and form into a loaf with about a ½-inch gap on the sides. 5. Spread the tomato purée on top of the meatloaf and sprinkle with goat cheese. Cover it and cook on low temperature setting for 7 to 8 hours. 6. Serve warm.
Per Serving: Calories 410; Fat 29g; Sodium 158mg; Carbs 4g; Fiber 1g; Sugar 1g; Protein 32g

Steak with Broccoli Noodles

Prep time: 15 minutes | Cook time: 15 minutes | Serves: 4

1 tablespoon vegetable oil
1 Thai chili, seeded and very finely chopped
1 pound thinly sliced steak
½ white onion, spiralized
2 garlic cloves, minced
2 teaspoons fish sauce
4 heads broccoli, florets removed,

stems peeled and spiralized
2 scallions, cut into 1- to 2-inch pieces
Salt
¼ cup soy sauce
2 tablespoons oyster sauce
Freshly ground black pepper
½ cup Thai basil leaves

1. Heat the vegetable oil. Add the onion noodles and sauté for 2 to 3 minutes. 2. Add in the chili and garlic, cook for just under 1 minute. Then add the beef in the pan and stir-fry for 4 to 5 minutes. 3. Add the fish sauce, broccoli florets, and broccoli noodles. Cook, for 3-4 minutes. Whisk the soy sauce and oyster sauce to combine. Whisk the soy sauce and oyster sauce to combine. 4. Pour the sauce and add the scallions in the pan. Toss to combine—cook for 1 to 2 minutes. Season with salt and pepper, as needed. 5. Add the basil, tossing until slightly wilted from the heat and remove from heat. Serve immediately.
Per Serving: Calories 355; Fat 17g; Sodium 796mg; Carbs 21g; Fiber 7g; Sugar 7g; Protein 33g

Cheesy Southwestern Meat Loaf

Prep time: 10 minutes | Cooking time: 60 minutes | Serves: 8

½ cup avocado oil or olive oil, extra-virgin
2 cups shredded (not spiralized) zucchini, from 2 small or 1 large zucchini
1½ teaspoons salt
1 pound ground beef, preferably grass-fed
1 pound ground pork chorizo
½ cup chopped cilantro
¼ cup chopped scallions, green

and white parts
1 large egg, beaten
1 tablespoon chopped chipotle pepper with adobo sauce
1 teaspoon garlic powder
¼ cup almond flour
2 cups shredded Mexican cheese blend or cheddar cheese
1 tablespoon tomato paste (no sugar added)

1. At 375°F/190°C, preheat your oven. Coat a loaf pan with 2 tablespoons of avocado oil. 2. Layer a colander with a layer of paper towels and add the shredded zucchini. Sprinkle with ½ teaspoon of salt, tossing to coat. Let sit for almost 10 minutes, then press down with another layer of paper towels to release some of the excess moisture. 3. While the zucchini drains, in a suitable bowl, mix the ground beef, chorizo, cilantro, scallions, ¼ cup of oil, egg, chipotle with adobo, garlic powder, and remaining 1 teaspoon of salt. Mix well with a fork. 4. Add the almond flour to the drained zucchini and toss to coat. Add the zucchini to the meat mixture and mix until well combined. Add half of the prepared mixture to the prepared pan and spread evenly. 5. Top with 1 cup of shredded cheese, spreading evenly. Top with the remaining half of the prepared mixture and spread evenly. 6. In a suitable bowl, beat the tomato paste and remaining 2 tablespoons of oil and spread evenly on top of the meat mixture. 7. Sprinkle with the remaining 1 cup of cheese. Bake for almost 50 to 55 minutes, or until cooked through. Let sit for almost 10 minutes before cutting.
Per Serving: Calories 589; Total Fat 18.2g; Sodium 513mg; Total Carbs 5.6g; Fiber 24.5g; Sugars 13.2g; Protein 26g

Shepherd's Pie

Prep time: 10 minutes | Cooking time: 70 minutes | Serves: 6

4 tablespoons olive oil, extra-virgin
2 cups cauliflower florets (from about half a head of cauliflower)
2 tablespoons unsalted butter
½ cup heavy cream
1 cup shredded cheddar cheese
2 teaspoons salt
2 teaspoons dried thyme
½ teaspoon black pepper, divided
1 pound ground beef, preferably grass-fed

½ small yellow onion, diced
1 cup chopped cabbage
1 carrot, peeled and diced
2 ribs celery, diced
4 ounces mushrooms, sliced
4 cloves garlic, minced
1 (14½-ounce) can diced tomatoes, with juices
2 tablespoons tomato paste
½ cup beef stock
8 ounces cream cheese, room temperature

1. At 375°F/190°C, preheat your oven. 2. Heat 2 tablespoons oil in a suitable saucepan over medium-low heat. Add the cauliflower and sauté until just tender, 6 to 8 minutes. Add the butter and heavy cream, cover, reduce heat to low, and cook until cauliflower is very tender, another 6 to 8 minutes. Remove it from the heat and allow to cool slightly. 3. Add the cheese, 1 teaspoon of salt, 1 teaspoon of thyme, and ¼ teaspoon of pepper to the cauliflower. 4. Using an immersion blender or hand mixer, puree until very smooth. Keep it aside. 5. In a suitable saucepan or skillet, heat the remaining 2 tablespoons of olive oil over medium heat. 6. Add the ground beef and sauté for almost 5 minutes, breaking apart the meat. 7. Add the onion, cabbage, carrot, celery, and mushrooms and sauté for another 5 to 6 minutes, or until the vegetables are just tender and the meat is browned. 8. Add the garlic, remaining 1 teaspoon of salt, remaining 1 teaspoon of thyme, and remaining ¼ teaspoon of pepper and sauté, stirring, for another 30 seconds. 9. Stir in the tomatoes with their juices and the tomato paste. 10. Bring to a simmer, reduce heat to low, cover, and simmer for almost 8 to 10 minutes, or until the vegetables are very tender and sauce has thickened. 11. In a suitable microwave-safe bowl, mix the stock and cream cheese and microwave on high for almost 1 minute or until cheese is melted. Whisk until creamy. 12. Add the cream cheese mixture to the meat and vegetables and stir to mix well. Place the prepared mixture in an 8-inch square glass baking dish or pie pan. 13. Spread the pureed cauliflower over the meat mixture and bake until golden, 25 to 30 minutes.
Per Serving: Calories 687; Total Fat 17.1g; Sodium 495mg; Total Carbs 2.7g; Fiber 27.3g; Sugars 12.9g; Protein 26g

Beef and Broccoli Foil Packs

Prep time: 10 minutes | Cooking time: 10 minutes | Serves: 4

¼ cup beef stock
¼ cup low-sodium soy sauce
¼ cup sesame oil
¼ cup plus 2 tablespoons olive oil, extra-virgin
4 cloves garlic, minced
2 tablespoons chopped fresh

ginger
1 pound flank steak, sliced
2 cups broccoli florets, cut into bite-size pieces
¼ cup minced scallion, green and white parts
2 tablespoons sesame seeds

1. In a suitable bowl, beat the stock, soy sauce, sesame oil, ¼ cup of olive oil, the garlic, and ginger. Pour half of the prepared mixture into a suitable zip-top plastic bag and add the steak slices. 2. Marinate in the refrigerator for 1 hour, or up to 24 hours. 3. Heat the remaining 2 tablespoons oil in a suitable skillet over high heat. Remove the steak from its marinade. Sear the steak for almost 2 to 3 minutes, until just browned per side, but not cooked through. 4. Lay four 8-inch squares of foil sheet on the counter. Place ½ cup of broccoli and a quarter of the seared steak in the middle of each piece of foil. 5. Pour a quarter of the remaining soy sauce mixture over each steak and broccoli pile, garnish with the scallions and sesame seeds, and cover with a second 8-inch foil square. Fold the foil up to about 1 inch from the prepared mixture per side. Fold in each corner once to secure and seal the foil pack. 6. Preheat the grill on medium-high heat. Place the prepared foil packs in a single layer on the grill and grill for almost 8 minutes.
Per Serving: Calories 483; Total Fat 6g; Sodium 184mg; Total Carbs 7.2g; Fiber 31.2g; Sugars 6g; Protein 30.4g

Slow Cooker Herb-and-Garlic Short Rib Stew

Prep time: 10 minutes | Cooking time: 6 hours | Serves: 4

1 pound boneless beef short ribs
1 teaspoon salt
½ teaspoon garlic powder
¼ teaspoon black pepper
4 tablespoons olive oil, extra-virgin
½ small yellow onion, diced
1 carrot, peeled and diced
2 ribs celery, diced
4 ounces sliced mushrooms

6 cloves garlic, minced
2 teaspoons dried thyme
2 teaspoons dried rosemary (or 2 tablespoons fresh)
1 teaspoon dried oregano
3 cups beef stock
1 (14½-ounce) can diced tomatoes, with juices
½ cup dry red wine (such as merlot)

1. Season the short ribs with the salt, garlic powder, and pepper. 2. Preheat 2 tablespoons oil in a suitable skillet over high heat. Add the short ribs and brown until dark in color, 2 to 3 minutes per side. Transfer to the bowl of a slow cooker. 3. Add the rest of the 2 tablespoons of oil to the skillet and reduce heat to medium. Add the onion, carrot, celery, and mushrooms and sauté until just tender but not fully cooked, 3 to 4 minutes. 4. Add the garlic and sauté, stirring, for an additional 30 seconds. Transfer the contents of the skillet to the slow cooker with the ribs. 5. Add the thyme, rosemary, oregano, stock, tomatoes with their juices, and wine, and cook on low for almost 4 to 6 hours, or until meat is very tender. 6. Remove the ribs from the stew and shred using two forks. Return the shredded meat to the stew and stir to mix well. 7. Serve warm.
Per Serving: Calories 426; Total Fat 8.6g; Sodium 588mg; Total Carbs 7g; Fiber 16.4g; Sugars 2.4g; Protein 23.2g

Corn Dogs

Prep time: 10 minutes | Cooking time: 8 minutes | Serves: 4

1½ cups shredded mozzarella cheese
1 ounce cream cheese

½ cup blanched finely ground almond flour
4 beef hot dogs

1. Place mozzarella, cream cheese, and flour in a suitable microwave-safe bowl. Microwave on high 45 seconds, then stir with a fork until a soft ball of dough forms. 2. Press dough out into a 12" × 6" rectangle, then use a knife to separate into four smaller rectangles. 3. Wrap each hot dog in one rectangle of dough and place into ungreased air fryer basket. Set the temperature to 400°F/200°C and set the timer for almost 8 minutes, turning corn dogs halfway through cooking. 4. Corn dogs will be golden brown when done. Serve warm.
Per Serving: Calories 161; Total Fat 12.4g; Sodium 375mg; Total Carbs 9.8g; Fiber 1.5g; Sugars 2.6g; Protein 3.8g

Weeknight Chili

Prep time: 10 minutes | Cooking time: 35 minutes | Serves: 6

¼ cup olive oil, extra-virgin
1 small yellow onion, diced
1 green bell pepper, diced
1 pound ground beef, preferably grass-fed
½ pound ground Italian sausage (hot or sweet)
1 tablespoon chili powder
2 teaspoons ground cumin

1½ teaspoons salt
6 cloves garlic, minced
1 (14½-ounce) can diced tomatoes, with juices
1 (6-ounce) can tomato paste
2 cups water
2 ripe avocados, pitted, peeled, and chopped
1 cup sour cream

1. Preheat the olive oil in a suitable pot over medium heat. Add the onion and bell pepper and sauté for almost 5 minutes, or until just tender. 2. Stir in the ground beef and sausage and cook until meat is browned, 5 to 6 minutes, stirring to break into small pieces. 3. Add the chili powder, cumin, salt, and garlic and sauté, stirring frequently, for almost 1 minute, until fragrant. Add the tomatoes and their juices, tomato paste, and water, stirring to mix well. 4. Bring the prepared mixture to a boil, reduce heat to low, cover, and simmer for almost 15 to 20 minutes, stirring occasionally. 5. Add additional water for a thinner chili if desired. Serve hot, garnished with chopped avocado and sour cream.

Per Serving: Calories 396; Total Fat 8.6g; Sodium 596mg; Total Carbs 5.9g; Fiber 3.4g; Sugars 3.8g; Protein 12.1g

Steak with Blue Cheese Butter

Prep time: 10 minutes | Cooking time: 10 minutes | Serves: 4

4 (4-ounce) filet mignon or New York strip steaks
1 teaspoon salt
1 teaspoon garlic powder
¼ teaspoon black pepper
¼ cup unsalted butter, room

temperature
¼ cup crumbled blue cheese
½ teaspoon dried thyme
2 tablespoons olive oil, extra-virgin

1. At 450°F/230°C, preheat your oven. Rub the steaks with the salt, ½ teaspoon of garlic powder, and the pepper. Let sit at room temperature for almost 15 to 30 minutes. 2. To make the blue cheese butter, in a suitable bowl, mix the butter, blue cheese, remaining ½ teaspoon of garlic powder, and thyme and whisk until well combined and smooth. Keep it aside. 3. Heat the olive oil in a suitable, oven-proof skillet over high heat. When the oil is very hot, add the steaks and sear for almost 1 minute per side. Transfer the skillet to your oven and roast to desired doneness. 4. For almost 1-inch-thick steaks, it will take 3 to 6 minutes for rare (130°F/55°C to 135°F/55°C), 6 to 8 minutes for medium-rare (140°F/60°C to 155°F/70°C), and 8 to 10 minutes for well-done (150°F/65°C to 155°F/70°C). For almost 1½-inch-thick steaks, cook 4 to 6 minutes for rare and 8 to 10 minutes for well-done. 5. Remove the prepared steaks from the skillet and place each on a separate plate. Top each with 2 tablespoons of blue cheese butter and allow the steak to rest and butter to melt for almost 5 minutes before serving.

Per Serving: Calories 336; Total Fat 9.9g; Sodium 1672mg; Total Carbs 2.6g; Fiber 1.7g; Sugars 2.1g; Protein 12.3g

Cheese-Stuffed Steak Burgers

Prep time: 10 minutes | Cooking time: 10 minutes | Serves: 4

1 pound ground sirloin
4 ounces mild cheddar cheese, cubed

½ teaspoon salt
¼ teaspoon ground black pepper

1. Form ground sirloin into four equal balls, then separate each ball in half and flatten into two thin patties, for eight total patties. 2. Place 1 ounce cheddar into center of one patty, then top with a second patty and press edges to seal burger closed. Repeat with remaining patties and cheddar to create four burgers. 3. Sprinkle black pepper and salt over both sides of burgers and carefully place burgers into ungreased air fryer basket. 4. Set the temperature to 350°F/175°C and set the timer for almost 10 minutes. Burgers will be done when browned on the edges and top. 5. Serve warm.

Per Serving: Calories 499; Total Fat 9.4g; Sodium 422mg; Total Carbs 3.4g; Fiber 17.2g; Sugars 1.6g; Protein 26.9g

Slow Cooker Swedish Meatballs

Prep time: 10 minutes | Cooking time: 4 hrs | Serves: 8

1 pound ground Italian pork sausage
1 pound ground beef, preferably grass-fed
½ small yellow onion, minced
¼ cup almond flour
1 large egg, beaten
3 teaspoons Worcestershire sauce
2 teaspoons salt
1 teaspoon ground allspice

½ teaspoon ground nutmeg
½ teaspoon ground ginger
½ teaspoon black pepper
1½ cups beef stock or broth
1 cup heavy cream
1 tablespoon Dijon mustard
4 ounces cream cheese, room temperature
1 cup sour cream, room temperature

1. In a suitable bowl, mix the pork, beef, onion, almond flour, egg, 1 teaspoon of Worcestershire, 1 teaspoon of salt, the allspice, nutmeg, ginger, and ¼ teaspoon of pepper and mix well with a fork. 2. Form the meat mixture into small 1-inch meatballs, and place on a suitable baking sheet or cutting board. 3. In the bowl of a 5- or 6-quart slow cooker, beat the stock, heavy cream, mustard, remaining 2 teaspoons of Worcestershire sauce, remaining 1 teaspoon of salt, and remaining ¼ teaspoon of pepper until smooth and creamy. Place the meatballs in the sauce, trying to not overcrowd. Set the slow cooker to low and cook for almost 4 hours. 4. After 4 hours of cooking, beat the cream cheese and sour cream and add to the warm mixture, gently stirring to incorporate well. 5. Serve the meatballs in their sauce with toothpicks, or over spiralized zucchini for a complete meal. Leftover meatballs and sauce can be frozen for up to 3 months.

Per Serving: Calories 371; Total Fat 4.9g; Sodium 1207mg; Total Carbs 7.5g; Fiber 25g; Sugars 7g; Protein 25.6g

Mozzarella-Stuffed Meatloaf

Prep time: 10 minutes | Cooking time: 30 minutes | Serves: 6

1 pound 80/20 ground beef
½ medium green bell pepper, seeded and chopped
¼ medium yellow onion, peeled and chopped

½ teaspoon salt
¼ teaspoon ground black pepper
2 ounces mozzarella cheese, sliced into ¼"-thick slices
¼ cup low-carb ketchup

1. In a suitable bowl, mix ground beef, bell pepper, onion, salt, and black pepper. Cut a piece of parchment to fit air fryer basket. Place half beef mixture on ungreased parchment and form a 9" × 4" loaf, for almost ½" thick. 2. Center mozzarella slices on beef loaf, leaving at least ¼" around each edge. 3. Press remaining beef into a second 9" × 4" loaf and place on top of mozzarella, pressing edges of loaves to seal. 4. Place parchment with meatloaf into air fryer basket. Set the temperature to 350°F/175°C and set the timer for almost 30 minutes, carefully turning loaf and brushing top with ketchup halfway through cooking. 5. Loaf will be browned and have an internal temperature of at least 180°F/80°C when done. Slice and serve warm.

Per Serving: Calories 542; Total Fat 17.8g; Sodium 801mg; Total Carbs 9g; Fiber 10.7g; Sugars 3.9g; Protein 19.2g

Marinated Steak Kebabs

Prep time: 10 minutes | Cooking time: 5 minutes | Serves: 4

1 pound strip steak, fat trimmed, cut into 1" cubes
½ cup soy sauce
¼ cup olive oil
1 tablespoon granular brown

erythritol
½ teaspoon salt
¼ teaspoon ground black pepper
1 medium green bell pepper, seeded and chopped into 1" cubes

1. Place steak into a suitable sealable bowl or bag and pour in soy sauce and olive oil. Add erythritol, then stir to coat steak. Marinate at room temperature 30 minutes. 2. Remove streak from marinade and sprinkle with salt and black pepper. 3. Place meat and vegetables onto 6" skewer sticks, alternating between steak and bell pepper. 4. Place kebabs into ungreased air fryer basket. Set the temperature to 400°F/200°C and set the timer for almost 5 minutes. Steak will be done when crispy at the edges and peppers are tender. Serve warm.

Per Serving: Calories 499; Total Fat 9.4g; Sodium 422mg; Total Carbs 3.4g; Fiber 17.2g; Sugars 1.6g; Protein 26.9g

Bacon and Blue Cheese Burgers

Prep time: 10 minutes | Cooking time: 15 minutes | Serves: 4

1 pound 70/30 ground beef	¼ cup peeled and chopped yellow
6 slices cooked sugar-free bacon,	onion
finely chopped	½ teaspoon salt
½ cup crumbled blue cheese	¼ teaspoon ground black pepper

1. In a suitable bowl, mix ground beef, bacon, blue cheese, and onion. Separate into four sections and shape each section into a patty. Sprinkle with black pepper and salt. 2. Place patties into ungreased air fryer basket. Set the temperature to 350°F/175°C and set the timer for almost 15 minutes, turning patties halfway through cooking. 3. Burgers will be done when internal temperature is at least 150°F/66°C for medium and 180°F/80°C for well. Serve warm.
Per Serving: Calories 254; Total Fat 2.6g; Sodium 482mg; Total Carbs 9.1g; Fiber 4.8g; Sugars 0.2g; Protein 7.8g

Blackened Steak Nuggets

Prep time: 10 minutes | Cooking time: 7 minutes | Serves: 2

1 pound rib eye steak, cut into 1"	½ teaspoon salt
cubes	¼ teaspoon garlic powder
2 tablespoons salted butter,	¼ teaspoon onion powder
melted	¼ teaspoon ground black pepper
½ teaspoon paprika	⅛ teaspoon cayenne pepper

1. Place steak into a suitable bowl and pour in butter. Toss to coat. Sprinkle with remaining ingredients. 2. Place bites into ungreased air fryer basket. Set the temperature to 400°F/200°C and set the timer for almost 7 minutes, shaking the basket three times during cooking. Steak will be crispy on the outside and browned when done and internal temperature is at least 150°F/65°C for medium and 180°F/80°C for well-done. Serve warm.
Per Serving: Calories 244; Total Fat 9.1g; Sodium 1399mg; Total Carbs 4.3g; Fiber 8.7g; Sugars 15.7g; Protein 8.3g

Spinach and Provolone Steak Rolls

Prep time: 10 minutes | Cooking time: 12 minutes | Serves: 8

1 (1-pound) flank steak,	1 cup fresh spinach leaves
butterflied	½ teaspoon salt
8 (1-ounce, ¼"-thick) deli slices	¼ teaspoon ground black pepper
provolone cheese	

1. Place steak on a suitable plate. Place provolone slices to cover steak, leaving 1" at the edges. Lay spinach leaves over cheese. 2. Gently roll steak and tie with kitchen twine or secure with toothpicks. Carefully slice into eight pieces. Sprinkle each with black pepper and salt. 3. Place rolls into ungreased air fryer basket, cut side up. Set the temperature to 400°F/200°C and set the timer for almost 12 minutes. Steak rolls will be browned and cheese will be melted when done and have an internal temperature of at least 150°F/65°C for medium steak and 180°F/80°C for well-done steak. Serve warm.
Per Serving: Calories 669; Total Fat 53.8g; Sodium 905mg; Total Carbs 1.7g; Fiber 8.6g; Sugars 12.3g; Protein 14g

Spicy Brisket

Prep time: 10 minutes | Cooking time: 110 minutes | Serves: 6

3 teaspoons salt	1 tablespoon avocado oil
2 teaspoons pepper	1 cup beef broth
1 teaspoon garlic powder	½ cup pickled jalapeño juice
1 teaspoon dried thyme	½ cup pickled jalapeños
½ teaspoon dried rosemary	½ medium onion, chopped
1 (4- to 5-pound) beef brisket	

1. In a suitable bowl mix salt, pepper, garlic powder, thyme, and rosemary. Sprinkle over brisket; keep it aside. 2. Hit the sauté button on the Instant Pot and add avocado oil to Instant Pot. Sear each side of brisket for almost 5 minutes. 3. Add beef broth, jalapeño juice, jalapeños, and onions to Instant Pot. Hit the cancel button and click to close lid. 4. Hit the manual button and adjust time to 100 minutes. When the pot beeps, allow pot to naturally release, for almost 30–40 minutes. Don't do a quick release; it will result in tougher meat. 5. Remove brisket, slice, and pour all the strained broth over meat for additional flavor.
Per Serving: Calories 541; Total Fat 12.4g; Sodium 250mg; Total Carbs 5.4g; Fiber 21.3g; Sugars 6.1g; Protein 26.5g

Marinated Rib Eye

Prep time: 10 minutes | Cooking time: 10 minutes | Serves: 4

1 pound rib eye steak	erythritol
¼ cup soy sauce	2 tablespoons olive oil
1 tablespoon Worcestershire sauce	½ teaspoon salt
1 tablespoon granular brown	¼ teaspoon ground black pepper

1. Place rib eye in a suitable sealable bowl or bag and pour in soy sauce, Worcestershire sauce, erythritol, and olive oil. Seal and let marinate 30 minutes in the refrigerator. 2. Remove rib eye from marinade, pat dry, and sprinkle on all sides with black pepper and salt. Place rib eye into ungreased air fryer basket. 3. Set the temperature to 400°F/200°C and set the timer for almost 10 minutes. Steak will be done when browned at the edges and has an internal temperature of 150°F/66°C for medium or 180°F/80°C for well-done. Serve warm.
Per Serving: Calories 339; Total Fat 14g; Sodium 556mg; Total Carbs 4.6g; Fiber 6.4g; Sugars 3.8g; Protein 10.5g

Roast Beef

Prep time: 10 minutes | Cooking time: 60 minutes | Serves: 6

1 (2-pound) top round beef roast	1 teaspoon dried rosemary
1 teaspoon salt	½ teaspoon garlic powder
½ teaspoon ground black pepper	1 tablespoon coconut oil, melted

1. Sprinkle all sides of roast with salt, pepper, rosemary, and garlic powder. Drizzle with coconut oil. 2. Place roast into ungreased air fryer basket, fatty side down. Set the temperature to 375°F/190°C and set the timer for almost 60 minutes, turning the roast halfway through cooking. Roast will be done when no pink remains and internal temperature is at least 180°F/82°C. Serve warm.
Per Serving: Calories 231; Total Fat 2.1g; Sodium 816mg; Total Carbs 8.1g; Fiber 14.4g; Sugars 4.5g; Protein 16.6g

Mexican-Style Shredded Beef

Prep time: 10 minutes | Cooking time: 35 minutes | Serves: 6

1 (2-pound) beef chuck roast, cut	½ teaspoon ground black pepper
into 2" cubes	½ cup no-sugar-added chipotle
1 teaspoon salt	sauce

1. In a suitable bowl, sprinkle beef cubes with black pepper and salt and toss to coat. 2. Place beef into ungreased air fryer basket. Set the temperature to 400°F/200°C and set the timer for almost 30 minutes, shaking the basket halfway through cooking. Beef will be done when internal temperature is at least 160°F/70°C. 3. Place cooked beef into a suitable bowl and shred with two forks. Pour in chipotle sauce and toss to coat. 4. Return beef to air fryer basket for an additional 5 minutes at 400°F/200°C to crisp with sauce. Serve warm.
Per Serving: Calories 373; Total Fat 3.1g; Sodium 687mg; Total Carbs 9.2g; Fiber 9.6g; Sugars 3.4g; Protein 17.8g

London Broil

Prep time: 10 minutes | Cooking time: 12 minutes | Serves: 4

1 pound top round steak	½ teaspoon ground black pepper
1 tablespoon Worcestershire sauce	½ teaspoon salt
¼ cup soy sauce	2 tablespoons salted butter,
2 cloves garlic, peeled and finely	melted
minced	

1. Place steak in a suitable sealable bowl or bag. Pour in Worcestershire sauce and soy sauce, then add garlic, pepper, and salt. Toss to coat. Seal and place into refrigerator to let marinate 2 hours. 2. Remove steak from marinade and pat dry. Drizzle top side with butter, then place into ungreased air fryer basket. Set the temperature to 375°F/190°C and set the timer for almost 12 minutes, turning steak halfway through cooking. 3. Steak will be done when browned at the edges and it has an internal temperature of 150°F/65°C for medium or 180°F/80°C for well-done. 4. Let steak rest on a suitable plate 10 minutes before slicing into thin pieces. Serve warm.
Per Serving: Calories 283; Total Fat 3.6g; Sodium 381mg; Total Carbs 5.4g; Fiber 8.1g; Sugars 3.1g; Protein 8.7g

Buttery Pot Roast

Prep time: 10 minutes | Cooking time: 90 minutes | Serves: 4

4 teaspoons onion powder	1 (2-pound) chuck roast
2 teaspoons dried parsley	1 tablespoon coconut oil
1 teaspoon salt	1 cup store-bought beef broth
1 teaspoon garlic powder	½ packet dry ranch seasoning
½ teaspoon dried oregano	1 stick butter
½ teaspoon pepper	10 pepperoncini

1. Hit the sauté button on the Instant Pot and allow to heat. In suitable bowl, mix onion powder, parsley, salt, garlic powder, oregano, and pepper. Rub seasoning onto roast. Add coconut oil to preheat. Place roast in pot and sear for almost 5 minutes each side; remove roast and keep it aside. 2. Hit the cancel button. Add broth to Instant Pot. Using rubber spatula or wooden spoon, scrape bottom to loosen any stuck-on seasoning or meat. 3. Place roast back into Instant Pot and sprinkle dry ranch powder on top. Place stick of butter on roast and add pepperoncini. Turn the pot's lid to close. Hit the manual button and adjust time for almost 90 minutes. 4. When the pot beeps, allow a natural release to retain meat tenderness. When pressure indicator drops, remove lid and remove cooked roast. Slice or shred and top with broth from pot.
Per Serving: Calories 344; Total Fat 3g; Sodium 603mg; Total Carbs 3.8g; Fiber 11.5g; Sugars 8.6g; Protein 9.4g

Creamy Mushroom Pot Roast

Prep time: 10 minutes | Cooking time: 90 minutes | Serves: 6

1 cup sliced button mushrooms	½ teaspoon dried oregano
½ medium onion, sliced	1 teaspoon salt
1 tablespoon coconut oil	1 (2–3-pound) chuck roast
2 teaspoons dried minced onion	1 cup beef broth
2 teaspoons dried parsley	4 tablespoons butter
1 teaspoon pepper	2 ounces cream cheese
1 teaspoon garlic powder	¼ cup heavy cream

1. Hit the sauté button on the Instant Pot and add mushrooms, onion, and coconut oil to Instant Pot. Stir-fry for almost 5 minutes or until onions turn translucent. While stir-frying, mix dried minced onion, parsley, pepper, garlic, oregano, and salt in suitable bowl. Rub into chuck roast. Hit the cancel button. 2. Add beef broth and roast into pot. Place butter and cream cheese on top. Turn the pot's lid to close. Hit the meat button and hit the adjust button to set heat to more. Set time to 90 minutes. 3. When the pot beeps allow a full natural release to retain moisture in meat. When pressure valve drops, stir in heavy cream. Remove roast carefully; it will be fall-apart tender. Hit the sauté button on the Instant Pot and reduce sauce in Instant Pot for almost 10 minutes, stirring occasionally. Hit the cancel button and spoon over roast to serve.
Per Serving: Calories 459; Total Fat 3.6g; Sodium 1614mg; Total Carbs 2g; Fiber 11.5g; Sugars 8.3g; Protein 25.9g

Broiled Lamb Chops with Mint Gremolata and Pan-Fried Zucchini

Prep time: 10 minutes | Cooking time: 20 minutes | Serves: 4

8 (4-ounce) bone-in lamb chops	½-inch-thick coins
Salt	½ cup fresh mint leaves
Black pepper	Grated zest of 1 lemon
2 tablespoons olive oil	2 teaspoons minced garlic
4 medium zucchini, sliced into	

1. Preheat the broiler to high. Season the lamb chops on both sides with black pepper and salt and place on a suitable baking sheet. 2. Broil for almost 4 minutes per side for rare, 5 minutes per side for medium-rare, 7 minutes per side for medium, and 9 minutes per side for well-done. Let rest for almost 5 minutes. 3. Meanwhile, in a suitable skillet, heat the oil over medium heat. 4. Add the zucchini and cook, stirring frequently, for almost 10 minutes, or to desired tenderness. 5. Finely chop the mint and place in a suitable bowl. Add the lemon zest and garlic and mix well.
Per Serving: Calories 396; Total Fat 11.4g; Sodium 448mg; Total Carbs 0.7g; Fiber 3.7g; Sugars 0.8g; Protein 40.2g

Quick Bratwurst

Prep time: 10 minutes | Cooking time: 8 minutes | Serves: 4

1 cup water	1 tablespoon coconut oil
4 (4-ounce) bratwursts	

1. Pour water into Instant Pot and place steam rack in bottom of pot. Put brats on steam rack and turn the pot's lid to close. Adjust time for almost 10 minutes. 2. When the pot beeps, quick-release the pressure. Remove brats and pour out water. 3. Replace inner pot and hit the sauté button. Place brats and coconut oil into Instant Pot. 4. Brown for almost 2–4 minutes or until golden. Remove brats with tongs when golden. 5. Serve alone or with buttered cabbage.
Per Serving: Calories 323; Total Fat 17.9g; Sodium 838mg; Total Carbs 4.3g; Fiber 1.5g; Sugars 1g; Protein 35.5g

Sausage Stuffing with Veggies

Prep time: 15 minutes | Cook time: 45 minutes | Serves: 4

4 cups cauliflower florets, broken or chopped into ½-inch pieces	1 tablespoon fresh sage, finely chopped
½ cup extra-virgin olive oil, divided	1 teaspoon dried thyme
1 teaspoon salt, divided	¼ teaspoon freshly ground black pepper
8 ounces bulk pork sausage	4 cloves garlic, minced
½ small onion, diced small	1 cup chicken or vegetable stock
4 ribs celery, diced small	¼ cup dry white wine
¼ cup chopped carrot	2 tablespoons fresh parsley, chopped
4 ounces chopped mushrooms	

1. Preheat the oven to 425°F/220°C. 2. Prepare a rimmed baking tray with aluminum foil. 3. In a large bowl, toss the cauliflower with ¼ cup of olive oil and ½ teaspoon of salt. Spread the cauliflower on the baking sheet, reserving the bowl. 4. Cook the cauliflower until golden brown and crispy but not soft, for 10 to 12 minutes. Remove from the oven, reduce temperature to 375°F/190°C, and allow the cauliflower to cool slightly before transferring back to the reserved bowl. 5. Heat the olive oil over medium-high heat. Add the sausage and sear for 10 minutes, breaking it into small pieces. Do not drain the rendered fat. 6. To the pan along with sausage, add onion, celery, carrot, mushrooms, sage, thyme, remaining ½ teaspoon of salt, and pepper, and sauté well until the vegetables begin to soften, 5 to 7 minutes. Add the garlic and sauté, stirring, for another 30 seconds. 7. Add the stock and white wine, increase heat to high, and sauté, continuously stirring, until half the liquid evaporates. 8. Transfer the sausage-and-vegetable mixture to the bowl with the cauliflower and stir in the parsley. Transfer the mixture to an 8-inch square glass baking dish. 9. Bake uncovered until the top is browned and crispy, for 15 to 20 minutes. Allow resting for 10 minutes before serving.
Per Serving: Calories 496; Fat 45g; Sodium 784mg; Carbs 10g; Fiber 3g; Sugar 6g; Protein 12g

Rosemary Mint Marinated Lamb Chops

Prep time: 10 minutes | Cooking time: 10 minutes | Serves: 4

3 tablespoons olive oil, extra-virgin, plus more for greasing	1 tablespoon chopped mint leaves
½ teaspoon sea salt	½ teaspoon garlic salt
1 tablespoon fresh rosemary leaves (from about 4 sprigs), plus more sprigs for garnish	4 (4-ounce) lamb chops (about ½-inch thick)
	Black pepper

1. In your high-speed blender, mix the olive oil, salt, rosemary, mint, and garlic salt and blend until smooth. 2. Rub the prepared mixture all over the lamb chops and let them marinate in an airtight container in the refrigerator for almost 30 minutes or up to 4 hours. 3. Oil a suitable skillet over medium-high heat. Add the lamb chops and cook for almost 3 minutes per side (for medium-rare), or to desired doneness. 4. Plate the chops and let them rest for almost 3 minutes. 5. Pour the leftover extra juices over the lamb chops and garnish with rosemary sprigs and pepper.
Per Serving: Calories 348; Total Fat 11.1g; Sodium 139mg; Total Carbs 7.9g; Fiber 3g; Sugars 1.6g; Protein 52.8g

Cheesy Bacon Stuffed Pork Chops

Prep time: 10 minutes | Cook time: 12 minutes | Serves: 4

½ ounce plain pork rinds, finely crushed
½ cup shredded sharp cheddar cheese
4 slices of cooked sugar-free

bacon, crumbled
4 (4-ounce) boneless pork chops
½ teaspoon salt
¼ teaspoon ground black pepper

1. In a small bowl, mix pork rinds, cheddar, and bacon. 2. Make a 3" slit in the side of each pork chop and stuff with ¼ pork rind mixture. Sprinkle pork chops with salt and pepper. 3. Place pork chops into an ungreased air fryer basket, stuffed side up. Set the temperature setting to 400°F/200°C and the timer for 12 minutes. 4. When done, pork chops will be browned and have an internal temperature of at least 145°F/65°C. 5. Serve warm.
Per Serving: Calories 348; Fat 22g; Sodium 694mg; Carbs 0g; Fiber 0g; Sugar 0g; Protein 33g

Parmesan Pork Chops

Prep time: 5 minutes | Cook time: 12 minutes | Serves: 4

1 large egg
½ cup grated Parmesan cheese
4 (4-ounce) boneless pork chops

½ teaspoon salt
¼ teaspoon ground black pepper

1. Whisk egg in a medium bowl and place Parmesan in a separate medium bowl. 2. Sprinkle pork chops on both sides with salt and pepper. Dip pork chop into the egg, then press both sides into Parmesan. 3. Place pork chops into an ungreased air fryer basket. Set the temperature setting to 400°F/200°C and the timer for 12 minutes, turning chops halfway through cooking. 4. When done, pork chops will be golden and have an internal temperature of at least 145°F/65°C. Serve warm.
Per Serving: Calories 298; Fat 17g; Sodium 626mg; Carbs 2g; Fiber 0g; Sugar 0g; Protein 29g

Crispy Pork

Prep time: 40 minutes | Cook time: 20 minutes | Serves: 4

1 pound pork belly, cut into 1" chunks
¼ cup soy sauce
1 tablespoon Worcestershire sauce

2 teaspoons sriracha hot chili sauce
½ teaspoon salt
¼ teaspoon ground black pepper

1. Place pork belly into a medium sealable bowl or bag and pour in soy sauce, Worcestershire sauce, and sriracha. Seal and let marinate for 30 minutes in the refrigerator. 2. Remove pork from marinade, pat dry with a paper towel, and sprinkle with salt and pepper. 3. Place pork in an ungreased air fryer basket. Set the temperature setting to 360°F/180°C and the timer for 20 minutes, shaking the basket halfway through cooking. Pork belly will be done with an internal temperature of at least 145°F/65°C and is golden brown. 4. Let pork belly rest on a large plate for 10 minutes. Serve warm.
Per Serving: Calories 588; Fat 56g; Sodium 423mg; Carbs 0g; Fiber 0g; Sugar 0g; Protein 11g

Pork Ribs

Prep time: 10 minutes | Cook time: 30 minutes | Serves: 4

1 (4-pound) rack pork spare ribs
1 teaspoon ground cumin
2 teaspoons salt
1 teaspoon ground black pepper

1 teaspoon garlic powder
½ teaspoon dry ground mustard
½ cup low-carb barbecue sauce

1. Place ribs on an ungreased aluminum foil sheet. Sprinkle meat evenly with cumin, salt, pepper, garlic powder, and ground mustard. 2. Cut the rack into portions that will fit in your air fryer, and wrap each piece in aluminum foil, working in batches if needed. 3. Place ribs into an ungreased air fryer basket. 4. Set the temperature setting to 400°F/200°C and the timer for 25 minutes. 5. When the timer beeps, carefully remove ribs from the foil and brush them with barbecue sauce. Return ribs back to the air fryer and cook at 400°F/200°C for an additional 5 minutes to brown. 6. Serve warm.
Per Serving: Calories 192; Fat 12g; Sodium 1374mg; Carbs 3g; Fiber 0g; Sugar 0g; Protein 13g

Crispy Baked Pork Chops with Veggie Gravy

Prep time: 10 minutes | Cook time: 25 minutes | Serves: 4

4 tablespoons extra-virgin olive oil, divided
½ cup almond flour
2 teaspoons dried sage, divided
1½ teaspoons salt, divided
½ teaspoon freshly ground black pepper, divided
1 large egg
¼ cup flax meal
¼ cup walnuts, very finely

chopped
4 (4-ounce) boneless pork chops
1 tablespoon unsalted butter
4 ounces chopped mushrooms
2 cloves garlic, minced
1 teaspoon dried thyme
8 ounces cream cheese, room temperature
½ cup heavy cream
¼ cup chicken stock

1. Preheat the oven to 400°F/220°C. Prepare a baking tray with aluminum foil lining and grease with 1 tablespoon of olive oil. 2. In a shallow bowl, Mix almond flour with 1 teaspoon of sage, ½ teaspoon of salt, and ¼ teaspoon of pepper. 3. In another bowl, whisk the egg. In another shallow bowl, stir the flax meal and walnuts. 4. Dredge each pork chop first in the flour mixture, then in the egg, then in the flax-and-walnut mixture to thoroughly coat all sides. Place the prepared baking sheet and drizzle the pork chops evenly with 1 tablespoon of olive oil. 5. Bake until cooked through and golden brown, for 18 to 25 minutes, depending on the thickness of the pork. 6. While the pork is baking, prepare the gravy. Heat the olive oil and the butter in a medium saucepan. 7. Add the mushrooms and sauté until very tender, for 4 to 6 minutes. Add the garlic, remaining 1 teaspoon of sage and 1 teaspoon of salt, thyme, and remaining ¼ teaspoon of pepper, and sauté for an additional 30 seconds. 8. Add the cream cheese to the mushrooms, reduce heat to low, and stir until melted and creamy, for 2 to 3 minutes. 9. Whisk in the cream and stock until smooth. Cook over low heat, frequently whisking, until the mixture is thick and creamy, another 3 to 4 minutes. 8. Serve each pork chop covered with a quarter of the mushroom gravy.
Per Serving: Calories 799; Fat 69g; Sodium 654mg; Carbs 11g; Fiber 4g; Sugar 4g; Protein 36g

Wrapped Pork Tenderloin

Prep time: 20 minutes | Cook time: 10 minutes | Serves: 6

1 (1-pound) pork tenderloin
½ teaspoon salt
½ teaspoon garlic powder

¼ teaspoon ground black pepper
8 slices sugar-free bacon

1. Sprinkle tenderloin with salt, garlic powder, and pepper. Wrap bacon around the tenderloin and secure it with toothpicks. 2. Place tenderloin into an ungreased air fryer basket. Set the temperature setting to 400°F/200°C and the timer for 20 minutes, turning the tenderloin after 15 minutes. 3. When done, bacon will be crispy, and tenderloin will have an internal temperature of at least 145°F/65°C. 4. Cut the tenderloin into six even portions, transfer each to a medium plate, and serve warm.
Per Serving: Calories 144; Fat 6g; Sodium 590mg; Carbs 0g; Fiber 0g; Sugar 0g; Protein 20g

Lamb Sausage

Prep time: 11 minutes | Cook time: 30 minutes | Serves: 4

1-pound ground lamb
½ onion, finely chopped
1 tablespoon chopped fresh parsley
2 teaspoons minced garlic
1 teaspoon dried basil
1 teaspoon paprika

¼ teaspoon sea salt
¼ teaspoon fennel seed
⅛ teaspoon freshly ground black pepper
Pinch ground cloves
2 tablespoons olive oil, divided

1. In a large bowl, stir the lamb, onion, parsley, garlic, basil, paprika, salt, fennel seed, pepper, and cloves until mixed well. 2. Divide the mix into 8 parts and form them into ½-inch-thick patties. Heat 1 tablespoon of olive oil in a large pan over medium-high heat and panfry the patties 4 times, turning once, until cooked through and golden, for about 15 minutes total. 3. Transfer the patties to a plate and repeat with the remaining patties and olive oil.
Per Serving: Calories 390; Fat 34g; Sodium 712mg; Carbs 2g; Fiber 1g; Sugar 1g; Protein 19g

Sweet and Spicy Ribs

Prep time: 10 minutes | Cook time: 30 minutes | Serves: 6

¼ cup granular brown erythritol
2 teaspoons paprika
2 teaspoons chili powder
1 teaspoon garlic powder

½ teaspoon cayenne pepper
2 teaspoons salt
1 teaspoon ground black pepper
1 (4-pound) rack pork spare ribs

1. Mix erythritol, paprika, chili powder, garlic powder, cayenne pepper, salt, and black pepper in a small bowl. Rub spice mix over ribs on both sides. Place ribs on an ungreased aluminum foil sheet and wrap to cover. 2. Place ribs into an ungreased air fryer basket. Set the temp setting to 400°F/200°C and the timer for 25 minutes. 3. When the timer beeps, remove ribs from the foil, then place them back into the air fryer basket to cook for an additional 5 minutes, turning halfway through cooking. 4. Ribs will be browned and have an internal temperature of at least 180°F/80°C when done. Serve warm.
Per Serving: Calories 474; Fat 32g; Sodium 898mg; Carbs 9g; Fiber 1g; Sugar 0g; Protein 35g

Delicious Pork Meatballs

Prep time: 10 minutes | Cook time: 12 minutes | Serves: 6

1 pound ground pork
1 large egg, whisked
½ teaspoon garlic powder
½ teaspoon salt
½ teaspoon ground ginger

¼ teaspoon crushed red pepper flakes
1 medium scallion, trimmed and sliced

1. Combine all ingredients in a large bowl. Spoon out 2 tablespoons of mixture and roll into a ball. Repeat to form eighteen meatballs total. 2. Place meatballs into an ungreased air fryer basket. Set the temperature setting to 400°F/200°C and the timer for 12 minutes, shaking the basket three times throughout the cooking. 3. When done, meatballs will be browned and have an internal temperature of at least 145°F/65°C when done. 4. Serve warm.
Per Serving: Calories 164; Fat 10g; Sodium 252mg; Carbs 1g; Fiber 0g; Sugar 0g; Protein 15g

Spiced Pork Loin

Prep time: 5 minutes | Cook time: 20 minutes | Serves: 6

1 teaspoon paprika
½ teaspoon ground cumin
½ teaspoon chili powder
½ teaspoon garlic powder

2 tablespoons coconut oil
1 (1½-pound) boneless pork loin
½ teaspoon salt
¼ teaspoon ground black pepper

1. Combine paprika, ground cumin, chili powder, and garlic powder in a small bowl. Drizzle coconut oil over pork. Spice pork loin with salt and pepper, then rub the spice mixture evenly on all sides. 2. Place pork loin into an ungreased air fryer basket. Set the temperature setting to 400°F/200°C and the timer for 20 minutes, turning the pork halfway through cooking. 3. When done, pork loin will be browned and have an internal temperature of at least 145°F/65°C when done. Serve warm.
Per Serving: Calories 249; Fat 16g; Sodium 278mg; Carbs 1g; Fiber 0g; Sugar 0g; Protein 24g

Tangy Pulled Pork

Prep time: 5 minutes | Cook time: 30 minutes | Serves: 4

1 tablespoon chili adobo sauce
1 tablespoon chili powder
2 teaspoons salt
1 teaspoon garlic powder
1 teaspoon cumin
½ teaspoon pepper

1 (2½–3 pound) cubed pork butt
1 tablespoon coconut oil
2 cups beef broth
1 lime, cut into wedges
¼ cup chopped cilantro

1. Mix adobo sauce, chili powder, salt, garlic powder, cumin, and pepper in a small bowl. 2. Press the Sauté button on Instant Pot and add coconut oil to the pot. Rub spice mixture onto the cubed pork butt. Place pork into pot and sear for 3–5 minutes per side. Add broth. 3. Press the Cancel button—lock Lid. Press the Manual setting of the pot and set the time to 30 minutes. When the timer beeps, let the pressure naturally release until the float valve drops and unlock the lid. 4. Shred pork with a fork. Pork should easily fall apart. For extra-crispy pork, place a single layer in a pan on the stove over medium heat. 5. Cook pork for 10–15 minutes or until water has cooked out and meat becomes brown and crisp. Serve warm with fresh lime wedges and cilantro garnish.
Per Serving: Calories 570; Fat 35g; Sodium 1725mg; Carbs 3.2g; Fiber 1.1g; Sugar 0.4g; Protein 55g

Pork Chops in Mushroom Gravy

Prep time: 10 minutes | Cooking time: 15 minutes | Serves: 4

4 (5-ounce) pork chops
1 teaspoon salt
½ teaspoon pepper
2 tablespoons avocado oil
1 cup chopped button mushrooms
½ medium onion, sliced
1 clove garlic, minced

1 cup chicken broth
¼ cup heavy cream
4 tablespoons butter
¼ teaspoon xanthan gum
1 tablespoon chopped fresh parsley

1. Sprinkle pork chops with black pepper and salt. Place avocado oil and mushrooms in Instant Pot and hit the sauté button. Sauté for 3–5 minutes until mushrooms begin to soften. 2. Add onions and pork chops. Sauté additional 3 minutes until pork chops reach a golden brown. 3. Add garlic and broth to Instant Pot. Turn the pot's lid to close. Hit the manual button and adjust time for almost 15 minutes. 4. When the pot beeps, allow a 10-minute natural release. Quick-release the remaining pressure. 5. Remove lid and place pork chops on plate. Hit the sauté button on the Instant Pot and add heavy cream, butter, and xanthan gum. 6. Reduce for almost 5–10 minutes or until sauce begins to thicken. 7. Add pork chops back into pot. Serve warm topped with mushroom sauce and parsley.
Per Serving: Calories 609; Total Fat 19.5g; Sodium 132mg; Total Carbs 9g; Fiber 6g; Sugars 13.3g; Protein 57.5g

Cabbage Egg Roll

Prep time: 10 minutes | Cooking time: 5 minutes | Serves: 4

1 pound 84% lean ground pork
2 tablespoons soy sauce
½ teaspoon salt
½ cup diced onion

1 clove garlic, minced
2 stalks green onion, sliced
8 cabbage leaves
1 cup water

1. Hit the sauté button on the Instant Pot and add ground pork, soy sauce, and salt to Instant Pot. Brown pork until no pink remains. Carefully drain grease. 2. Add diced onion and continue cooking until translucent, 2–4 minutes. Add garlic and cook for additional 30 seconds. Hit the cancel button. 3. Pour mixture into suitable bowl; keep it aside. Mix green onions into pork. Rinse pot and replace. Add water and steam rack. 4. Take 2–3 tablespoons of pork mixture and spoon it into cabbage leaf in rectangle shape, off to one side of the leaf. 5. Fold the short ends of the leaf toward the middle. Complete the roll by starting at the filled edge and rolling toward the empty side, as you would get a burrito. 6. Place rolls onto steam rack. Turn the pot's lid to close. Hit the manual button and adjust time for almost 1 minute. 7. When the pot beeps, quick-release the steam. Serve warm.
Per Serving: Calories 570; Total Fat 29.3g; Sodium 845mg; Total Carbs 5.8g; Fiber 1.6g; Sugars 2.7g; Protein 68.6g

Chipotle Pork Chops

Prep time: 10 minutes | Cooking time: 15 minutes | Serves: 4

2 tablespoons coconut oil
3 chipotle chilies
2 tablespoons adobo sauce
2 teaspoons cumin
1 teaspoon dried thyme
1 teaspoon salt
4 (5-ounce) boneless pork chops

½ medium onion, chopped
2 bay leaves
1 cup chicken broth
½ (7-ounce) can fire-roasted diced tomatoes
⅓ cup chopped cilantro

1. Hit the sauté button on the Instant Pot and add coconut oil to preheat. While it heats, add chilies, adobo sauce, cumin, thyme, and salt to food processor. Pulse to make paste. 2. Rub paste into pork chops. Place in Instant Pot and sear each side 5 minutes or until browned. 3. Hit the cancel button and add onion, bay leaves, broth, tomatoes, and cilantro to Instant Pot. 4. Turn the pot's lid to close. Hit the manual button and adjust time for almost 15 minutes. 5. When the pot beeps, allow a 10-minute natural release, then quick-release the remaining pressure. 6. Serve warm with additional cilantro as garnish if desired.
Per Serving: Calories 419; Total Fat 15.8g; Sodium 3342mg; Total Carbs 0.4g; Fiber 0.2g; Sugars 0g; Protein 65.4g

Dijon Pork Chops

Prep time: 10 minutes | Cooking time: 8 hours | Serves: 4

1 tablespoon olive oil, extra-virgin
1 cup chicken broth
1 sweet onion, chopped
¼ cup Dijon mustard
1 teaspoon minced garlic
1 teaspoon maple extract
4 (4-ounce) boneless pork chops
1 cup heavy (whipping) cream
1 teaspoon chopped fresh thyme, for garnish

1. Lightly grease the insert of the slow cooker with the olive oil. 2. Add the broth, onion, Dijon mustard, garlic, and maple extract to the insert, and stir to combine. Add the pork chops. 3. Cover and cook on low for almost 8 hours. 4. Stir in the heavy cream. 5. Serve topped with the thyme. (Make it paleo: replace the heavy cream with coconut milk to create a lovely sauce with very little change in flavor. Dijon mustard is strong enough to mask the coconut taste, especially when it is reduced in a slow cooker.)
Per Serving: Calories 305; Total Fat 16.7g; Sodium 148mg; Total Carbs 2.5g; Fiber 1.1g; Sugars 0.1g; Protein 36.5g

Roasted Pork Loin with Grainy Mustard Sauce

Prep time: 10 minutes | Cooking time: 70 minutes | Serves: 8

1 (2-pound) boneless pork loin roast
Sea salt
Black pepper
3 tablespoons olive oil
1½ cups heavy (whipping) cream
3 tablespoons grainy mustard

1. At 375°F/190°C, preheat your oven. 2. Season the pork roast all over with sea black pepper and salt. 3. Place a suitable skillet over medium-high heat and add the olive oil. 4. Brown the roast on all sides in the skillet. for almost 6 minutes in total, and place the roast in a baking dish. Roast until a meat thermometer inserted in the thickest part of the roast reads 155°F/70°C, for almost 1 hour. 5. When there is approximately 15 minutes of roasting time left, place a suitable saucepan over medium heat and add the heavy cream and mustard. 6. Mix the sauce until it simmers, then reduce its heat to low. Simmer the sauce until it is very rich and thick, for almost 5 minutes. Remove this pan from the heat and keep it aside. 7. Let the pork rest for almost 10 minutes before slicing and serve with the sauce.
Per Serving: Calories 506; Total Fat 23.9g; Sodium 197mg; Total Carbs 3.6g; Fiber 0.7g; Sugars 1.2g; Protein 66.1g

Herb-Crusted Lamb Chops

Prep time: 10 minutes | Cooking time: 15 minutes | Serves: 3

1 pound lamb chops
2 tablespoons Dijon mustard
4 fresh rosemary sprigs, chopped
4 fresh thyme sprigs, chopped
3 tablespoons almond flour
4 garlic cloves, minced
1 teaspoon onion powder
¼ teaspoon salt
¼ teaspoon black pepper
¼ cup olive oil

1. At 350°F/175°C, preheat your oven. 2. Coat the lamb chops with the mustard. Keep it aside. 3. To your high-speed blender or food processor, add the rosemary, thyme, almond flour, garlic, onion powder, salt, and pepper. Pulse until finely chopped. 4. Slowly add about 2 tablespoons of olive oil to form a thick paste. 5. Hit the herb paste firmly around the edges of the mustard-coated chops, creating a crust. In a suitable oven-safe skillet over medium heat, heat the remaining 2 tablespoons of olive oil for almost 2 minutes. 6. Add the chops to the skillet on their sides to brown. 7. Cook, undisturbed, for almost 2 to 3 minutes so the crust adheres properly to the meat. Turn and cook on the opposite edge for almost 2 to 3 minutes more. 8. Transfer the chops to a suitable baking sheet. Place the sheet in the preheated oven. 9. Cook for almost 7 to 8 minutes, for medium. Remove the sheet from your oven. Serve immediately.
Per Serving: Calories 348; Total Fat 11.1g; Sodium 139mg; Total Carbs 7.9g; Fiber 3g; Sugars 1.6g; Protein 52.8g

Herb-Braised Pork Chops

Prep time: 10 minutes | Cooking time: 8 hours | Serves: 6

¼ cup olive oil
1½ pounds pork loin chops
Salt, for seasoning
Black pepper, for seasoning
1 cup chicken broth
½ sweet onion, chopped
2 teaspoons minced garlic
1 teaspoon dried thyme
1 teaspoon dried oregano
1 cup heavy (whipping) cream
1 tablespoon chopped fresh basil, for garnish

1. Lightly grease the insert of the slow cooker with 1 tablespoon of the olive oil. 2. In a suitable skillet over medium-high heat, heat the remaining 3 tablespoons of the olive oil. 3. Rub the pork with black pepper and salt. Add the pork to the skillet and brown for almost 5 minutes. Transfer the chops to the insert. 4. In a suitable bowl, stir the broth, onion, garlic, thyme, and oregano. 5. Add the broth mixture to the chops. Cover and cook on low for almost 7 to 8 hours. 6. Stir in the heavy cream. Serve topped with the basil.
Per Serving: Calories 404; Total Fat 19.4g; Sodium 187mg; Total Carbs 5g; Fiber 1.1g; Sugars 0.8g; Protein 52g

Rack of Lamb with Kalamata Tapenade

Prep time: 10 minutes | Cooking time: 25 minutes | Serves: 4

For the tapenade
1 cup pitted Kalamata olives
2 tablespoons chopped fresh parsley
2 tablespoons olive oil, extra-virgin
2 teaspoons minced garlic
2 teaspoons freshly squeezed lemon juice
For the lamb chops
2 (1-pound) racks French-cut lamb chops (8 bones each)
Sea salt
Black pepper
1 tablespoon olive oil

1. Place the olives, parsley, olive oil, garlic, and lemon juice in a food processor and process until the prepared mixture is puréed but still slightly chunky. 2. Transfer the tapenade to a container and store sealed in the refrigerator until needed. At 450°F/230°C, preheat your oven. 3. Rub the lamb racks with black pepper and salt. Place a suitable ovenproof skillet over medium-high heat and add the olive oil. 4. Pan sear the lamb racks on all sides until browned. for almost 5 minutes in total. 5. Arrange the racks upright in the skillet, with the bones interlaced, and roast them in your oven until they reach your desired doneness. 6. For almost 20 minutes for medium-rare or until the internal temperature reaches 125°F/50°C. 7. Let the lamb rest for almost 10 minutes and then cut the lamb racks into chops. 8. Top with the Kalamata tapenade.
Per Serving: Calories 841; Fat 65.7g; Sodium 1153mg; Carbs 2.9g; Fiber 1.2g; Sugar 0.1g; Protein 57g

Italian-Spiced Pork Tenderloin

Prep time: 10 minutes | Cooking time: 20 minutes | Serves: 2

1 teaspoon dried oregano
1 slice gluten-free bread (use ½ cup of almond flour for a paleo version)
1 garlic clove, peeled and minced
1 large egg white, beaten
½ pound pork tenderloin, trimmed of excess fat
Essentials
Salt and ground black pepper, to taste
1 onion, peeled and diced
Cooking spray (use coconut oil for a paleo version)

1. At 400°F/200°C, preheat your oven. Spray a broiler pan with cooking oil spray. 2. Mix the oregano, onion, garlic, and bread in a food processor and process until finely ground. You should have about ⅓ cup breadcrumbs. 3. Transfer the breadcrumbs to a plate. 4. Season the pork with salt and black pepper. 5. Dip the meat into the beaten egg white, and then roll in the bread crumb mixture until coated evenly. 6. Place the pork on the broiler pan and roast for almost 20 minutes. Remove from your oven and let rest for almost 5 minutes. 7. Cut the pork into ¼-inch thick slices and serve.
Per Serving: Calories 494; Total Fat 27.1g; Sodium 106mg; Total Carbs 23.4g; Fiber 7.5g; Sugars 10.5g; Protein 42.7g

Nut-stuffed pork chops

Prep time: 10 minutes | Cooking time: 30 minutes | Serves: 4

3 ounces goat cheese
½ cup chopped walnuts
¼ cup toasted chopped almonds
1 teaspoon chopped fresh thyme
4 center-cut pork chops,

butterflied
Sea salt
Black pepper
2 tablespoons olive oil

1. At 400°F/200°C, preheat your oven. 2. In a suitable bowl, make the filling by stirring the goat cheese, walnuts, almonds, and thyme until well mixed. 3. Rub the pork chops inside and outside with black pepper and salt. 4. Stuff each pork chop, pushing the filling to the bottom of the cut section. Secure the stuffing with toothpicks through the meat. 5. Place a suitable skillet over medium-high heat and add the olive oil. 6. Pan-sear the pork chops until they're browned per side, for almost 10 minutes in total. 7. Transfer the prepared pork chops to a baking dish and roast the chops in your oven until cooked through. for almost 20 minutes. 8. Serve after removing the toothpicks.
Per Serving: Calories 414; Total Fat 20.8g; Sodium 156mg; Total Carbs 4.5g; Fiber 0.4g; Sugars 1.6g; Protein 49.8g

Lamb Dogs with Tzatziki

Prep time: 10 minutes | Cooking time: 25 minutes | Serves: 10

For the tzatziki
½ medium cucumber, peeled and grated on the large holes of a box grater
1 cup full-fat plain Greek yogurt
1 tablespoon olive oil, extra-virgin
1 tablespoon chopped fresh dill (or
For the lamb dogs
Oil or cooking spray, for greasing
2 pounds ground lamb
2 eggs
2 tablespoons Italian seasoning
2 tablespoons olive oil
2 scallions, finely chopped

½ teaspoon dried dill weed)
1 teaspoon freshly squeezed lemon juice
1 garlic clove, minced (or ½ teaspoon garlic powder)
½ teaspoon sea salt
¼ teaspoon black pepper

¼ cup chopped fresh mint
2 teaspoons lemon-pepper seasoning
1 teaspoon garlic powder
1 teaspoon sea salt
½ teaspoon black pepper

1. Wrap the cucumber shreds in a clean dishtowel and squeeze out as much liquid as possible. 2. In a suitable bowl, beat the cucumber, yogurt, oil, lemon juice, dill, garlic, salt, and pepper. Cover and keep it in the refrigerator while you prepare the lamb dogs. 3. At 350°F/175°C, preheat your oven. Layer a suitable baking sheet with foil sheet and a baking rack. 4. Grease or spray the rack with oil to prevent the lamb from sticking. 5. In a suitable bowl, mix the ground meat, eggs, Italian seasoning, oil, scallions, mint (if using), lemon-pepper seasoning, garlic powder, salt, and pepper. 6. Divide the meat mixture into 10 equal portions. 7. Form the prepared mixture into one large, flat rectangle. 8. Score it with your hand down the middle lengthwise and then score it 4 more times in the opposite direction so that you end up with 10 squares. 9. Form each portion into a log (or hot dog shape) and place on the prepared baking rack. 10. Bake for almost 20 to 25 minutes until browned and cooked through. 11. Serve the lamb dogs topped with the sauce.
Per Serving: Calories 397; Total Fat 19.1g; Sodium 431mg; Total Carbs 6.8g; Fiber 5.3g; Sugars 6.4g; Protein 39.4g

Pork-and-Sauerkraut Casserole

Prep time: 10 minutes | Cooking time: 10 hours | Serves: 6

3 tablespoons olive oil, extra-virgin
2 tablespoons butter
2 pounds pork shoulder roast
1 (28-ounce) jar sauerkraut,

drained
1 cup chicken broth
½ sweet onion, sliced
¼ cup granulated erythritol

1. Lightly grease the insert of the slow cooker with 1 tablespoon of the olive oil. 2. In a suitable skillet over medium-high heat, heat the remaining 2 tablespoons of the olive oil and the butter. 3. Add the pork to the skillet and brown on all sides for almost 10 minutes. 4. Transfer to the insert and add the sauerkraut, broth, onion, and erythritol. 5. Cover and cook on low for almost 9 to 10 hours. Serve warm.
Per Serving: Calories 636; Total Fat 25g; Sodium 259mg; Total Carbs 0.9g; Fiber 0.5g; Sugars 0g; Protein 95.6g

Cranberry Pork Roast

Prep time: 10 minutes | Cooking time: 8 hours 10 minutes | Serves: 6

3 tablespoons olive oil, extra-virgin
2 tablespoons butter
2 pounds pork shoulder roast
1 teaspoon ground cinnamon
¼ teaspoon allspice
¼ teaspoon salt
⅛ teaspoon black pepper, freshly

ground
½ cup cranberries
½ cup chicken broth
½ cup granulated erythritol
2 tablespoons Dijon mustard
Juice and zest of ½ orange
1 scallion, white and green parts, chopped, for garnish

1. Lightly grease the insert of the slow cooker with 1 tablespoon of the olive oil. 2. In a suitable skillet over medium-high heat, heat the remaining 2 tablespoons of the olive oil and the butter. 3. Lightly season the pork with cinnamon, allspice, salt, and pepper. Add the pork to the skillet and brown on all sides for almost 10 minutes. Transfer to the insert. 4. In a suitable bowl, stir the cranberries, broth, erythritol, mustard, and orange juice and zest, and add the prepared mixture to the pork. 5. Cover and cook on low for almost 7 to 8 hours. Serve topped with the scallion.
Per Serving: Calories 367; Total Fat 22.9g; Sodium 101mg; Total Carbs 8g; Fiber 1.9g; Sugars 3g; Protein 31.8g

Pancetta-And-Brie–Stuffed Pork Tenderloin

Prep time: 10 minutes | Cooking time: 8 hours | Serves: 4

1 tablespoon olive oil
2 (½-pound) pork tenderloins
4 ounces pancetta, cooked crispy and chopped

4 ounces triple-cream brie
1 teaspoon minced garlic
1 teaspoon chopped fresh basil
⅛ teaspoon black pepper

1. Lightly grease the insert of the slow cooker with the olive oil. 2. Place the pork on a cutting board and make a lengthwise cut, holding the knife parallel to the board, through the center of the meat without cutting right through. Open the meat up like a book and cover it with plastic wrap. 3. Pound the meat with a mallet or rolling pin until each piece is about ½ inch thick. Lay the butterflied pork on a clean work surface. 4. In a suitable bowl, stir this pancetta, brie, garlic, basil, and pepper. 5. Divide the cheese mixture between the tenderloins and spread it evenly over the meat leaving about 1 inch around the edges. 6. Roll the tenderloin up and secure with toothpicks. 7. Place the pork in the insert, cover, and cook on low for almost 8 hours. Remove the toothpicks and serve.
Per Serving: Calories 315; Total Fat 15g; Sodium 91mg; Total Carbs 0g; Fiber 0g; Sugars 0g; Protein 42.3g

Carnitas

Prep time: 10 minutes | Cooking time: 10 hours 10 minutes | Serves: 8

3 tablespoons olive oil, extra-virgin
2 pounds pork shoulder, cut into 2-inch cubes
2 cups diced tomatoes
2 cups chicken broth
½ sweet onion, chopped
2 fresh chipotle peppers, chopped
Juice of 1 lime

1 teaspoon ground coriander
1 teaspoon ground cumin
½ teaspoon salt
1 avocado, peeled, pitted, and diced, for garnish
1 cup sour cream, for garnish
2 tablespoons chopped cilantro, for garnish

1. Lightly grease the insert of the slow cooker with 1 tablespoon of the olive oil. 2. In a suitable skillet over medium-high heat, heat the remaining 2 tablespoons of the olive oil. 3. Add the pork meat and brown on all sides for almost 10 minutes. 4. Transfer to the insert and add the tomatoes, broth, onion, peppers, lime juice, coriander, cumin, and salt. 5. Cover and cook on low for almost 9 to 10 hours. 6. Shred the cooked pork with a fork and mix the meat into the sauce. 7. Serve topped with the avocado, sour cream, and cilantro.
Per Serving: Calories 278; Total Fat 15.4g; Sodium 321mg; Total Carbs 1.3g; Fiber 0.5g; Sugars 0.1g; Protein 32.1g

Chops with Kalamata Tapenade

Prep time: 15 minutes | Cook time: 25 minutes | Serves: 4

For the tapenade
1 cup pitted Kalamata olives
2 tablespoons chopped fresh parsley
2 tablespoons extra-virgin olive oil
2 teaspoons minced garlic
2 teaspoons freshly squeezed lemon juice

For the lamb chops
2 (1-pound) racks French-cut lamb chops (8 bones each)
Sea salt
Freshly ground black pepper
1 tablespoon olive oil

To make the tapenade: 1. Place the olives, parsley, olive oil, garlic, and lemon juice in a food processor and process until the mixture is puréed but still slightly chunky. 2. Transfer the tapenade to a container and store sealed in the refrigerator until needed

To make the lamb chops: 1. Preheat the oven to 450°F/230°C. 2. Spice the lamb racks with salt and pepper. Place a large ovenproof pan over medium-high heat and add the olive oil. 3. Sear the lamb racks brown, about 5 minutes. 4. Arrange the racks upright in the pan, with the bones interlaced, and roast them in the oven about 20 minutes for medium-rare or until the internal temperature reaches 125°F/50°C. 5. Let the roasted lamb rest for 10 minutes, and then cut the lamb racks into chops. Arrange 4 chops per person on the plate and top with the Kalamata tapenade.

Per Serving: Calories 348; Fat 28g; Sodium 987mg; Carbs 2g; Fiber 1g; Sugar 1g; Protein 21g

Herbed Lamb Racks

Prep time: 1 hour 10 minutes | Cook time: 25 minutes | Serves: 4

4 tablespoons extra-virgin olive oil
2 tablespoons finely chopped fresh rosemary
2 teaspoons minced garlic
Pinch sea salt
2 (1-pound) racks French-cut lamb chops (8 bones each)

1. Whisk the olive oil, rosemary, garlic, and salt in a small bowl. Place the racks in a sealable freezer bag and pour the olive oil mixture into the bag. 2. Massage the meat through the bag so it is coated with the marinade. Press the air out of the bag and seal it. 3. Marinate the lamb racks in the refrigerator for 1 to 2 hours. 4. Preheat the oven to 450°F/230°C. 5. Place a large ovenproof pan over medium-high heat. Take the lamb racks out of the bag and sear them in the pan on all sides, about 5 minutes. 6. Arrange the racks upright in the pan, with the bones interlaced, and roast for about 20 minutes for medium-rare. 7. Let the roasted lamb rest for 10 minutes, and then cut the racks into chops. 8. Serve 4 chops per person.

Per Serving: Calories 354; Fat 30g; Sodium 687mg; Carbs 0g; Fiber 0g; Sugar 0g; Protein 21g

Lamb Leg with Red Pesto

Prep time: 15 minutes | Cook time: 70 minutes | Serves: 8

For the pesto
1 cup sun-dried tomatoes packed in oil
¼ cup pine nuts
2 tablespoons extra-virgin olive oil
2 tablespoons chopped fresh basil
2 teaspoons minced garlic

For the lamb leg
1 (2-pound) lamb leg
Sea salt
Freshly ground black pepper
2 tablespoons olive oil

To make the pesto: 1. Place the sun-dried tomatoes, pine nuts, olive oil, basil, and garlic in a blender or food processor; process until smooth. 2. Set aside until needed.

To make the lamb leg: 1. Preheat the oven to 400°F/200°C. Season the lamb leg all over with salt and pepper. 2. Place a large ovenproof pan over medium-high heat and add the olive oil. 3. Sear the lamb on all sides until nicely browned, about 6 minutes. 4. Spread the sun-dried tomato pesto all over the lamb and place the lamb on a baking sheet. 5. Roast for about 1 hour for medium. 6. Let the roasted lamb rest for 10 minutes before slicing and serving.

Per Serving: Calories 352; Fat 29g; Sodium 1024mg; Carbs 5g; Fiber 2g; Sugar 3g; Protein 17g

Shepherd's Pie with Cauliflower Mash

Prep time: 10 minutes | Cooking time: 30 minutes | Serves: 8

6 cups fresh or frozen cauliflower florets or rice
2 pounds ground beef or lamb
1 tablespoon butter or ghee, plus ¼ cup, melted
½ cup chopped onion
3 garlic cloves, minced
2 tablespoons Italian seasoning
1 tablespoon tomato paste
2 cups chopped mushrooms
2 teaspoons sea salt
1 teaspoon black pepper
4 ounces cream cheese, at room temperature
1 tablespoon Italian seasoning
1 teaspoon garlic powder
½ cup grated parmesan or white cheddar cheese

1. Preheat your oven to 375°F/190°C. 2. Place the cauliflower in a microwave-safe dish and cook on high for almost 6 to 8 minutes if using frozen (10 to 15 minutes if using fresh), until tender. Transfer to a colander to drain. 3. Meanwhile, in a suitable skillet over medium heat, cook the ground meat until browned, for 5 to 7 minutes. Drain the excess liquid and transfer the meat to a bowl. 4. In the same skillet, melt 1 tablespoon of butter and add the onion. Cook for almost 3 minutes over medium-high heat. 5. Add the garlic, Italian seasoning, tomato paste, mushrooms, 1 teaspoon of salt, and ½ teaspoon of pepper and cook for another 5 to 8 minutes until the mushrooms are cooked down. 6. While the mushrooms are cooking, strain off any excess liquid from the cauliflower and add it to your high-speed blender or food processor with the remaining ¼ cup of melted butter, cream cheese, Italian seasoning, garlic powder, remaining 1 teaspoon of salt, and remaining ½ teaspoon of pepper. Blend until smooth. Taste and set the seasoning. 7. Return the meat to the skillet with the mushrooms and onions and stir well. 8. Transfer the meat mixture to a 9-by-13-inch baking dish. Spoon the cauliflower mixture over the top and smooth it into an even layer. Sprinkle with the cheese and bake for almost 20 minutes. 9. Let cool and cut into 8 squares.

Per Serving: Calories 681; Total Fat 30.7g; Sodium 1245mg; Total Carbs 4.9g; Fiber 9.9g; Sugars 5g; Protein 42.5g

Rosemary Lamb Chops

Prep time: 10 minutes | Cooking time: 6 hours | Serves: 4

3 tablespoons olive oil, extra-virgin
1½ pounds lamb shoulder chops
Salt, for seasoning
Black pepper, for seasoning
½ cup chicken broth
1 sweet onion, sliced
2 teaspoons minced garlic
2 teaspoons dried rosemary
1 teaspoon dried thyme

1. Lightly grease the insert of the slow cooker with 1 tablespoon of the olive oil. 2. In a suitable skillet over medium-high heat, heat the remaining 2 tablespoons of the olive oil. 3. Season the lamb with black pepper and salt. Add the lamb to the skillet and brown for almost 6 minutes, turning once. 4. Transfer the lamb to the insert, and add the broth, onion, garlic, rosemary, and thyme. 5. Cover and cook on low for almost 6 hours. Serve warm.

Per Serving: Calories 443; Total Fat 16.3g; Sodium 305mg; Total Carbs 7.4g; Fiber 7.8g; Sugars 11.4g; Protein 38.5g

Tender Lamb Roast

Prep time: 10 minutes | Cooking time: 7 to 8 hours | Serves: 6

1 tablespoon olive oil, extra-virgin
2 pounds lamb shoulder roast
Salt, for seasoning
Black pepper, for seasoning
1 (14.5-ounce) can diced tomatoes
1 tablespoon cumin
2 teaspoons minced garlic
1 teaspoon paprika
1 teaspoon chili powder
1 cup sour cream
2 teaspoons chopped fresh parsley, for garnish

1. Lightly grease the insert of the slow cooker with the olive oil. 2. Lightly season the lamb with black pepper and salt. 3. Place the lamb in the insert and add the tomatoes, cumin, garlic, paprika, and chili powder. 4. Cover and cook on low for almost 7 to 8 hours. 5. Stir in the sour cream. Serve topped with the parsley.

Per Serving: Calories 392; Total Fat 23.4g; Sodium 88mg; Total Carbs 1.4g; Fiber 1.9g; Sugars 3.7g; Protein 34.5g

Lamb-Vegetable

Prep time: 10 minutes | Cook time: 6 hours | Serves: 4

¼ cup extra-virgin olive oil, divided
1 pound boneless lamb chops, about ½-inch thick
Salt, for seasoning
Freshly ground black pepper, for seasoning

½ sweet onion, sliced
½ fennel bulb, cut into 2-inch chunks
1 zucchini, cut into 1-inch chunks
¼ cup chicken broth
2 tablespoons chopped fresh basil for garnish

1. Lightly grease the slow cooker with 1 tablespoon of olive oil. 2. Spiced the lamb with salt and pepper. 3. In a medium bowl, toss the onion along with fennel, and zucchini with the olive oil, and then place half of the vegetables in the cooker. 4. Place the lamb on the vegetables, cover with the remaining vegetables, and add the broth. 5. Cover it and cook on low temperature setting for 6 hours. Cover the pot and cook. 6. Serve topped with the basil.
Per Serving: Calories 431; Fat 37g; Sodium 972mg; Carbs 5g; Fiber 2g; Sugar 2g; Protein 21g

Lamb Kebabs with Mint Pesto

Prep time: 15 minutes plus 1 hour to marinate | Cook time: 15 minutes | Serves: 4

1½ cups fresh mint leaves
¼ cup shelled pistachios
2 cloves garlic, chopped
Zest and juice of 1 orange
¼ cup sesame oil
1 teaspoon salt

¼ teaspoon freshly ground black pepper
¼ cup extra-virgin olive oil
½ cup apple cider vinegar
1 pound leg of lamb, boneless, cut into 1-inch cubes

1. In a food processor, combine the mint, pistachios, and garlic in a bowl and process until very finely chopped. 2. Add the orange zest and juice, sesame oil, salt, and pepper, and pulse until smooth. With the processor running, stream in the olive oil until soft. 3. Place ¼ cup of the mint pesto in a small bowl, add the vinegar, and whisk to form a marinade. 4. Place the lamb cubes in the marinade and toss to coat. Cover and refrigerate for at least 1 hour, up to 24 hours. 5. While the lamb is marinating, soak four wooden skewers in water for 30 to 60 minutes—Preheat the oven to 450°F/230°C. 6. Thread the lamb cubes onto the soaked skewers, dividing evenly among the four. Place the skewers on a broiler pan or rimmed baking sheet lined with foil. 7. Cook until browned and cooked through, for 12 to 15 minutes, flipping halfway through cooking time. 8. Serve the skewers drizzled with the remaining mint pesto.
Per Serving: Calories 592; Fat 52g; Sodium 1745mg; Carbs 5g; Fiber 1g; Sugar 1g; Protein 22g

Lamb Shanks with Mushrooms

Prep time: 15 minutes | Cook time: 7-8 hours | Serves: 6

3 tablespoons extra-virgin olive oil, divided
2 pounds lamb shanks
½ pound wild mushrooms, sliced
1 leek, thoroughly cleaned and chopped
2 celery stalks, chopped
1 carrot, diced

1 tablespoon minced garlic
1 (15-ounce) can crushed tomatoes
½ cup beef broth
2 tablespoons apple cider vinegar
1 teaspoon dried rosemary
½ cup sour cream, for garnish

1. Lightly grease the slow cooker with 1 tablespoon of olive oil. 2. In a large pan over medium-high heat, heat the remaining 2 tablespoons of the olive oil. Add the lamb; sear for 6 minutes, turning once; and transfer to the insert. In the pan, sauté the mushrooms, leek, celery, carrot, and garlic for 5 minutes. 3. Transfer the vegetables to the insert and the tomatoes, broth, apple cider vinegar, and rosemary. 4. Cover it and cook on low temperature setting for 7 to 8 hours. 5. Serve topped with sour cream.
Per Serving: Calories 475; Fat 36g; Sodium 666mg; Carbs 11g; Fiber 5g; Sugar 6g; Protein 31g

Spiced Curried Lamb

Prep time: 15 minutes | Cook time: 7-8 hours | Serves: 6

3 tablespoons extra-virgin olive oil, divided
1½ pounds lamb shoulder chops
Salt, for seasoning
Freshly ground black pepper, for seasoning
3 cups coconut milk

½ sweet onion, sliced
¼ cup curry powder
1 tablespoon grated fresh ginger
2 teaspoons minced garlic
1 carrot, diced
2 tablespoons chopped cilantro for garnish

1. Lightly grease the slow cooker with 1 tablespoon of olive oil. 2. In a large pan over medium-high heat, heat the remaining 2 tablespoons of the olive oil. 3. Season the lamb with salt and pepper. Season the lamb with salt and pepper. Sear it for 6 minutes, turning once. Transfer to the insert. Stir together the coconut milk, onion, curry, ginger, and garlic in a medium bowl. 4. Add the mixture to the lamb along with the carrot. 5. Cover it and cook on low temperature setting for 7 to 8 hours. 6. Serve topped with cilantro.
Per Serving: Calories 490; Fat 41g; Sodium 500mg; Carbs 10g; Fiber 5g; Sugar 2g; Protein 26g

Herbed Lamb Chops

Prep time: 10 minutes | Cook time: 25 minutes | Serves: 2

4 lamb chops
2 teaspoons fresh rosemary
1 tablespoon extra-virgin olive oil
1 tablespoon butter (use extra olive oil for a paleo version),

optional
Fresh garlic, to taste
Salt and ground black pepper, to taste

1. Add the butter along with olive oil to a pan and place over medium-high heat. Place the lamb chops in the hot pan, cook for 2-3 minutes, and flip. 2. Sprinkle the top side with ¾ of the fresh rosemary, cook for 7-8 minutes, and flip to sear the other side. 3. Once the chops are golden brown, reduce the heat to low and cook for another 4-5 minutes until they are cooked through. 4. Place the chops on a serving plate, garnish with the remaining rosemary and serve.
Per Serving: Calories 198; Fat 15g; Sodium 865mg; Carbs 0g; Fiber 0g; Sugar 0g; Protein 16g

Keto Crusted Lamb Chops

Prep time: 10 minutes | Cook time: 75 minutes | Serves: 2

2 lamb chops, 1-inch thick
2 teaspoons Dijon mustard
½ cup ground almonds
10 asparagus spears, trimmed

4 cherry tomatoes
Salt and ground black pepper to taste

1. Preheat the oven to 350°F/175°C. 2. Spice the lamb chops with salt and pepper. Coat the chops with mustard and sprinkle with ground almonds until covered. Reserve a bit of the almond for the vegetables. 3. Arrange the lamb chops in a roasting pan and roast for about 50-60 minutes until they acquire a golden crust. 4. Coat the asparagus and cherry tomatoes with oil, and then sprinkle the remaining ground almonds over the vegetables—roast next to the chops for about 15 minutes. Serve hot.
Per Serving: Calories 219; Fat 14g; Sodium 1714mg; Carbs 6g; Fiber 4g; Sugar 2g; Protein 15g

Tunisian Lamb Ragout

Prep time: 10 minutes | Cooking time: 8 hours | Serves: 6

¼ cup olive oil
1½ pounds lamb shoulder, cut into 1-inch chunks
1 sweet onion, chopped
1 tablespoon minced garlic
4 cups pumpkin, cut into 1-inch pieces

2 carrots, diced
1 (14.5-ounce) can diced tomatoes
3 cups beef broth
2 tablespoons Ras el Hanout
1 teaspoon hot chili powder
1 teaspoon salt
1 cup Greek yogurt

1. Lightly grease the slow cooker insert with 1 tablespoon olive oil. 2. Place a suitable skillet over medium–high heat and add the remaining oil. 3. Brown the lamb for almost 6 minutes, then add the onion and garlic. 4. Sauté for 3 minutes more, then transfer the lamb and vegetables to the insert. 5. Add the pumpkin, carrots, tomatoes, broth, Ras el Hanout, chili powder, and salt to the insert and stir to combine. 6. Cover and cook on low for almost 8 hours. Serve topped with yogurt.
Per Serving: Calories 423; Total Fat 18.4g; Sodium 137mg; Total Carbs 4.6g; Fiber 1.9g; Sugars 0.8g; Protein 56.2g

Sweet-and-Sour Pork Chops

Prep time: 10 minutes | Cooking time: 6 hours | Serves: 4

3 tablespoons olive oil, extra-virgin
1 pound boneless pork chops
½ cup granulated erythritol
¼ cup chicken broth
¼ cup tomato paste
2 tablespoons coconut aminos
2 tablespoons red chili paste
2 teaspoons minced garlic
¼ teaspoon salt
¼ teaspoon black pepper

1. Lightly grease the insert of the slow cooker with 1 tablespoon of the olive oil. 2. In a suitable skillet over medium-high heat, heat the remaining 2 tablespoons of the olive oil. Add the pork chops, brown for almost 5 minutes, and transfer to the insert. 3. In a suitable bowl, stir the erythritol, broth, tomato paste, coconut aminos, chili paste, garlic, salt, and pepper. Add the sauce to the chops. 4. Cover and cook on low for almost 6 hours. Serve warm.
Per Serving: Calories 340; Total Fat 27.7g; Sodium 109mg; Total Carbs 2.6g; Fiber 0.3g; Sugars 3g; Protein 15.7g

Cheese-Stuffed Tenderloin

Prep time: 10 minutes | Cooking time: 25 minutes | Serves: 2

½ pound pork tenderloin
2 tablespoons grated pecorino cheese
2 tablespoons crumbled feta cheese
1 green onion, chopped
1 tablespoon cashews, finely crushed
½ teaspoon onion, diced

Essentials
Salt and ground black pepper, to taste

1. Preheat grill. 2. Using a sharp knife, cut a pocket, running lengthwise, into the pork tenderloin. 3. Place the green onion, onions, crushed cashews, pecorino cheese, and feta cheese in a suitable bowl and mix well to combine. 4. Spoon the prepared mixture into the pocket and secure the pocket with a skewer or wrap in butcher's twine. 5. Sprinkle the pork with salt and freshly ground pepper and grill until golden brown and juices run clear.
Per Serving: Calories 347; Total Fat 17.7g; Sodium 1655mg; Total Carbs 6.8g; Fiber 1.2g; Sugars 2.8g; Protein 33.3g

Lemon Pork

Prep time: 10 minutes | Cooking time: 8 hours 10 minutes | Serves: 6

3 tablespoons olive oil
1 tablespoon butter
2 pounds pork loin roast
½ teaspoon salt
¼ teaspoon black pepper
¼ cup chicken broth
Juice and zest of 1 lemon
1 tablespoon minced garlic
½ cup heavy (whipping) cream

1. Lightly grease the insert of the slow cooker with 1 tablespoon of the olive oil. 2. In a suitable skillet over medium-high heat, heat the remaining 2 tablespoons of the olive oil and the butter. 3. Rub the pork with black pepper and salt. 4. Add the pork to the skillet and brown the roast on all sides for almost 10 minutes. Transfer it to the insert. 5. In a suitable bowl, stir the broth, lemon juice and zest, and garlic. 6. Add the broth mixture to the roast. 7. Cover, and cook on low for almost 7 to 8 hours. 8. Stir in the heavy cream and serve.
Per Serving: Calories 786; Total Fat 24.2g; Sodium 252mg; Total Carbs 1.6g; Fiber 3.9g; Sugars 22.8g; Protein 106.9g

Chapter 6 Fish and Seafood

Buttery Snow Crab Legs 72

Delicious Shrimp Stir-Fry 72

Silky Buttered Scallops 72

Garlic Butter Shrimp with Asparagus ... 72

Tangy Buttery Lobster Tail 72

Lobster in Mac 'N' Cheese................. 72

Salmon Burger 72

Spicy Creamy Shrimp 73

Shrimp with Cauliflower Rice 73

Tangy Dill Salmon......................... 73

Foiled Salmon 73

Nutty Pesto Salmon 73

Blackened Salmon......................... 73

Salmon Stuffed Avocado Boats........... 73

Fish in Taco Bowls 73

Tangy Cod 74

Redfish with Spicy Crawfish Cream Sauce 74

Golden Coconut Mahi-Mahi 74

Macadamia Halibut with Mango Coulis 74

Seared Mackerel 74

Baked Mackerel with Green Veggies ... 74

Garlicky Parmesan Crusted Salmon 75

Salmon in Creamy Sauce 75

Roasted Sea Bass 75

Delicious Sesame Salmon 75

Ginger Steamed Fish 75

Teriyaki Salmon with Spicy Mayo and Vegetables 75

Classical Salmon Poke 75

Charred Salmon with Garlic Green Beans 76

Traditional Sushi 76

Smoked Salmon Sushi Roll 76

Salmon with Cauliflower Pilaf 76

Pepper-Crusted Salmon 76

Sheet Pan Salmon with Beans 76

Salmon in Brown Butter Sauce 77

Roasted Salmon with Olive Salsa 77

Tangy Salmon and Asparagus 77

Dijon-Ginger Salmon 77

Delicious Glazed Salmon 77

Pan-Seared Garlicky Salmon.............. 77

Salmon with Delicious Tarragon-Dijon Sauce 77

Nut-Crusted Salmon 77

Grilled Salmon Packets 78

Classical Salmon Gratin 78

Seared Salmon 78

Roasted Herb-Crusted Salmon with Colors 78

Traditional Salmon Cakes 78

Curried Salmon Cakes 78

Tropical Ginger Salmon Burgers 78

Salmon Cakes 79

Chef's Snapper Veracruz 79

Salmon-Stuffed Mushrooms 79

Crispy Fish Sticks 79

Ahi Tuna Steaks with Bagel Seasoning... 79

Hot and Tangy Shrimp 79

Traditional Fish Tacos 79

Crispy Coconut Shrimp.................... 80

Wrapped Scallops 80

Garlic Scallops 80

Crab-Stuffed Boats 80

Traditional Lobster Tails 80

Delicious Tuna Cakes 80

Yummy Italian Baked Cod 80

Citrus-Marinated Tilapia 80

Delicious Rainbow Salmon Kebabs 81

Spicy Fish Bowl 81

Delicious Cajun Salmon 81

Southern-Style Catfish Steak 81

Sweet Buttery Salmon 81

Cheesy Lobster Tails 81

Regular Crab Cakes 81

Spiced Snow Crab Legs 81

Lemon Butter Cod Steak 82

Tuna Tomatoes 82

Nut-Crusted Mahi Mahi 82

Regular Salmon Patties 82

Halibut in a Blanket 82

Crispy Fish with Tartar Sauce 82

Instant Shrimp 82

Shrimp Alfredo and Zoodles 83

Cajun Crab Legs And Veggies 83

Delicious Shrimp Scampi 83

Crispy Keto Baked Fish 83

Oven-Fried Catfish 83

Nutty Halibut Curry 83

Nut-Crusted Catfish 84

Crispy Fried Cod Sticks 84

Cream-Poached Trout 84

Cod with Green Pistou 84

Roasted Cod with Garlic Butter 84

Pan-Fried Shrimp Balls over Garlicky Greens 84

Crispy Cod Cakes 85

Baked Halibut Steak with Herb Sauce ... 85

Pesto Flounder with Greens 85

Baked Haddock 85

Cheesy Fried Haddock 85

Seared Cod with Coconut-Mushroom Sauce 85

Teriyaki Halibut............................. 86

Baked Keto Halibut 86

Pan-Fried Salmon and Bok Choy

In Miso Vinaigrette 86

Halibut with Tangy Basil Sauce 86

Crispy Haddock............................. 86

Thai-Inspired Seafood Chowder 86

Buttery Snow Crab Legs

Prep time: 4 minutes | Cook time: 7 minutes | Serves: 2

2 pounds crab legs
1 cup water
4 tablespoons butter

1 garlic clove, finely minced
½ lemon, juiced
4 lemon wedges

1. Rinse crab legs. Pour water into Instant Pot. Place steamer basket and crab legs into Instant Pot. Click lid closed. 2. Select the Steam setting and adjust the time for 7 minutes. When the timer beeps, quick-release the pressure. Crab legs will be bright pink when done. 3. In a bowl, melt butter and add garlic. 4. Squeeze lemon juice into butter or over legs and crack legs open. Serve with butter sauce and lemon wedges.

Per Serving: Calories 511; Fat 22.5g; Sodium 3036mg; Carbs 1g; Fiber 0.1g; Sugar 0.1g; Protein 66.7g

Delicious Shrimp Stir-Fry

Prep time: 11 minutes | Cook time: 10 minutes | Serves: 4

2 tablespoons coconut oil
1-pound medium shrimp, shelled and deveined
½ cup button mushrooms
½ cup diced zucchini

2 cups broccoli florets
¼ cup soy sauce or liquid aminos
2 cloves garlic, minced
⅛ teaspoon red pepper flakes
2 cups cooked cauliflower rice

1. Press the Sauté button of the instant pot and add coconut oil. 2. Cook shrimp in it for 5 minutes until fully cooked. 3. Remove from pot and set aside. 4. Add mushrooms with zucchini, broccoli, soy sauce, garlic, and red pepper flakes to pot and stir-fry for 3–5 minutes until fork-tender. 5. Add shrimp back to pot. 6. Separate premade, warmed cauliflower rice into each plate and top with a portion of stir-fry. Serve warm.

Per Serving: Calories 173; Fat 7.4g; Sodium 1538mg; Carbs 7g; Fiber 1.4g; Sugar 1.6g; Protein 19g

Silky Buttered Scallops

Prep time: 5 minutes | Cook time: 5 minutes | Serves: 4

2 tablespoons avocado oil
1-pound large sea scallops
⅛ teaspoon salt

⅛ teaspoon pepper
2 tablespoons melted butter

1. Press the Sauté button and add avocado oil to Instant Pot. Allow to fully preheat. 2. Remove side muscle from scallops. Pat dry with towel and sprinkle with salt and pepper. 3. When Instant Pot reads "hot," carefully add scallops to the pan and sear for 2 minutes. 4. Carefully turn and sear opposite side for 2–3 minutes. They will appear opaque all the way through when finished. 5. Pour butter over scallops and serve hot.

Per Serving: Calories 190; Fat 12.4g; Sodium 517mg; Carbs 3.7g; Fiber 0g; Sugar 0g; Protein 13g

Garlic Butter Shrimp with Asparagus

Prep time: 5 minutes | Cook time: 3 minutes | Serves: 2

1-pound uncooked peeled shrimp, deveined
1 clove garlic, finely minced
½ teaspoon salt
¼ teaspoon pepper
¼ teaspoon paprika
⅛ teaspoon red pepper flakes

½ pound asparagus, cut into bite-sized pieces
Juice of ½ lemon
4 tablespoons butter
2 teaspoons chopped fresh parsley
1 cup water

1. Sprinkle shrimp with garlic, salt, pepper, paprika, and red pepper flakes and place in 7-cup glass bowl. Place asparagus in bowl. 2. Squeeze lemon juice over shrimp and asparagus and gently mix. Cut butter into cubes and place around dish. 3. Sprinkle with parsley. Cover with foil. Place steam rack and add water to Instant Pot. 4. Carefully place dish on steam rack and click lid closed. 5. Select the Steam setting and adjust the time for 3 minutes. When the timer beeps, quick-release the pressure. 6. Remove dish from pot. Serve warm.

Per Serving: Calories 381; Fat 23.3g; Sodium 1868mg; Carbs 5.9g; Fiber 1.6g; Sugar 1.5g; Protein 32.7g

Tangy Buttery Lobster Tail

Prep time: 5 minutes | Cook time: 4 minutes | Serves: 2

1 cup chicken broth
½ cup water
1 teaspoon Old Bay seasoning
2 (12-ounce) fresh lobster tails
Juice of ½ lemon

2 tablespoons butter, melted
¼ teaspoon salt
¼ teaspoon dried parsley
⅛ teaspoon pepper

1. Pour broth, water, and Old Bay seasoning into Instant Pot. Place steam rack in bottom. Place lobster tails on a steam rack, shell side down. Click lid closed. 2. Select the Manual setting of the pot and adjust the time for 4 minutes. When the timer beeps, quick-release the pressure. 3. In small bowl, combine lemon juice, butter, salt, parsley, and pepper. 4. Crack open tail and dip into butter sauce.

Per Serving: Calories 259; Fat 17.3g; Sodium 1160mg; Carbs 0.8g; Fiber 0.1g; Sugar 0.3g; Protein 32.9g

Lobster in Mac 'N' Cheese

Prep time: 11 minutes | Cook time: 15 minutes | Serves: 4

1 head cauliflower, chopped into bite-sized pieces
1 cup water
4 tablespoons butter
½ medium onion, diced
4 ounces cream cheese
¼ cup heavy cream

½ cup grated Gruyère cheese
½ cup shredded sharp cheddar cheese
1 teaspoon hot sauce
1 teaspoon salt
½ teaspoon pepper
1-pound cooked lobster meat

1. Place cauliflower on steamer basket. Add water to Instant Pot and place a steamer basket in bottom of pot. Click lid closed. Select the Steam setting and adjust the time for 1 minute. 2. When the timer beeps, quick-release the pressure and remove steamer basket. Set cauliflower aside. Pour water out of the pot and wipe dry. 3. Replace pot and press the Sauté button. Press the Adjust setting to set heat to Less. Add butter and onion. Sauté for 3–5 minutes or until onion becomes soft and fragrant. 4. Soften cream cheese in microwave and stir with spoon until smooth. Add cream cheese to Instant Pot. 5. Press the Cancel button. Press the Sauté button and Press the Adjust setting to set heat to Normal. 6. Add heavy cream to pot and simmer. Continuously stir until ingredients are fully incorporated. Press the Cancel button. 7. Add shredded cheeses and stir quickly to melt. Add cooked cauliflower into pot, stirring until fully coated with cheese. 8. Add hot sauce and seasoning. Chop lobster into bite-sized pieces and fold into pot. 9. Serve warm.

Per Serving: Calories 521; Fat 33.8g; Sodium 1500mg; Carbs 9g; Fiber 4.5g; Sugar 6g; Protein 35.3g

Salmon Burger

Prep time: 11 minutes | Cook time: 5 minutes | Serves: 4

2 tablespoons coconut oil
1-pound salmon filets
½ teaspoon salt
¼ teaspoon garlic powder
¼ teaspoon chili powder
2 tablespoons finely diced onion

1 egg
2 tablespoons mayo
⅓ cup finely ground pork rinds
1 avocado
Juice of ½ lime

1. Press the Sauté button and Press the Adjust setting to set heat to Less. Add coconut oil to Instant Pot. Allow to fully preheat to become nonstick. 2. Remove skin from salmon filet. Finely mince salmon and place in a large bowl. Add remaining ingredients except avocado and lime to a bowl and form 4 patties. 3. Place burgers into the pot and sear each side for about 3–4 minutes until center feels firm and reads 145°F/65°C on meat thermometer. Press the Cancel button and set aside. 4. Scoop out avocado flesh. In a bowl, mash avocado and squeeze in juice from lime. Divide mash into four sections and place on top of salmon burgers. 5. Serve warm.

Per Serving: Calories 425; Fat 27.6g; Sodium 668mg; Carbs 3.8g; Fiber 2.5g; Sugar 0.4g; Protein 35.6g

Spicy Creamy Shrimp

Prep time: 5 minutes | Cook time: 7 minutes | Serves: 2

1-pound shrimp, peeled and
deveined
½ teaspoon Old Bay seasoning
¼ teaspoon salt
¼ teaspoon pepper

⅛ teaspoon cayenne
⅛ teaspoon garlic powder
1 cup water
¼ cup mayo
2 tablespoons chili paste

1. Toss shrimp in a 7-cup glass bowl with Old Bay seasoning, salt, pepper, cayenne, and garlic. 2. Pour water into Instant Pot. Place steam rack into pot and place bowl with shrimp on top. Click lid closed and press the Steam button. Adjust time for 7 minutes. 3. When the timer beeps, do a quick release and carefully remove bowl from Instant Pot. Drain water. 4. In a bowl, mix mayo and chili paste. Add to shrimp and toss to coat. Serve warm.
Per Serving: Calories 399; Fat 34.3g; Sodium 2259mg; Carbs 8.6g; Fiber 0.1g; Sugar 4.2g; Protein 32.2g

Shrimp with Cauliflower Rice

Prep time: 4 minutes | Cook time: 5 minutes | Serves: 2

1-pound shrimp, peeled and
deveined
½ teaspoon salt
¼ teaspoon pepper
¼ teaspoon garlic powder

¼ teaspoon dried parsley
6 asparagus spears
1 cup water
2 tablespoons butter
1 cup uncooked cauliflower rice

1. Sprinkle seasoning on shrimp and place on steamer basket. Cut asparagus into bite-sized pieces and add to steamer basket. 2. Pour water into Instant Pot and place steamer basket in bottom. Select the Steam setting and adjust the time for 5 minutes. 3. When the timer beeps, quick-release the pressure. Remove steamer basket and pour water out of Instant Pot. Replace pot and press the Sauté button. 4. Add butter to Instant Pot, cauliflower rice, cooked shrimp, and asparagus. Stir-fry for 3–5 minutes until cauliflower is tender.
Per Serving: Calories 283; Fat 12.4g; Sodium 1876mg; Carbs 6.4g; Fiber 2.1g; Sugar 1.9g; Protein 33.1g

Tangy Dill Salmon

Prep time: 4 minutes | Cook time: 5 minutes | Serves: 2

2 (1-inch-thick, 3-ounce) salmon
filets
1 teaspoon fresh dill
½ teaspoon salt

¼ teaspoon pepper
1 cup water
2 tablespoons lemon juice
½ lemon, sliced

1. Spice salmon with dill, salt to taste, and pepper. 2. Place steam rack in the Instant Pot and add water in it. 3. Place spiced salmon on steam rack, skin side down. 4. Spread lemon juice over filets and lemon slices on top. 5. Press the Steam button setting and adjust the time to 5 minutes. Quick-release the pressure. 6. Serve with additional dill and lemon slices.
Per Serving: Calories 127; Fat 4.9g; Sodium 618mg; Carbs 1.8g; Fiber 0.3g; Sugar 0.4g; Protein 17g

Foiled Salmon

Prep time: 2 minutes | Cook time: 7 minutes | Serves: 2

2 (3-ounce) salmon filets
1 teaspoon salt
¼ teaspoon pepper
¼ teaspoon garlic powder

¼ teaspoon dried dill
½ lemon
1 cup water

1. Place each filet of salmon skin side down on a square of foil. Sprinkle with seasoning and squeeze lemon juice over fish. 2. Slice lemon into four pieces and place two on each filet. Close foil packet by folding over edges. 3. Pour water into Instant Pot and place steam rack in bottom of pot. Place foil packets on the steam rack. Select the Steam setting and adjust the time for 7 minutes. 4. When the timer beeps, quick-release the pressure. 5. Salmon should easily flake when fully cooked.
Per Serving: Calories 125; Fat 4.6g; Sodium 1201mg; Carbs 0.5g; Fiber 0.1g; Sugar 0g; Protein 18g

Nutty Pesto Salmon

Prep time: 5 minutes | Cook time: 7 minutes | Serves: 4

¼ cup sliced almonds
1 tablespoon butter
4 (3-ounce) salmon filets
½ cup pesto

½ teaspoon salt
¼ teaspoon pepper
1 cup water

1. Place almonds and butter into Instant Pot. Press the Sauté button. Sauté almonds for 3–5 minutes until they begin to soften. Remove and set aside. Press the Cancel button. 2. Brush salmon filets with pesto and add salt and pepper. Pour water into Instant Pot and place steam rack in bottom. 3. Add salmon to steam rack. Select the Steam setting and adjust the time for 7 minutes. 4. Serve warm with almond slices on top.
Per Serving: Calories 182; Fat 20g; Sodium 689mg; Carbs 4.3g; Fiber 1.3g; Sugar 1.3g; Protein 21g

Blackened Salmon

Prep time: 5 minutes | Cook time: 5 minutes | Serves: 2

2 (3-ounce) salmon filets
1 tablespoon avocado oil
1 teaspoon paprika
½ teaspoon salt

¼ teaspoon pepper
¼ teaspoon onion powder
¼ teaspoon dried thyme
⅛ teaspoon cayenne pepper

1. Drizzle avocado oil over salmon. Mix remaining ingredients in a bowl and rub over filets. 2. Press the Sauté button and place salmon into Instant Pot. Sear for 2–5 minutes until seasoning is blackened and easily flakes with fork.
Per Serving: Calories 190; Fat 11.4g; Sodium 620mg; Carbs 1.1g; Fiber 0.6g; Sugar 0.2g; Protein 18.6g

Salmon Stuffed Avocado Boats

Prep time: 11 minutes | Cook time: 7 minutes | Serves: 2

2 (3-ounce) salmon filets
½ teaspoon salt
¼ teaspoon pepper
1 cup water

⅓ cup mayo
Juice of ½ lemon
2 avocados
½ teaspoon fresh dill, chopped

1. Sprinkle salt and pepper over salmon filets. Pour water into Instant Pot and place steam rack on bottom. 2. Place salmon skin side down on steam rack. Click lid closed. Press the Steam button and adjust the timer for 7 minutes. 3. When the timer beeps, quick-release the pressure. Check to ensure salmon is fully cooked, with an internal temperature reaching 145°F/65°C. Set aside to cool. 4. In a large bowl, mix mayo with lemon juice. Cut avocados in half. Remove pits and dice avocados. Add avocados to a large bowl and gently fold into mixture. 5. Use a fork to flake apart salmon into bite-sized pieces, and gently fold into mixture. 6. Serve garnished with fresh dill.
Per Serving: Calories 602; Fat 50g; Sodium 863mg; Carbs 12.8g; Fiber 39.4g; Sugar 0.8g; Protein 21.5g

Fish in Taco Bowls

Prep time: 16 minutes | Cook time: 5 minutes | Serves: 4

4 cups shredded cabbage
¼ cup mayo
2 tablespoons sour cream
1 lime, halved
2 tablespoons chopped pickled
jalapeños
3 (4-ounce) tilapia filets
2 teaspoons chili powder

1 teaspoon cumin
1 teaspoon garlic powder
1 teaspoon salt
2 tablespoons coconut oil
1 avocado, diced
4 tablespoons fresh chopped
cilantro

1. Mix cabbage, mayo, sour cream, lime juice, and jalapeños. Chill for at least 30 minutes before serving. 2. Select the Sauté setting on Instant Pot. Pat dry fillet and sprinkle evenly with spices. 3. Add oil to the pot and heat it. Add tilapia fillet and sear each side for 2–4 minutes. 4. Cut fish into bite-sized pieces. Divide slaw into four bowls and place fish on top. 5. Cut avocado and scoop out flesh. Divide avocado among bowls. 6. Squeeze lime juice over fish and slaw and sprinkle with cilantro.
Per Serving: Calories 328; Fat 23.8g; Sodium 259mg; Carbs 9g; Fiber 4.8g; Sugar 2.8g; Protein 19.4g

Tangy Cod

Prep time: 5 minutes | Cook time: 15 minutes | Serves: 4

2 tablespoons butter
¼ cup diced onion
1 clove garlic, minced
1 cup cherry tomatoes
¼ teaspoon salt
⅛ teaspoon pepper
¼ teaspoon dried thyme

¼ cup chicken broth
1 tablespoon capers
4 (4-ounce) cod filets
1 cup water
¼ cup fresh chopped Italian parsley

1. Press the Sauté button and add butter and onions to Instant Pot. Add garlic in the cooked onion and cook additional 30 seconds. 2. Slice tomatoes in half and add salt, pepper, thyme, and chicken broth to the pot. Continue cooking sauce for 5–7 minutes or until tomatoes soften. Press the Cancel button. 3. Pour sauce into 7-cup glass bowl. Add capers and fish filets. Cover with foil. Pour water into Instant Pot and place steam rack on bottom. Place bowl on top. 4. Click lid closed. Select the Manual setting of the pot and adjust the time for 3 minutes. If using a frozen filet, add 2–3 additional minutes. 5. When the timer beeps, quick-release the pressure. Sprinkle with fresh parsley and serve.

Per Serving: Calories 157; Fat 7.3g; Sodium 261mg; Carbs 2.2g; Fiber 0.9g; Sugar 1.5g; Protein 21g

Redfish with Spicy Crawfish Cream Sauce

Prep time: 11 minutes | Cook time: 20 minutes | Serves: 4

For the blackened redfish
1 tablespoon paprika
2 teaspoons kosher salt
1 teaspoon onion powder
1 teaspoon garlic powder
1 teaspoon freshly ground black pepper
For the cream sauce
2 tablespoons butter
¼ cup sliced scallion
2 garlic cloves, finely minced
⅓ cup chicken broth

½ teaspoon dried thyme
½ teaspoon dried oregano
¼ teaspoon cayenne pepper
4 (4-ounce) redfish fillets, skinned and boned
5 tablespoons butter, melted

2 tablespoons white wine
1 cup heavy (whipping) cream
1-pound crawfish tails, thawed if frozen

1. In a small bowl, stir the paprika, salt, onion powder, garlic powder, black pepper, thyme, oregano, and cayenne. Set aside. 2. Place the fillets on paper towels and pat dry. Place the 3 tablespoons melted butter in a shallow dish. 3. Dredge each fillet in the melted butter, coating each side well. Liberally sprinkle both sides of the fillets with the blackening seasoning. 4. Reserve ½ teaspoon of seasoning. Preheat a heavy skillet over medium to medium-high heat for 2 to 3 minutes. Add the remaining 2 tablespoons of butter to the pan to melt. Quickly add the fillets to the hot pan and sear for 2 to 3 minutes per side, or until done. 5. Remove the fillets from the pan. 6. Add the butter, scallion, garlic, and reserved ½ teaspoon of seasoning in same skillet. Sauté for 1 to 2 minutes. Add the chicken broth and wine. Cook until reduced by half, stirring constantly to pick up the browned parts left on the bottom of the pan. 7. Add the heavy cream and simmer the sauce for 3 to 4 minutes, stirring constantly until thickened. Add the crawfish tails and stir until heated through. 8. Serve the sauce over the blackened fillets.

Per Serving: Calories 670; Fat 46g; Sodium 812mg; Carbs 6g; Fiber 1g; Sugar 1g; Protein 58g

Golden Coconut Mahi-Mahi

Prep time: 5 minutes | Cook time: 25 minutes | Serves: 1

1 tablespoon coconut oil
1 teaspoon ground turmeric
½ teaspoon smoked paprika

1 (6-ounce) mahi-mahi fillet
Pink Himalayan salt
Freshly ground black pepper

1. Preheat the oven to 425°F/220°C. Line a baking sheet with parchment paper. Mix coconut oil, turmeric, and paprika in a small bowl. 2. Place the mahi-mahi on the prepared baking sheet. Season with salt and pepper to taste. Rub the mahi-mahi with the coconut oil mixture and evenly coat. 3. Roast for 20 to 25 minutes, or until the mahi-mahi is cooked through.

Per Serving: Calories 308; Fat 16g; Sodium 853mg; Carbs 2g; Fiber 1g; Sugar 0.2g; Protein 40g

Macadamia Halibut with Mango Coulis

Prep time: 11 minutes | Cook time: 10 minutes | Serves: 4

½ cup finely chopped macadamia nuts
½ teaspoon sea salt
¼ teaspoon freshly ground black pepper
¼ teaspoon garlic powder
½ teaspoon onion powder

1¼ pounds halibut, cut into 4 (5-ounce) fillets
2 tablespoons coconut oil
½ cup diced mango
1 tablespoon lime juice
½ cup full-fat coconut milk
4 sprigs fresh cilantro, for garnish

1. Preheat the oven to 425°F/220°C. Prepare a rimmed baking sheet with parchment lining. 2. Mix the macadamia nuts, salt, pepper, garlic powder, and onion powder in a shallow dish. Coat the halibut fillets in the coconut oil and then dredge in the nut mixture. 3. Place the fillets onto the baking sheet, and bake for 12 minutes until the fish flakes easily with a fork. 4. While the halibut is cooking, in a blender, purée the mango, lime juice, and coconut milk until very smooth. 5. Drizzle a few tablespoons of the mango coulis over each plate and then top with the baked halibut and a sprig of cilantro.

Per Serving: Calories 423; Fat 27g; Sodium 632mg; Carbs 6g; Fiber 2g; Sugar 2g; Protein 40g

Seared Mackerel

Prep time: 11 minutes | Cook time: 20 minutes | Serves: 4

1-pound wild-caught mackerel fillets, cut into 4 pieces
1 teaspoon salt
½ teaspoon freshly ground black pepper
½ cup extra-virgin olive oil, divided
1 bunch asparagus, trimmed, cut

into 2-inch pieces
1 can artichoke hearts
4 large garlic cloves, peeled and crushed
2 bay leaves
¼ cup red wine vinegar
½ teaspoon smoked paprika

1. Season the fish fillets generously and let sit at room temperature for 5 minutes. 2. Heat oil and cook the fish skin side up for 5 minutes. Flip and cook for 5 minutes on the other side, until browned and cooked through. 3. Heat the oil in the same skillet and add the asparagus, artichokes, garlic, bay leaves, and sauté until the vegetables are tender for 6 to 8 minutes. 4. Using a slotted spoon, top the fish with the cooked vegetables, reserving the oil in the skillet. 5. Add the vinegar and paprika to the oil and whisk to combine well. Pour the vinaigrette over the fish and vegetables and let sit at room temperature. 6. Remove the bay leaf before serving.

Per Serving: Calories 578; Fat 50g; Sodium 589mg; Carbs 12g; Fiber 5g; Sugar 2g; Protein 26g

Baked Mackerel with Green Veggies

Prep time: 22 minutes | Cook time: 15 minutes | Serves: 4

2 cups chopped kale
1 cup asparagus, cut into 1-inch pieces
¼ onion, thinly sliced
2 teaspoons chopped fresh basil

4 (3-ounce) mackerel fillets
Sea salt
Freshly ground black pepper
¼ cup olive oil
1 lemon, cut into thin slices

1. Preheat the oven to 400°F/200°C. Lay out sheets of aluminum foil, each about 12-inches long. 2. Place ½ cup kale, ¼ cup asparagus, a quarter of the onion slices, and ½ teaspoon of basil in the middle of each piece of foil. 3. Place a fillet on the vegetables and season the fish with salt and pepper. Drizzle the fish with olive oil and arrange lemon slices on top. 4. Fold the foil up to form loose packets. Set the packets on a baking sheet and bake until the fish is opaque, for about 15 minutes. 5. Open the packets carefully and serve.

Per Serving: Calories 327; Fat 26g; Sodium 744mg; Carbs 9g; Fiber 3g; Sugar 2g; Protein 18g

Garlicky Parmesan Crusted Salmon

Prep time: 16 minutes | Cook time: 15 minutes | Serves: 8

4 pounds salmon fillets, skin on
½ cup (1 stick) butter, melted
3 garlic cloves, minced
1 teaspoon salt
½ teaspoon freshly ground black

pepper
½ cup finely crushed pork skins
½ cup grated Parmesan cheese
1 lemon, for squeezing

1. Preheat the oven to 350°F/175°C temperature setting, and prepare a baking sheet with parchment paper. Place the salmon fillets, skin-side down, on the lined baking sheet. 2. In a small bowl, mix the butter and garlic. 3. Spread or brush over the salmon. Season the fillets with spices, and then sprinkle with the crushed pork skins and Parmesan. 4. Bake the fish for 15 minutes and remove from the oven, and squeeze lemon over the top.
Per Serving: Calories 532; Fat 32g; Sodium 622mg; Carbs 1g; Fiber 0g; Sugar 0g; Protein 56g

Salmon in Creamy Sauce

Prep time: 11 minutes | Cook time: 10 minutes | Serves: 4

4 (5- to 6-ounce) fillets, about an inch thick, patted dry
1 tablespoon olive oil
¼ teaspoon salt
⅛ teaspoon freshly ground black

pepper
⅓ cup sour cream
⅓ cup mayonnaise
½ teaspoon Dijon mustard
½ cup heavy (whipping) cream

1. Heat a nonstick skillet over medium heat. 2. Drizzle the fillet with olive oil, and spice both sides with salt and pepper. Place each fillet, skin-side up, in the hot pan, and allow to sear, undisturbed, for about 4 minutes. Flip, and cook until cooked through. 3. Transfer the fillets to a serving plate. Meanwhile whisk the sour cream, mayonnaise, and Dijon mustard. 4. Beat the cream with an electric hand mixer on high, until soft peaks form, about 1 minute, and fold into the sour cream mixture. 5. Pour the sauce into the skillet and warm over low heat for 1 to 2 minutes. Serve the salmon topped with the cream sauce.
Per Serving: Calories 530; Fat 42g; Sodium 633mg; Carbs 2g; Fiber 0g; Sugar 0g; Protein 34g

Roasted Sea Bass

Prep time: 16 minutes | Cook time: 25 minutes | Serves: 4

2 whole sea bass (about 2 pounds), cleaned and scaled
2 tablespoons olive or avocado oil
Salt
Freshly ground black pepper
1 red onion, cut into ¼-inch slices

3 lemons, sliced into rounds
1 large leek, sliced into rounds
8 dried bay leaves
3 tablespoons fresh oregano
Nut-free pesto, for serving

1. Preheat the oven to 425°F/220°C. Place the fish in a dish and brush the fish with the oil. Season with salt and pepper. 2. Fill the cavity of fish with the onion, lemon, and leek slices, and the bay leaves and oregano. 3. Roast the fish for about 25 minutes, or until the skin is crispy and the fish is flaky. 4. To serve, remove the head and tail, then cut the fish into 4 equal-size fillets. 5. Serve with nut-free pesto, if desired.
Per Serving: Calories 307; Fat 19g; Sodium 541mg; Carbs 8g; Fiber 3g; Sugar 2g; Protein 26g

Delicious Sesame Salmon

Prep time: 16 minutes | Cook time: 15 minutes | Serves: 4

Olive oil, for greasing
2 tablespoons soy sauce
2 tablespoons rice vinegar
4 teaspoons sesame oil
4 (5-ounce) boneless salmon

fillets
Sea salt
Freshly ground black pepper
¼ cup sesame seeds
2 teaspoons chopped fresh thyme

1. Preheat the oven to 425°F/220°C. Grease a 9-by-13-inch baking dish with oil, and set aside. 2. Whisk the soy sauce, rice vinegar, and sesame oil in a small bowl. Dry the salmon with paper towels, and lightly season both sides of the fillets with salt and pepper. 3. Place the salmon in the baking dish. Pour the soy mixture over the salmon, and bake the fish in the oven until it is just cooked through, for about 13 to 15 minutes. 4. Top the salmon with sesame seeds and chopped thyme, and serve.
Per Serving: Calories 303; Fat 19g; Sodium 1002mg; Carbs 3g; Fiber 1g; Sugar 0g; Protein 30g

Ginger Steamed Fish

Prep time: 5 minutes | Cook time: 25 minutes | Serves: 4

4 scallions, white part chopped, green part cut in 2- to 3-inch pieces and sliced lengthwise in half
2 garlic cloves, minced
1½ thumb-size pieces fresh

ginger, thinly sliced
1 (4- to 5-pound) head-on tilapia
1 tablespoon soy sauce
2 teaspoons rice wine vinegar
2 teaspoons sesame oil

1. Preheat the oven to 400°F/200°C temperature setting, and put parchment paper in a large baking tray, with a little extra room for the foil on the ends and sides. Place a piece of aluminum foil, large enough to fold over the fish and seal, on top of the parchment paper. 2. Place one-third of the green and white scallions, garlic, and ginger across the bottom of the foil, and then place the fish on top. 3. Open the fish cavity, and place another third of the scallions, garlic, and ginger inside. 4. Close the fish, and top with the remaining garlic and ginger, reserving the remaining scallions for garnish. 5. Whisk the soy sauce, vinegar, and sesame oil in a small bowl, and drizzle over the fish. 6. Fold the foil over and roll the edges a couple of times to seal the foil pouch. Bake for 25 minutes. Remove the foil, plate the fish, and sprinkle the remaining scallions on top.
Per Serving: Calories 272; Fat 7g; Sodium 556mg; Carbs 3g; Fiber 1g; Sugar 0.1g; Protein 51g

Teriyaki Salmon with Spicy Mayo and Vegetables

Prep time: 22 minutes | Cook time: 25 minutes | Serves: 2

For the spicy mayo
2 teaspoons minced garlic
1 tablespoon freshly squeezed lemon juice
1 large egg
½ teaspoon salt
For salmon and asparagus
12 asparagus spears, trimmed
½ teaspoon minced fresh ginger
2 teaspoons olive oil, divided
½ teaspoon rice wine vinegar
¼ teaspoon freshly ground black

1 tablespoon cayenne pepper
⅛ teaspoon freshly ground black pepper
½ cup olive oil

pepper
¼ cup sugar-free teriyaki sauce
2 (8-ounce) salmon fillets
Sliced scallions, for garnish

1. In a food processor, add garlic and lemon juice with the egg, salt, cayenne pepper, and black pepper to the garlic and lemon juice purée. 2. While puréeing, slowly add the olive oil until the mayo forms. Refrigerate while the fillets cook. Preheat the oven to 400°F/200°C. 3. Mix the ginger, 1 teaspoon of olive oil, rice wine vinegar, pepper, and the teriyaki sauce in a medium bowl. 4. Cover the salmon completely with the sauce. Line a baking dish with aluminum foil. 5. Move the salmon from the sauce to the baking dish. Pour any remaining sauce on top of the fillets. Stack the asparagus around the fillets and drizzle them with the olive oil. 6. Bake the fish with veggies for 15 to 20 minutes. Remove the fish from the oven. 7. Serve immediately with the spicy mayo. Garnish with the scallions.
Per Serving: Calories 577; Fat 42g; Sodium 689mg; Carbs 13g; Fiber 3g; Sugar 2g; Protein 42g

Classical Salmon Poke

Prep time: 5 minutes | Cook time: 0 minutes | Serves: 2

½ pound sushi-grade salmon, chopped into ½-inch cubes
¼ red onion, finely chopped
1 tablespoon dried chives
½ tablespoon capers
1 tablespoon dried basil
1 teaspoon Dijon mustard

½ teaspoon olive oil
Juice of ½ small lemon
Salt
Freshly ground black pepper
1 cucumber, sliced into rounds, for serving

1. Mix the salmon, red onion, chives, capers, basil, mustard, olive oil, and lemon juice in a bowl, and spice with salt and pepper. 2. If desired, spoon the poke onto cucumber rounds.
Per Serving: Calories 177; Fat 9g; Sodium 834mg; Carbs 1g; Fiber 0g; Sugar 0g; Protein 23g

Charred Salmon with Garlic Green Beans

Prep time: 16 minutes | Cook time: 25 minutes | Serves: 4

For the rub
2 tablespoons stevia, or other sugar substitute
1 tablespoon chili powder
1 teaspoon freshly ground black pepper
½ tablespoon ground cumin
½ tablespoon paprika
½ tablespoon salt
¼ teaspoon dry mustard
Dash cinnamon

For the salmon
¼ cup coconut oil
4 (4- to 6-ounce) salmon fillets
¼ cup Dijon mustard, divided
For the green beans
3 tablespoons butter
1 tablespoon olive oil
4 garlic cloves, minced
1-pound green beans
½ teaspoon salt
¼ teaspoon freshly ground black pepper

1. Combine the stevia and spices in a bowl. 2. Heat the oil in a skillet for about 5 minutes. 3. Coat each salmon fillet with mustard. 4. Add the salmon in the hot oil and sear for about 2 minutes. 5. Flip and reduce the heat to medium. 6. Cook the fish for 6 -minutes more, until the fish is opaque. 7. In another large skillet over medium heat, heat the butter and olive oil. Cook the garlic and cook until fragrant, about 1 minute. 8. Add the green beans, salt, and pepper. Cover and reduce the heat to medium-low. Cook it for 12 minutes, stirring occasionally. 9. Serve immediately alongside the salmon.
Per Serving: Calories 539; Fat 42g; Sodium 903mg; Carbs 12g; Fiber 6g; Sugar 2g; Protein 31g

Traditional Sushi

Prep time: 16 minutes | Cook time: 5 minutes | Serves: 2 to 4

4 cups cauliflower rice
2 tablespoons gelatin
1 tablespoon apple cider vinegar
1 teaspoon salt
2 to 4 nori sheets
½ pound sushi-grade fish, thinly sliced
1 avocado, halved
1 small cucumber (or any other vegetable you'd like), thinly sliced
Sesame seeds, for topping
Coconut aminos or tamari, wasabi, sugar-free pickled ginger, sliced avocado, and/or avocado oil mayonnaise mixed with sugar-free hot sauce, for serving

1. In a shallow saucepan with a lid, combine the cauliflower with 3 tablespoons of water. Turn the heat to medium, cover, and steam for 3 to 5 minutes. 2. Drain the cauliflower and transfer to a medium bowl. Stir in the gelatin, vinegar, and salt until the mixture is smooth and sticky. Set aside. 3. Spread a nori sheet on top of the plastic wrap, then spread with a layer of the cauliflower rice. Layer slices of fish, avocado, and cucumber over the cauliflower on the end of the nori sheet closest to you. 4. Gently roll the nori sheet over all the ingredients, using the towel as your rolling aid. 5. When you're done rolling, remove the towel and plastic wrap as you slide the roll onto a plate or cutting board. 6. With a knife, cut the roll into equal pieces. Repeat with the remaining nori and filling ingredients. Sprinkle sesame seeds on top of your sushi, if desired.
Per Serving: Calories 295; Fat 15g; Sodium 911mg; Carbs 10g; Fiber 8g; Sugar 2g; Protein 30g

Smoked Salmon Sushi Roll

Prep time: 16 minutes plus 20 minutes for refrigerating | Cook time: None | Serves: 4

14 ounces smoked salmon
1 tablespoon wasabi paste
¾ cup cream cheese, at room
temperature
½ avocado, sliced
1 tablespoon sesame seeds

1. Place the salmon on the plastic wrap, overlapping, to create a large rectangle 6 to 7 inches long and 4 inches wide. 2. Mix the wasabi paste and the cream cheese. 3. Spread the cream cheese mix evenly over the smoked salmon rectangle. 4. Place the avocado slices over the cream cheese, in the center of the fish. Roll the wrap into sushi. 5. Cover the salmon sushi roll in sesame seeds. 6. Refrigerate the sushi roll for 15 to 20 minutes. With a knife, slice into pieces and serve.
Per Serving: Calories 539; Fat 42g; Sodium 966mg; Carbs 12g; Fiber 6g; Sugar 6g; Protein 31g

Salmon with Cauliflower Pilaf

Prep time: 5 minutes | Cook time: 10 minutes | Serves: 4

1 medium head of cauliflower, riced
3 tablespoons coconut oil, melted, divided
1 tablespoon extra-virgin olive oil
1 teaspoon white wine vinegar
1 tablespoon minced preserved lemons
¼ cup roughly chopped mint
¼ cup roughly chopped pistachios
½ teaspoon salt, plus more for pilaf, divided
Freshly ground black pepper
4 (5-ounce) salmon fillets
1 teaspoon ground cumin
1 teaspoon ground coriander
1 teaspoon ground ginger
1 teaspoon paprika

1. Heat the oil and stir-fry the cauliflower for 5 minutes, until just heated through. Sprinkle in the olive oil, white wine vinegar, preserved lemons, mint, and pistachios, and toss gently to mix. Season with salt and pepper. Set aside. 2. Heat a large skillet until hot. In a bowl, combine the salt, cumin, coriander, ginger, and paprika. Coat the salmon fillets with the remaining 2 tablespoons of coconut oil and season with the spice mixture, ½ teaspoon salt, and pepper. 3. Sear the salmon fillet for about 2 minutes on each side, until it flakes easily with a fork but is still a deeper shade of pink on the inside. 4. Serve each salmon fillet alongside a serving of the cauliflower rice.
Per Serving: Calories 409; Fat 24g; Sodium 1003mg; Carbs 10g; Fiber 5g; Sugar 0.8g; Protein 41g

Pepper-Crusted Salmon

Prep time: 5 minutes | Cook time: 5 minutes | Serves: 4

4 (6-ounce) salmon fillets
2 tablespoons coconut oil, melted
1 tablespoon freshly ground black pepper
½ teaspoon coarse sea salt, divided
1 bunch kale, tough ribs removed
and roughly chopped
2 tablespoons extra-virgin olive oil
1 teaspoon red wine vinegar
¼ cup roughly chopped hazelnuts
½ cup fresh blueberries

1. Preheat a large skillet over medium-high heat. Coat the salmon fillets with the oil and then season liberally with the pepper and salt. 2. In the hot skillet, sear the salmon for about 2 minutes on each side, until it flakes easily and deeper shade of pink on the inside. 3. While the salmon is cooking, place the kale in a large bowl, season with a generous pinch of sea salt, and drizzle with the olive oil. 4. Using your hands, massage the oil and salt into the kale until it releases some of its liquid and becomes soft. Season with the red wine vinegar. 5. Divide the kale on serving plates and top with equal amounts of the hazelnuts and blueberries. Serve the salmon fillets alongside the kale.
Per Serving: Calories 442; Fat 29g; Sodium 568mg; Carbs 8g; Fiber 3g; Sugar 0.4g; Protein 37g

Sheet Pan Salmon with Beans

Prep time: 11 minutes| Cook time: 25 minutes| Serves: 4

3 tablespoons butter
3 garlic cloves, finely chopped
1½ tablespoons freshly squeezed lemon juice
¾ teaspoon kosher salt, plus more for seasoning
½ teaspoon paprika
½ teaspoon garlic powder
¼ teaspoon onion powder
4 (4-ounce) salmon fillets
12 ounces fresh green beans, trimmed
2 tablespoons olive oil
Freshly ground black pepper
Lemon wedges, for serving

1. Preheat the oven to 400°F/200°C. Line a baking sheet with parchment paper. 2. In a bowl, mix the butter with garlic, lemon juice, salt, paprika, garlic powder, and onion powder. Microwave until the butter melts. 3. Grease the salmon with the spiced butter and place the fish, skin-side down, on the baking sheet. 4. In a bowl, toss the green beans and olive oil. 5. Season with spices. Spread the beans around the salmon. 6. Bake for 12 minutes. Flip the salmon over and stir the green beans. Bake for 10 minutes more, or until the salmon is cooked to your desired doneness. 7. To crisp the skin, broil the salmon for 2 to 3 minutes before removing it from the oven. 8. Serve immediately with lemon wedges for squeezing.
Per Serving: Calories 408; Fat 32g; Sodium 866mg; Carbs 9g; Fiber 4g; Sugar 0.8g; Protein 21g

Salmon in Brown Butter Sauce

Prep time: 11 minutes | Cook time: 15 minutes | Serves: 4

½ cup butter, cut into pieces	4 (4-ounce) salmon fillets
Juice and zest of 1 lime	Sea salt
1 tablespoon capers	Freshly ground black pepper
Sea salt	2 tablespoons coconut oil
Freshly ground black pepper	

1. Melt the butter in a small saucepan over medium heat. 2. Continue to heat the butter, occasionally stirring, until it is golden brown and very fragrant, for about 4 minutes. 3. Remove the brown butter from the heat. 4. Stir the lime zest with lime juice, and capers. Spice with salt and pepper and set aside. 5. Pat the fish dry and season lightly with spices. Heat the oil and add the salmon and panfry until crispy and golden on both sides, turning once, for 6 to 7 minutes per side. 6. Transfer the fish to a serving plate, drizzle with the sauce, and serve.
Per Serving: Calories 485; Fat 44g; Sodium 904mg; Carbs 0g; Fiber 0g; Sugar 0g; Protein 23g

Roasted Salmon with Olive Salsa

Prep time: 25 minutes | Cook time: 16 minutes | Serves: 4

½ cup sliced black olives	1 teaspoon chopped fresh basil
½ English cucumber, chopped	1 teaspoon chopped fresh oregano
¼ cup chopped sun-dried tomatoes packed in oil	4 (4-ounce) salmon fillets
1 scallion, white and green parts, chopped	2 tablespoons olive oil
	Sea salt
¼ cup avocado oil	Freshly ground black pepper

1. Mix the olives, cucumber, sun-dried tomatoes, scallion, avocado oil, basil, and oregano in a medium bowl. 2. Preheat the oven to 350°F/175°C. Prepare a baking sheet with aluminum foil. 3. Place the fish on the sheet and drizzle them with olive oil. Season the fish with salt and pepper. 4. Bake the fish until it is opaque, turning once, about 5 minutes per side or until the fish flakes easily with a fork. 5. Serve the fish topped with salsa.
Per Serving: Calories 457; Fat 39g; Sodium 714mg; Carbs 4g; Fiber 1g; Sugar 0.2g; Protein 24g

Tangy Salmon and Asparagus

Prep time: 5 minutes | Cook time: 15 minutes | Serves: 1

2 tablespoons avocado oil, divided	Juice of ½ lemon
2 garlic cloves, minced	6 asparagus spears, woody ends removed
1 (6-ounce) salmon fillet	Half a lemon, sliced thinly

1. Preheat the oven to 425°F/220°C. 2. Combine 1 tablespoon of avocado oil and the garlic in a bowl. 3. Place the salmon on the baking sheet. Rub the salmon with the garlic and oil mixture until it is evenly coated. 4. Squeeze the lemon juice over the salmon, and season with salt and pepper. 5. Stack the asparagus around the salmon in a single layer, drizzle the spears with the remaining 1 tablespoon of avocado oil, and place the lemon slices over them. 6. Roast for 12 to 15 minutes, until the salmon is cooked through.
Per Serving: Calories 527; Fat 39g; Sodium 620mg; Carbs 8g; Fiber 3g; Sugar 1g; Protein 36g

Dijon-Ginger Salmon

Prep time: 11 minutes | Cook time: 10 minutes | Serves: 1

1 teaspoon Dijon mustard	¼ teaspoon freshly grated ginger root
1 teaspoon coconut aminos	
1 teaspoon avocado oil	1 (6-ounce) salmon fillet
1 garlic clove, minced	

1. Combine mustard, oil, coconut aminos, garlic, and ginger to make a marinade. Drizzle over the salmon, and allow it to sit for 10 minutes. 2. Heat a skillet over medium-high heat. Place the salmon in the skillet; discard any leftover marinade. 3. Cook for 4 to 5 minutes, depending on the thickness of the fish. 4. Turn the salmon carefully with a spatula, then cook for another 4 to 5 minutes or until it is cooked.
Per Serving: Calories 355; Fat 23g; Sodium 844mg; Carbs 3g; Fiber 0g; Sugar 0g; Protein 34g

Delicious Glazed Salmon

Prep time: 11 minutes | Cook time: 15 minutes | Serves: 4

Nonstick cooking spray	4 skinless salmon fillets
2 tablespoons sugar-free maple syrup	1 teaspoon sea salt
2 tablespoons Dijon mustard	¼ teaspoon freshly ground black pepper
2 teaspoons melted coconut oil	

1. Preheat the oven to 400°F/200°C. 2. Lightly spray the aluminum foiled baking tray with cooking spray. 3. Whisk together the sugar-free maple syrup, mustard, and coconut oil in a small bowl. Season the salmon with spices. 4. Spoon half the sauce evenly over each fillet. Place the salmon skin-side down on the foiled baking sheet. Bake for 8 minutes. 5. Spoon the remaining sauce evenly over each fillet, and then bake for another 3 to 4 minutes or until the fish flakes easily.
Per Serving: Calories 230; Fat 9g; Sodium 788mg; Carbs 2g; Fiber 2g; Sugar 0.5g; Protein 3g

Pan-Seared Garlicky Salmon

Prep time: 5 minutes | Cook time: 10 minutes | Serves: 2

1 tablespoon extra-virgin olive oil	2 tablespoons butter
2 (8-ounce) salmon fillets	1 tablespoon chopped fresh parsley
1 lemon, halved	
Pink Himalayan sea salt	2 garlic cloves, minced
Freshly ground black pepper	

1. Heat the olive oil over medium-high heat. Squeeze the lemon juice over the fillets. 2. Season the salmon with salt and pepper. Place the fillet skin-side up in the hot oil. Cook for 4-5 minutes, flip the fish, and cook for another 2 to 3 minutes on the other side. 3. Add the butter, the juice from the other lemon half, the parsley, and garlic to the pan. Toss to combine. 4. Cook the fish for 2 to 3 more minutes, until the flesh flakes easily with a fork. 5. Transfer the fish to a serving plate, then top with the butter sauce and serve.
Per Serving: Calories 489; Fat 33g; Sodium 963mg; Carbs 1g; Fiber 0g; Sugar 0g; Protein 45g

Salmon with Delicious Tarragon-Dijon Sauce

Prep time: 5 minutes| Cook time: 15 minutes| Serves: 4

1¼ pounds salmon fillet (skin on or removed), cut into 4 equal pieces	tarragon or 1 to 2 teaspoons dried tarragon
¼ cup avocado oil mayonnaise	½ teaspoon salt
¼ cup Dijon or stone-ground mustard	¼ teaspoon freshly ground black pepper
Zest and juice of ½ lemon	¼ cup extra-virgin olive oil, for serving
2 tablespoons chopped fresh	

1. Preheat the oven to 425°F/220°C. Line a baking sheet with parchment paper. Place the salmon pieces, skin-side down, on a baking sheet. 2. Whisk the mayonnaise, mustard, lemon zest, juice, tarragon, salt, and pepper in a small bowl. 3. Top the salmon evenly with the sauce mixture. Bake until lightly browned on top and slightly translucent in the center, for 10 to 12 minutes, depending on the thickness of the salmon. 4. Drizzle each fillet with olive oil before serving.
Per Serving: Calories 387; Fat 28g; Sodium 909mg; Carbs 4g; Fiber 1g; Sugar 0.9g; Protein 29g

Nut-Crusted Salmon

Prep time: 5 minutes | Cook time: 15 minutes | Serves: 4

1 tablespoon butter, melted, plus more for greasing the pan	2 tablespoons cream cheese, at room temperature
12 ounces salmon fillet (skin-on)	1 teaspoon garlic salt
½ cup finely chopped pecans	1 teaspoon freshly ground black pepper
¼ cup grated Parmesan cheese	

1. Preheat the oven to 425°F/220°C. Lightly grease a 13-by-9-inch baking dish. Place the fillet skin-side down in the baking dish. 2. In a small bowl, mix the pecans, Parmesan cheese, cream cheese, melted butter, garlic salt, and pepper over the top of the salmon. 3. Bake it for about 15 minutes or until the salmon flakes easily with a fork.
Per Serving: Calories 303; Fat 24g; Sodium 793mg; Carbs 3g; Fiber 1g; Sugar 1g; Protein 21g

Grilled Salmon Packets

Prep time: 11 minutes | Cook time: 21 minutes | Serves: 4

1½ pounds salmon, skin removed
Extra-virgin olive oil, for greasing
1 small bunch fresh dill, divided
1 medium lemon, thinly sliced, divided

2 tablespoons unsalted butter, melted
3 garlic cloves, minced
¾ teaspoon salt
¼ teaspoon ground black pepper

1. Preheat a grill to medium heat, about 375°F/190°C. Lightly spray the aluminum foiled baking tray with cooking spray. Arrange half of the dill sprigs down the middle of the baking sheet, add half of the lemon slices. 2. Place the salmon on lemon slices. 3. Drizzle the salmon with the melted butter and sprinkle it with the garlic, salt, and pepper. Top with the remaining half of the dill and the remaining lemon slices. 4. Fold the foil's sides up and over the top of the salmon until the fish is completely enclosed. 5. Flip the wrapped salmon onto the grill. Grill the salmon for 14 to 18 minutes, or until the salmon is almost cooked. Then carefully open the foil so that the top of the fish is uncovered. 6. Continue grilling until the fish cooked. To serve, cut the salmon into 4 portions.
Per Serving: Calories 308; Fat 18g; Sodium 832mg; Carbs 2g; Fiber 0g; Sugar 0g; Protein 34g

Classical Salmon Gratin

Prep time: 5 minutes plus 10 minutes to marinate | Cook time: 10 minutes | Serves: 4

1-pound skinless salmon fillets, cut into 1-inch cubes
Grated zest and juice of 1 lemon
¾ cup heavy (whipping) cream
2 tablespoons chopped fresh tarragon

1 teaspoon onion powder
1 teaspoon minced garlic
Salt
Freshly ground black pepper
½ cup shredded Swiss cheese

1. Preheat the broiler to high. Place an oven rack about a third of the way down. 2. Place the salmon in a 7-by-11-inch broiler-safe baking dish and add the lemon zest and juice. Cover and let marinate for 10 minutes, stirring halfway through. 3. Meanwhile, in a medium bowl, combine the heavy cream, tarragon, onion powder, garlic, and salt and pepper to taste. Mix well. 4. Drain the juice from the salmon and return it to the baking dish. Pour the cream mixture over the salmon. Top with the Swiss cheese. 5. Broil the cheese for about 10 minutes, or until the cheese has melted and has turned golden brown.
Per Serving: Calories 375; Fat 28g; Sodium 689mg; Carbs 4g; Fiber 0g; Sugar 0g; Protein 27g

Seared Salmon

Prep time: 5 minutes | Cook time: 20 minutes | Serves: 2

¼ cup (½ stick) butter
1 tablespoon finely minced onion
1½ teaspoons white wine vinegar
1 teaspoon freshly squeezed lemon juice
½ teaspoon dried tarragon
¼ teaspoon dried parsley
1 large egg yolk

2 tablespoons heavy whipping cream
1 tablespoon extra-virgin olive oil
2 (8-ounce) salmon fillets
Pink Himalayan sea salt
Freshly ground black pepper
1 (6- to 8-ounce) container lump crab meat

1. Melt the butter in a pan and cook the onion for 3 to 5 minutes, until it turns translucent. Add the vinegar, lemon juice, tarragon, and parsley. Stir to combine. 2. Whisk the egg yolk and cream. Once the mixture in the saucepan starts to simmer, remove it from the heat and slowly add the egg mixture, whisking while you pour. 3. Whisk until the sauce thickens. Cover and set aside. Season the salmon fillets. 4. Heat the olive oil and place the fillets skin-side up in the skillet. Cook for 4 to 5 minutes, then turn and cook until the flesh flakes easily with a fork. 5. Transfer the salmon to a serving plate, then place the crab in the skillet and quickly heat it, stirring gently. 6. Top the salmon fillets with the crab, then drizzle on the sauce.
Per Serving: Calories 741; Fat 53g; Sodium 1023mg; Carbs 1g; Fiber 0g; Sugar 0g; Protein 62g

Roasted Herb-Crusted Salmon with Colors

Prep time: 11 minutes | Cook time: 15 minutes | Serves: 4

¼ cup chopped fresh parsley
¼ cup chopped fresh chives
¼ cup fresh oregano leaves
2 tablespoons mayonnaise
4 (3- to 4-ounce) salmon fillets
20 asparagus spears, ends

trimmed
16 cherry tomatoes, halved
2 tablespoons olive oil
Salt
Freshly ground black pepper

1. Preheat the oven to 400°F/200°C. Prepare a baking sheet with aluminum foil. Mix the parsley, chives, oregano, and mayonnaise in a medium bowl. 2. Place the salmon fillets in the baking sheet and spread the herb mixture over the salmon. 3. Cover the salmon with asparagus and tomatoes. 4. Drizzle the oil over the veggies and spice everything with salt and pepper. Cook for about 12 minutes.
Per Serving: Calories 258; Fat 18g; Sodium 695mg; Carbs 6g; Fiber 3g; Sugar 1g; Protein 19g

Traditional Salmon Cakes

Prep time: 11 minutes | Cook time: 15 minutes | Serves: 4

1 (16-ounce) can pink salmon, drained and bones removed
¼ cup almond flour
¼ cup crushed pork rinds
2 scallions, diced
1 large egg

3 tablespoons mayonnaise
1 teaspoon garlic salt
1 teaspoon freshly ground black pepper
2 tablespoons extra-virgin olive oil

1. In a bowl, combine the salmon, almond flour, pork rinds, scallions, egg, mayonnaise, garlic salt, and pepper, and mix well. 2. Form 8 small patties or 4 large patties. Heat the oil. Cook the patties for 7-8 minutes until crispy. 3. Larger parties may need to cook a little longer. Transfer the patties to the lined plate to drain.
Per Serving: Calories 313; Fat 21g; Sodium 752mg; Carbs 5g; Fiber 0g; Sugar 0g; Protein 26g

Curried Salmon Cakes

Prep time: 5 minutes | Cook time: 25 minutes | Serves: 4

1-pound skinless salmon fillets, roughly chopped
2 large eggs
2 tablespoons chopped fresh cilantro

4 scallions, green and white parts, roughly chopped
1 teaspoon Thai red curry paste
2 tablespoons olive oil

1. Place parchment paper on a large plate and set aside. In a food processor or blender, combine the salmon, eggs, cilantro, scallions, and curry paste and process until smooth. 2. Divide the mixture into 8 parts on the lined plate. Flatten them into patties and place another layer of paper on top. Spoon out the remaining 4 portions, flatten, and top with paper. 3. Chill for at least 1 hour. Heat oil in a large pot over medium heat. 4. Cook the cakes on one side for 5 minutes, flip, and cook for another 5 minutes, or until cooked through.
Per Serving: Calories 305; Fat 21g; Sodium 805mg; Carbs 2g; Fiber 1g; Sugar 0.6g; Protein 26g

Tropical Ginger Salmon Burgers

Prep time: 16 minutes | Cook time: 20 minutes | Serves: 4

12 ounces fresh salmon, chopped
1 egg, beaten
2 tablespoons coconut flour
1 scallion, finely chopped
Juice of 1 lemon
2 teaspoons peeled, grated fresh

ginger
½ teaspoon ground coriander
Pinch sea salt
Pinch freshly ground black pepper
¼ cup coconut oil
¼ cup mayonnaise

1. Combine the salmon, egg, coconut flour, scallion, lemon juice, ginger, coriander, salt, and pepper until well mixed. Form the mixture into 8 equal patties, each ½-inch thick. 2. Chill the salmon patties in the refrigerator until firm, about 1 hour. Heat the oil over medium-high heat. 3. Panfry the salmon burgers, turning once, until cooked through and lightly browned, for about 10 minutes per side. 4. Serve 2 burgers per person topped with mayonnaise.
Per Serving: Calories 369; Fat 31g; Sodium 756mg; Carbs 4g; Fiber 2g; Sugar 0g; Protein 20g

Salmon Cakes

Prep time: 16 minutes | Cook time: 15 minutes | Serves: 4

1 (14.5-ounce) can red salmon or 1-pound wild-caught salmon fillet, skin removed
½ cup minced red onion
1 large egg
2 tablespoons avocado oil mayonnaise, plus more for serving
1 very ripe avocado, pitted, peeled, and mashed
½ cup almond flour
1 to 2 teaspoons dried dill
1 teaspoon garlic powder
1 teaspoon salt
½ teaspoon paprika
½ teaspoon freshly ground black pepper
Zest and juice of 1 lemon
¼ cup extra-virgin olive oil

1. Remove the spine, large bones, and pieces of skin from the salmon. Place the salmon and red onion in a large bowl and break up any lumps using a fork. 2. Add the egg, mayonnaise, and avocado and combine well. Whisk the almond flour, dill, garlic powder, salt, paprika, and pepper in a small bowl. 3. Add the dry ingredients, lemon zest, and juice to the salmon and combine well. Form into 8 small patties, about 2 inches in diameter and place on a plate. Let rest for 15 minutes. 4. Fry the patties in oil until browned, for 2 to 3 minutes per side. 5. Cover the pan and lower the heat, and cook for another 6 to 8 minutes. Serve warm with mayonnaise or aioli.
Per Serving: Calories 343; Fat 26g; Sodium 856mg; Carbs 5g; Fiber 1g; Sugar 1g; Protein 23g

Chef's Snapper Veracruz

Prep time: 11 minutes | Cook time: 22 minutes | Serves: 4

¼ cup extra-virgin olive oil
¼ cup diced yellow onion
2 teaspoons roughly chopped garlic
Pinch red pepper flakes
2 tablespoons minced fresh parsley
1 teaspoon minced oregano
¼ cup pitted green olives
2 tablespoons drained capers
1 cup canned plum tomatoes with juices, hand crushed
1 tablespoon red wine vinegar
1¼ pounds red snapper, cut into 4 (5-ounce) fillets
3 tablespoons cold butter, cut into pieces
Sea salt
Freshly ground black pepper

1. Heat the olive oil over medium heat. Cook the onion with garlic, and red pepper flakes until softened, for about 5 minutes. 2. Add the parsley, oregano, olives, capers, tomatoes, and vinegar to the skillet and cook for 10 minutes, until the sauce has reduced somewhat and the tomatoes are pulpy. 3. Season the fish generously on both sides with salt and pepper, then add the fillets to the pan, scooping some of the sauce over the fish. 4. Cook for about 3 minutes on each side, or until the fish flakes easily with a fork. 5. Whisk in the cold butter into the tomato mixture one tablespoon at a time. Pour the buttery sauce over the cooked fish and serve immediately.
Per Serving: Calories 434; Fat 27g; Sodium 965mg; Carbs 8g; Fiber 2g; Sugar 2g; Protein 38g

Salmon-Stuffed Mushrooms

Prep time: 5 minutes | Cook time: 25 minutes | Serves: 4

4 portabella mushroom caps
2 (6-ounce) cans wild-caught salmon (or freshly cooked wild-caught salmon)
4 ounces cream cheese, at room temperature
¼ cup mayonnaise
2 scallions, chopped
½ teaspoon paprika
½ teaspoon garlic powder
½ teaspoon sea salt
¼ teaspoon freshly ground black pepper
1 cup freshly grated Parmesan cheese

1. Preheat the oven to 350ºF/175°C. 2. Prepare a baking sheet with parchment paper. Clean the mushrooms, remove the stems, and carefully scrape the gills away with a spoon. Place them top down on the baking sheet. 3. Combine the salmon, cream cheese, mayonnaise, scallions, paprika, garlic powder, salt, and pepper in a large bowl. Mix well to combine. 4. Spoon the salmon mixture into the mushroom caps, dividing equally. 5. Sprinkle with the Parmesan and bake for 20 to 25 minutes until the mushrooms are tender and the cheese is bubbly.
Per Serving: Calories 385; Fat 29g; Sodium 468mg; Carbs 5g; Fiber 1g; Sugar 2g; Protein 26g

Crispy Fish Sticks

Prep time: 15 minutes | Cook time: 12 minutes | Serves: 4

1 large egg
½ teaspoon old bay seasoning
1½ ounces plain pork rinds, finely
crushed
4 (4-ounce) cod fillets, cut into 1"
× 2" sticks

1. In a medium bowl, whisk egg. In a separate medium bowl, combine old bay seasoning and pork rinds. 2. Dip each fish stick into the egg, then gently press it into the pork rind mixture to coat all sides. Place fish sticks into an ungreased air fryer basket. 3. Set the temperature setting to 400°F/200°C and the timer for 12 minutes, turning fish sticks halfway through cooking. 4. When done, fish sticks will be golden brown and have an internal temperature of at least 145°F/65°C when done. Serve warm.
Per Serving: Calories 156; Fat 5g; Sodium 605mg; Carbs 0g; Fiber 0g; Sugar 0g; Protein 25g

Ahi Tuna Steaks with Bagel Seasoning

Prep time: 5 minutes | Cook time: 14 minutes | Serves: 2

2 (6-ounce) ahi tuna steaks
2 tablespoons olive oil
3 tablespoons of everything bagel seasoning

1. Drizzle each steak with olive oil. Place seasoning on a medium plate and press each side of tuna steaks into seasoning to form a thick layer. 2. Place steaks into an ungreased air fryer basket. 3. Set the temperature setting to 400°F/200°C and the timer for 14 minutes, turning steaks halfway through cooking. 4. Steaks will be done when the internal temperature is at least 145°F/65°C for well-done. Serve warm.
Per Serving: Calories 385; Fat 14g; Sodium 1513mg; Carbs 0g; Fiber 0g; Sugar 0g; Protein 40g

Hot and Tangy Shrimp

Prep time: 5 minutes | Cook time: 5 minutes | Serves: 4

1-pound medium shrimp, peeled and deveined
1 tablespoon salted butter, melted
2 teaspoons chili powder
¼ teaspoon garlic powder
¼ teaspoon salt
¼ teaspoon ground black pepper
½ small lime, zested and juiced, divided

1. In a medium bowl, toss shrimp with butter, then sprinkle with chili powder, garlic powder, salt, pepper, and lime zest. 2. Place shrimp into an ungreased air fryer basket. 3. Set the temperature setting to 400°F/200°C and the timer for 5 minutes. Shrimp will be firm and form a "C" shape when done. 4. Transfer shrimp to serving dish and drizzle with lime juice. Serve warm.
Per Serving: Calories 98; Fat 4g; Sodium 752mg; Carbs 2g; Fiber 1g; Sugar 0g; Protein 13g

Traditional Fish Tacos

Prep time: 15 minutes | Cook time: 20 minutes | Serves: 4

1 large egg, beaten
½ cup coconut flour, divided
1 teaspoon salt
1 teaspoon ground cumin
¼ teaspoon paprika
⅛ teaspoon chili powder
1-pound skinless, boneless cod,
cut into 1-inch pieces, patted dry
8 large butter lettuce leaves
½ cup coleslaw, divided
1 sliced avocado
¼ cup Pico de Gallo, divided
1 lime, quartered

1. Preheat the oven to 400°F/200°C. Prepare a baking sheet with parchment paper. Pour the egg into a small bowl. Pour ¼ cup of coconut flour into a medium bowl. 2. In a second medium bowl, thoroughly combine the remaining ¼ cup of coconut flour, salt, cumin, paprika, and chili powder. 3. Dip the cod pieces into the plain coconut flour, the egg, and finally the seasoned flour. Place the cod on the baking sheet in a single layer. Bake for 10 minutes, flip, and then bake for another 10 minutes. Let cool for 2 minutes. 4. To assemble the tacos, lay out the lettuce leaves and top with equal amounts of cod, coleslaw, avocado, and Pico de Gallo. Squeeze lime juice on top. Serve immediately.
Per Serving: Calories 344; Fat 22g; Sodium 478mg; Carbs 19g; Fiber 9g; Sugar 4g; Protein 25g

Crispy Coconut Shrimp

Prep time: 5 minutes | Cook time: 8 minutes | Serves: 2

8 ounces jumbo shrimp, peeled and deveined
2 tablespoons salted butter, melted
½ teaspoon old bay seasoning
¼ cup unsweetened shredded coconut
¼ cup coconut flour

1. In a large bowl, toss shrimp in butter and old bay seasoning. 2. In a medium bowl, combine shredded coconut with coconut flour. Coat each piece of shrimp in coconut mixture. 3. Place shrimp into an ungreased air fryer basket. Set the temperature setting to 400°F/200°C and the timer for 8 minutes, gently turning the shrimp halfway through cooking. 4. The shrimp will be pink and C-shaped when done. Serve warm.
Per Serving: Calories 296; Fat 19g; Sodium 786mg; Carbs 13g; Fiber 7g; Sugar 4g; Protein 17g

Wrapped Scallops

Prep time: 5 minutes | Cook time: 10 minutes | Serves: 4

8 (1-ounce) sea scallops, cleaned and patted dry
8 slices of sugar-free bacon
¼ teaspoon salt
¼ teaspoon ground black pepper

1. Wrap scallop in 1 slice of bacon and secure with a toothpick. Sprinkle with salt and pepper. 2. Place scallops into an ungreased air fryer basket. 3. Set the temp setting to 360°F/180°C and the timer for 10 minutes. When done, scallops will be opaque and firm and have an internal temperature of 130°F/55°C. 4. Serve warm.
Per Serving: Calories 125; Fat 6g; Sodium 691mg; Carbs 2g; Fiber 0g; Sugar 0g; Protein 14g

Garlic Scallops

Prep time: 5 minutes | Cook time: 10 minutes | Serves: 4

4 tablespoons salted butter, melted
4 teaspoons peeled and finely minced garlic
½ small lemon, zested and juiced
8 (1-ounce) sea scallops, cleaned and patted dry
¼ teaspoon salt
¼ teaspoon ground black pepper

1. Mix butter, garlic, lemon zest, and lemon juice in a small bowl. Place scallops in an ungreased 6" round nonstick baking dish. Pour butter mixture over scallops, then sprinkle with salt and pepper. 2. Place dish into air fryer basket. Set the temperature setting to 360°F/180°C and the timer for 10 minutes. 3. When done, scallops will be opaque and firm and have an internal temperature of 130°F/55°C. 4. Serve warm.
Per Serving: Calories 145; Fat 11g; Sodium 458mg; Carbs 3g; Fiber 0g; Sugar 0g; Protein 7g

Crab-Stuffed Boats

Prep time: 5 minutes | Cook time: 7 minutes | Serves: 4

2 medium avocados, halved and pitted
8 ounces cooked crab meat
¼ teaspoon old bay seasoning
2 tablespoons peeled and diced yellow onion
2 tablespoons mayonnaise

1. Scoop out avocado flesh in each avocado half, leaving ½" around the edges to form a shell. Chop scooped-out avocado. 2. Combine crab meat, old bay seasoning, onion, mayonnaise, and chopped avocado in a medium bowl. Place ¼ mixture into each avocado shell. 3. Place avocado boats into an ungreased air fryer basket. Set the temperature to 350°F/175°C and the timer for 7 minutes. 4. The avocado will be browned on the top, and the mixture will be bubbling when done. 5. Serve warm.
Per Serving: Calories 209; Fat 15g; Sodium 307mg; Carbs 1g; Fiber 5g; Sugar 0g; Protein 12g

Traditional Lobster Tails

Prep time: 5 minutes | Cook time: 9 minutes | Serves: 4

4 (6-ounce) lobster tails
2 tablespoons salted butter, melted
1 tablespoon peeled and finely
minced garlic
¼ teaspoon salt
¼ teaspoon ground black pepper
2 tablespoons lemon juice

1. Carefully cut open lobster tails with scissors and pull back the shell to expose the meat. Pour butter over each tail, then sprinkle with garlic, salt, and pepper. 2. Place tails into an ungreased air fryer basket. Set the temperature setting to 400°F/200°C and the timer for 9 minutes. The lobster, will be firm and opaque when done. 3. Transfer tails to four medium plates and pour lemon juice over lobster meat. Serve warm.
Per Serving: Calories 186; Fat 7g; Sodium 910mg; Carbs 1g; Fiber 0g; Sugar 0g; Protein 28g

Delicious Tuna Cakes

Prep time: 10 minutes | Cook time: 10 minutes | Serves: 4

4 (3-ounce) pouches tuna, drained
1 large egg, whisked
2 tablespoons peeled and chopped
white onion
½ teaspoon old bay seasoning

1. In a large bowl, mix all patties ingredients and form into four beautiful patties. 2. Place patties into an ungreased air fryer basket. 3. Set the temperature setting to 400°F/200°C and the timer for 10 minutes. 4. Cakes will be browned and crispy when done. Let cool for 5 minutes before serving.
Per Serving: Calories 100; Fat 2g; Sodium 432mg; Carbs 1g; Fiber 0g; Sugar 0g; Protein 21g

Yummy Italian Baked Cod

Prep time: 5 minutes | Cook time: 12 minutes | Serves: 4

4 (6-ounce) cod fillets
2 tablespoons salted butter, melted
1 teaspoon Italian seasoning
¼ teaspoon salt
½ cup low-carb marinara sauce

1. Place cod into an ungreased 6" round nonstick baking dish. Pour butter over cod and sprinkle with Italian seasoning and salt. Top with marinara. 2. Place dish into air fryer basket. Set the temperature to 350°F/175°C and the timer for 12 minutes. 3. Fillets will be lightly browned, easily flake, and have an internal temperature of at least 145°F/65°C when done. 4. Serve warm.
Per Serving: Calories 193; Fat 8g; Sodium 811mg; Carbs 2g; Fiber 0g; Sugar 0g; Protein 27g

Citrus-Marinated Tilapia

Prep time: 10 minutes | Cooking time: 30 minutes | Serves: 4

4 tilapia fillets., for almost 4 ounces each
¼ cup lime juice
Essentials
2 tablespoons coconut oil, for cooking
¼ cup green onions, chopped
1 tablespoon fresh dill, chopped
½ teaspoon garlic powder

1 tablespoon water
Salt and black pepper, to taste

1. Mix the coconut oil, green onions, lime juice or lemon juice, dill, garlic powder, and water in a baking dish. Add the fish fillets and toss with your hands to coat. Season with salt. 2. Cover with foil sheet and let marinate in the refrigerator for at least 1 hour. 3. When ready to cook, at 350°F/175°C, preheat your oven, remove the fish from the refrigerator, and bake covered in your oven for almost 30 minutes until the fillets are cooked through. 4. Place the fillets on a serving plate, season with black pepper and serve. Garnish with dill, if desired.
Per serving: Calories: 403; Total fat 21.8g; Sodium 355mg; Total Carbs 2.3g; Fiber 4.4g; Sugars 4.8g; Protein 43.5g

Delicious Rainbow Salmon Kebabs

Prep time: 10 minutes | Cook time: 8 minutes | Serves: 2

6 ounces boneless, skinless salmon, cut into 1" cubes	½ medium zucchini, trimmed and cut into ½" slices
¼ medium red onion, peeled and cut into 1" pieces	1 tablespoon olive oil
½ yellow bell pepper, seeded and cut into 1" pieces	½ teaspoon salt
	¼ teaspoon ground black pepper

1. Using one 6" skewer, skewer 1 piece salmon, then 1 piece onion, 1 piece bell pepper, and finally 1 piece zucchini. 2. Repeat this pattern with additional skewers to make four kebabs total. Grease with olive oil and sprinkle with salt and black pepper. 3. Place kebabs into an ungreased air fryer basket. Set the temperature setting to 400°F/200°C and the timer for 8 minutes, turning kebabs halfway through cooking. 4. Salmon will easily flake and have an internal temperature of at least 145°F/65°C when done; vegetables will be tender. 5. Serve warm.
Per Serving: Calories 183; Fat 9g; Sodium 642mg; Carbs 6g; Fiber 1g; Sugar 2g; Protein 17g

Spicy Fish Bowl

Prep time: 10 minutes | Cook time: 12 minutes | Serves: 4

½ teaspoon salt	cabbage
¼ teaspoon garlic powder	⅓ cup mayonnaise
¼ teaspoon ground cumin	¼ teaspoon ground black pepper
4 (4-ounce) cod fillets	¼ cup chopped pickled jalapeños
4 cups finely shredded green	

1. Sprinkle salt, garlic powder, and cumin over cod and place them into an ungreased air fryer basket. Set the temperature to 350°F/175°C and the timer for 12 minutes, turning fillets halfway through cooking. 2. Cod will flake easily and have an internal temperature of at least 145°F/65°C when done. 3. In a large bowl, toss cabbage with mayonnaise, pepper, and jalapeños until fully coated. 4. Serve cod warm over cabbage slaw on four medium plates.
Per Serving: Calories 221; Fat 14g; Sodium 850mg; Carbs 4g; Fiber 2g; Sugar 2g; Protein 18g

Delicious Cajun Salmon

Prep time: 5 minutes | Cook time: 7 minutes | Serves: 2

2 (4-ounce) boneless, skinless salmon fillets	⅛ teaspoon cayenne pepper
2 tablespoons salted butter, softened	½ teaspoon garlic powder
	1 teaspoon paprika
	¼ teaspoon ground black pepper

1. Brush each fillet with butter. Mix all other ingredients except butter and rub them into the fish on both sides. 2. Place fillets into an ungreased air fryer basket. Set the temperature setting to 390°F/200°C and the timer for 7 minutes. 3. The internal temperature will be 145°F/65°C when done. Serve warm.
Per Serving: Calories 248; Fat 14g; Sodium 174mg; Carbs 1g; Fiber 1g; Sugar 0g; Protein 23g

Southern-Style Catfish Steak

Prep time: 10 minutes | Cook time: 12 minutes | Serves: 4

4 (7-ounce) catfish fillets	almond flour
⅓ cup heavy whipping cream	2 teaspoons old bay seasoning
1 tablespoon lemon juice	½ teaspoon salt
1 cup blanched finely ground	¼ teaspoon ground black pepper

1. Place catfish fillets into a large bowl with cream and pour lemon juice. Stir to coat. 2. In a separate bowl, mix flour along with old bay seasoning. Remove each fillet and gently shake off excess cream. 3. Sprinkle with salt and pepper. Press each fillet gently into the flour mixture on both sides to coat. 4. Place fillets into an ungreased air fryer basket. Set the temperature setting to 400°F/200°C and the timer for 12 minutes, turning fillets halfway through cooking. 5. Catfish will be golden brown and have an internal temperature of at least 145°F/65°C when done. 6. Serve warm.
Per Serving: Calories 284; Fat 14g; Sodium 625mg; Carbs 1g; Fiber 1g; Sugar 1g; Protein 32g

Sweet Buttery Salmon

Prep time: 5 minutes | Cook time: 12 minutes | Serves: 4

2 tablespoons salted butter, melted	4 (4-ounce) boneless, skinless salmon fillets
1 teaspoon low-carb maple syrup	½ teaspoon salt
1 teaspoon yellow mustard	

1. In a small bowl, whisk together butter, syrup, and mustard—brush ½ mixture over each fillet on both sides. Sprinkle fillets with salt on both sides. 2. Place salmon into an ungreased air fryer basket. Set the temperature setting to 400°F/200°C and the timer for 12 minutes. 3. Halfway through cooking, brush fillets on both sides with the remaining syrup mixture. 4. Salmon will easily flake and have an internal temperature of at least 145°F/65°C when done. 5. Serve warm.
Per Serving: Calories 193; Fat 9g; Sodium 435mg; Carbs 1g; Fiber 0g; Sugar 0g; Protein 23g

Cheesy Lobster Tails

Prep time: 5 minutes | Cook time: 7 minutes | Serves: 4

4 (4-ounce) lobster tails	¼ teaspoon salt
2 tablespoons salted butter, melted	¼ teaspoon ground black pepper
1½ teaspoons Cajun seasoning, divided	¼ cup grated Parmesan cheese
	½ ounce plain pork rinds, finely crushed

1. Cut lobster tails open carefully with scissors and gently pull the meat away from the shells, resting meat on top of the shells. 2. Grease lobster meat with butter and spice with 1 teaspoon of Cajun seasoning, ¼ teaspoon per tail. Mix remaining Cajun seasoning, salt, pepper, Parmesan, and pork rinds in a small bowl. Gently press ¼ mixture onto the meat on each lobster's tail. 3. Carefully place tails into an air fryer basket. Set the temperature setting to 400°F/200°C and the timer for 7 minutes. 4. Lobster tails will be crispy and golden on top and have an internal temperature of at least 145°F/65°C when done. Serve warm.
Per Serving: Calories 184; Fat 0g; Sodium 931mg; Carbs 1g; Fiber 0g; Sugar 0g; Protein 23g

Regular Crab Cakes

Prep time: 10 minutes | Cook time: 10 minutes | Serves: 4

8 ounces fresh lump crabmeat	crushed
2 tablespoons mayonnaise	¼ cup seeded and chopped red bell pepper
1 teaspoon old bay seasoning	
½ ounce plain pork rinds, finely	

1. In a large bowl, mix all ingredients. Separate into four equal sections and form into patties. 2. Cut a piece of parchment to fit the air fryer basket. Place patties onto ungreased parchment and into an air fryer basket. 3. Set the temperature setting to 380°F/195°C and the timer for 10 minutes, turning the patties halfway through cooking. 4. Crab cakes will be golden when done. Serve warm.
Per Serving: Calories 116; Fat 7g; Sodium 561mg; Carbs 0g; Fiber 0g; Sugar 0g; Protein 12g

Spiced Snow Crab Legs

Prep time: 5 minutes | Cook time: 15 minutes | Serves: 4

8 pounds fresh shell-on snow crab legs	4 tablespoons salted butter, melted
2 tablespoons coconut oil	2 teaspoons lemon juice
2 teaspoons old bay seasoning	

1. Place crab legs into an ungreased air fryer basket, working in batches if needed. Drizzle legs with coconut oil and sprinkle with old bay seasoning. 2. Set the temperature setting to 400°F/200°C and the timer for 15 minutes, shaking the basket three times during cooking. 3. Legs will turn a bright red-orange when done. Serve warm. 4. In a separate small bowl, whisk butter and lemon juice for dipping. 5. Serve on the side.
Per Serving: Calories 284; Fat 13g; Sodium 1186mg; Carbs 0g; Fiber 0g; Sugar 0g; Protein 38g

Lemon Butter Cod Steak

Prep time: 5 minutes | Cook time: 12 minutes | Serves: 4

4 (4-ounce) cod fillets
2 tablespoons salted butter, melted

1 teaspoon old bay seasoning
½ medium lemon, cut into 4 slices

1. Place cod fillets into an ungreased 6" round nonstick baking dish. Brush tops of fillets with butter and sprinkle with old bay seasoning. Lay 1 lemon slice on each fillet. 2. Cover the spiced fillet with aluminum foil and place into air fryer basket. Set the temperature to 350°F/175°C and the timer for 12 minutes, turning fillets halfway through cooking. When done, fish will be opaque and have an internal temperature of at least 145°F/63°C when done. Serve warm.
Per Serving: Calories 128; Fat 6g; Sodium 529mg; Carbs 0g; Fiber 0g; Sugar 0g; Protein 17g

Tuna Tomatoes

Prep time: 5 minutes | Cook time: 5 minutes | Serves: 2

2 medium beefsteak tomatoes, tops removed, seeded, membranes removed
2 (2.6-ounce) pouches tuna packed in water, drained
1 medium stalk celery, trimmed and chopped

2 tablespoons mayonnaise
¼ teaspoon salt
¼ teaspoon ground black pepper
2 teaspoons coconut oil
¼ cup shredded mild cheddar cheese

1. Scoop pulp out of each tomato, leaving ½" shell. 2. Mix tuna, celery, mayonnaise, salt, and pepper in a medium bowl. Drizzle with coconut oil. Spoon ½ mixture into each tomato and top each with 2 tablespoons of cheddar. 3. Place tomatoes into an ungreased air fryer basket. Set the temperature setting to 320°F/160°C and the timer for 5 minutes. 4. The cheese will be melted when done. Serve warm.
Per Serving: Calories 219; Fat 15g; Sodium 697mg; Carbs 4g; Fiber 1g; Sugar 2g; Protein 18g

Nut-Crusted Mahi Mahi

Prep time: 5 minutes | Cook time: 15 minutes | Serves: 4

Coconut oil, for greasing
4 (4-ounce) Mahi Mahi fillets, rinsed and patted dry
1 teaspoon sea salt, plus a pinch
½ teaspoon black pepper, plus a pinch
½ cup macadamia nuts, salted,

roasted, coarsely chopped
2 tablespoons almond flour (or crushed pork rinds)
½ teaspoon garlic powder
½ teaspoon onion powder
4 tablespoons mayonnaise

1. Preheat the oven to 400°F/200°C. 2. With coconut oil, grease an 8-inch square baking dish. 3. Place the mahi-mahi in the prepared baking dish. Spice fillet with salt and pepper on both sides. 4. In small bowl, mix the macadamia nuts, almond flour, garlic powder, onion powder, and a pinch salt and pepper. 5. Spread 1 tablespoon of mayonnaise on each fillet. Divide the nut mixture among the top of the 4 fillets, gently patting it down to adhere to the mayonnaise. 6. Bake for about 15 minutes until golden brown and cooked through.
Per Serving: Calories 364; Fat 28g; Sodium 689mg; Carbs 4g; Fiber 2g; Sugar 1g; Protein 24g

Regular Salmon Patties

Prep time: 5 minutes | Cook time: 8 minutes | Serves: 4

12 ounces pouched pink salmon
3 tablespoons mayonnaise
⅓ cup blanched finely ground almond flour

½ teaspoon Cajun seasoning
1 medium avocado, peeled, pitted, and sliced

1. Mix salmon, mayonnaise, flour, and Cajun seasoning in a medium bowl. Form mixture into four patties. 2. Place patties into an ungreased air fryer basket. Set the temperature setting to 400°F/200°C and the timer for 8 minutes, turning patties halfway through cooking. Cakes will be made when firm and golden brown. 3. Transfer patties to four medium plates and serve warm with avocado slices.
Per Serving: Calories 263; Fat 18g; Sodium 589mg; Carbs 5g; Fiber 3g; Sugar 0g; Protein 20g

Halibut in a Blanket

Prep time: 10 minutes | Cook time: 20 minutes | Serves: 4

Coconut oil, for greasing
4 (4-ounce) halibut fillets, about 1-inch thick
½ cup (1 stick) butter, cut into squares
2 tablespoons finely chopped

scallion
1 tablespoon minced garlic
½ lemon
Sea salt
Freshly ground black pepper

1. Preheat the oven to 400°F/200°C. 2. Cut out four 12-inch squares of aluminum foil, and grease them with coconut oil. Place one halibut fillet on each foil square. 3. Place two pats of butter on each fillet. Sprinkle the scallion and garlic over the fillets, dividing equally, and then squeeze the lemon half over the fillets, finally topping with a healthy sprinkle of salt and pepper. 4. Pull the sides of each foil square up to create a pouch around the halibut, and then roll the top like a paper lunch bag. 5. The fish should be thoroughly enclosed, but there should be room in the foil pouches to allow steam to circulate and cook the fish. 6. Place the foil pouches on a large baking sheet. Bake it for 20 minutes until it opaque throughout. 7. Remove the fish from the foil pouches before serving but save the "juice" to serve over any veggies you choose to serve with the dish.
Per Serving: Calories 313; Fat 25g; Sodium 632mg; Carbs 1g; Fiber 0g; Sugar 0g; Protein 21g

Crispy Fish with Tartar Sauce

Prep time: 10 minutes | Cook time: 15 minutes | Serves: 4

For the fish sticks

Avocado or coconut oil, for greasing
1 egg, lightly beaten
1 scoop unflavored MCT powder (or collagen powder)
Pinch sea salt
Pinch freshly ground black pepper
1 cup freshly grated Parmesan

cheese
½ cup crushed pork rinds
1 teaspoon garlic powder
1 teaspoon onion powder
1 teaspoon paprika
1-pound cod fillets, rinsed, patted dry, and cut into 1-by-4-inch pieces

For the sauce

4 tablespoons mayonnaise
1 pickle spear, finely chopped
1 teaspoon freshly squeezed lemon juice
½ teaspoon onion powder

½ teaspoon garlic powder
Pinch sea salt
Pinch freshly ground black pepper
1 teaspoon chopped fresh dill
Dash low-carb sweetener

To make the fish sticks: 1. Preheat the oven to 400°F/200°C. Prepare a rimmed baking tray with aluminum foil. Place a wire rack over the baking sheet and lightly grease the rack with oil. 2. Put the lightly beaten egg in a shallow bowl. Combine the MCT powder, salt, and pepper in another shallow bowl. 3. Combine the Parmesan, pork rinds, garlic powder, onion powder, and paprika in a third bowl. 4. Dip the fish in the MCT mixture to coat both sides, shaking off the excess. Next, dip in the egg and then into the Parmesan mixture, patting to help the coating adhere. Place the fish on the wire rack. 5. Bake the fish for 12 - 15 minutes until golden brown.
To make the sauce: 1. Mix together the mayonnaise, chopped pickle, lemon juice, onion powder, and garlic powder in a small bowl. Add the salt, pepper, dill, and sweetener. 2. Serve immediately
Per Serving: Calories 314; Fat 20g; Sodium 698mg; Carbs 2g; Fiber 0g; Sugar 0g; Protein 31g

Instant Shrimp

Prep time: 2 minutes | Cook time: 5 minutes | Serves: 4

1-pound medium shrimp, peeled and deveined
2 tablespoons salted butter,

melted
¼ teaspoon salt
¼ teaspoon ground black pepper

1. Toss shrimp in butter in a large bowl, then sprinkle with salt and pepper. 2. Place shrimp into an ungreased air fryer basket. 3. Set the temperature setting to 400°F/200°C and the timer for 5 minutes, shaking the basket halfway through cooking. 4. Shrimp will be pink when done. Serve warm.
Per Serving: Calories 119; Fat 6g; Sodium 736mg; Carbs 1g; Fiber 0g; Sugar 0g; Protein 13g

Shrimp Alfredo and Zoodles

Prep time: 10 minutes | Cook time: 25 minutes | Serves: 5

For zoodles
3 medium zucchinis
1 teaspoon salt
For shrimp and sauce
2 tablespoons ghee
3 garlic cloves, minced
1-pound shrimp, peeled and deveined
4 ounces cream cheese, at room temperature
½ cup heavy (whipping) cream
½ teaspoon sea salt
¼ teaspoon freshly ground black pepper
1 cup freshly grated Parmesan cheese
¼ teaspoon cayenne pepper

To make the zoodles: 1. Trim off the ends of the zucchinis. Swirl the zucchini into noodle shapes (zoodles) using a vegetable spiral slicer. 2. Lay the zoodles on a kitchen towel and sprinkle with the salt. 3. While the sauce is simmering, fold the zoodles up in the towel and squeeze out as much water as possible.
To make the shrimp and sauce: 1. In a cooking pan melt the ghee and cook the garlic for 3 minutes until fragrant. 2. Add the shrimp in it and cook for 4-6 minutes, until the shrimp turn pink. 3. Remove the cooked shrimp to a plate. 4. In the same cooking pan, add the cream cheese and whisk until melted. 5. Pour in the cream, whisking constantly. 6. Spice with the salt and pepper. 7. Let the creamy sauce simmer for 5-10 minutes, often whisking, until thickened. 8. Remove the cooking pan from the heat and stir in the Parmesan and cayenne. Adjust the seasoning as per taste. 8. Add the zoodles, cover, and cook for 5 minutes. 9. The zoodles will release a bit of water, thin out the thick sauce a bit. 10. Add the cooked shrimp and toss before serving.
Per Serving: Calories 329; Fat 25g; Sodium 489mg; Carbs 6g; Fiber 1g; Sugar 2g; Protein 20g

Cajun Crab Legs And Veggies

Prep time: 15 minutes | Cook time: 30 minutes | Serves: 6

Coconut oil, for greasing
2 zucchinis, halved lengthwise and sliced
3 cups roughly chopped cauliflower
10 tablespoons butter or ghee, melted, divided
2 tablespoons Cajun seasoning
1 tablespoon mince or chopped garlic
6 ounces sausages or bratwurst, cut into rounds ½-inch thick2 pounds of frozen snow crab legs (about two clusters)
½ lemon
Chopped fresh parsley for garnish

1. Preheat the oven to 450ºF/230°C temperature setting. Prepare a large baking sheet by lining it with aluminum foil and then grease the foil with oil. 2. Arrange the zucchini halves cut-side up on the baking sheet. Spread the cauliflower in an even layer. In a bowl, stir 5 tablespoons of melted butter with Cajun seasoning, and garlic. 3. Pour half of the spiced butter mixture over the veggies. 4. Bake the veggies for 15-20 minutes until tender. 5. Place the sausage slices on the vegetables. 6. Break the crab legs and put them in a pan. Drizzle with the remaining spiced butter mixture—bake them all for another 10 minutes. 7. Squeeze the lemon juice and sprinkle parsley, and serve immediately with the remaining butter for dipping.
Per Serving: Calories 415; Fat 29g; Sodium 845mg; Carbs 5g; Fiber 2g; Sugar 0g; Protein 33g

Delicious Shrimp Scampi

Prep time: 5 minutes | Cook time: 10 minutes | Serves: 4

4 tablespoons butter or ghee
4 garlic cloves, minced
½ cup bone broth
½ teaspoon sea salt
¼ teaspoon freshly ground black pepper
2 pounds shrimp, peeled and deveined
¼ cup freshly squeezed lemon juice
Chopped fresh parsley, for garnish

1. Cook garlic in the butter for 3 minutes until fragrant over medium heat. 2. Add the bone broth, salt, and pepper, and bring to a simmer for about 2 minutes. 3. Add the shrimp and cook for 4- 6 minutes, until the shrimp turn pink. Add the lemon juice. Sprinkle parsley over the shrimp to serve.
Per Serving: Calories 253; Fat 13g; Sodium 698mg; Carbs 3g; Fiber 0g; Sugar 0g; Protein 31g

Crispy Keto Baked Fish

Prep time: 10 minutes | Cook time: 20 minutes | Serves: 4

½ cup extra-virgin olive oil, divided
1-pound flaky white fish (such as cod, haddock, or halibut), skin removed
½ cup shelled finely chopped pistachios
½ cup ground flaxseed
Zest and juice of 1 lemon, divided
1 teaspoon ground cumin
1 teaspoon ground allspice
½ teaspoon salt (use 1 teaspoon if pistachios are unsalted)
¼ teaspoon freshly ground black pepper

1. Preheat the oven to 400°F/200°C. 2. Manage a baking sheet with parchment lining and drizzle 2 tablespoons olive oil over the sheet, spreading to coat the bottom evenly. 3. Cut the fish into 4 dense pieces. Place on the prepared baking sheet. Combine the pistachios, flaxseed, lemon zest, cumin, allspice, salt, and pepper in a small bowl. 4. Drizzle in ¼ cup olive oil and stir well. Divide the nut mixture evenly atop the fish pieces. 5. Drizzle the lemon juice and remaining 2 tablespoons oil over the fish and bake until cooked for about 15 -20 minutes.
Per Serving: Calories 509; Fat 41g; Sodium 745mg; Carbs 9g; Fiber 2g; Sugar 2g; Protein 26g

Oven-Fried Catfish

Prep time: 10 minutes plus 3 hours to soak | Cook time: 30 minutes | Serves: 4

4 catfish fillets
2 teaspoons baking soda
Avocado oil
½ cup almond flour
¼ cup crushed pork rinds
¼ teaspoon paprika
¼ teaspoon garlic powder
¼ teaspoon kosher salt
⅛ teaspoon cayenne pepper
2 eggs, lightly beaten

1. Place the catfish in a large bowl of cold water, add the baking soda, and stir to combine. Let it marinate for overnight. 2. Preheat the oven to 350°F/175°C. Manage a baking sheet with parchment lining and brush it liberally with avocado oil. Drain the catfish, rinse it, and pat it dry with a paper towel. 3. Stir the almond flour, pork rinds, paprika, garlic powder, salt, and cayenne in a shallow pie plate. Whisk the beaten eggs and 1 tablespoon water to combine in another shallow dish. 4. Coat each catfish fillet in the egg mixture and dredge it in the almond flour mixture, coating both sides well. Place the fillets, not touching, on the baking sheet. 5. Bake the fish for 25-30 minutes until the fish is cooked through and flaky, turning the fish halfway through the baking time. Serve with tartar sauce.
Per Serving: Calories 308; Fat 20g; Sodium 689mg; Carbs 2g; Fiber 1g; Sugar 1g; Protein 30g

Nutty Halibut Curry

Prep time: 5 minutes | Cook time: 35 minutes | Serves: 4

1 tablespoon avocado oil
½ cup finely chopped celery
½ cup frozen butternut squash cubes
1 cup full-fat canned coconut milk
½ cup seafood stock
1½ tablespoons curry powder
1 tablespoon dried cilantro
½ tablespoon garlic powder
½ tablespoon ground turmeric
1 teaspoon ground ginger
1-pound skinless halibut fillet, cut into chunks
Cooked cauliflower rice, for serving

1. Heat the avocado oil in a saucepan with a lid. Add the celery and cook for about 3 minutes. Add the squash and cook for 5 minutes. Add the coconut milk and seafood stock and cook, stirring, for 3 minutes. 2. Stir in the curry powder, cilantro, garlic, turmeric, and ginger. Add the halibut to the pot, reduce the heat to medium, cover, and cook for 15 -20 minutes until the fish is thoroughly white and flakes easily with a fork. 3. Serve the halibut curry over cauliflower rice if you'd like, or just eat it by itself!
Per Serving: Calories 362; Fat 22g; Sodium 986mg; Carbs 8g; Fiber 3g; Sugar 1g; Protein 33g

Nut-Crusted Catfish

Prep time: 20 minutes | Cook time: 25 minutes | Serves: 4

4 catfish fillets, about 4 ounces each, rinsed and dry
2 cups chopped pecans
1½ teaspoons gluten-free Worcestershire sauce
1¼ teaspoons garlic powder
1¼ teaspoons paprika
1 teaspoon salt, plus more for seasoning

½ teaspoon black pepper, plus more for seasoning
¼ teaspoon onion powder
¼ teaspoon cayenne pepper
2 eggs, lightly beaten
1 teaspoon hot sauce
Chopped fresh parsley, for serving
Lemon wedges, for serving

1. Preheat the oven to 375°F/190°C. Prepare a baking sheet with parchment paper. Set aside. Combine the pecans, Worcestershire sauce, garlic powder, paprika, salt, black pepper, onion powder, and cayenne in a food processor. 2. Pulse until the pecans are finely chopped. Pour the mixture into a shallow pie plate and set aside. In a separate shallow dish, whisk the eggs and hot sauce. 3. Dip each catfish fillet into the egg, coating it on both sides, and dredge in the pecan mixture, pressing the pecan coating onto the fish to make sure the top of the fillet is well coated. Place the fillets onto the baking sheet. 4. Bake for 20-25 minutes until done and the pecan crust is golden brown and fragrant. The thickest part of the fish should flake easily and will be opaque all the way through. 5. Garnish with parsley and lemon wedges for squeezing.
Per Serving: Calories 647; Fat 55g; Sodium 1104mg; Carbs 11g; Fiber 7g; Sugar 5g; Protein 27g

Crispy Fried Cod Sticks

Prep time: 15 minutes | Cook time: 15 minutes | Serves: 4

1 cup crushed pork rinds
¼ cup grated Parmesan cheese
½ cup heavy (whipping) cream
1 large egg
4 (4-ounce) cod fillets, patted dry

Extra-virgin olive oil, for frying
1 (10-ounce) can original Ro-Tel (drained)
2 tablespoons lemon juice

1. Combine the pork rinds and grated Parmesan. In another bowl, whisk the heavy cream and egg. 2. Dip each cod fillet thoroughly in the egg mixture, then dip on both sides into the pork rind mixture, making sure the entire fillet is covered. 3. Put the fillet in fridge to refrigerate while the oil heats. Heat the oil to 365°F/185°C. Working in batches if necessary, fry each fillet for about 2 minutes on each side or until the outside is golden brown. 4. Drain on a paper towel if needed, then plate and serve, topping each fillet with one-quarter of the can of Ro-Tel.
Per Serving: Calories 375; Fat 28g; Sodium 455mg; Carbs 6g; Fiber 0g; Sugar 0g; Protein 36g

Cream-Poached Trout

Prep time: 10 minutes | Cooking time: 20 minutes | Serves: 4

4 (4-ounce) skinless trout fillets
Sea salt
Black pepper, freshly ground
3 tablespoons butter
1 teaspoon chopped fresh parsley, for garnish

1 leek, white and green parts, halved lengthwise, sliced, and thoroughly washed
1 teaspoon minced garlic
1 cup heavy (whipping) cream
Juice of 1 lemon

1. At 400°F/200°C, preheat your oven. 2. Pat the trout fillets dry with paper towels and lightly season with black pepper and salt. 3. Place them in a 9-inch-square baking dish in one layer. Keep it aside. 4. Place a suitable saucepan over medium-high heat and melt the butter. 5. Sauté the leek and garlic until softened, for almost 6 minutes. 6. Add the heavy cream and lemon juice to the saucepan and cook to a boil, whisking. 7. Pour the sauce over the fish and bake until the fish is just cooked through, for 10 to 12 minutes. 8. Serve topped with the parsley.
Per serving: Calories: 383; Total fat: 19g; saturated fat: 3g; cholesterol: 64mg; carbohydrates: 26g; Fiber: 1g; Protein: 21g

Cod with Green Pistou

Prep time: 15 minutes | Cook time: 10 minutes | Serves: 4

1 cup roughly chopped fresh Italian parsley
1 to 2 garlic cloves, minced
Zest and juice of 1 lemon
1 teaspoon salt
½ teaspoon freshly ground black

pepper
1 cup extra-virgin olive oil, divided
1-pound cod fillets, cut into 4 equal-sized pieces

1. Pulse the parsley, garlic, lemon zest and juice, salt, and pepper in a food processor. While the food processor is blending, slowly stream in ¾ cup of olive oil until well combined. 2. In a large pan, heat the remaining ¼ cup of olive oil over medium-high heat. Add the cod fillets, cover, and cook for 4 to 5 minutes on each side, or until cooked through. 3. Remove from the heat and keep warm. Add the pistou to the pan and heat over medium-low heat. Return the cooked fish to the pan, flipping to coat in the sauce. 4. Serve warm, covered with pistou.
Per Serving: Calories 581; Fat 55g; Sodium 714mg; Carbs 3g; Fiber 1g; Sugar 1g; Protein 21g

Roasted Cod with Garlic Butter

Prep time: 5 minutes | Cook time: 20 minutes | Serves: 2

2 (8-ounce) cod fillets
¼ cup (½ stick) butter, thinly sliced
1 tablespoon minced garlic
½ pound baby bok choy, halved

lengthwise
¼ teaspoon salt
¼ teaspoon freshly ground black pepper

1. Preheat the oven to 400°F/200°C temperature setting. 2. Make a pouch with aluminum foil. Place the cod inside the pouch. 3. Top the cod with slices of butter and the garlic, evenly divided. Tuck the bok choy around the fillets. Season with salt and pepper. 4. Close the aluminum pouch with the two ends of the foil so the butter remains in it. Place the sealed pouches in a baking dish. 5. Bake the fish pouches for 15 to 20 minutes, depending on the thickness of the fillets. 6. Serve immediately.
Per Serving: Calories 317; Fat 24g; Sodium 478mg; Carbs 4g; Fiber 1g; Sugar 2g; Protein 23g

Pan-Fried Shrimp Balls over Garlicky Greens

Prep time: 10 minutes | Cooking time: 25 minutes | Serves: 4

1 pound wild-caught shrimp, peeled, deveined, and finely chopped
¼ cup coconut or almond flour
1 large egg, lightly beaten
1 (2-inch) piece fresh ginger, peeled and minced
¼ cup minced scallion, green part only
1 teaspoon garlic powder
Grated zest of 1 lime

½ teaspoon salt
¼ to ½ teaspoon red pepper flakes
10 tablespoons olive oil, plus more for frying as needed
8 cups kale or spinach, torn into bite-size pieces
6 garlic cloves, minced
¼ cup soy sauce
2 tablespoons rice vinegar
2 tablespoons sesame oil

1. In a suitable bowl, mix the shrimp, coconut flour, egg, ginger, 2 tablespoons of scallion, garlic powder, lime zest, salt, and red pepper flakes, mixing well with a fork. 2. Using your hands, form the shrimp mixture into about a dozen (1-inch) balls and place them on a cutting board or baking sheet lined with parchment paper. Allow to rest for almost 10 minutes. 3. In a suitable skillet or saucepan, heat 4 tablespoons of olive oil over medium-high heat. Working in batches of three to four balls, panfry them for almost 5 to 7 minutes total, carefully turning to brown all sides. Repeat until all the shrimp balls have been fried, adding additional oil with each batch as needed. Keep the shrimp balls warm. 4. In a suitable skillet, heat 2 tablespoons of olive oil over medium-high heat. Add the greens and sauté for almost 5 minutes. Add the garlic and sauté for almost 2 to 4 minutes, or until the greens are wilted. 5. In a suitable bowl, beat the soy sauce, vinegar, and sesame oil. 6. To serve, divide the sautéed greens between plates and top with three shrimp balls drizzled with the sauce.
Per serving: Calories: 210; Total fat 9.1g; Sodium 282mg; Total Carbs 3.8g; Fiber 3g; Sugars 8.5g; Protein 22.8g

Crispy Cod Cakes

Prep time: 5 minutes | Cook time: 20 minutes | Serves: 2

3 tablespoons extra-virgin olive oil
¼ medium onion, chopped
1 garlic clove, minced
1 cup cauliflower rice
1-pound cod fillets
½ cup almond flour
1 large egg
2 tablespoons chopped fresh parsley

2 tablespoons ground flaxseed
1 tablespoon freshly squeezed lemon juice
1 teaspoon dried dill
½ teaspoon ground cumin
½ teaspoon pink Himalayan sea salt
¼ teaspoon freshly ground black pepper
Tartar sauce

1. Heat oil and cook the onion and garlic for about 7 minutes, until tender over medium heat. Add in the cauliflower rice stir for 5 to 7 minutes, until warmed through and tender. Transfer to a large bowl. 2. Heat 1 teaspoon of olive oil in the same pan over medium-high heat. Cook the cod for 4 to 5 minutes on each side, until cooked through. 3. Let the cod cool for a couple of minutes. Add the almond flour, egg, parsley, flaxseed, lemon juice, dill, cumin, salt, and pepper to the bowl with the cauliflower rice. Mix until the ingredients are well combined. 4. Add the fish to the bowl and mix well. Heat the remaining 1 tablespoon of olive oil in the pan over medium heat. 5. Using a ½ cup measuring cup, form 4 fish cakes by packing the mixture into the cup, then slipping the cake out of the cup onto a plate. 6. Place the fish cakes in the hot oil and cook for about 5 minutes per side, flipping once, until golden brown on both sides. 7. Place the cod cakes on serving plates, and do help with tartar sauce.
Per Serving: Calories 531; Fat 34g; Sodium 359mg; Carbs 12g; Fiber 6g; Sugar 2g; Protein 45g

Baked Halibut Steak with Herb Sauce

Prep time: 15 minutes | Cook time: 18 minutes | Serves: 4

4 (5-ounce) halibut fillets
1 tablespoon extra-virgin olive oil
Sea salt
Freshly ground black pepper
½ cup plain Greek yogurt
¼ cup mayonnaise

2 tablespoons sour cream
Juice and zest of 1 lemon
1 tablespoon chopped fresh dill
1 teaspoon chopped fresh basil
1 teaspoon chopped fresh chives

1. Preheat the oven to 400°F/200°C. Prepare a baking sheet with parchment paper. 2. Pat dry fish with paper towels and lightly oil with olive oil. Season both sides of the fish with salt and pepper. 3. Place the spiced fillets on the baking sheet, and bake until cooked through about 15 to 18 minutes. 4. While the fish is cooking, stir the yogurt, mayonnaise, sour cream, lemon juice, lemon zest, dill, basil, and chives in a small bowl. 5. Serve the fish with a generous dollop of sauce.
Per Serving: Calories 374; Fat 25g; Sodium 236mg; Carbs 2g; Fiber 0g; Sugar 0g; Protein 33g

Pesto Flounder with Greens

Prep time: 10 minutes | Cook time: 10 minutes | Serves: 6

2 pounds bok choy (about 1 large head)
6 skinless flounder fillets (4 ounces each)
6 tablespoons pesto
6 tablespoons finely grated

Parmesan cheese
Freshly ground black pepper
2 tablespoons olive oil
1 garlic clove, minced
Salt

1. Preheat the broiler to high. Prepare a baking sheet with aluminum foil. Trim off the thick root end of the bok choy. 2. Slice stalks into quarters, then cut into rough chunks. 3. Pat dry the fish dry with paper towels and place it on the baking sheet. 4. Spread a tablespoon pesto over each fillet. Sprinkle 1 tablespoon of Parmesan on each fillet. 5. Spice it with pepper. Cook it under the broiler for 5 to 7 minutes until is opaque. Heat the olive oil and cook bok choy with garlic, frequently stirring, for about 5 minutes. 6. When done, remove it from the broiler and transfer to serving plates. Add cooked garlicky bok choy and season with salt.
Per Serving: Calories 264; Fat 17g; Sodium 354mg; Carbs 10g; Fiber 4g; Sugar 3g; Protein 19g

Baked Haddock

Prep time: 10 minutes | Cook time: 27 minutes | Serves: 4

2 tablespoons olive oil
1 onion, thinly sliced
1 tablespoon minced garlic
4 (3-ounce) haddock fillets
2 cups canned coconut milk
2 tablespoons chopped fresh cilantro

1 teaspoon ground coriander
½ teaspoon ground cumin
Sea salt
Freshly ground black pepper

1. Preheat the oven to 350°F/175°C. Heat the olive oil in ovenproof pan over medium-high heat. Sauté the onion and garlic until lightly caramelized, about 7 minutes. 2. Pan sear the fish, turning once, about 8 minutes. Add the coconut milk, coriander, and cumin, stirring carefully. 3. Cover and bake until the fish flake with a fork, for about 12 minutes. Season with salt and pepper, and serve topped with cilantro.
Per Serving: Calories 381; Fat 29g; Sodium 632mg; Carbs 6g; Fiber 1g; Sugar 1g; Protein 23g

Cheesy Fried Haddock

Prep time: 15 minutes | Cook time: 12 minutes | Serves: 4

1-pound boneless haddock fillets, cut into 4 equal pieces
¼ cup almond flour, divided
1 large egg
1 tablespoon water
½ cup Parmesan cheese

¼ cup flaxseed meal
¼ teaspoon freshly ground black pepper
Pinch ground cayenne pepper
½ cup extra-virgin olive oil
Lemon wedges, for garnish

1. Put 2 tablespoons of almond flour in a small bowl, and set it next to the fish. 2. Stir the eggs and water in another small bowl, and set the mixture next to the almond flour. 3. Stir the remaining 2 tablespoons of almond flour with the Parmesan cheese, flaxseed meal, black pepper, and cayenne pepper in a medium bowl. 4. Set the bowl next to the egg mixture. Dredge the fish pieces in the almond flour, the egg mixture, and the flour mixture, in that order, until all 4 pieces are coated. 5. Heat the olive oil. When the oil is hot, fry the fish, turning once, until both sides are golden and crispy for about 6 minutes per side, depending on the thickness of the fish. 6. Transfer the fish to a paper towel-lined plate, and use paper towels to blot off the excess oil. 7. Serve with lemon wedges.
Per Serving: Calories 349; Fat 25g; Sodium 741mg; Carbs 4g; Fiber 3g; Sugar 1g; Protein 27g

Seared Cod with Coconut-Mushroom Sauce

Prep time: 10 minutes | Cooking time: 20 minutes | Serves: 4

1 pound cod fillet
½ teaspoon salt
¼ teaspoon black pepper, freshly ground
½ cup coconut oil
Grated zest and juice of 1 lime
4 ounces shiitake mushrooms, sliced
2 garlic cloves, minced

1 (13.5-ounce) can full-fat coconut milk
1 teaspoon ground ginger
1 teaspoon red pepper flakes
2 tablespoons tamari (or 1 tablespoon miso paste and 1 tablespoon water)
2 tablespoons toasted sesame oil

1. Cut the cod into four equal pieces and season with black pepper and salt. 2. In a suitable skillet, heat 4 tablespoons of coconut oil over high heat until just before smoking. 3. Add the cod, skin-side up, cover to prevent splattering and sear for almost 4 to 5 minutes, until it's golden brown. Remove the fish from the skillet, drizzle with the juice of ½ lime, and let rest. 4. In the same skillet, add the remaining 4 tablespoons of coconut oil and heat over medium. Add the mushrooms and sauté for almost 5 to 6 minutes, until they are just tender. Add the garlic and sauté for almost 1 minute, until fragrant. 5. Whisk in the coconut milk, ginger, red pepper flakes, tamari, and remaining lime zest and juice and reduce its heat to low. 6. Return the cod to the skillet, skin-side down, cover and simmer for almost 3 to 4 minutes, until the fish is cooked through. 7. To serve, place the cod on rimmed plates or in shallow bowls and spoon the sauce over the fish. Drizzle with the sesame oil.
Per serving: Calories: 456; Total fat 26.2g; Sodium 119mg; Total Carbs 3.5g; Fiber 1.5g; Sugars 2.3g; Protein 28.8g

Teriyaki Halibut

Prep time: 5 minutes | Cook time: 15 minutes | Serves: 1

1 tablespoon balsamic vinegar
1 tablespoon coconut aminos
1 teaspoon grated ginger root
1 tablespoon avocado oil

1 (6-ounce) halibut fillet
Pink Himalayan salt
Freshly ground black pepper

1. In a saucepan heat the balsamic vinegar, coconut aminos, and grated ginger until bubbling. Reduce the heat to low and simmer for 5 minutes. 2. Transfer to a bowl and set aside. Heat the oil in a sauté pan or pan. 3. Season the halibut with salt and pepper and add the fish to the pan. Sear the halibut for about 3 minutes and then flip and sear the other side for 3 more minutes. 4. Flip once more and brush 1 tablespoon of teriyaki sauce over the top and sides of the fish. Lower the heat to medium flame and cook for another 2 minutes on each side, or until the center is opaque. 5. Remove the halibut from the pan and top with the remaining sauce before serving.
Per Serving: Calories 393; Fat 19g; Sodium 698mg; Carbs 5g; Fiber 0g; Sugar 0g; Protein 45g

Baked Keto Halibut

Prep time: 20 minutes | Cook time: 15 minutes | Serves: 4

½ cup heavy (whipping) cream
½ cup finely chopped pecans
¼ cup finely chopped almonds
4 (4-ounce) boneless halibut fillets

Sea salt
Freshly ground black pepper
2 tablespoons extra-virgin olive oil

1. Preheat the oven to 400°F/200°C. Prepare a baking sheet with parchment. Pour the heavy cream into a bowl and set it on your work surface. 2. Stir the pecans and almonds in another bowl and set beside the cream. Pat dry the halibut fillets with paper towels and lightly season with salt and pepper. 3. Dip the fillets in the cream, shaking off the excess; then dredge the fish in the nut mixture so that both sides of each piece are thickly coated. 4. Place the fish on the prepared baking sheet and brush both sides of the pieces generously with olive oil. 5. Bake the fish until the topping is golden, and the fish flakes easily with a fork, for 12 to 15 minutes. Serve.
Per Serving: Calories 392; Fat 31g; Sodium 698mg; Carbs 3g; Fiber 2g; Sugar 1g; Protein 26g

Pan-Fried Salmon and Bok Choy In Miso Vinaigrette

Prep time: 10 minutes | Cooking time: 25 minutes | Serves: 4

¼ cup miso paste
2 tablespoons rice wine vinegar or dry white wine
6 tablespoons toasted sesame oil
2 teaspoons ground ginger
1 teaspoon red pepper flakes
2 garlic cloves, minced

1 pound wild-caught salmon fillet, skin removed
½ cup avocado oil or olive oil, extra-virgin
8 heads baby bok choy, quartered
2 tablespoons tamari or water
2 tablespoons sesame seeds

1. In a suitable bowl, mix the miso, vinegar, 2 tablespoons of sesame oil, ginger, red pepper flakes, and garlic and whisk until smooth. 2. In a glass baking dish or resealable storage bag, place the salmon and pour the marinade over it. 3. Refrigerate for 30 minutes or up to overnight. To cook the fish, in a suitable skillet heat 4 tablespoons of avocado oil over medium-high heat. 4. Remove the salmon from the marinade, reserving the liquid, and fry for almost 3 to 5 minutes per side, until the fish is crispy and golden brown. The time depends on your desired doneness and the thickness of the fish. 5. Transfer the fish to a suitable platter and keep warm. 6. In the same skillet, add the remaining 4 tablespoons of avocado oil over medium-high heat. Add the bok choy and fry for almost 7 minutes, until it is crispy and just tender. 7. Transfer it to the platter with the salmon. Reduce its heat to low. 8. Add the reserved miso marinade and tamari to the oil in the skillet and whisk to mix well. Simmer, uncovered, for almost 4 to 5 minutes, until slightly thickened. 9. Whisk in the remaining 4 tablespoons of sesame oil until smooth. 10. Serve the salmon and bok choy drizzled with the warm miso vinaigrette and sprinkled with the sesame seeds.
Per serving: Calories: 305; Total fat 5.7g; Sodium 307mg; Total Carbs 4g; Fiber 1.8g; Sugars 4.4g; Protein 20.8g

Halibut with Tangy Basil Sauce

Prep time: 10 minutes | Cook time: 20 minutes | Serves: 4

½ cup extra-virgin olive oil, divided
2 large garlic cloves, minced
1-pint grape tomatoes halved
¼ cup dry white wine
Juice of 1 lemon

½ cup roughly chopped fresh basil
Sea salt
Freshly ground black pepper
1¼ pounds halibut, cut into 4 (5-ounce) fillets

1. Heat olive oil in a saucepan. Cook the garlic until fragrant. 2. Cook the tomatoes for 10 minutes until they partially break down. Stir in the wine and simmer for 1 to 2 minutes to cook off the alcohol. 3. Stir in basil along with lemon juice and season generously with salt and pepper. While the sauce is cooking, heat the remaining 2 tablespoons of olive oil in a large pan over medium-high heat. 4. Season the halibut fillets liberally with salt and pepper. Sear on each side for 3 to 4 minutes, or until the fish flakes easily with a fork.
Per Serving: Calories 467; Fat 31g; Sodium 412mg; Carbs 5g; Fiber 0g; Sugar 0g; Protein 38g

Crispy Haddock

Prep time: 20 minutes | Cook time: 12 minutes | Serves: 4

16 ounces boneless, skinless haddock fillet, cut into 4 pieces
1 cup almond flour
½ teaspoon paprika
⅛ teaspoon ground cardamom

⅛ teaspoon sea salt
Pinch freshly ground black pepper
½ cup heavy (whipping) cream
¼ cup coconut oil

1. Rinse the fillets and pat them thoroughly dry with paper towels. In a medium bowl, stir the almond flour, paprika, cardamom, salt, and pepper until well blended. 2. Pour the cream into another medium bowl and set it beside the almond flour mixture. Dredge one fish fillet in the flour mixture, shaking off the excess. 3. Then dip the fillet into the cream, shaking off the excess liquid. Finally, dredge the fish in the flour again to coat thoroughly and set aside. 4. Repeat with the remaining fillets. Fry the fillets until the fish is golden and crispy, turning once about 12 minutes total.
Per Serving: Calories 475; Fat 39g; Sodium 845mg; Carbs 7g; Fiber 3g; Sugar 2g; Protein 28g

Thai-Inspired Seafood Chowder

Prep time: 10 minutes | Cooking time: 15 minutes | Serves: 4

2 tablespoons coconut oil
1 red bell pepper, coarsely chopped
1 (2-inch) piece fresh ginger, peeled and minced
6 garlic cloves, sliced
1 jalapeño, finely chopped (seeded for less heat, if preferred)
2 teaspoons Thai green curry paste
2 (13.5-ounce) cans full-fat coconut milk

¼ cup tamari (or 2 tablespoons miso paste and 2 tablespoons water)
1 to 2 teaspoons monk fruit extract
8 ounces wild-caught shrimp, peeled and deveined
8 ounces cod fillet, skinned and cut into bite-size chunks
Grated zest and juice of 1 lime
½ to 1 cup sliced fresh basil
Sliced jalapeño, for garnish

1. In a suitable stockpot, heat the coconut oil over medium heat. Add the bell pepper, ginger, garlic, and jalapeño and sauté for almost 4 to 5 minutes, until the vegetables are tender. 2. Add the curry paste and sauté for almost 1 minute, then add the coconut milk and tamari and whisk to mix well. Stir in the monk fruit extract (if using). 3. Bring the prepared mixture to a boil, reduce its heat to low, add the shrimp and cod, cover and simmer for almost 3 to 4 minutes, until the seafood is cooked through but not overly done. 4. Remove the shrimp from the heat and stir in the lime zest and juice and basil. Serve warm, garnished with the jalapeño (if using).
Per serving: Calories: 232; Total fat 9.7g; Sodium 389mg; Total carbs 1.1g; Fiber 0.5g; Sugars 0.2g; Protein 33.1g

Chapter 7 Vegetables and Sides

Zucchini Boats ………………… 88

Parmesan Cauliflower ……………… 88

Pesto Pasta…………………………… 88

Keto Tater Tots …………………… 88

Fried Zuck Patties ………………… 88

Zucchini Fries ……………………… 88

Radish Potatoes …………………… 88

Smashed Cauliflower………………… 88

Creamed Spinach ………………… 89

Baked Jalapeño and Cheese Cauliflower
Mash ………………………… 89

Burger Bun for One ……………… 89

Oven-Safe Baking Dishes …………… 89

Roasted Asparagus ……………… 89

Cheesy Baked Asparagus …………… 89

Dijon Roast Cabbage………………… 89

Garlic Parmesan–Roasted Cauliflower … 89

Cauliflower Rice Balls ……………… 90

Cheesy Loaded Broccoli …………… 90

Buttery Mushrooms ……………… 90

"Faux-Tato" Hash ………………… 90

Savory Zucchini Boats …………… 90

Roasted Broccoli Salad …………… 90

Bacon-Jalapeño Cheesy "Breadsticks" … 90

Onion Rings ……………………… 90

Dinner Rolls …………………… 91

A Go-To Bread! …………………… 91

Crispy Green Beans ……………… 91

Flatbread Dippers ………………… 91

Mini Spinach and Sweet Pepper Poppers 91

Roasted Brussels Sprouts ………… 91

Roasted Salsa……………………… 91

Sweet Pepper Nachos …………… 91

Spinach and Artichoke–Stuffed Peppers 92

Pesto Vegetable Skewers ………… 92

Lemon Caper Cauliflower Steaks ……… 92

Crispy Eggplant Rounds ………… 92

Cauliflower Rice–Stuffed Peppers …… 92

Pan Pizza ………………………… 92

Vegetable Burgers ………………… 92

Stuffed Portobello Mushrooms ……… 92

Crustless Spinach and Cheese Frittata … 93

Cauliflower Pizza Crust………………… 93

Roasted Spaghetti Squash ………… 93

Alfredo Eggplant Stacks ………… 93

White Cheddar and Mushroom Soufflés 93

Cheesy Broccoli Sticks …………… 93

Zucchini Fritters ………………… 93

Herb Cloud Eggs ………………… 93

Crispy Cabbage Steaks …………… 94

Cheesy Cabbage Cribbage……………… 94

Steamed Cauliflower………………… 94

Zucchini Boats

Prep time: 10 minutes | Cook time: 30 minutes | Serves: 4

2 medium zucchinis
½ cup grated cheddar cheese
2 ounces full-fat cream cheese, softened
¼ cup diced onion
¼ cup full-fat sour cream
2 tablespoons melted unsalted butter
¼ teaspoon salt
4 strips no-sugar-added bacon, cooked and crumbled
1 medium jalapeño pepper, deveined, seeded, and finely chopped

1. Preheat the oven to 350°F/175°C. 2. Cut the zucchinis in half lengthwise. Cut in half at the midpoint to create eight "boats" 3" to 4" long to be hollowed out. 3. With a spoon, scoop out each boat; try to get the most out but leave enough so the sides aren't too thin (about ¼" max). Chop the removed flesh finely and put in a medium bowl. 4. Place eight scooped-out boats in a large greased baking dish. 5. Add remaining ingredients except bacon and jalapeños to the bowl with zucchini flesh and mix well. Divide the mixture evenly and scoop it into the boats. 6. Top with crumbled bacon and jalapeño. 7. Bake it for 30 minutes until filling bubbles up, and zucchini boats are softened. Remove from oven and let cool for 5 minutes. Serve.
Per Serving: Calories 259; Fat 20g; Sodium 496mg; Carbs 6g; Fiber 1g; Sugar 4g; Protein 10g

Parmesan Cauliflower

Prep time: 10 minutes | Cook time: 35 minutes | Serves: 4

16 ounces cauliflower, cut into bite-sized florets
4 tablespoons melted unsalted butter
2 tablespoons olive oil
¼ teaspoon salt
¼ teaspoon black pepper
1 cup grated Parmesan cheese
2 teaspoons parsley flakes

1. Preheat the oven to 400°F/200°C. Prepare a baking sheet with parchment paper. 2. Toss cauliflower, melted butter, and olive oil in a large mixing bowl. Add salt and pepper. 3. Place coated cauliflower on the baking sheet. Keep cauliflower in a single layer so it cooks evenly. Bake for 25–30 minutes or until soft. 4. Remove from oven and dust with Parmesan cheese and parsley. Return to oven for 5 minutes to melt the cheese. 5. Remove from the oven and serve warm.
Per Serving: Calories 294; Fat 23g; Sodium 632mg; Carbs 9g; Fiber 2g; Sugar 2g; Protein 9g

Pesto Pasta

Prep time: 5 minutes | Cook time: 15 minutes | Serves: 6

¼ cup pine nuts
4 cloves garlic, peeled and chopped
1½ cups fresh basil leaves
½ cup olive oil
½ cup grated or shredded Parmesan cheese, divided
1 head cauliflower, cut into florets

1. Pulse the pine nuts, garlic, basil, oil, and ¼ cup Parmesan cheese in a small blender until liquefied, about 1–2 minutes. 2. Steam florets until tender, for about 10–15 minutes. Place florets in a medium mixing bowl and gently fold in pesto sauce. 3. Serve warm and sprinkle with remaining Parmesan cheese.
Per Serving: Calories 270; Fat 23g; Sodium 193mg; Carbs 10g; Fiber 3g; Sugar 3g; Protein 6g

Keto Tater Tots

Prep time: 5 minutes | Cook time: 30 minutes | Serves: 8

1½ pounds riced cauliflower
4 tablespoons avocado oil, divided
1 large egg
1½ cups shredded whole milk mozzarella cheese
2 cloves minced garlic
¾ teaspoon salt, divided

1. In a pan, fry cauliflower rice with 2 tablespoons oil for 5–10 minutes until soft and brown. 2. In a bowl, whisk egg and mix in cheese, garlic, and ½ teaspoon salt. 3. Combine browned cauliflower rice with egg mixture. Stir the mixture well to melt the cheese. 4. Form cauliflower tots using a spoon or melon scoop. 5. In a pan over medium heat, fry tots using the remaining 2 tablespoons of oil. 6. Space tots apart in a single layer, turning every 3–5 minutes until browned on all sides. 7. Repeat until all tots are cooked. Sprinkle with remaining ¼ teaspoon salt and serve hot.
Per Serving: Calories 154; Fat 12g; Sodium 378mg; Carbs 5g; Fiber 2g; Sugar 2g; Protein 7g

Fried Zuck Patties

Prep time: 30 minutes | Cook time: 15 minutes | Serves: 8

1 pound zucchini
1 teaspoon salt
2 large beaten eggs
2 medium green onions, chopped
1½ teaspoons lemon pepper
1 cup shredded whole milk
mozzarella cheese
½ cup blanched almond flour
¼ cup grated Parmesan cheese
¼ cup flaxseed meal
4 tablespoons coconut oil

1. Grate zucchini and sprinkle with salt. Drain the grated zucchini for 15 minutes or more in a large colander. Turn shreds often to speed up drainage. Squeeze the mixture using a cheesecloth to remove excess moisture. 2. Mix grated zucchini with beaten eggs and green onions in a large bowl. 3. Mix all ingredients except for the oil. Add to zucchini mixture, stirring well. 4. Form "zuck" patties 3" in diameter and ½" thick. 5. In a pan heat oil. Fry patties for 3–5 minutes per side. 6. When "Zuck" patties are thoroughly cooked and firm throughout, place on a paper towel-lined plate to drain and cool.
Per Serving: Calories 199; Fat 16g; Sodium 457mg; Carbs 5g; Fiber 2g; Sugar 2g; Protein 8g

Zucchini Fries

Prep time: 10 minutes | Cook time: 23 minutes | Serves: 4

2 medium zucchinis
¼ teaspoon salt
¼ teaspoon black pepper
¼ teaspoon garlic powder
¾ cup grated Parmesan cheese
1 large egg, beaten

1. Preheat the oven to 425°F/220°C. Prepare a baking sheet with foil. Place a rack onto a baking sheet. 2. Slice zucchini in half, lengthwise, until you have created eight long sticks of similar size. Then cut bars in half across the middle, making sixteen pieces (per zucchini). 3. Mix salt, pepper, garlic powder, and cheese in a medium bowl. 4. In a separate bowl, beat egg. 5. First, dip stick in the egg. Second, press each side into the spices. 6. Place spaced apart on the rack in a layer. 7. Bake the chips for 20 minutes, flipping fries and rotating pan halfway through until browned and crispy. 8. Then broil fries for 2–3 minutes until dark golden.
Per Serving: Calories 113; Fat 6g; Sodium 509mg; Carbs 6g; Fiber 1g; Sugar 3g; Protein 8g

Radish Potatoes

Prep time: 5 minutes | Cook time: 50 minutes | Serves: 4

20 medium radishes, trimmed and halved
2 tablespoons olive oil
2 teaspoons Italian seasoning,
divided
¼ teaspoon salt
¼ teaspoon black pepper
¼ cup grated Parmesan cheese

1. Preheat the oven to 400°F/200°C. Grease a baking pan with olive oil. Add halved radishes to the baking dish, brush with olive oil, and dust with half of the Italian seasoning, salt, and pepper. 2. Bake for 45 minutes until light brown and crisp. Toss and re-season halfway through. 3. Add Parmesan on top and bake for 5 more minutes. Remove from the oven and your golden radishes are ready to serve.
Per Serving: Calories 89; Fat 8g; Sodium 266mg; Carbs 2g; Fiber 0g; Sugar 0g; Protein 2g

Smashed Cauliflower

Prep time: 10 minutes | Cook time: 18 minutes | Serves: 6

1 pound cauliflower florets
3 tablespoons unsalted butter
¼ teaspoon garlic powder
½ cup fat-free sour cream
2 tablespoons chopped green
onion, divided
1 cup shredded cheddar cheese, divided
¼ teaspoon salt

1. Steam florets for 10–15 minutes until very soft. Remove from heat and let sit in a metal colander for 10–15 minutes to release water. 2. Pulse florets in a food processor for 2–3 minutes until fluffy. Add butter, garlic powder, and sour cream and process for 2–3 more minutes until it resembles mashed potatoes. 3. Scoop cauliflower into a medium microwave-safe bowl and mix in two-thirds of the green onion and ½ cup cheese and salt. Microwave for 2–3 minutes. 4. Serve and sprinkle remaining cheese and green onion on top.
Per Serving: Calories 183; Fat 14g; Sodium 250mg; Carbs 5g; Fiber 2g; Sugar 2g; Protein 6g

Creamed Spinach

Prep time: 5 minutes | Cook time: 15 minutes | Serves: 6

20 ounces fresh spinach, finely chopped
⅓ cup grated Parmesan cheese
6 ounces full-fat cream cheese, softened

4 tablespoons full-fat sour cream
½ teaspoon garlic powder
½ teaspoon onion powder
¼ teaspoon salt
¼ teaspoon black pepper

1. In a nonstick pan, add spinach. Cook for 3–5 minutes while stirring until wilted and excess water is removed. 2. Add remaining ingredients and stir for 5–10 minutes until cheeses are melted and are blended. Serve.
Per Serving: Calories 158; Fat 11g; Sodium 378mg; Carbs 6g; Fiber 2g; Sugar 2g; Protein 6g

Baked Jalapeño and Cheese Cauliflower Mash

Prep time: 10 minutes | Cooking time: 15 minutes | Serves: 6

1 (12-ounce) steamer bag cauliflower florets, cooked according to package instructions
2 tablespoons salted butter, softened
2 ounces cream cheese, softened

½ cup shredded sharp cheddar cheese
¼ cup pickled jalapeños
½ teaspoon salt
¼ teaspoon ground black pepper

1. Place cooked cauliflower into a food processor with remaining ingredients. Pulse twenty times until cauliflower is smooth and all the recipe ingredients are combined. 2. Spoon mash into an ungreased 6" round nonstick baking dish. Place dish into air fryer basket. 3. Set the temperature to 380°F/195°C and set the timer for almost 15 minutes. 4. The top will be golden brown when done. Serve warm.
Per serving: Calories: 393; Total fat 8.9g; Sodium 124mg; Total Carbs 4.7g; Fiber 8.1g; Sugars 2.6g; Protein 14.7g

Burger Bun for One

Prep time: 10 minutes | Cooking time: 5 minutes | Serves: 1

2 tablespoons salted butter, melted
¼ cup blanched finely ground almond flour

¼ teaspoon baking powder
⅛ teaspoon apple cider vinegar
1 large egg, whisked

1. Pour butter into an ungreased 4" ramekin. Add flour, baking powder, and vinegar to ramekin and stir until well-mixed. Add egg and stir until batter is mostly smooth. 2. Place ramekin into air fryer basket. Set the temperature to 350°F/175°C and set the timer for almost 5 minutes. 3. When done, the center will be firm and the top slightly browned. Let cool. 4. For almost 5 minutes, then remove from ramekin and slice in half. Serve.
Per serving: Calories: 162; Total fat 9.8g; Sodium 359mg; Total Carbs 7.7g; Fiber 5.1g; Sugars 6.1g; Protein 6.3g

Oven-Safe Baking Dishes

Prep time: 10 minutes | Cooking time: 12 minutes | Serves: 4

2 cups trimmed and halved fresh Brussels sprouts
2 tablespoons olive oil
¼ teaspoon salt

¼ teaspoon ground black pepper
2 tablespoons balsamic vinegar
2 slices cooked sugar-free bacon, crumbled

1. In a suitable bowl, toss Brussels sprouts in olive oil, then sprinkle with black pepper and salt. 2. Place into ungreased air fryer basket. Set the temperature to 375°F/190°C and set the timer for almost 12 minutes, shaking the basket halfway through cooking. Brussels sprouts will be tender and browned when done. 3. Place sprouts in a suitable serving dish and drizzle with balsamic vinegar. Sprinkle bacon over top. 4. Serve warm.
Per serving: Calories: 393; Total fat 8.9g; Sodium 124mg; Total Carbs 4.7g; Fiber 8.1g; Sugars 2.6g; Protein 14.7g

Roasted Asparagus

Prep time: 10 minutes | Cooking time: 12 minutes | Serves: 4

1 tablespoon olive oil
1 pound asparagus spears, ends trimmed

¼ teaspoon salt
¼ teaspoon ground black pepper
1 tablespoon salted butter, melted

1. In a suitable bowl, drizzle olive oil over asparagus spears and sprinkle with black pepper and salt. 2. Place spears into ungreased air fryer basket. Set the temperature to 375°F/190°C and set the timer for almost 12 minutes, shaking the basket halfway through cooking. Asparagus will be lightly browned and tender when done. 3. Transfer to a suitable dish and drizzle with butter. Serve warm.
Per serving: Calories: 121; Total fat 9.5g; Sodium 266mg; Total carbs 5.4g; Fiber 1.8g; Sugars 1.7g; Protein 5.9g

Cheesy Baked Asparagus

Prep time: 10 minutes | Cooking time: 18 minutes | Serves: 4

½ cup heavy whipping cream
½ cup grated parmesan cheese
2 ounces cream cheese, softened
1 pound asparagus, ends trimmed,

chopped into 1" pieces
¼ teaspoon salt
¼ teaspoon ground black pepper

1. In a suitable bowl, beat heavy cream, parmesan, and cream cheese until well-mixed. 2. Place asparagus into an ungreased 6" round nonstick baking dish. Pour cheese mixture over top and sprinkle with black pepper and salt. 3. Place dish into air fryer basket. Set the temperature to 350°F/175°C and set the timer for almost 18 minutes. 4. Asparagus will be tender when done. Serve warm.
Per serving: Calories: 144; Total fat 10.6g; Sodium 528mg; Total Carbs 1.8g; Fiber 1.2g; Sugars 4.9g; Protein 4.3g

Dijon Roast Cabbage

Prep time: 10 minutes | Cooking time: 10 minutes | Serves: 4

1 small head cabbage, cored and sliced into 1"-thick slices
2 tablespoons olive oil
½ teaspoon salt

1 tablespoon Dijon mustard
1 teaspoon apple cider vinegar
1 teaspoon granular erythritol

1. Drizzle each cabbage slice with 1 tablespoon olive oil, then sprinkle with salt. Place slices into ungreased air fryer basket, working in batches if needed. 2. Set the temperature to 350°F/175°C and set the timer for almost 10 minutes. Cabbage will be tender and edges will begin to brown when done. 3. In a suitable bowl, whisk remaining olive oil with mustard, vinegar, and erythritol. Drizzle over cabbage in a suitable serving dish. 4. Serve warm.
Per serving: Calories: 196; Total fat 13.9g; Sodium 479mg; Total carbs 7g; Fiber 0.6g; Sugars 2.9g; Protein 11.7g

Garlic Parmesan–Roasted Cauliflower

Prep time: 10 minutes | Cooking time: 15 minutes | Serves: 6

1 medium head cauliflower, leaves and core removed, cut into florets
2 tablespoons salted butter, melted

½ tablespoon salt
2 cloves garlic, peeled and finely minced
½ cup grated parmesan cheese

1. Toss cauliflower in a suitable bowl with butter. Sprinkle with salt, garlic, and ¼ cup parmesan. 2. Place florets into ungreased air fryer basket. Set the temperature to 350°F/175°C and set the timer for almost 15 minutes, shaking basket halfway through cooking. 3. Cauliflower will be browned at the edges and tender when done. 4. Transfer florets to a suitable serving dish and sprinkle with remaining parmesan. 5. Serve warm.
Per serving: Calories: 207; Total fat 15.9g; Sodium 366mg; Total carbs 5.4g; Fiber 1.3g; Sugars 2.4g; Protein 12.1g

Cauliflower Rice Balls

Prep time: 10 minutes | Cooking time: 8 minutes | Serves: 4

1 (10-ounce) steamer bag cauliflower rice, cooked according to package instructions	1 large egg
	2 ounces plain pork rinds, finely crushed
½ cup shredded mozzarella cheese	¼ teaspoon salt
	½ teaspoon Italian seasoning

1. Place cauliflower into a suitable bowl and mix with mozzarella. 2. Whisk egg in a separate suitable bowl. Place pork rinds into another suitable bowl with salt and Italian seasoning. 3. Separate cauliflower mixture into four equal sections and form each into a ball. Carefully dip a ball into whisked egg, then roll in pork rinds. Repeat with remaining balls. 4. Place cauliflower balls into ungreased air fryer basket. Set the temperature to 400°F/200°C and set the timer for almost 8 minutes. Rice balls will be golden when done. 5. Use a spatula to carefully move cauliflower balls to a suitable dish for serving. Serve warm.
Per serving: Calories: 259; Total fat 14.9g; Sodium 325mg; Total Carbs 6.2g; Fiber 4.9g; Sugars 7.4g; Protein 8.5g

Cheesy Loaded Broccoli

Prep time: 10 minutes | Cooking time: 10 minutes | Serves: 2

3 cups fresh broccoli florets	¼ cup sour cream
1 tablespoon coconut oil	4 slices cooked sugar-free bacon, crumbled
¼ teaspoon salt	
½ cup shredded sharp cheddar cheese	1 medium scallion, trimmed and sliced

1. Place broccoli into ungreased air fryer basket, drizzle with coconut oil, and sprinkle with salt. 2. Set the temperature to 350°F/175°C and set the timer for almost 8 minutes. Shake basket three times during cooking to avoid burned spots. 3. When the pot beeps, sprinkle broccoli with cheddar and set the timer for almost 2 additional minutes. When done, cheese will be melted and broccoli will be tender. 4. Serve warm in a suitable serving dish, topped with sour cream, crumbled bacon, and scallion slices.
Per serving: Calories: 211; Total fat 10.3g; Sodium 645mg; Total Carbs 1.3g; Fiber 8.3g; Sugars 13.1g; Protein 11.2g

Buttery Mushrooms

Prep time: 10 minutes | Cooking time: 10 minutes | Serves: 4

8 ounces cremini mushrooms, halved	melted
	¼ teaspoon salt
2 tablespoons salted butter,	¼ teaspoon ground black pepper

1. In a suitable bowl, toss mushrooms with butter, then sprinkle with black pepper and salt. 2. Place into ungreased air fryer basket. Set the temperature to 400°F/200°C and set the timer for almost 10 minutes, shaking the basket halfway through cooking. Mushrooms will be tender when done. 3. Serve warm.
Per serving: Calories: 222; Total fat 14.3g; Sodium 343mg; Total Carbs 4.8g; Fiber 5g; Sugars 9.7g; Protein 12.3g

"Faux-Tato" Hash

Prep time: 10 minutes | Cooking time: 12 minutes | Serves: 4

1 pound radishes, ends removed, quartered	seeded and chopped
	2 tablespoons salted butter, melted
¼ medium yellow onion, peeled and diced	
½ medium green bell pepper,	½ teaspoon garlic powder
	¼ teaspoon ground black pepper

1. In a suitable bowl, mix radishes, onion, and bell pepper. Toss with butter. 2. Sprinkle garlic powder and black pepper over mixture in bowl, then spoon into ungreased air fryer basket. 3. Set the temperature to 320°F/160°C and set the timer for almost 12 minutes. Shake basket halfway through cooking. Radishes will be tender when done. 4. Serve warm.
Per serving: Calories: 333; Total fat 18.5g; Sodium 576mg; Total Carbs 8.2g; Fiber 5g; Sugars 10g; Protein 8.1g

Savory Zucchini Boats

Prep time: 10 minutes | Cooking time: 10 minutes | Serves: 4

1 large zucchini, ends removed, halved lengthwise	¼ cup feta cheese
	1 tablespoon balsamic vinegar
6 grape tomatoes, quartered	1 tablespoon olive oil
¼ teaspoon salt	

1. Use a spoon to scoop out 2 tablespoons from center of each zucchini half, making just enough space to fill with tomatoes and feta. 2. Place tomatoes evenly in centers of zucchini halves and sprinkle with salt. Place into ungreased air fryer basket. Set the temperature to 350°F/175°C and set the timer for almost 10 minutes. When done, zucchini will be tender. 3. Transfer boats to a serving tray and sprinkle with feta, then drizzle with vinegar and olive oil. 4. Serve warm.
Per serving: Calories: 263; Total fat 10.6g; Sodium 718mg; Total Carbs 3g; Fiber 7.1g; Sugars 9.9g; Protein 4.3g

Roasted Broccoli Salad

Prep time: 10 minutes | Cooking time: 7 minutes | Serves: 4

2 cups fresh broccoli florets, chopped	⅛ teaspoon ground black pepper
	¼ cup lemon juice
1 tablespoon olive oil	¼ cup shredded parmesan cheese
¼ teaspoon salt	¼ cup sliced roasted almonds

1. In a suitable bowl, toss broccoli and olive oil. Sprinkle with black pepper and salt, then drizzle with 2 tablespoons lemon juice. 2. Place broccoli into ungreased air fryer basket. Set the temperature to 350°F/175°C and set the timer for almost 7 minutes, shaking the basket halfway through cooking. Broccoli will be golden on the edges when done. 3. Place broccoli into a suitable serving bowl and drizzle with remaining lemon juice. Sprinkle with parmesan and almonds. 4. Serve warm.
Per serving: Calories: 190; Total fat 11.5g; Sodium 639mg; Total Carbs 8g; Fiber 1.9g; Sugars 13.5g; Protein 7.5g

Bacon-Jalapeño Cheesy "Breadsticks"

Prep time: 10 minutes | Cooking time: 15 minutes | Serves: 8

2 cups shredded mozzarella cheese	2 large eggs, whisked
	4 slices cooked sugar-free bacon, chopped
¼ cup grated parmesan cheese	
¼ cup chopped pickled jalapeños	

1. Mix all the recipe ingredients in a suitable bowl. 2. Cut a suitable piece of parchment paper to fit inside air fryer basket. 3. Dampen your hands with a bit of water and press out mixture into a circle to fit on ungreased parchment. You may need to separate into two smaller circles, depending on the size of air fryer. 4. Place parchment with cheese mixture into air fryer basket. Set the temperature to 320°F/160°C and set the timer for almost 15 minutes. Carefully flip when 5 minutes remain on timer. 5. The top will be golden brown when done. Slice into eight sticks. Serve warm.
Per serving: Calories: 161; Total fat 12.7g; Sodium 355mg; Total carbs 7.1g; Fiber 2.4g; Sugars 2.2g; Protein 7.9g

Onion Rings

Prep time: 10 minutes | Cooking time: 5 minutes | Serves: 8

1 large egg	crushed
¼ cup coconut flour	1 large white onion, peeled and sliced into 8 (¼") rings
2 ounces plain pork rinds, finely	

1. Whisk egg in a suitable bowl. Place coconut flour and pork rinds in two separate suitable bowls. 2. Dip each onion ring into egg, then coat in coconut flour. Dip coated onion ring in egg once more, then press gently into pork rinds to cover all sides. 3. Place rings into ungreased air fryer basket. Set the temperature to 400°F/200°C and set the timer for almost 5 minutes, turning the onion rings halfway through cooking. 4. Onion rings will be golden and crispy when done. 5. Serve warm.
Per serving: Calories: 361; Total fat 10.3g; Sodium 1557mg; Total Carbs 2.2g; Fiber 5.7g; Sugars 3.6g; Protein 16.7g

Dinner Rolls

Prep time: 10 minutes | Cooking time: 12 minutes | Serves: 6

1 cup shredded mozzarella cheese
1 ounce cream cheese, broken into small pieces
1 cup blanched finely ground

almond flour
¼ cup ground flaxseed
½ teaspoon baking powder
1 large egg, whisked

1. Place mozzarella, cream cheese, and flour in a suitable microwave-safe bowl. Microwave on high 1 minute. Mix until smooth. 2. Add flaxseed, baking powder, and egg to mixture until fully combined and smooth. Microwave an additional 15 seconds if dough becomes too firm. 3. Separate dough into six equal pieces and roll each into a ball. Place rolls into ungreased air fryer basket. 4. Set the temperature to 320°F/160°C and set the timer for almost 12 minutes, turning rolls halfway through cooking. 5. Allow rolls to cool completely before serving for almost 5 minutes.
Per serving: Calories: 448; Total fat 8.5g; Sodium 247mg; Total Carbs 7.7g; Fiber 32.5g; Sugars 6g; Protein 27g

A Go-To Bread!

Prep time: 10 minutes | Cooking time: 10 minutes | Serves: 6

1 pound radishes, ends removed, quartered
2 tablespoons salted butter, melted
½ teaspoon garlic powder

½ teaspoon dried parsley
¼ teaspoon dried oregano
¼ teaspoon ground black pepper
¼ cup grated parmesan cheese

1. Place radishes into a suitable bowl and drizzle with butter. Sprinkle with garlic powder, parsley, oregano, and pepper, then place into ungreased air fryer basket. 2. Set the temperature to 350°F/175°C and set the timer for almost 10 minutes, shaking the basket three times during cooking. Radishes will be done when tender and golden. 3. Place radishes into a suitable serving dish and sprinkle with parmesan. 4. Serve warm.
Per serving: Calories: 373; Total fat 12g; Sodium 1364mg; Total Carbs 3.3g; Fiber 31.3g; Sugars 6.4g; Protein 19.1g

Crispy Green Beans

Prep time: 10 minutes | Cooking time: 8 minutes | Serves: 4

2 teaspoons olive oil
½ pound fresh green beans, ends trimmed

¼ teaspoon salt
¼ teaspoon ground black pepper

1. In a suitable bowl, drizzle olive oil over green beans and sprinkle with black pepper and salt. 2. Place green beans into air fryer basket. 3. Set the temperature to 350°F/175°C and set the timer for almost 8 minutes. 4. Serve.
Per serving: Calories: 277; Total fat 21g; Sodium 925mg; Total Carbs 0.1g; Fiber 4.8g; Sugars 8.1g; Protein 6.7g

Flatbread Dippers

Prep time: 10 minutes | Cooking time: 8 minutes | Serves: 4

1 cup shredded mozzarella cheese
1 ounce cream cheese, broken into small pieces

½ cup blanched finely ground almond flour

1. Place mozzarella into a suitable microwave-safe bowl. Add cream cheese pieces. Microwave on high 60 seconds, then stir to combine. Add flour and stir until a soft ball of dough forms. 2. Cut dough ball into two equal pieces. Cut a piece of parchment to fit into air fryer basket. Press each dough piece into a 5" round on ungreased parchment. 3. Place parchment with dough into air fryer basket. Set the temperature to 350°F/175°C and set the timer for almost 8 minutes. Carefully flip the flatbread over halfway through cooking. Flatbread will be golden brown when done. 4. Let flatbread cool 5 minutes, then slice each round into six triangles. Serve warm.
Per serving: Calories: 114; Total fat 2.6g; Sodium 242mg; Total Carbs 12.5g; Fiber 1.6g; Sugars 0.8g; Protein 10.5g

Mini Spinach and Sweet Pepper Poppers

Prep time: 10 minutes | Cooking time: 8 minutes | Serves: 4

4 ounces cream cheese, softened
1 cup chopped fresh spinach leaves
½ teaspoon garlic powder

8 mini sweet bell peppers, tops removed, seeded, and halved lengthwise

1. In a suitable bowl, mix cream cheese, spinach, and garlic powder. Place 1 tablespoon mixture into each sweet pepper half and press down to smooth. 2. Place poppers into ungreased air fryer basket. Set the temperature to 400°F/200°C and set the timer for almost 8 minutes. 3. Poppers will be done when cheese is browned on top and peppers are tender-crisp. 4. Serve warm.
Per serving: Calories: 162; Total fat 8.7g; Sodium 135mg; Total carbs 19g; Fiber 2.7g; Sugars 1g; Protein 5g

Roasted Brussels Sprouts

Prep time: 10 minutes | Cooking time: 10 minutes | Serves: 6

1 pound fresh Brussels sprouts, halved
2 tablespoons coconut oil
½ teaspoon salt

¼ teaspoon ground black pepper
½ teaspoon garlic powder
1 tablespoon salted butter, melted

1. Place Brussels sprouts into a suitable bowl. 2. Drizzle with coconut oil and sprinkle with salt, pepper, and garlic powder. 3. Place Brussels sprouts into ungreased air fryer basket. Set the temperature to 350°F/175°C and set the timer for almost 10 minutes, shaking the basket three times during cooking. 4. Brussels sprouts will be dark golden and tender when done. 5. Place cooked sprouts in a suitable serving dish and drizzle with butter. Serve warm.
Per serving: Calories: 229; Total fat 12.6g; Sodium 875mg; Total Carbs 6.2g; Fiber 4.6g; Sugars 8.9g; Protein 5.4g

Roasted Salsa

Prep time: 10 minutes | Cooking time: 30 minutes | Serves: 8

2 large San Marzano tomatoes, cored and cut into large chunks
½ medium white onion, peeled and large-diced
½ medium jalapeño, seeded and

large-diced
2 cloves garlic, peeled and diced
½ teaspoon salt
1 tablespoon coconut oil
¼ cup fresh lime juice

1. Place tomatoes, onion, and jalapeño into an ungreased 6" round nonstick baking dish. Add garlic, then sprinkle with salt and drizzle with coconut oil. 2. Place dish into air fryer basket. Set the temperature to 300°F/150°C and set the timer for almost 30 minutes. Vegetables will be dark brown around the edges and tender when done. 3. Pour the prepared mixture into a food processor or blender. Add lime juice. Process on low speed 30 seconds until only a few chunks remain. 4. Transfer salsa to a sealable container and refrigerate at least 1 hour. Serve chilled.
Per serving: Calories: 229; Total fat 12.6g; Sodium 875mg; Total Carbs 6.2g; Fiber 4.6g; Sugars 8.9g; Protein 5.4g

Sweet Pepper Nachos

Prep time: 10 minutes | Cooking time: 5 minutes | Serves: 2

6 mini sweet peppers, seeded and sliced in half
¾ cup shredded Colby jack cheese

¼ cup sliced pickled jalapeños
½ medium avocado, peeled, pitted, and diced
2 tablespoons sour cream

1. Place peppers into an ungreased 6" round nonstick baking dish. Sprinkle with Colby jack cheese and top with jalapeños. 2. Place dish into air fryer basket. Set the temperature to 350°F/175°C and set the timer for almost 5 minutes. Cheese will be melted and bubbly when done. 3. Remove dish from air fryer and top with avocado. Drizzle with sour cream. Serve warm.
Per serving: Calories: 111; Total fat 5.4g; Sodium 1357mg; Total carbs 8.7g; Fiber 2g; Sugars 3.9g; Protein 9.1g

Spinach and Artichoke–Stuffed Peppers

Prep time: 10 minutes | Cooking time: 15 minutes | Serves: 4

2 ounces cream cheese, softened
½ cup shredded mozzarella cheese
½ cup chopped fresh spinach leaves

¼ cup chopped canned artichoke hearts
2 medium green bell peppers, halved and seeded

1. In a suitable bowl, mix cream cheese, mozzarella, spinach, and artichokes. Spoon ¼ cheese mixture into each pepper half. 2. Place peppers into ungreased air fryer basket. Set the temperature to 320°F/160°C and set the timer for almost 15 minutes. 3. Peppers will be tender and cheese will be bubbling and brown when done. Serve warm.
Per serving: Calories: 197; Total fat 17g; Sodium 426mg; Total Carbs 2.5g; Fiber 3g; Sugars 4.8g; Protein 1.9g

Pesto Vegetable Skewers

Prep time: 10 minutes | Cooking time: 8 minutes | Serves: 4

1 medium zucchini, trimmed and cut into ½" slices
½ medium yellow onion, peeled and cut into 1" squares
1 medium red bell pepper, seeded

and cut into 1" squares
16 whole cremini mushrooms
⅓ cup basil pesto
½ teaspoon salt
¼ teaspoon ground black pepper

1. Divide zucchini slices, onion, and bell pepper into eight even portions. 2. Place on 6" skewers for a total of eight kebabs. 3. Add 2 mushrooms to each skewer and brush kebabs generously with pesto. 4. Sprinkle each kebab with salt and black pepper on all sides, then place into ungreased air fryer basket. 5. Set the temperature to 375°F/190°C and set the timer for almost 8 minutes, turning kebabs halfway through cooking. 6. Vegetables will be browned at the edges and tender-crisp when done. Serve warm.
Per serving: Calories: 60; Total fat 0.3g; Sodium 295mg; Total Carbs 14g; Fiber 2.6g; Sugars 2.3g; Protein 2g

Lemon Caper Cauliflower Steaks

Prep time: 10 minutes | Cooking time: 15 minutes | Serves: 4

1 small head cauliflower, leaves and core removed, cut into 4 (½"-thick) "steaks"
4 tablespoons olive oil
1 medium lemon, zested and

juiced
¼ teaspoon salt
⅛ teaspoon ground black pepper
1 tablespoon salted butter, melted
1 tablespoon capers, rinsed

1. Brush each cauliflower "steak" with ½ tablespoon olive oil on both sides and sprinkle with lemon zest, salt, and pepper on both sides. 2. Place cauliflower into ungreased air fryer basket. Set the temperature to 400°F/200°C and set the timer for almost 15 minutes, turning cauliflower halfway through cooking. 3. Steaks will be golden at the edges and browned when done. Transfer steaks to four medium plates. 4. In a suitable bowl, whisk remaining olive oil, butter, lemon juice, and capers, and pour evenly over steaks. 5. Serve warm.
Per serving: Calories: 240; Total fat 11.8g; Sodium 440mg; Total Carbs 3.9g; Fiber 6.7g; Sugars 8.8g; Protein 2.2g

Crispy Eggplant Rounds

Prep time: 10 minutes | Cooking time: 10 minutes | Serves: 4

1 large eggplant, ends trimmed, cut into ½" slices
½ teaspoon salt
2 ounces parmesan 100% cheese

crisps, finely ground
½ teaspoon paprika
¼ teaspoon garlic powder
1 large egg

1. Sprinkle eggplant rounds with salt. 2. Place rounds on a kitchen towel for almost 30 minutes to draw out excess water. 3. Pat rounds dry. 4. In a suitable bowl, mix cheese crisps, paprika, and garlic powder. 5. In a separate suitable bowl, whisk egg. 6. Dip each eggplant slice in egg, then gently press into cheese crisps to coat both sides. 7. Set eggplant rounds into ungreased air fryer basket. 8. Set the temperature to 400°F/200°C and set the timer for 10 minutes. Serve warm.
Per serving: Calories: 400; Total fat 15.2g; Sodium 644mg; Total Carbs 3.6g; Fiber 6.3g; Sugars 2.3g; Protein 42.2g

Cauliflower Rice–Stuffed Peppers

Prep time: 10 minutes | Cooking time: 15 minutes | Serves: 4

2 cups uncooked cauliflower rice
¾ cup drained canned petite diced tomatoes
2 tablespoons olive oil
1 cup shredded mozzarella cheese

¼ teaspoon salt
¼ teaspoon ground black pepper
4 medium green bell peppers, tops removed, seeded

1. In a suitable bowl, mix all the recipe ingredients except bell peppers. Scoop mixture evenly into peppers. 2. Place peppers into ungreased air fryer basket. Set the temperature to 350°F/175°C and set the timer for almost 15 minutes. 3. Peppers will be tender and cheese will be melted when done. Serve warm.
Per serving: Calories: 223; Total fat 13.1g; Sodium 591mg; Total Carbs 2.5g; Fiber 4.2g; Sugars 1g; Protein 5.3g

Pan Pizza

Prep time: 10 minutes | Cooking time: 8 minutes | Serves: 2

1 cup shredded mozzarella cheese
¼ medium red bell pepper, seeded and chopped
½ cup chopped fresh spinach leaves

2 tablespoons chopped black olives
2 tablespoons crumbled feta cheese

1. Sprinkle mozzarella into an ungreased 6" round nonstick baking dish in an even layer. Add remaining ingredients on top. 2. Place dish into air fryer basket. Set the temperature to 350°F/175°C. 3. Set the timer for almost 8 minutes. Slice and serve.
Per serving: Calories: 203; Total fat 13.5g; Sodium 990mg; Total Carbs 7.9g; Fiber 4.4g; Sugars 8.9g; Protein 5.9g

Vegetable Burgers

Prep time: 10 minutes | Cooking time: 12 minutes | Serves: 4

8 ounces cremini mushrooms
2 large egg yolks
½ medium zucchini, trimmed and chopped
¼ cup peeled and chopped yellow

onion
1 clove garlic, peeled and finely minced
½ teaspoon salt
¼ teaspoon ground black pepper

1. Place all the recipe ingredients into a food processor and pulse twenty times until finely chopped and combined. 2. Separate mixture into four equal sections and press each into a burger shape. Place burgers into ungreased air fryer basket. 3. Set the temperature to 375°F/190°C and set the timer for almost 12 minutes, turning burgers halfway through cooking. Burgers will be browned and firm when done. 4. Place burgers on a suitable plate and let cool 5 minutes before serving.
Per serving: Calories: 241; Total fat 20.1g; Sodium 608mg; Total Carbs 3.4g; Fiber 2.9g; Sugars 8g; Protein 4.5g

Stuffed Portobello Mushrooms

Prep time: 10 minutes | Cooking time: 8 minutes | Serves: 4

3 ounces cream cheese, softened
½ medium zucchini, trimmed and chopped
¼ cup seeded and chopped red bell pepper
1½ cups chopped fresh spinach

leaves
4 large Portobello mushrooms, stems removed
2 tablespoons coconut oil, melted
½ teaspoon salt

1. In a suitable bowl, mix cream cheese, zucchini, pepper, and spinach. 2. Drizzle mushrooms with coconut oil and sprinkle with salt. 3. Scoop ¼ zucchini mixture into each mushroom. 4. Place mushrooms into ungreased air fryer basket. Set the temperature to 400°F/204°C and set the timer for almost 8 minutes. 5. Portobellos will be tender and tops will be browned when done. Serve warm.
Per serving: Calories: 200; Total fat 6.3g; Sodium 647mg; Total Carbs 3g; Fiber 7g; Sugars 18.6g; Protein 7g

Crustless Spinach and Cheese Frittata

Prep time: 10 minutes | Cooking time: 20 minutes | Serves: 4

6 large eggs
½ cup heavy whipping cream
1 cup frozen chopped spinach, drained
1 cup shredded sharp cheddar
cheese
¼ cup peeled and diced yellow onion
½ teaspoon salt
¼ teaspoon ground black pepper

1. In a suitable bowl, whisk eggs and cream. Whisk in spinach, cheddar, onion, salt, and pepper. 2. Pour mixture into an ungreased 6" round nonstick baking dish. Place dish into air fryer basket. 3. Set the temperature to 320°F/160°C and set the timer for almost 20 minutes. Eggs will be firm and slightly browned when done. 4. Serve immediately.
Per serving: Calories: 161; Total fat 8.1g; Sodium 692mg; Total Carbs 0.6g; Fiber 5g; Sugars 8.2g; Protein 5.2g

Cauliflower Pizza Crust

Prep time: 10 minutes | Cooking time: 7 minutes | Serves: 2

1 (12-ounce) steamer bag cauliflower, cooked according to package instructions
½ cup shredded sharp cheddar cheese
1 large egg
2 tablespoons blanched finely ground almond flour
1 teaspoon Italian seasoning

1. Let cooked cauliflower cool for almost 10 minutes. Using a kitchen towel, wring out excess moisture from cauliflower and place into food processor. 2. Add cheddar, egg, flour, and Italian seasoning to processor and pulse ten times until cauliflower is smooth and all the recipe ingredients are combined. 3. Cut two pieces of parchment paper to fit air fryer basket. Divide cauliflower mixture into two equal portions and press each into a 6" round on ungreased parchment. 4. Place crusts on parchment into air fryer basket. Set the temperature to 360°F/180°C and set the timer for almost 7 minutes, gently turning crusts halfway through cooking. 5. Store crusts in refrigerator in an airtight container up to 4 days or freeze between sheets of parchment in a sealable storage bag for up to 2 months.
Per serving: Calories: 357; Total fat 8.5g; Sodium 168mg; Total Carbs 4.1g; Fiber 10g; Sugars 54.7g; Protein 6.5g

Roasted Spaghetti Squash

Prep time: 10 minutes | Cooking time: 45 minutes | Serves: 6

1 (4-pound) spaghetti squash, halved and seeded
2 tablespoons coconut oil
4 tablespoons salted butter,
melted
1 teaspoon garlic powder
2 teaspoons dried parsley

1. Brush shell of spaghetti squash with coconut oil. Brush inside with butter. Sprinkle inside with garlic powder and parsley. 2. Place squash skin side down into ungreased air fryer basket, working in batches if needed. Set the temperature to 350°F/175°C and set the timer for almost 30 minutes. 3. When the timer beeps, flip squash and cook an additional 15 minutes until fork-tender. 4. Use a fork to remove spaghetti strands from shell and serve warm.
Per serving: Calories: 310; Total fat 25.9g; Sodium 131mg; Total carbs 9.7g; Fiber 5.1g; Sugars 3.4g; Protein 13g

Alfredo Eggplant Stacks

Prep time: 10 minutes | Cooking time: 12 minutes | Serves: 6

1 large eggplant, ends trimmed, cut into ¼" slices
1 medium beefsteak tomato, cored and cut into ¼" slices
1 cup alfredo sauce
8 ounces fresh mozzarella cheese, cut into 18 slices
2 tablespoons fresh parsley leaves

1. Place 6 slices eggplant in bottom of an ungreased 6" round nonstick baking dish. Place 1 slice tomato on top of each eggplant round, followed by 1 tablespoon alfredo and 1 slice mozzarella. Repeat with remaining ingredients. for almost three repetitions. 2. Cover dish with foil sheet and place dish into air fryer basket. Set the temperature to 350°F/175°C and set the timer for almost 12 minutes. Eggplant will be tender when done. 3. Sprinkle parsley evenly over each stack. Serve warm.
Per serving: Calories: 327; Total fat 17.6g; Sodium 654mg; Total Carbs 6.7g; Fiber 3.4g; Sugars 17.8g; Protein 7.8g

White Cheddar and Mushroom Soufflés

Prep time: 10 minutes | Cooking time: 12 minutes | Serves: 4

3 large eggs, whites and yolks separated
½ cup sharp white cheddar cheese
3 ounces cream cheese, softened
¼ teaspoon cream of tartar
¼ teaspoon salt
¼ teaspoon ground black pepper
½ cup cremini mushrooms, sliced

1. In a suitable bowl, whip egg whites until stiff peaks form. for almost 2 minutes. In a separate suitable bowl, beat cheddar, egg yolks, cream cheese, cream of tartar, salt, and pepper until well-mixed. 2. Fold egg whites into cheese mixture, being careful not to stir. Fold in mushrooms, then pour mixture evenly into four ungreased 4" ramekins. 3. Place ramekins into air fryer basket. Set the temperature to 350°F/175°C and set the timer for almost 12 minutes. 4. Eggs will be browned on the top and firm in the center when done. Serve warm.
Per serving: Calories: 180; Total fat 10.3g; Sodium 672mg; Total Carbs 4.6g; Fiber 6g; Sugars 3.5g; Protein 7.8g

Cheesy Broccoli Sticks

Prep time: 10 minutes | Cooking time: 16 minutes | Serves: 2

1 (10-ounce) steamer bag broccoli florets, cooked according to package instructions
1 large egg
1 ounce parmesan 100% cheese
crisps, finely ground
½ cup shredded sharp cheddar cheese
½ teaspoon salt
½ cup ranch dressing

1. Let cooked broccoli cool 5 minutes, then place into a food processor with egg, cheese crisps, cheddar, and salt. Process on low for almost 30 seconds until all the recipe ingredients are combined and begin to stick. 2. Cut a sheet of parchment paper to fit air fryer basket. Take one scoop of mixture, for almost 3 tablespoons, and roll into a 4" stick shape, pressing down gently to flatten the top. 3. Place stick on ungreased parchment into air fryer basket. Repeat with remaining mixture to form eight sticks. 4. Set the temperature to 350°F/177°C and set the timer for almost 16 minutes, turning sticks halfway through cooking. Sticks will be golden brown when done. 5. Serve warm with ranch dressing on the side for dipping.
Per serving: Calories: 282; Total fat 4g; Sodium 684mg; Total Carbs 4.7g; Fiber 5.5g; Sugars 6.9g; Protein 8.9g

Zucchini Fritters

Prep time: 10 minutes | Cooking time: 12 minutes | Serves: 4

1½ medium zucchini, trimmed and grated
½ teaspoon salt
1 large egg, whisked
¼ teaspoon garlic powder
¼ cup grated parmesan cheese

1. Place grated zucchini on a kitchen towel and sprinkle with ¼ teaspoon salt. Wrap in towel and let sit 30 minutes, then wring out as much excess moisture as possible. 2. Place zucchini into a suitable bowl and mix with egg, remaining salt, garlic powder, and parmesan. 3. Cut a piece of parchment to fit air fryer basket. Divide mixture into four mounds, for almost ⅓ cup each, and press out into 4" rounds on ungreased parchment. 4. Place parchment with rounds into air fryer basket. Set the temperature to 400°F/200°C and set the timer for almost 12 minutes, turning fritters halfway through cooking. 5. Fritters will be crispy on the edges and tender but firm in the center when done. Serve warm.
Per serving: Calories: 366; Total fat 15g; Sodium 67mg; Total Carbs 8.9g; Fiber 14g; Sugars 24.4g; Protein 7.5g

Herb Cloud Eggs

Prep time: 10 minutes | Cooking time: 8 minutes | Serves: 2

2 large eggs, whites and yolks separated
¼ teaspoon salt
¼ teaspoon dried oregano
2 tablespoons chopped fresh chives
2 teaspoons salted butter, melted

1. In a suitable bowl, whip egg whites until stiff peaks form, for almost 3 minutes. 2. Place egg whites evenly into two ungreased 4" ramekins. 3. Sprinkle evenly with salt, oregano, and chives. 4. Place 1 whole egg yolk in center of each ramekin and drizzle with butter. 5. Place ramekins into air fryer basket. Set the temperature to 350°F/177°C and set the timer for almost 8 minutes. 6. Egg whites will be fluffy and browned when done. Serve warm.
Per serving: Calories: 264; Total fat 10g; Sodium 9mg; Total Carbs 5.4g; Fiber 6.8g; Sugars 3.5g; Protein 8g

Crispy Cabbage Steaks

Prep time: 10 minutes | Cooking time: 10 minutes | Serves: 4

1 small head green cabbage, cored and cut into ½"-thick slices
¼ teaspoon salt
¼ teaspoon ground black pepper
2 tablespoons olive oil

1 clove garlic, peeled and finely minced
½ teaspoon dried thyme
½ teaspoon dried parsley

1. Sprinkle each side of cabbage with black pepper and salt, then place into ungreased air fryer basket, working in batches if needed. 2. Drizzle each side of cabbage with olive oil, then sprinkle with remaining ingredients on both sides. 3. Set the temperature to 350°F/175°C and set the timer for almost 10 minutes, turning "steaks" halfway through cooking. 4. Cabbage will be browned at the edges and tender when done. Serve warm.

Per serving: Calories: 441; Total fat 33.9g; Sodium 759mg; Total Carbs 4.9g; Fiber 2.2g; Sugars 3.6g; Protein 21.4g

Cheesy Cabbage Cribbage

Prep time: 10 minutes | Cook time: 40 minutes | Serves: 4

3 tablespoons unsalted butter, melted
¼ teaspoon garlic powder
¼ teaspoon salt
⅛ teaspoon ground black pepper

½ large cabbage, cut through the stem into 4 wedges
1 cup grated Parmesan cheese, divided

1. Preheat oven to 375°F/190°C. Prepare a baking sheet with parchment paper. 2. Whisk to combine butter, garlic powder, salt, and pepper in a small bowl. Brush mixture onto both cut sides of each cabbage wedge. 3. Sprinkle ¾ cup Parmesan evenly onto both cut sides of each wedge. 4. Bake for 40 minutes, flipping wedges halfway through, until they start to brown. 5. Sprinkle with remaining cheese and serve warm.

Per Serving: Calories 220; Fat 14g; Sodium 625mg; Carbs 13g; Fiber 4g; Sugar 5g; Protein 9g

Steamed Cauliflower

Prep time: 4 minutes | Cook time: 1 minutes | Serves: 2

1 cup water
½ large head of cauliflower,

chopped

1. Add water to Instant Pot and place steamer basket inside pot. Put cauliflower into steamer basket. 2. Select the Steam setting and adjust the time for 1 minute. When the timer beeps, quick-release the steam. 3. When pressure indicator drops, remove steamer basket. 4. Feel free to season with your choice of herbs, salt, and butter.

Per Serving: Calories 52; Fat 0.4g; Sodium 62mg; Carbs 10g; Fiber 4.2g; Sugar g; Protein 4g

Chapter 8 Dessert and Drinks

Peanut Butter Cheesecake 96
Pecan Cookies 96
Chocolate Doughnut 96
Heavenly Chocolate Lava Cakes 96
Silky Chocolate Soufflés 96
Strawberry Pie 96
Pumpkin Pie with Spiced Pork Rinds ... 96
Brown Cookies 96
Delicious Peanut Butter Cookies 97
Beautiful Chocolate Chip Cookie Cake 97
Cake in Olive Oil 97
Roasted Nut Clusters 97
Brownies 97
Simple Cinnamon Pretzels 97
Keto Danish 97
Coconut Cake 97
Delicious Strawberry Shortcake 98
Creamy Shortbread Cookies 98
Pumpkin Pie Cake 98
Tangy Lime Bars 98
Apple Crisp 98
Economical Peanut Butter Pie 98
Berries Mascarpone 98
Doodles 98
German Chocolate Cookie 99
Candy Almonds 99
Chocolate Puddin' Cake 99
Chocolate Peanut Butter Cupcake 99
Lemonade Strawberry Shortcake 99
Crème Brûlée 99
Coffee Cake Bites 99
Refreshing Mint Smoothie 100
Hot Cider 100
Chai Latte 100
Keto Martini 100
Energy Booster Drink 100
Strawberry Cheesecakes 100

Three-Layered Chocolate Cream Cake ... 100
Coconut Nut Cookies 100
Chocolaty Cheesecake Bars 101
Chocolate Pudding 101
Strawberries Coconut Whip 101
Nutty Chocolate Milkshake 101
Buttery Pecan Ice Cream 101
Blueberry Ice Cream 101
Chocolate Truffles 101
Chocolate Coconut Torts 101
Peanut Butter with Jelly Cookies 102
Nutty Chocolate Fudge 102
Nuts Squares 102
Regular Peanut Butter Cookies 102
Creamy Coconut Brownies 102
Regular Carrot Cake with
Cream Cheese Frosting 102
Mini Chocolaty Avocado Tarts 102
Chocolate Macaroons 103
Chocolate Tart 103
Peanut Butter Bars 103
Minty Chocolate Shake 103
Chocolate Almonds 103
Healthy Almond Cookies 103
Snicker Bites 103
Delicious Swoop Cream 103
Strawberry Milkshake 103
Blueberry Smoothie 104
Caramel Macchiato 104
Piña Colada 104
Sweet Iced Tea 104
Hibiscus Tea 104
Fast Fudge 104
Cayenne Chocolate Pudding 104
Salty Pecan Bark 104
Peanut Butter Cheesecake Bites 104

Peanut Butter Cheesecake

Prep time: 11 minutes | Cook time: 10 minutes | Serves: 2

4 ounces cream cheese, softened
2 tablespoons confectioners' erythritol
1 tablespoon all-natural, no-sugar-

added peanut butter
½ teaspoon vanilla extract
1 large egg, whisked

1. Mix cream cheese and erythritol until smooth. Add peanut butter with vanilla, mix them until smooth. Add egg and stir just until combined. 2. Spoon mixture into an ungreased 4" springform nonstick pan and place into the air fryer basket. 3. Set the temperature setting to 300°F/150°C and the timer for 10 minutes. 4. Edges will be firm, but the center will be mostly set with only a small amount of jiggle when done. 5. Let the pan cool at room temperature 30 minutes, cover with plastic wrap, then place into refrigerator for at least 2 hours. 6. Serve chilled.
Per Serving: Calories 282; Fat 23g; Sodium 242mg; Carbs 13g; Fiber 1g; Sugar 2g; Protein 9g

Pecan Cookies

Prep time: 5 minutes | Cook time: 24 minutes | Serves: 12

1 cup chopped pecans
½ cup salted butter, melted
½ cup coconut flour

¾ cup confectioners' erythritol, divided
1 teaspoon vanilla extract

1. In a food processor, blend together pecans, butter, flour, ½ cup erythritol, and vanilla for 1 minute until a dough forms. 2. Form dough into twelve individual cookie balls, about 1 tablespoon each. 3. Cut three pieces of parchment to fit the air fryer basket. Place four cookies on each the ungreased parchment and place one piece of parchment with cookies into the air fryer basket. Adjust the air fryer temperature to 325°F/160°C and timer for 8 minutes. Repeat cooking with remaining batches. 4. When the timer goes off, allow cookies to cool for 5 minutes on a large serving plate until cool enough to handle. 5. While still warm, dust cookies with remaining erythritol. Allow to cool completely, for about 15 minutes, before serving.
Per Serving: Calories 151; Fat 14g; Sodium 64mg; Carbs 13g; Fiber 3g; Sugar 1g; Protein 2g

Chocolate Doughnut

Prep time: 11 minutes | Cook time: 6 minutes | Serves: 10

1 cup blanched finely ground almond flour
½ cup low-carb vanilla protein powder
½ cup granular erythritol

¼ cup unsweetened cocoa powder
½ teaspoon baking powder
2 large eggs, whisked
½ teaspoon vanilla extract

1. Mix all ingredients into a soft dough. Separate and roll dough into twenty balls, about 2 tablespoons each. 2. Place the parchment paper in the air fryer basket and place doughnut holes into the air fryer basket on the ungreased parchment. 3. Set the temperature setting to 380°F/195°C and timer for 6 minutes, flipping doughnut holes halfway through cooking. 4. Doughnut holes will be golden and firm when done. Cool completely before serving.
Per Serving: Calories 103; Fat 7g; Sodium 59mg; Carbs 13g; Fiber 2g; Sugar 1g; Protein 8g

Heavenly Chocolate Lava Cakes

Prep time: 5 minutes | Cook time: 15 minutes | Serves: 2

2 large eggs, whisked
¼ cup blanched finely ground almond flour

½ teaspoon vanilla extract
2 ounces low-carb chocolate chips, melted

1. In a medium bowl, mix eggs with flour and vanilla. Fold in chocolate until fully combined. 2. Pour batter into two 4" ramekins greased with cooking spray. Place ramekins into the air fryer basket. 3. Set the temperature setting to 320°F/160°C and timer for 15 minutes. 4. Cakes will be set at the edges and firm in the center when done. Let cool for 5 minutes before serving.
Per Serving: Calories 260; Fat 21g; Sodium 71mg; Carbs 21g; Fiber 10g; Sugar 1g; Protein 11g

Silky Chocolate Soufflés

Prep time: 5 minutes | Cook time: 15 minutes | Serves: 2

2 large eggs, whites and yolks separated
1 teaspoon vanilla extract

2 ounces low-carb chocolate chips
2 teaspoons coconut oil, melted

1. Beat egg whites until stiff peaks form in a medium bowl. 2. In a bowl, mix egg yolks and vanilla. Set aside. Place chocolate chips in a separate medium microwave-safe bowl and drizzle with coconut oil. 3. Microwave on high 20 seconds, then stir and continue cooking in 10-second increments until melted, being careful not to overheat chocolate. Let cool for 1 minute. 4. Slowly pour melted chocolate into egg yolks and whisk until smooth. Then, slowly begin adding egg white mixture to chocolate mixture, about ¼ cup at a time, folding in gently. 5. Pour mixture into two 4" ramekins greased with cooking spray. Place ramekins into the air fryer basket. Set the temperature setting to 400°F/200°C and timer for 15 minutes. 6. Soufflés will puff up while cooking and deflate a little once cooled. The center will be set when done. Let cool for 10 minutes, then serve warm.
Per Serving: Calories 217; Fat 18g; Sodium 71mg; Carbs 19g; Fiber 8g; Sugar 0g; Protein 8g

Strawberry Pie

Prep time: 16 minutes | Cook time: 10 minutes | Serves: 6

1½ cups whole shelled pecans
1 tablespoon unsalted butter, softened
1 cup heavy whipping cream

12 medium fresh strawberries, hulled
2 tablespoons sour cream

1. Place pecans and butter into a food processor and pulse ten times until a dough forms. Press dough into the bottom of an ungreased 6" round nonstick baking dish. 2. Place dish into the air fryer basket. Set the temperature setting to 320°F/160°C and timer for 10 minutes. Crust will be firm and golden when done. Let cool for 20 minutes. 3. In a large bowl, whisk cream until fluffy and doubled in size, about 2 minutes. 4. In a separate large bowl, mash strawberries until mostly liquid. Fold strawberries and sour cream into whipped cream. 5. Spoon mixture into cooled crust, cover, and place into refrigerator for at least 30 minutes to set. Serve chilled.
Per Serving: Calories 340; Fat 33g; Sodium 17mg; Carbs 7g; Fiber 3g; Sugar 3g; Protein 3g

Pumpkin Pie with Spiced Pork Rinds

Prep time: 5 minutes | Cook time: 5 minutes | Serves: 4

3 ounces plain pork rinds
2 tablespoons salted butter, melted

1 teaspoon pumpkin pie spice
¼ cup confectioners' erythritol

1. In a large bowl, toss pork rinds in butter. Sprinkle with pumpkin pie spice, then toss to evenly coat. 2. Place pork rinds into the ungreased the air fryer basket. Set the temperature setting to 400°F/200°C and timer for 5 minutes. 3. Pork rinds will be golden when done. Transfer rinds to a medium serving bowl and sprinkle with erythritol. 4. Serve immediately.
Per Serving: Calories 173; Fat 13g; Sodium 394mg; Carbs 9g; Fiber 0g; Sugar 0g; Protein 12g

Brown Cookies

Prep time: 5 minutes | Cook time: 27 minutes | Serves: 9

4 tablespoons salted butter, melted
⅓ cup granular brown erythritol
1 large egg

½ teaspoon vanilla extract
1 cup blanched finely ground almond flour
½ teaspoon baking powder

1. Whisk together butter, erythritol, egg, and vanilla in a large bowl. Stir in the flour and baking powder until combined. 2. Separate dough into nine pieces and roll into balls, about 2 tablespoons each. 3. Cut pieces of parchment to fit your air fryer basket and place three cookies on each the ungreased piece. 4. Place one piece of parchment into the air fryer basket. Adjust the temperature setting to 300°F/150°C and timer for 9 minutes. 5. Edges of cookies will be browned when done. Repeat with remaining cookies. Serve warm.
Per Serving: Calories 129; Fat 12g; Sodium 75mg; Carbs 9g; Fiber 1g; Sugar 1g; Protein 3g

Delicious Peanut Butter Cookies

Prep time: 5 minutes | Cook time: 27 minutes | Serves: 9

2 tablespoons salted butter, melted
2 tablespoons all-natural, no-sugar-added peanut butter
⅓ cup granular brown erythritol
1 large egg
½ teaspoon vanilla extract
1 cup blanched finely ground almond flour
½ teaspoon baking powder

1. Whisk together butter, peanut butter, erythritol, egg, and vanilla in a large bowl. 2. Stir in the flour and baking powder until combined. 3. Separate the dough into nine equal pieces and roll each into a ball, about 2 tablespoons each. 4. Cut three pieces of parchment to fit your air fryer basket and place three cookies on each the ungreased piece. 5. Place one piece of parchment with cookies into the air fryer basket. Adjust the temperature setting to 300°F/150°C and timer for 9 minutes. 6. Edges of cookies will be browned when done. Repeat with remaining cookies. Serve warm.
Per Serving: Calories 129; Fat 11g; Sodium 55mg; Carbs 10g; Fiber 2g; Sugar 1g; Protein 4g

Beautiful Chocolate Chip Cookie Cake

Prep time: 5 minutes | Cook time: 15 minutes | Serves: 8

4 tablespoons salted butter, melted
⅓ cup granular brown erythritol
1 large egg
½ teaspoon vanilla extract
1 cup blanched finely ground almond flour
½ teaspoon baking powder
¼ cup low-carb chocolate chips

1. Whisk together butter, erythritol, egg, and vanilla in a large bowl. Stir in the flour and baking powder until combined. 2. Fold in chocolate chips, then spoon batter into an ungreased 6" round nonstick baking dish. 3. Place dish into the air fryer basket. Set the temperature setting to 300°F/150°C and timer for 15 minutes. When edges are browned, cookie cake will be done. 4. Slice and serve warm.
Per Serving: Calories 170; Fat 16g; Sodium 84mg; Carbs 15g; Fiber 4g; Sugar 1g; Protein 4g

Cake in Olive Oil

Prep time: 11 minutes | Cook time: 30 minutes | Serves: 8

2 cups blanched finely ground almond flour
5 large eggs, whisked
¾ cup extra-virgin olive oil
⅓ cup granular erythritol
1 teaspoon vanilla extract
1 teaspoon baking powder

1. In a large bowl, mix all ingredients. Pour batter into an ungreased 6" round nonstick baking dish. 2. Place dish into the air fryer basket. Set the temperature setting to 300°F/150°C and timer for 30 minutes. When done, the cake will be golden on top and firm in the center. 3. Let cake cool in dish for 30 minutes before slicing and serving.
Per Serving: Calories 395; Fat 37g; Sodium 105mg; Carbs 13g; Fiber 3g; Sugar 1g; Protein 10g

Roasted Nut Clusters

Prep time: 35 minutes | Cook time: 8 minutes | Serves: 8

3 ounces whole shelled pecans
1 tablespoon salted butter, melted
2 teaspoons confectioners'
erythritol
½ teaspoon ground cinnamon
½ cup low-carb chocolate chips

1. In a medium bowl, toss pecans with butter, then sprinkle with erythritol and cinnamon. 2. Place pecans into the ungreased air fryer basket. Set the temperature setting to 350°F/175°C and timer for 8 minutes, shaking the basket two times during cooking. They will feel soft initially but get crunchy as they cool. 3. Prepare a baking sheet with parchment paper. 4. Place chocolate in a medium microwave-safe bowl. Microwave on high, heating in 20-second increments and stirring until melted. Place 1 teaspoon chocolate in a rounded mound on the ungreased parchment-lined baking sheet, then press 1 pecan into top, repeating with remaining chocolate and pecans. 5. Place baking sheet into refrigerator to cool at least 30 minutes. 6. Once cooled, store clusters in a large sealed container in refrigerator up to 5 days.
Per Serving: Calories 136; Fat 13g; Sodium 11mg; Carbs 11g; Fiber 5g; Sugar 0g; Protein 2g

Brownies

Prep time: 5 minutes | Cook time: 15 minutes | Serves: 2

½ cup blanched finely ground almond flour
3 tablespoons granular erythritol
3 tablespoons unsweetened cocoa powder
½ teaspoon baking powder
1 teaspoon vanilla extract
2 large eggs, whisked
2 tablespoons salted butter, melted

1. Mix flour, erythritol, cocoa powder, and baking powder in a medium bowl. 2. Add in vanilla, eggs, and butter, and stir until a thick batter forms. 3. Pour batter into two 4" ramekins greased with cooking spray and place ramekins into the air fryer basket. Adjust the temperature setting to 325°F/160°C and timer for 15 minutes. 4. Centers will be firm when done. Let the ramekins cool for 5 minutes before serving.
Per Serving: Calories 367; Fat 31g; Sodium 285mg; Carbs 29g; Fiber 6g; Sugar 2g; Protein 14g

Simple Cinnamon Pretzels

Prep time: 11 minutes | Cook time: 10 minutes | Serves: 6

1½ cups shredded mozzarella cheese
1 cup blanched finely ground almond flour
2 tablespoons salted butter, melted, divided
¼ cup granular erythritol, divided
1 teaspoon ground cinnamon

1. Place mozzarella, flour, 1 tablespoon butter, and 2 tablespoons erythritol in a large microwave-safe bowl. Microwave on high 45 seconds, then stir with a fork until a smooth dough ball forms. 2. Separate dough into six equal sections. Gently roll each section into a 12" rope, then fold into a pretzel shape. 3. Place pretzels into the ungreased air fryer basket. Set the temperature setting to 370°F/175°C and timer for 8 minutes, turning pretzels halfway through cooking. 4. In a small bowl, combine remaining butter, remaining erythritol, and cinnamon. Brush ½ mixture on both sides of pretzels. 5. Place pretzels back into the air fryer and cook for an additional 2 minutes at 370°F/175°C. 6. Transfer pretzels to a large plate. Brush on both sides with remaining butter mixture, then let cool 5 minutes before serving.
Per Serving: Calories 223; Fat 19g; Sodium 222mg; Carbs 13g; Fiber 2g; Sugar 1g; Protein 11g

Keto Danish

Prep time: 11 minutes | Cook time: 12 minutes | Serves: 6

1½ cups shredded mozzarella cheese
½ cup blanched finely ground almond flour
3 ounces cream cheese, divided
¼ cup confectioners' erythritol
1 tablespoon lemon juice

1. Place mozzarella, flour, and 1 ounce cream cheese in a large microwave-safe bowl. Microwave on high 45 seconds, then stir with a fork until a soft dough forms. 2. Separate dough into six equal sections and press each in a single layer into an ungreased 4" × 4" square nonstick baking dish to form six even squares that touch. 3. Mix remaining cream cheese, erythritol, and lemon juice in a small bowl. Place a tablespoon mixture in center of each dough in a baking dish. 4. Fold all four corners of each dough piece halfway to center to reach the cream cheese mixture. 5. Place the dish into your air fryer. Set the temperature setting to 320°F/160°C and timer for 12 minutes. 6. The center and edges will be browned when done. Let cool for 10 minutes before serving.
Per Serving: Calories 190; Fat 14g; Sodium 244mg; Carbs 10g; Fiber 1g; Sugar 1g; Protein 10g

Coconut Cake

Prep time: 11 minutes | Cook time: 25 minutes | Serves: 6

2 tablespoons salted butter, melted
⅓ cup coconut flour
2 large eggs, whisked
½ cup granular erythritol
1 teaspoon baking powder
1 teaspoon vanilla extract
½ cup sour cream

1. Mix all ingredients in a large bowl. Pour batter into an ungreased 6" round nonstick baking dish. 2. Place the dish in the air fryer basket. Set the temperature setting to 300°F/150°C and timer for 25 minutes. 3. The cake will be dark golden on top, and a toothpick inserted in the center should come out clean when done. 4. Let cool in dish for 15 minutes before slicing and serving.
Per Serving: Calories 123; Fat 9g; Sodium 148mg; Carbs 21g; Fiber 2g; Sugar 2g; Protein 4g

Delicious Strawberry Shortcake

Prep time: 1 hour 10 minutes | Cook time: 25 minutes | Serves: 6

2 tablespoons coconut oil
1 cup blanched finely ground almond flour
2 large eggs, whisked
½ cup granular erythritol

1 teaspoon baking powder
1 teaspoon vanilla extract
2 cups sugar-free whipped cream
6 medium fresh strawberries, hulled and sliced

1. Mix coconut oil with flour, eggs, erythritol, baking powder, and vanilla. Pour the shortcake batter into an ungreased 6" round nonstick baking dish. 2. Place dish into the air fryer basket. 3. Set the temperature setting to 300°F/150°C and timer for 25 minutes. 4. Cool the shortcakes for about 1 hour. 5. Once cooled, top cake with delicious whipped cream and strawberries to serve.
Per Serving: Calories 235; Fat 21g; Sodium 104mg; Carbs 21g; Fiber 2g; Sugar 1g; Protein 6g

Creamy Shortbread Cookies

Prep time: 40 minutes | Cook time: 20 minutes | Serves: 12

¼ cup coconut oil, melted
2 ounces cream cheese, softened
½ cup granular erythritol
1 large egg, whisked

2 cups blanched finely ground almond flour
1 teaspoon almond extract

1. Combine all ingredients to form a firm ball. 2. Place dough on a sheet of plastic wrap and roll into a 12"-long log shape. Roll log in plastic wrap and place in refrigerator for 30 minutes to chill. 3. Remove log from plastic and slice into twelve equal cookies. Place six cookies on each the ungreased sheet. Place one sheet with cookies into the air fryer basket. 4. Set the temperature setting to 320°F/160°C and timer for 10 minutes, turning cookies halfway through cooking. They will be lightly golden when done. Repeat with remaining cookies. 5. Let cool for 15 minutes before serving to avoid crumbling.
Per Serving: Calories 175; Fat 16g; Sodium 23mg; Carbs 12g; Fiber 2g; Sugar 1g; Protein 5g

Pumpkin Pie Cake

Prep time: 11 minutes | Cook time: 25 minutes | Serves: 8

4 tablespoons salted butter, melted
½ cup granular brown erythritol
¼ cup pure pumpkin puree
1 cup blanched finely ground

almond flour
½ teaspoon baking powder
⅛ teaspoon salt
1 teaspoon pumpkin pie spice

1. Mix all ingredients in a large bowl. Pour batter into an ungreased 6" round nonstick baking dish. 2. Place dish into the air fryer basket. Set the temperature setting to 300°F/150°C and timer for 25 minutes. 3. The top will be dark brown, and a toothpick inserted in the center should come out clean when done. 4. Let cool for 30 minutes before serving.
Per Serving: Calories 139; Fat 13g; Sodium 112mg; Carbs 15g; Fiber 2g; Sugar 1g; Protein 3g

Tangy Lime Bars

Prep time: 11 minutes | Cook time: 33 minutes | Serves: 12

1½ cups blanched finely ground almond flour, divided
¾ cup confectioners' erythritol, divided

4 tablespoons salted butter, melted
½ cup fresh lime juice
2 large eggs, whisked

1. Mix 1 cup flour, ¼ cup erythritol, and butter in a medium bowl. Press mixture into bottom of an ungreased 6" round nonstick cake pan. 2. Place pan into the air fryer basket. Set the temperature setting to 300°F/150°C and timer for 13 minutes. Crust will be brown and set in the middle when done. 3. Allow to cool in pan for 10 minutes. 4. In a medium bowl, Add the remaining flour, remaining erythritol, lime juice, and eggs. 5. Pour mixture over cooled crust and return to the air fryer for 20 minutes at 300°F/150°C. 6. Top will be browned and firm when done. Let cool completely in pan for about 30 minutes, then chill covered in the refrigerator for 1 hour. 7. Serve chilled.
Per Serving: Calories 133; Fat 12g; Sodium 42mg; Carbs 12g; Fiber 2g; Sugar 1g; Protein 4g

Apple Crisp

Prep time: 11 minutes | Cook time: 40 minutes | Serves: 6

1 pound frozen sliced rhubarb
¼ cup superfine blanched almond flour
2 tablespoons coconut flour
½ cup 0g net carbs sweetener
2 ounces unsalted butter, cubed

3 tablespoons 0g net carbs brown sugar alternative
½ cup unsweetened flaked coconut
⅛ teaspoon ground cinnamon

1. Preheat oven to 375°F/190°C. Grease a 9" × 9" × 2" dish. 2. Combine rhubarb, almond flour, coconut flour, and sweetener in a large mixing bowl. Spread evenly into baking dish. 3. In a food processor, pulse butter and brown sugar alternative for 1–2 minutes until mixture forms crumble of desired texture. Briefly pulse in flaked coconut and cinnamon until blended. 4. Spread crumble evenly into a baking dish. 5. Bake for 30–40 minutes until bubbling and golden on top. 6. Let cool and serve warm.
Per Serving: Calories 167; Fat 13g; Sodium 2mg; Carbs 22g; Fiber 4g; Sugar 2g; Protein 2g

Economical Peanut Butter Pie

Prep time: 130 minutes | Cook time: 0 minutes | Serves: 8

Pie Crust
1 cup superfine blanched almond flour
3½ tablespoons 100% cocoa powder
3 tablespoons 0g net carbs

Pie Filling
¾ cup no-sugar-added peanut butter, softened
¾ cup 0g net carbs sweetener
1½ (8-ounce) packages full-fat

sweetener
½ tablespoon pure vanilla extract
2½ tablespoons unsalted butter, softened

cream cheese, softened
½ tablespoon pure vanilla extract
½ cup heavy whipping cream
¼ teaspoon 100% cocoa powder

1. In a bowl, mix all crust ingredients. Form crust into bottom of a greased 9" pie tin. 2. In a bowl, mix peanut butter with sweetener, cream cheese, and vanilla. Pour in cream in the butter mix and mix until blended. 3. Pour filling onto crust evenly and top sprinkle with cocoa. Chill in refrigerator 2 hours until set. 4. Cut into slices and serve chilled.
Per Serving: Calories 474; Fat 40g; Sodium 202mg; Carbs 23g; Fiber 5g; Sugar 4g; Protein 12g

Berries Mascarpone

Prep time: 5 minutes | Cook time: 0 minutes | Serves: 4

2 cups fresh raspberries
8 ounces mascarpone cheese, softened

2 (3.9-gram) packets sugar-free lemonade drink mix, single serving

1. Distribute raspberries evenly into four dessert bowls. 2. In a bowl blend mascarpone cheese with drink mix with aid of electric beater. 3. Dollop equal amounts of cheese mixture on top of berry bowls. 4. Serve chilled.
Per Serving: Calories 211; Fat 16g; Sodium 67mg; Carbs 13g; Fiber 4g; Sugar 5g; Protein 5g

Doodles

Prep time: 11 minutes | Cook time: 15 minutes | Serves: 12

3 ounces (6 tablespoons) unsalted butter, softened
10 tablespoons 0g net carbs sweetener, divided
½ teaspoon xanthan gum
1½ teaspoons ground cinnamon, divided

1 large egg, beaten
1 teaspoon baking powder
⅛ teaspoon salt
½ tablespoon pure vanilla extract
2 cups superfine blanched almond flour

1. Preheat oven to 375°F/190°C. Line a baking sheet with parchment paper. 2. In a medium bowl, whip butter using a mixer. Fold in 8 tablespoons (½ cup) sweetener, xanthan gum, 1 teaspoon cinnamon, egg, baking powder, salt, and vanilla. 3. Slowly stir in almond flour until dough forms. 4. In a bowl, stir remaining sweetener with remaining ½ teaspoon cinnamon until well mixed. Scoop out cookie dough with a spoon and form into 1" balls. Roll to coat in cinnamon and sweetener mix. 5. Place balls on sheet and flatten with hand to desired thickness. Space cookies ½" apart and bake 12–15 minutes until golden. 6. Let cool and serve.
Per Serving: Calories 184; Fat 16g; Sodium 72mg; Carbs 9g; Fiber 2g; Sugar 1g; Protein 5g

German Chocolate Cookie

Prep time: 5 minutes | Cook time: 20 minutes | Serves: 12

¼ cup superfine blanched almond flour
3 tablespoons 100% cocoa powder
1 teaspoon dry coffee grounds
½ cup 0g net carbs sweetener
⅛ teaspoon salt
3 tablespoons unsalted butter, melted
⅓ cup heavy whipping cream
½ teaspoon pure vanilla extract
1 large egg, beaten
1 cup shredded unsweetened coconut
¼ cup finely chopped pecans

1. Preheat oven to 350°F/175°C. Line a baking sheet with parchment paper. 2. Mix almond flour, cocoa, coffee, sweetener, and salt in a medium bowl. Add remaining ingredients and stir to mix until dough forms. 3. Form dough into 1"–1½" balls and place on the baking sheet. Flatten to desired thickness and separate by at least ½". 4. Bake for 15–20 minutes until set. Serve warm.
Per Serving: Calories 136; Fat 12g; Sodium 33mg; Carbs 8g; Fiber 2g; Sugar 1g; Protein 2g

Candy Almonds

Prep time: 5 minutes | Cook time: 22 minutes | Serves: 8

8 ounces whole almonds
1 tablespoon unsalted butter, melted
1 tablespoon 100% cocoa powder
4 tablespoons 0g net carbs sweetener
⅛ teaspoon salt
⅛ teaspoon cayenne pepper

1. Preheat oven to 375°F/190°C. Line a baking sheet with parchment paper. 2. Spread almonds on a baking sheet for roasting in a single layer. Toast almonds in oven for 10–15 minutes, turning almonds halfway through cooking time. 3. Mix hot toasted almonds with melted butter in a medium bowl and stir to coat. 4. Thoroughly mix cocoa, sweetener, salt, and cayenne pepper in a medium bowl. Add buttery nuts to dry mix and stir to evenly coat. 5. Return single layer of chocolate-covered almonds to the baking sheet and bake for an additional 7 minutes, stirring once. 6. Let cool before eating. Coating will harden as it cools.
Per Serving: Calories 181; Fat 15g; Sodium 36mg; Carbs 10g; Fiber 4g; Sugar 1g; Protein 6g

Chocolate Puddin' Cake

Prep time: 11 minutes | Cook time: 30 minutes | Serves: 8

1 cup superfine blanched almond flour
⅓ cup coconut flour
½ cup 100% cocoa powder
4 tablespoons 0g net carbs sweetener
1½ teaspoons baking powder
1 cup unsweetened canned coconut milk
1 (4-ounce) stick unsalted butter, melted
1 teaspoon pure vanilla extract
4 medium eggs, beaten

1. Combine almond flour with coconut flour, cocoa powder, sweetener, and baking powder. Whisk in remaining ingredients until thoroughly blended. 2. Spray a baking pan that will fit your pressure cooker with nonstick cooking spray. 3. Add batter and cover baking pan with foil. 4. Add 1 cup water to bottom of pressure cooker and place baking pan in cooker on top of trivet. 5. Close lid, close vent, and cook on high pressure for 30 minutes. 6. Release pressure and remove lid. When cool enough to handle, remove cake and remove foil. 7. Serve warm.
Per Serving: Calories 297; Fat 25g; Sodium 143mg; Carbs 12g; Fiber 5g; Sugar 2g; Protein 8g

Chocolate Peanut Butter Cupcake

Prep time: 5 minutes | Cook time: 2 minutes | Serves: 1

2 tablespoons no-sugar-added peanut butter
3 (1-gram) packets 0g net carbs sweetener
1 large egg, beaten
¼ teaspoon baking powder
1 tablespoon sugar-free chocolate chips

1. Spray a medium microwave-safe coffee mug with nonstick cooking spray. 2. Add peanut butter. Microwave for 45–60 seconds to soften. 3. Stir all ingredients well to mix. Microwave for 60 seconds. 4. Serve warm.
Per Serving: Calories 304; Fat 24g; Sodium 247mg; Carbs 20g; Fiber 7g; Sugar 6g; Protein 15g

Lemonade Strawberry Shortcake

Prep time: 40 minutes | Cook time: 21 minutes | Serves: 4

Shortcake
2 ounces full-fat cream cheese, softened
6 ounces shredded whole milk mozzarella cheese
1 large egg, beaten
1 (3.9-gram) packet sugar-free lemonade drink mix, single serving
⅓ cup superfine blanched almond flour
4 (1-gram) packets 0g net carbs sweetener
1 tablespoon baking powder
Topping
1 cup chopped fresh strawberries
3 tablespoons no-sugar-added red raspberry jam
8 tablespoons canned unsweetened whipped cream

1. In a microwave-safe bowl, add cream cheese and mozzarella cheese. Microwave 30 seconds and stir. Repeat. In a large bowl, whisk together remaining shortcake ingredients. 2. Combine cheeses with the shortcake ingredients and mix well. 3. Form resulting dough into a large ball and refrigerate for 30 minutes. 4. Preheat oven to 425°F/220°C. Cover a baking sheet with greased foil. 5. In a small bowl, add strawberries and jam. Gently stir to evenly coat berries. Set aside. 6. Divide dough into four even balls. 7. Put balls on the baking sheet with 2" in between to account for spreading. 8. Bake 15–20 minutes until browned. Let cool for 10 minutes. 9. Place buns into four bowls and top evenly with strawberry mixture and whipped cream. 10. Serve chilled.
Per Serving: Calories 298; Fat 21g; Sodium 708mg; Carbs 13g; Fiber 2g; Sugar 3g; Protein 14g

Crème Brûlée

Prep time: 11 minutes | Cook time: 27 minutes | Serves: 6

2 large egg yolks, beaten
½ teaspoon pure vanilla extract
1 cup heavy whipping cream
¼ cup 0g net carbs sweetener
⅛ teaspoon salt
1 tablespoon 0g net carbs brown sugar substitute

1. Preheat oven to 350°F/175°C. Insert silicone liners into muffin tin cups. 2. Whisk egg yolks and vanilla together. 3. Add cream, sweetener, and salt to a medium saucepan over medium heat. Bring to boil and immediately remove from heat while stirring to combine and dissolve sweetener and salt. 4. Slowly stir in yolk mixture and whisk until thoroughly combined. Pour mixture evenly into muffin cups. 5. Bake for 20–25 minutes until baked throughout. 6. Remove from oven and top evenly with brown sugar substitute. 7. Preheat oven broiler on high. 8. Briefly place muffin cups under broiler, for 1–2 minutes, until top layer browns and becomes hard. Monitor this last step carefully to prevent burning. 9. Let cool slightly and serve (while still in liner).
Per Serving: Calories 160; Fat 15g; Sodium 66mg; Carbs 6g; Fiber 0g; Sugar 1g; Protein 2g

Coffee Cake Bites

Prep time: 11 minutes | Cook time: 20 minutes | Serves: 10

1½ cups superfine blanched almond flour
⅔ cup 0g net carbs sweetener, divided
1 teaspoon baking powder
¼ teaspoon salt
2 large eggs
3 tablespoons unsalted butter, softened, divided
1 teaspoon pure vanilla extract
¼ cup unsweetened almond milk
1½ tablespoons ground cinnamon

1. Preheat oven to 375°F/190°C. Grease a large muffin tin. 2. Whisk almond flour, ⅓ cup sweetener, baking powder, and salt in a medium bowl. 3. Add eggs, 2 tablespoons butter, vanilla, and almond milk and fold until well mixed. 4. Mix 1 tablespoon butter, cinnamon, and ⅓ cup sweetener in a separate medium bowl. 5. Fill ten cups of the muffin tin about ⅓ full with almond flour batter. Add approximately 2 teaspoons of cinnamon batter and top with a large dollop of almond flour batter that is equal to about ⅓ of muffin cup. 6. Bake for 15–20 minutes until a toothpick inserted into the center comes out clean. Serve warm.
Per Serving: Calories 164; Fat 13g; Sodium 126mg; Carbs 11g; Fiber 2g; Sugar 1g; Protein 5g

Refreshing Mint Smoothie

Prep time: 11 minutes | Cook time: 0 minutes | Serves: 2

1 cup ice
1 cup unsweetened almond milk
½ cup full-fat plain Greek yogurt
½ cup unsweetened canned
coconut milk
½ medium avocado, peeled and

pitted
½ cup chopped fresh mint
1 cup chopped fresh spinach
1 cup chopped fresh kale
4 (1-gram) packets 0g net carbs
sweetener

1. In a large blender, pulse all ingredients at once until desired consistency is reached. 2. Pour into two pint glasses and enjoy with a friend.
Per Serving: Calories 285; Fat 24g; Sodium 188mg; Carbs 9g; Fiber 4g; Sugar 2g; Protein 9g

Hot Cider

Prep time: 5 minutes | Cook time: 10 minutes | Serves: 4

3 cups water
6 cinnamon sticks
14 whole cloves

8 (1-gram) packets 0g net carbs
sweetener
3 tablespoons apple cider vinegar

1. In a pot, add water with cinnamon sticks, cloves, and sweetener. Bring to boil and simmer for 10 minutes, stirring regularly. 2. Remove from heat and let cool. Add apple cider vinegar and stir to mix when liquid is warm but cool enough to drink. 3. Using strainer to remove seasonings, pour liquid evenly into four glass mugs and serve warm.
Per Serving: Calories 2; Fat 0g; Sodium 0mg; Carbs 0g; Fiber 0g; Sugar 0g; Protein 0g

Chai Latte

Prep time: 11 minutes | Cook time: 2 hours 5 minutes | Serves: 4

2 cups water
4 tea bags black tea
3 cinnamon sticks
⅛ teaspoon ground cardamom
⅛ teaspoon allspice
⅛ teaspoon ground anise

1 tablespoon coconut butter
1½ cups unsweetened almond
milk
6 (1-gram) packets 0g net carbs
sweetener

1. In a small pot, boil water and steep tea bags in. 2. Pour hot tea into a slow cooker. 3. Add other ingredients to the slow cooker and stir until sweetener is dissolved and all ingredients are well mixed. 4. Close slow cooker and cook on high for 2 hours. 5. Remove lid, whisk, and let cool. 6. When cooled, stir again and pour through a strainer into four glass mugs with handles. Serve warm.
Per Serving: Calories 37; Fat 3g; Sodium 72mg; Carbs 2g; Fiber 1g; Sugar 0g; Protein 1g

Keto Martini

Prep time: 5 minutes | Cook time: 0 minutes | Serves: 2

2 (1½-ounce) shots unflavored
gin
½ ounce olive brine
½ ounce dry vermouth

6 stuffed green olives
2 slices cooked (crispy) no-sugar-
added bacon
4 (1") chunks avocado

1. Shake gin, brine, and vermouth together in a large covered glass over a few ice cubes. 2. Strain chilled liquids quickly into two martini glasses (leaving ice behind). 3. Use decorative skewer to pierce (in a fun pattern) olives, bacon, and avocado chunks. 4. Insert skewer into glass as drink stirrer. Serve immediately.
Per Serving: Calories 220; Fat 7g; Sodium 433mg; Carbs 4g; Fiber 1g; Sugar 2g; Protein 4g

Energy Booster Drink

Prep time: 5 minutes | Cook time: 0 minutes | Serves: 1

2½ cups water
3 tablespoons fresh lemon juice
1 teaspoon apple cider vinegar
2 (1-gram) packets 0g net carbs

sweetener
½ teaspoon salt
1 cup ice

1. Combine all ingredients (including the lemon rinds if you squeezed your own juice) in a pitcher and stir until sweetener and salt are dissolved. 2. Serve immediately.
Per Serving: Calories 11; Fat 0g; Sodium 1162mg; Carbs 3g; Fiber 0g; Sugar 1g; Protein 0g

Strawberry Cheesecakes

Prep time: 10 minutes | Cook time: 0 minutes | Serves: 4

Crust
½ cup almond flour
3 tablespoons butter, melted

¼ cup sugar substitute

Filling
6 strawberries
3 tablespoons sugar
8 ounces cream cheese
⅓ cup sour cream

½ teaspoon pure vanilla extract
4 strawberries, quartered (for
garnish)
Fresh mint leaves (for garnish)

1. To prepare the crust, place the almond flour, melted butter, and sugar substitute in a medium bowl and mix well to combine. 2. Divide the mixture evenly into 4 small serving bowls or ramekins, lightly pressing with your hands. 3. To prepare the filling, puree the strawberries in a food processor. 4. Add the sugar substitute, vanilla extract, cream cheese, and sour cream. Blend until smooth and creamy. 5. Spoon the mixture over the crust and chill for at least 1 hour.
Per Serving: Calories 489; Fat 47g; Sodium 678mg; Carbs 12g; Fiber 3g; Sugar 6g; Protein 8g

Three-Layered Chocolate Cream Cake

Prep time: 30 minutes | Cook time: 60 minutes | Serves: 8

4 ounces unsweetened chocolate
½ cup butter
1½ cups powdered sweetener,
divided
3 eggs
½ cup + 8 tablespoons raw
unsweetened cocoa powder

1 vanilla pod
Pinch of sea salt
1 cup whipping cream
Coconut whipped cream
1 can coconut milk, refrigerated
overnight

1. Preheat the oven to 325°F/165°C. Spray a little cooking oil into a pan smaller than 8 inches. 2. Combine the chocolate and butter in a double boiler and melt them together. Stir in ½ cup of sweetener and stirring over low heat until everything is well combined. Remove from heat and let cool a little bit. 3. Separate the eggs, and beat the whites until stiff peaks form. Add ¼ cup of sweetener little by little. 4. Whisk the yolks together with another ¼ cup of sweetener. Add the chocolate mixture to the yolks and stir well. Mix in ½ cup cocoa, and then scrape the vanilla seeds from the pod and add to the mix along with salt. 5. Fold in egg whites slowly to the chocolate mixture, but do not over mix. 6. Bake it for 1 hour. Let it cool thoroughly, and then remove it from the pan. Let it cool thoroughly, and then remove it from the pan.
Cream: 1. To prepare the 3 types of filling, beat the whipping cream for about 6-7 minutes until it gets very thick. Slowly add ½ cup of sweetener. 2. Divide the cream into halves and place one half in a bowl. Divide the remaining cream into halves again, and remember to put in the other 2 separate bowls. You will have 3 bowls, one with ½ of the cream and two with ¼ of the cream. 3. Take a bowl with ¼ cream, add 1 tablespoon of cocoa powder and mix well. This will be the lightest-colored cream. 4. Add ½ the cream to the bowl, and add 3 tablespoons of cocoa powder. Mix until well distributed. This will be the middle-colored cream. 5. Add to the last bowl with ¼ cream. This will be the darkest cream.
Assembling: 1. Slice the cake horizontally into 3 slices using a very sharp knife. 2. Place the bottom part on a serving plate and cover with the middle-colored cream. Repeat with the second cake layer. 3. Top the third cake layer and cover it with the light-colored cream on top, followed by the darkest cream. 4. Cut into 8 slices and enjoy
Per Serving: Calories 304; Fat 27g; Sodium 678mg; Carbs 11g; Fiber 6g; Sugar 2g; Protein 7g

Coconut Nut Cookies

Prep time: 10 minutes | Cook time: 15 minutes | Serves: 6

1¼ cups almond flour
½ cup unsweetened, shredded
coconut
3 large eggs
6 tablespoons butter, softened

⅓ cup pure Grade B maple syrup
1 teaspoon almond extract
¼ teaspoon ground cinnamon
¼ teaspoon sea salt

1. Preheat the oven to 350°F/175°C. Prepare a metal baking sheet with parchment paper or non-stick spray. 2. Use a hand mixer to blend the maple syrup with the softened butter until smooth and creamy. 3. Add the eggs and mix well. Add the almond flour, almond extract, cinnamon, and salt with the mixer on low, mixing until combined. 4. Stir in the shredded coconut. Drop the spoonful onto the baking sheet. 5. Bake for 12-15 minutes, until golden brown around the edges.
Per Serving: Calories 271; Fat 25g; Sodium 347mg; Carbs 5g; Fiber 3g; Sugar 5g; Protein 7g

Chocolaty Cheesecake Bars

Prep time: 50 minutes | Cook time: 55 minutes | Serves: 6

Brownie layer

2 ounces bittersweet chocolate, chopped
½ cup butter softened
⅓ cup raw unsweetened cocoa powder
Cheesecake layer
2 large eggs
16 ounces cream cheese, softened
⅓ cup sugar substitute

½ cup almond flour
2 large eggs
½ cup sugar substitute
½ teaspoon pure vanilla extract
¼ teaspoon salt

¼ cup heavy cream
½ teaspoon pure vanilla extract

1. Preheat the oven to 325°F/165°C. 2. Grease an 8x8 baking dish oil. 3. Melt the butter along with chocolate and stir until well combined. 4. Whisk the almond flour, cocoa powder, and salt together in a small bowl. 5. Whisk the eggs along with sugar substitute, and vanilla extract in a large bowl until frothy. Slowly whisk in the melted chocolate mixture. 6. Add in the flour mix and stir until smooth. Pour into the prepared baking dish and bake for 20 minutes. Cool the cake completely. 7. Mix together the cream cheese, eggs, sugar substitute, heavy cream, and vanilla extract with an electric mixer for the cheesecake layer. 8. Reduce the oven heat to 300°F/150°C. Pour the batter over the baked brownies and return to the oven for 40 to 45 minutes or until set. 9. Cool it before serving.
Per Serving: Calories 556; Fat 54g; Sodium 489mg; Carbs 12g; Fiber 3g; Sugar 5g; Protein 13g

Chocolate Pudding

Prep time: 5 minutes | Cook time: 5 minutes | Serves: 4

2 cups coconut milk, canned
¼ cup raw unsweetened cocoa powder
1 tablespoon stevia
2 tablespoons gelatin

4 tablespoons water
½ cup whipping cream
1 ounce chopped bittersweet chocolate (optional for garnish)

1. Heat the coconut milk, cocoa powder, and stevia in a small saucepan. Stir until the cocoa powder and stevia have dissolved. 2. Mix the gelatin with the water and add to the saucepan. Stir until well combined. 3. Pour the mixture into 4 small ramekins or glasses. 4. Place the hot ramekins in the refrigerator to cool for at least 1 hour.
Per Serving: Calories 389; Fat 37g; Sodium 894mg; Carbs 14g; Fiber 5g; Sugar 7g; Protein 8g

Strawberries Coconut Whip

Prep time: 5 minutes | Cook time: 3 minutes | Serves: 4

2 cans coconut cream, refrigerated
4 cups strawberries

1 ounce chopped unsweetened 70% dark chocolate

1. Scoop the solidified coconut cream into a large bowl and blend with a hand mixer for about 5 minutes until stiff peaks form. Slice the strawberries and arrange them in 4 small serving bowls. 2. Dollop the coconut whipped cream on top of the strawberries. 3. Garnish with chopped dark chocolate and additional berries. 4. Serve and enjoy!
Per Serving: Calories 342; Fat 31g; Sodium 532mg; Carbs 15g; Fiber 5g; Sugar 6g; Protein 15g

Nutty Chocolate Milkshake

Prep time: 5 minutes | Cook time: 0 minutes | Serves: 4

2 cups unsweetened coconut, almond, or dairy-free milk of choice
1 banana, sliced and frozen
¼ cup unsweetened coconut flakes
1 cup ice cubes

¼ cup macadamia nuts, chopped
3 tablespoons sugar-free sweetener
2 tablespoons raw unsweetened cocoa powder
Whipped coconut cream (optional for garnish)

1. Mix all the ingredients in blender until smooth and creamy. If desired, divide evenly between 4 "mocktail" glasses and top with whipped coconut cream. 2. Add a cocktail umbrella and toasted coconut for added flair. 3. Enjoy your delicious Choco-nut smoothie!
Per Serving: Calories 199; Fat 17g; Sodium 347mg; Carbs 12g; Fiber 4g; Sugar 8g; Protein 3g

Buttery Pecan Ice Cream

Prep time: 10 minutes | Cook time: 0 minutes | Serves: 4

½ cup chopped pecans
⅛ teaspoon xanthan gum
2 egg yolks
1 teaspoon pure vanilla extract

¼ cup sugar substitute
2 tablespoons butter
1 cup heavy cream

1. Melt butter over medium heat. Whisk the heavy cream into the butter after it has melted and become slightly brown. 2. Stir in the sugar substitute and mix until dissolved. 3. Add the xanthan gum and whisk until well combined. Transfer to a large metal bowl and allow to cool. 4. Add the egg yolks slowly, one at a time, using a hand mixer. 5. Stir in the pecans and vanilla extract. 6. Place the bowl in the freezer for at least 4 hours, stirring well every hour. 7. Remove from the freezer and scoop into serving bowls. 8. Garnish with additional chopped pecans, if desired, and serve!
Per Serving: Calories 230; Fat 24g; Sodium 421mg; Carbs 2g; Fiber 1g; Sugar 2g; Protein 3g

Blueberry Ice Cream

Prep time: 15 minutes | Cook time: 0 minutes | Serves: 4

¼ cup sour cream
1 cup heavy whipping cream
¼ cup fresh blueberries

1 egg yolk, beaten
2 teaspoons pure vanilla extract

1. Whip the sour cream with a hand mixer until frothy. 2. Whip the heavy cream in a separate bowl until soft peaks form. 3. Fold the sour cream with the whipped cream carefully. Puree the blueberries in a food processor or blender until smooth. 4. Stir the blueberry puree, egg yolk, and vanilla extract into the whipped cream mixture. Mix until just combined. 5. Transfer mixture into a loaf pan and freeze for 2 hours, stirring well every 30 minutes. 6. Scoop into serving bowls and enjoy your fresh blueberry ice cream!
Per Serving: Calories 153; Fat 15g; Sodium 690mg; Carbs 3g; Fiber 0g; Sugar 3g; Protein 2g

Chocolate Truffles

Prep time: 10 minutes | Cook time: 20 minutes | Serves: 6

4 ounces unsweetened dark chocolate
1 tablespoon raw unsweetened cocoa powder
1 tablespoon pure maple syrup

1½ tablespoons butter
⅓ cup heavy cream
¼ teaspoon pure vanilla extract
¼ teaspoon ground cinnamon
Pinch of sea salt

1. Chop the dark chocolate finely. 2. Heat the cream in a saucepan. Mix in the chopped chocolate and butter. Stir until melted and well combined. Mix in the chopped chocolate and butter. Stir until melted and well combined. 3. Remove from heat and stir the vanilla extract, maple syrup, salt, and cinnamon. 4. Place mixture in the fridge for at least 2 hours. 5. Remove the mixture from the fridge once cooled and shape them into small balls using your palms. 6. Roll balls in cocoa powder until coated fully. Store in an airtight container in the fridge.
Per Serving: Calories 160; Fat 11g; Sodium 333mg; Carbs 11g; Fiber 1g; Sugar 2g; Protein 2g

Chocolate Coconut Torts

Prep time: 5 minutes | Cook time: 7 minutes | Serves: 6

4 ounces unsweetened dark chocolate
¼ cup unsweetened, shredded coconut
1 cup coconut flour

1 tablespoon chocolate protein powder
4 tablespoons coconut oil
⅓ cup heavy cream

1. Chop the dark chocolate into small pieces. 2. Heat the cream in a pan over medium-low heat. Add the chocolate and coconut oil and stir until melted and well combined. 3. Stir in the coconut flour and protein powder while removed from heat. Cool the mix for at least 2 hours in fridge. 4. Once cooled, shape into small balls using your palms. 5. Roll balls in the shredded coconut until coated fully.
Per Serving: Calories 326; Fat 27g; Sodium 348mg; Carbs 12g; Fiber 3g; Sugar 6g; Protein 9g

Peanut Butter with Jelly Cookies

Prep time: 10 minutes | Cook time: 12 minutes | Serves: 6

⅔ cup creamy peanut butter
⅓ cup sugar-free strawberry preserves
⅓ cup almond flour
1 egg

½ cup sugar substitute
¼ teaspoon pure vanilla extract
¼ teaspoon baking powder
¼ teaspoon sea salt

1. Preheat the oven to 350°F/175°C. Prepare a metal baking sheet by lining it with parchment paper or nonstick spray. 2. Beat the egg with the peanut butter and sugar substitute in a large bowl until smooth and creamy. Add the almond flour along with baking powder, salt, and vanilla extract. Mix well to form a dough. 3. Shape mix into balls and place them on the prepared baking sheet. 4. Make a small well in the middle of each cookie and fill with about 1 teaspoon of the preserves. 5. Bake it for 10-12 minutes, until the cookies are golden brown. Cool on a wire rack, and enjoy!
Per Serving: Calories 209; Fat 18g; Sodium 452mg; Carbs 7g; Fiber 2g; Sugar 8g; Protein 9g

Nutty Chocolate Fudge

Prep time: 10 minutes | Cook time: 5 minutes | Serves: 4

2 tablespoons raw unsweetened cocoa powder
2 tablespoons sugar substitute
3 tablespoons coconut oil

¼ cup chopped walnuts
¼ cup heavy cream
1 teaspoon pure vanilla extract

1. Place the coconut oil in a metal bowl atop a pot of simmering water. Stir until melted. 2. Whisk in the cocoa powder along with sugar substitute. Remove from heat and stir in the walnuts, heavy cream, and vanilla extract. 3. Stir until well combined and pour into chocolate molds or a square tray. 4. Let cool, then transfer to the fridge to harden. 5. Remove from the fridge and enjoy your delicious chocolate walnut fudge.
Per Serving: Calories 168; Fat 18g; Sodium 478mg; Carbs 3g; Fiber 1g; Sugar 2g; Protein 3g

Nuts Squares

Prep time: 10 minutes | Cook time: 25 minutes | Serves: 6

1 cup pecans (halved)
3 tablespoons pure Grade B maple syrup
½ cup almond flour
¼ cup flax meal
¼ cup unsweetened, shredded

coconut
¼ cup coconut oil, melted
1 egg, beaten
2 tablespoons sugar substitute
⅓ cup sugar-free chocolate chips

1. Preheat the oven to 350°F/ 175°C. Prepare a baking sheet by lining it with parchment paper. Place the pecans on the baking sheet and bake for 7 minutes, until toasted and fragrant. 2. Allow the pecans to cool when done. Chop the pecans once cooled, reserving a few halves for garnish. 3. Mix the flax meal, almond flour, chopped pecans, and shredded coconut in a large bowl. 4. Stir in the maple syrup, coconut oil, egg, and sugar substitute. Mix well. Add the sugar-free chocolate chips if using. 5. Transfer the dough into a 9-inch by 3-inch loaf pan that has been prepared with nonstick cooking spray. 6. Bake at 350°F/175°C temperature setting for 20 minutes, or until a toothpick inserted comes out clean. 7. Remove from oven and allow to cool. 8. Cut into squares and enjoy!
Per Serving: Calories 233; Fat 21g; Sodium 433mg; Carbs 12g; Fiber 4g; Sugar 4g; Protein 5g

Regular Peanut Butter Cookies

Prep time: 10 minutes | Cook time: 14 to 16 minutes | Serves: 6

½ cup creamy peanut butter
½ cup coconut flour
¼ cup sugar substitute

1 egg
¼ teaspoon pure vanilla extract
Pinch of sea salt

1. Preheat the oven to 350°F/175°C. Prepare a metal baking sheet by lining it with parchment paper or non-stick cooking spray. 2. Using an electric mixer, blend all ingredients until a smooth dough forms. 3. Shape the dough into walnut-size balls and arrange them on the prepared baking sheet. 4. Using a fork, make crisscross marks on top of the balls to form cookies and bake for 14-16 minutes, until golden brown.
Per Serving: Calories 160; Fat 14g; Sodium 421mg; Carbs 5g; Fiber 3g; Sugar 3g; Protein 7g

Creamy Coconut Brownies

Prep time: 10 minutes | Cook time: 25 minutes | Serves: 6

¾ cup coconut butter, melted
⅓ cup coconut cream
¼ cup raw unsweetened cocoa powder
¼ cup coconut flour
2 tablespoons butter, melted

½ cup sugar substitute
1 egg
1 teaspoon pure vanilla extract
¼ teaspoon baking soda
Pinch of sea salt

1. Whisk the coconut flour, cocoa powder, sugar substitute, baking soda, and salt together in a large bowl. 2. Whisk the coconut butter, coconut cream, and butter together in a separate bowl until well combined. Whisk in the egg and vanilla extract. 3. Stir in the dry ingredients slowly into the wet ingredients and mix well. 4. Transfer the mixture into a 9-inch by 3-inch loaf pan that has been prepared with nonstick cooking spray. 5. Bake at 350°F/175°C temperature setting for 20 minutes or until a toothpick inserted comes out clean. 6. Cut into squares and enjoy!
Per Serving: Calories 175; Fat 17g; Sodium 541mg; Carbs 5g; Fiber 3g; Sugar 8g; Protein 3g

Regular Carrot Cake with Cream Cheese Frosting

Prep time: 15 minutes | Cook time: 30 minutes | Serves: 6

Carrot cake
1½ cups carrots, grated finely
¾ cups sugar substitute
¼ cup brown sugar substitute
½ cup coconut oil, melted
2 large eggs

¼ cup flax meal
½ teaspoon baking soda
½ teaspoon ground cinnamon
¼ teaspoon ground nutmeg
¾ cup almond flour

Cream cheese frosting
8 ounces cream cheese, softened
2 tablespoons pure Grade B maple syrup

¼ teaspoon pure vanilla extract
¼ cup toasted walnuts, chopped (optional for garnish)

1. Preheat the oven to 350°F/175°C temperature setting and grease a 9-inch round cake pan with oil. 2. Blend the sugars, coconut oil, and eggs using a hand mixer. 3. Whisk the all dry ingredients together until well combined. Add the dry ingredients slowly and keep blending until no lumps remain. 4. Add in the grated carrots and pour the cake batter into the cake pan. Bake the cake for 30 minutes. 5. Remove from oven and allow to cool. Beat the cream cheese, maple syrup, and vanilla extract until light and fluffy to prepare the frosting. 6. Top the cake with the frosting, sprinkle with toasted walnuts, slice, and serve!
Per Serving: Calories 479; Fat 45g; Sodium 236mg; Carbs 14g; Fiber 5g; Sugar 7g; Protein 11g

Mini Chocolaty Avocado Tarts

Prep time: 15 minutes | Cook time: 8 minutes | Serves: 4

Tart crust
2 tablespoons almond flour
1 tablespoon maple syrup

1 large egg white
¼ cup flax meal

Middle layer
4 tablespoons creamy peanut butter

2 tablespoons butter

Top layer
1 medium avocado
4 tablespoons raw unsweetened cocoa powder

¼ cup sugar substitute
2 tablespoons heavy cream
½ teaspoon pure vanilla extract

1. Preheat the oven to 350°F/175°C. 2. Mix the almond flour, flax meal, 1 tablespoon of sugar substitute, and egg white in a small bowl. 3. Press the mix into 4 small tart tins. Bake for about 8 minutes, until golden. Remove from oven and allow to cool slightly. 4. Melt the peanut butter with regular butter in a small saucepan over medium-low heat and stir until well combined. Divide evenly between the baked tart shells. Chill for 30 minutes. 5. Mix the avocado, cocoa powder, sugar substitute, heavy cream, and vanilla extract in a blender or food processor. 6. Remove the chilled tarts from the fridge, top with the blended avocado mixture, and return to the refrigerator for at least 1 hour. 7. Serve and enjoy!
Per Serving: Calories 367; Fat 33g; Sodium 357mg; Carbs 5g; Fiber 10g; Sugar 3g; Protein 11g

Chocolate Macaroons

Prep time: 10 minutes | Cook time: 25 minutes | Serves: 3

1 cup unsweetened shredded coconut
2 ounces dark chocolate (80% cocoa or higher)
2 large egg whites

¼ cup sugar substitute
2 tablespoons coconut oil
1 teaspoon pure vanilla extract
Pinch of sea salt

1. Preheat the oven to 350°F/175°C. Prepare a metal baking sheet by lining it with parchment paper. 2. Spread the shredded coconut evenly onto the baking sheet and place in the oven to toast for 3-5 minutes or until light brown and fragrant. 3. Beat the egg whites with an electric mixer in a large mixing bowl. Add the sugar substitute slowly and continue mixing until stiff peaks form. 4. Stir in the coconut along with vanilla extract, and salt. 5. Prepare a baking sheet with parchment paper. Shape into balls and drop them onto the prepared baking sheet. 6. Bake for 15-18 minutes until golden brown. Cool it on a wire rack. 7. Melt the chocolate with the coconut oil. Stir until well combined. 8. Drizzle the macaroons with the melted chocolate and enjoy!
Per Serving: Calories 143; Fat 12g; Sodium 689mg; Carbs 8g; Fiber 2g; Sugar 6g; Protein 3g

Chocolate Tart

Prep time: 20 minutes | Cook time: 30 minutes | Serves: 4

Crust
1 cup coconut flour
¼ cup flaxseed meal
3 tablespoons sugar substitute
Filling
½ cup raw unsweetened cocoa powder
1 cup heavy cream
2½ teaspoons gelatin powder

½ cup butter
4 egg whites

¼ cup sugar substitute
1 teaspoon pure vanilla extract
¼ cup pistachios, sliced

For the crust: 1. Preheat the oven to 375°F/190°C. Prepare a tiny tart or pie pan with nonstick cooking spray. Prepare a tiny tart or pie pan with nonstick cooking spray. 2. Combine all the crust in a food processor and pulse until well combined. Press the mix in tart pan and bake it for about 15 minutes. 3. Remove from oven and allow to cool.
To prepare the filling: 1. Combine all stuffing (reserving the pistachios) in a blender or food processor and blend until smooth and creamy. 2. Pour the mixture into the crust, cover with plastic wrap, and refrigerate for at least 2 hours. 3. Sprinkle with the reserved pistachios, and serve!
Per Serving: Calories 490; Fat 46g; Sodium 235mg; Carbs 13g; Fiber 7g; Sugar 8g; Protein 13g

Peanut Butter Bars

Prep time: 10 minutes | Cook time: 5 minutes | Serves: 24

½ cup unsweetened dark chocolate baking chips
½ cup coconut oil
½ cup unsweetened peanut butter

1 teaspoon pure vanilla extract
2 tablespoons sugar substitute
1 teaspoon sea salt

1. Prepare a mini muffin tin with liners. 2. Add the dark chocolate, coconut oil, vanilla extract, sugar substitute, and sea salt to a stockpot and stir until thoroughly melted. 3. Pour 2 teaspoons of the chocolate mix into the base of each lined muffin tin and top with a scoop of peanut butter. Set in the freezer for about 5 minutes to harden. 4. Remove the muffin pan from the freezer and top with another 2 teaspoons of the melted chocolate mixture to thoroughly cover the peanut butter. 5. Set the pan in the freezer and freeze for another 15-20 minutes or until the peanut butter cups are hardened. 6. Store leftovers in the fridge.
Per Serving: Calories 107; Fat 10g; Sodium 714mg; Carbs 4g; Fiber 1g; Sugar 3g; Protein 2g

Minty Chocolate Shake

Prep time: 5 minutes | Cook time: 0 minutes | Serves: 2

1 cup full-fat coconut milk
2 tablespoons unsweetened dark chocolate, chopped
½ cup mint leaves

½ avocado pitted
1 teaspoon pure vanilla extract
1 tablespoon sugar substitute
½ cup ice

1. Add all the ingredients into blender. 2. Blend them until smooth. 3. Enjoy right away.
Per Serving: Calories 247; Fat 21g; Sodium 314mg; Carbs 18g; Fiber 7g; Sugar 8g; Protein 4g

Chocolate Almonds

Prep time: 10 minutes | Cook time: 5 minutes | Serves: 8

¾ cup unsweetened dark chocolate baking chips
1½ cups whole raw almonds

1 teaspoon pure vanilla extract
Pinch of sea salt

1. Prepare a baking sheet by paper lining and add the chocolate chips to a stockpot with the vanilla extract over low heat. Stir the chocolate until melted. 2. Add the almonds to the stockpot with the melted chocolate and stir until the almonds are coated. 3. Place the almonds onto the lined baking sheet. 4. Sprinkle with salt and set in the fridge for at least 30 minutes before serving.
Per Serving: Calories 183; Fat 15g; Sodium 314mg; Carbs 7g; Fiber 4g; Sugar 7g; Protein 4g

Healthy Almond Cookies

Prep time: 10 minutes | Cook time: 10 minutes | Serves: 18

1 cup unsweetened almond butter
½ cup sugar substitute
¼ cup unsweetened dark chocolate baking chips

1 egg
1 teaspoon baking soda
1 teaspoon pure vanilla extract
Pinch of sea salt

1. Preheat the oven to 350°F/190°C temperature setting and prepare a baking sheet by lining it with parchment paper. 2. Add the almond butter, egg, sugar substitute, and vanilla to a large mixing bowl and stir well. Add in the remaining ingredients and stir. 3. Drop the dough by 1-inch rounds onto the baking sheet and bake for 10 minutes or until the edges are brown and lightly crispy.
Per Serving: Calories 137; Fat 10g; Sodium 236mg; Carbs 10g; Fiber 1g; Sugar 3g; Protein 3g

Snicker Bites

Prep time: 10 minutes | Cook time: 0 minutes | Serves: 12

1 cup unsweetened peanut butter
¼ cup sugar substitute
¼ cup unsweetened dark chocolate baking chips
3 tablespoons coconut flour

2 tablespoons unsweetened almond milk
1 teaspoon ground cinnamon
1 teaspoon pure vanilla extract
Pinch of sea salt

1. Prepare a baking sheet with parchment paper. 2. Mix all the ingredients well. Set in the fridge for 30 minutes. 3. Remove from the fridge, roll into 12 bite-sized balls, and place on the lined baking sheet. 4. Set in the refrigerator for another hour before serving.
Per Serving: Calories 194; Fat 14g; Sodium 259mg; Carbs 12g; Fiber 3g; Sugar 5g; Protein 7g

Delicious Swoop Cream

Prep time: 10 minutes | Cook time: 0 minutes | Serves: 8

1 cup heavy whipping cream
¼ teaspoon liquid sweetener, 0g

net carbs
½ teaspoon pure vanilla extract

1. In a medium bowl of an electric mixer, whip all ingredients on high speed 1–2 minutes until soft peaks form. 2. Serve cool.
Per Serving: Calories 103; Fat 10g; Sodium 11mg; Carbs 1g; Fiber 0g; Sugar 1g; Protein 1g

Strawberry Milkshake

Prep time: 2 minutes | Cook time: 0 minutes | Serves: 2

1 cup crushed ice cubes
½ cup sliced strawberries, divided
¼ cup heavy whipping cream
1 tablespoon full-fat cream cheese, softened
2 cups unsweetened vanilla

almond milk
1 scoop of low-carb vanilla protein powder
1 teaspoon pure vanilla extract
4 (1-gram) packets of sweetener, 0g net carbs

1. In a blender, add ice, then remaining ingredients, holding back 2 strawberry slices, and blend 1–2 minutes until creamy. 2. Divide evenly between two tall glasses. Garnish each glass with 1 strawberry slice. Serve immediately.
Per Serving: Calories 231; Fat 16g; Sodium 287mg; Carbs 8g; Fiber 2g; Sugar 4g; Protein 14g

Blueberry Smoothie

Prep time: 3 minutes | Cook time: 0 minutes | Serves: 2

1 cup ice cubes
¼ cup blueberries
1 cup spinach
1 cup unsweetened vanilla almond milk
1 scoop berry-flavored low-carb

protein powder
3 tablespoons heavy whipping cream
½ teaspoon pure vanilla extract
4 (1-gram) packets of sweetener, 0g net carbs

1. In a blender, add ice, then the remaining ingredients. 2. Pulse 1–2 minutes until desired consistency is reached. 3. Serve immediately.
Per Serving: Calories 328; Fat 19g; Sodium 360mg; Carbs 12g; Fiber 3g; Sugar 7g; Protein 27g

Caramel Macchiato

Prep time: 3 minutes | Cook time: 3 minutes | Serves: 2

14 ounces brewed macchiato, hot and unsweetened
¼ cup heavy whipping cream
½ teaspoon pure vanilla extract

1 (1-gram) packet sweetener, 0g net carbs
2 tablespoons sugar-free caramel syrup

1. In an emersion blender, add all and pulse 15–30 seconds to blend. 2. Serve immediately in two coffee mugs while still hot.
Per Serving: Calories 125; Fat 11g; Sodium 41mg; Carbs 5g; Fiber 0g; Sugar 1g; Protein 1g

Piña Colada

Prep time: 3 minutes | Cook time: 0 minutes | Serves: 2

1½ cups ice
½ teaspoon sugar-free pineapple drink enhancer
1 cup unsweetened canned coconut milk (12–14% coconut fat)

1 (1½-ounce) shot of unflavored white rum
1 teaspoon 100% lemon juice
4 whole raspberries
2 green leaves from a pineapple crown

1. Add ice and remaining ingredients except for raspberries and pineapple leaves in a blender. 2. Pulse 1–2 minutes until desired consistency is reached, adding water if needed. Divide evenly between two tall glasses. 3. Using a toothpick, pierce two raspberries and one pineapple leaf—balance garnish on the lip of the glass. Repeat for a second glass. 4. Serve immediately.
Per Serving: Calories 199; Fat 15g; Sodium 60mg; Carbs 2g; Fiber 0g; Sugar 0g; Protein 2g

Sweet Iced Tea

Prep time: 5 minutes | Cook time: 0 minutes | Serves: 4

4 cups unsweetened brewed herbal tea, chilled
4 cups sugar-free lemonade, chilled

3 (1-gram) packets of sweetener, 0g net carbs
8 thin slices of lemon

1. Add all tea ingredients in a pitcher and stir to combine until sweetener is dissolved. 2. Divide evenly among four tall glasses and serve immediately while still chilled.
Per Serving: Calories 6; Fat 0g; Sodium 34mg; Carbs 2g; Fiber 0g; Sugar 0g; Protein 0g

Hibiscus Tea

Prep time: 10 minutes | Cook time: 0 minutes | Serves: 4

6 cups unsweetened brewed hibiscus tea
¾ cup unsweetened canned coconut milk, Premium 12–14% coconut fat

6 (1-gram) packets of sweetener, 0g net carbs
2 teaspoons pure vanilla extract
1½ cups ice cubes
¼ cup fresh mint leaves

1. Add tea, coconut milk, sweetener, and vanilla to a pitcher and stir to combine until sweetener is dissolved. 2. Divide evenly among four tall glasses over ice. Top with mint leaves and serve.
Per Serving: Calories 66; Fat 6g; Sodium 26mg; Carbs 2g; Fiber 0g; Sugar 0g; Protein 1g

Fast Fudge

Prep time: 15 minutes | Cook time: 10 minutes | Serves: 20

2 cups unsweetened 100% cocoa powder
¾ cup unsalted butter, softened
1 cup water

⅔ cup whole milk
1 cup sweetener, 0g net carbs
1 teaspoon pure vanilla extract
¼ teaspoon salt

1. Grease a 9" × 9" baking dish. 2. Add cocoa powder and butter in the top pan of a double boiler and stir to combine. 3. Boil water over medium-high heat for a double boiler. Reduce heat to low and cover with the top pan. Stir cocoa mixture constantly while slowly adding milk, sweetener, vanilla, and salt until fudge is thoroughly blended and creamy, approximately 10 minutes. Fudge will become increasingly more and challenging to stir. 4. Transfer fudge to prepared baking dish. Using a spatula, evenly press fudge into all corners of the container. Cover and refrigerate. 5. Serve cold. Cut into serving-sized squares right before serving.
Per Serving: Calories 90; Fat 8g; Sodium 35mg; Carbs 10g; Fiber 3g; Sugar 1g; Protein 2g

Cayenne Chocolate Pudding

Prep time: 10 minutes | Cook time: 0 minutes | Serves: 2

3 tablespoons unsweetened canned coconut milk
2 medium avocados, peeled and pitted
½ cup ice cubes
2 tablespoons unsweetened 100% cocoa powder

1 teaspoon pure vanilla extract
1 teaspoon ground cinnamon
2 tablespoons sweetener, 0g net carbs
⅛ teaspoon salt
⅛ teaspoon ground cayenne pepper

1. Add all chocolate pudding ingredients to a food processor and pulse until even and creamy, 2–3 minutes, stopping midway from scraping down sides with a rubber spatula. 2. Serve immediately.
Per Serving: Calories 299; Fat 24g; Sodium 159mg; Carbs 18g; Fiber 12g; Sugar 2g; Protein 4g

Salty Pecan Bark

Prep time: 25 minutes | Cook time: 1 minutes | Serves: 6

1 cup sugar-free chocolate chips
1 tablespoon coconut oil

1 cup pecan halves
⅛ teaspoon salt

1. Prepare a baking sheet with parchment paper. 2. In a microwave-safe bowl, add chocolate chips with oil and microwave on high 30 seconds. Stir and microwave again 30 seconds. 3. Stir in pecans until coated. 4. Spread the mixture in even layer on the prepared baking sheet. Sprinkle with salt. 5. Freeze at least 20 minutes to harden. 6. Break into 1"–2" pieces and serve—store leftovers in a medium resealable container.
Per Serving: Calories 276; Fat 24g; Sodium 48mg; Carbs 21g; Fiber 11g; Sugar 1g; Protein 4g

Peanut Butter Cheesecake Bites

Prep time: 10 minutes | Cooking time: 15 minutes | Serves: 8

16 ounces cream cheese, softened
1 cup powdered erythritol
½ cup peanut flour
¼ cup sour cream
2 teaspoons vanilla extract

2 eggs
2 cups water
¼ cup low-carb chocolate chips
1 tablespoon coconut oil

1. In suitable bowl, beat cream cheese and erythritol until smooth. Gently fold in peanut flour, sour cream, and vanilla. Fold in eggs slowly until well-mixed. 2. Pour batter into four 4-inch springform pans or silicone cupcake molds. Cover with foil. Pour water into Instant Pot and place steam rack in pot. 3. Carefully lower pan into the pot. Hit the cake button and hit the adjust button to set heat to more. Set time for almost 15 minutes. 4. When the pot beeps, allow a full natural release. Carefully lift cups from Instant Pot and allow to cool completely before refrigerating. 5. In suitable bowl, microwave chocolate chips and coconut oil for almost 30 seconds and whisk until smooth. 6. Drizzle over cheesecakes. Chill in fridge.
Per serving: Calories 284; Total Fat 23g; Sodium 14mg; Total Carbs 7.5g; Fiber 11.1g; Sugars 4g; Protein 6.1g

Chapter 9 Sauces, Staples, and Dressings

Sriracha Mayo 106

Avocado Mayo 106

Peanut Sauce 106

Garlic Aioli 106

Tzatziki 106

Alfredo Sauce 106

Basic Broth 106

90-Second Bread 106

Taco Seasoning 107

Guacamole 107

Butternut Squash "Cheese" Sauce 107

Keto Mayonnaise 107

Ranch Dressing 107

Avocado-Kale Pesto 107

Tahini Goddess Dressing 107

Avocado-Herb Butter....................... 107

Cinnamon Butter 107

Italian Seasoning 107

Horseradish Butter....................... 108

Strawberry Butter 108

Beef Bone Broth 108

Beef Stock 108

Chicken Bone Broth 108

Herbed Chicken Stock 108

Harissa Oil....................... 108

Buttermilk Ranch Dressing 108

Lemon-Garlic Dressing 109

Basil Dressing 109

Grapefruit-Tarragon Dressing 109

Ranch Seasoning 109

Chimichurri 109

Traditional Caesar Dressing 109

Ranch Dressing with Buttermilk 109

Mustard Shallot Vinaigrette 109

Herbed Balsamic Dressing 109

Herbed Infused Olive Oil 109

Ginger with Lime Dressing 110

Garlic and Herb Marinade................. 110

Lemon-Tahini Dressing..................... 110

Cashew Hummus 110

Any-Herb Pesto 110

Keto Peanut Butter Cups 110

Basic Marinara 110

Bolognese Sauce 110

Bacon Jam 111

Roasted Garlic 111

Spinach-Cheese Spread..................... 111

Marinara Sauce 111

Ghee 111

Crab Sauce....................... 111

Enchilada Sauce 111

Queso Sauce 111

Golden Caramelized Onions 111

Coconut-Curry Simmer Sauce 112

Red Wine Vinaigrette 112

Easiest Creamy Caesar Dressing 112

Tangy Citrus-Poppyseed Dressing 112

Herbed Vegetable Broth 112

Herbed Beef Bone Broth 112

Carolina Barbecue Sauce 112

Sriracha Mayo

Prep time: 5 minutes | Cook time: 0 minutes | Serves: 4

½ cup mayonnaise
2 tablespoons Sriracha sauce
½ teaspoon garlic powder

½ teaspoon onion powder
¼ teaspoon paprika

1. Whisk the mayonnaise, Sriracha, garlic powder, onion powder, and paprika until well mixed. 2. Pour into an airtight glass container, and keep in the refrigerator for up to 1 week.
Per Serving: Calories 201; Fat 22g; Sodium 633mg; Carbs 1g; Fiber 0g; Sugar 0.6g; Protein 1g

Avocado Mayo

Prep time: 5 minutes | Cook time: 0 minutes | Serves: 4

1 medium avocado, cut into chunks
½ teaspoon ground cayenne pepper

Juice of ½ lime
2 tablespoons fresh cilantro leaves
Pinch pink Himalayan salt
¼ cup olive oil

1. In a food processor, blend the avocado, cayenne pepper, lime juice, cilantro, and pink Himalayan salt until all the ingredients are well combined. 2. Slowly incorporate the olive oil, adding 1 tablespoon at a time and pulsing the food processor. 3. Keep in an airtight glass container in the refrigerator for up to 1 week.
Per Serving: Calories 58; Fat 5g; Sodium 411mg; Carbs 4g; Fiber 3g; Sugar 1g; Protein 1g

Peanut Sauce

Prep time: 5 minutes | Cook time: 0 minutes | Serves: 4

½ cup creamy peanut butter
2 tablespoons soy sauce
1 teaspoon Sriracha sauce

1 teaspoon toasted sesame oil
1 teaspoon garlic powder

1. Blend the peanut butter, soy sauce, Sriracha sauce, sesame oil, and garlic powder until thoroughly mixed. 2. Pour into an airtight glass container and keep in the refrigerator for up to 1 week.
Per Serving: Calories 185; Fat 15g; Sodium 356mg; Carbs 6g; Fiber 2g; Sugar 1.5g; Protein 7g

Garlic Aioli

Prep time: 5 minutes | Cook time: 0 minutes | Serves: 4

½ cup mayonnaise
2 garlic cloves, minced
Juice of 1 lemon
1 tablespoon chopped fresh flat-

leaf Italian parsley
1 teaspoon chopped chives
Pink Himalayan salt
Freshly ground black pepper

1. Combine the mayonnaise along with garlic, lemon juice, parsley, and chives, and season with pink Himalayan salt and pepper. Blend until fully combined. 2. Pour into a sealed glass container and chill in the refrigerator for at least 30 minutes before serving.
Per Serving: Calories 204; Fat 22g; Sodium 175mg; Carbs 3g; Fiber 1g; Sugar 0.5g; Protein 1g

Tzatziki

Prep time: 11 minutes | Cook time: 0 minutes | Serves: 4

½ large English cucumber, unpeeled
1½ cups Greek yogurt
2 tablespoons olive oil
Large pinch of pink Himalayan salt

A large pinch of freshly ground black pepper
Juice of ½ lemon
2 garlic cloves, finely minced
1 tablespoon fresh dill

1. Halve the cucumber lengthwise and discard the seeds. 2. Grate the cucumber with a zester or grater onto a large plate lined with a few layers of paper towels. Close the paper towels around the grated cucumber, and squeeze as much water out of it as possible. 3. Blend the yogurt, olive oil, pink Himalayan salt, pepper, lemon juice, and garlic until combined. 4. Mix the fresh dill and grated cucumber in the mixture and transfer to bowl. I like to chill this sauce for at least 30 minutes before serving. 5. Keep in an airtight glass container in the refrigerator for up to 1 week.
Per Serving: Calories 149; Fat 11g; Sodium 657mg; Carbs 5g; Fiber 1g; Sugar 0.5g; Protein 8g

Alfredo Sauce

Prep time: 5 minutes | Cook time: 10 minutes | Serves: 2

4 tablespoons butter
2 ounces cream cheese
1 cup heavy (whipping) cream
½ cup grated Parmesan cheese

1 garlic clove, finely minced
1 teaspoon dried Italian seasoning
Pink Himalayan salt
Freshly ground black pepper

1. Combine the butter with cream cheese, and heavy cream in a saucepan over medium heat. Whisk slowly and constantly until the butter and cream cheese melt. 2. Add the Parmesan, garlic, and Italian seasoning. Continue to whisk until everything is well blended. 3. Turn the heat to medium-low and simmer, occasionally stirring, for 5 to 8 minutes to allow the sauce to blend and thicken. 4. Season with pink Himalayan salt and pepper, and stir to combine. 5. Toss with your favorite hot, pre-cooked, keto-friendly noodles and serve. 6. Keep this sauce in an airtight glass container in the refrigerator for up to 4 days.
Per Serving: Calories 294; Fat 30g; Sodium 865mg; Carbs 2g; Fiber 0g; Sugar 0g; Protein 5g

Basic Broth

Prep time: 16 minutes | Cook time: 2-3 hours | Serves: 8

3 celery stalks with greens, roughly chopped
2 carrots, roughly chopped
1 medium yellow onion, peeled and quartered
½ cup chopped fresh parsley

4 garlic cloves, crushed
4 thyme sprigs
2 bay leaves
½ teaspoon black peppercorns
½ teaspoon salt
8 cups water

1. In a large pot, combine the celery, carrots, onion, parsley, garlic, thyme, bay leaves, peppercorns, and salt. 2. Add water, cover, and boil. Simmer gently for 2 to 3 hours on low heat. 3. Strain the broth and discard the solids. Store the broth in sealed containers in the refrigerator for up to 5 days or in the freezer for up to 1 month.
Per Serving (1 cup): Calories 24; Fat 0g; Sodium 1011mg; Carbs 4g; Fiber 0g; Sugar 0g; Protein 2g

1-Beef Broth Variation
Add 2 to 3 pounds of beef bones (beef marrow, knuckle bones, ribs, and other bones) and apple cider vinegar in step 1 of the Basic Broth recipe and enough water to cover the extra ingredients Simmer, scooping off any accumulating foam, for 6 to 7 hours. Strain the broth, discarding the solids.
Per Serving: Calories 42; Fat 1g; Sodium 1201mg; Carbs 0g; Fiber 0g; Sugar 0g; Protein 8g

2-Chicken Broth Variation
Add 2 chicken carcasses and 2 tablespoons of apple cider vinegar in step 1 of the Basic Broth recipe and enough water to cover the extra ingredients. Simmer, scooping off any accumulating foam, for 4 to 5 hours. (Don't scoop if using a slow cooker.) Strain the broth, discarding the solids.
Per Serving: Calories 38; Fat 0g; Sodium 1011mg; Carbs 0g; Fiber 0g; Sugar 0g; Protein 9g

3-Fish Broth Variation
Add 3 to 4 pounds of fish bones and heads to the Basic Broth recipe and enough water to cover the extra ingredients. Simmer for 1 hour and then strain the broth through a fine-mesh sieve, discarding the solids.
Per Serving: Calories 34; Fat 1g; Sodium 1011mg; Carbs 0g; Fiber 0g; Sugar 0g; Protein 7g

90-Second Bread

Prep time: 4 minutes | Cook time: 90 seconds | Serves: 1

1 large egg
3 tablespoons almond flour
1 tablespoon melted butter

¼ teaspoon baking powder
Pinch sea salt
Nonstick cooking spray

1. Beat the egg with a fork. Whisk in the almond flour, butter, baking powder, and salt until thoroughly combined. 2. Grease the inside of a large coffee mug with cooking spray. 3. Microwave the mixture into the mug for 90 seconds. Cool the bread slightly, and then remove it from the coffee mug. It should slide right out. 4. Slice the bread in half and either enjoy it with your preferred toppings or toasted for some extra crunch.
Per Serving: Calories 300; Fat 27g; Sodium 547mg; Carbs 5g; Fiber 2g; Sugar 2g; Protein 11g

Taco Seasoning

Prep time: 5 minutes | Cook time: 0 minutes | Serves: 4

4 tablespoons ground cumin
1 tablespoon garlic powder
1 tablespoon chili powder

1 tablespoon onion powder
2 teaspoons dried oregano
2 teaspoons smoked paprika

1. In a sealable container, combine the cumin, garlic powder, chili powder, onion powder, oregano, and paprika. 2. Store the container at room temperature for up to 6 days.
Per Serving: Calories 29; Fat 1g; Sodium 322mg; Carbs 4g; Fiber 1g; Sugar 0.5g; Protein 1g

Guacamole

Prep time: 16 minutes | Cook time: 0 minutes | Serves: 2

1 avocado, pitted and peeled
¼ medium red onion, diced
1 teaspoon freshly squeezed lime juice

¼ tablespoon ground cumin
¼ tablespoon garlic powder
1 teaspoon minced fresh cilantro
Salt

1. Put the avocado in a medium bowl. With a fork, mash to your preferred consistency. 2. Add the onion, lime juice, cumin, garlic powder, and cilantro. Mix well. 3. Season with salt to taste. Serve immediately.
Per Serving: Calories 165; Fat 13g; Sodium 411mg; Carbs 10g; Fiber 6g; Sugar 2g; Protein 2g

Butternut Squash "Cheese" Sauce

Prep time: 11 minutes | Cook time: 10 minutes | Serves: 6

1 tablespoon coconut oil
2 cups frozen, cubed butternut squash
2 tablespoons nutritional yeast
1 tablespoon tahini
1 teaspoon garlic powder

½ teaspoon onion powder
½ teaspoon smoked paprika
¼ teaspoon salt
¼ teaspoon freshly ground black pepper

1. In a shallow sauté pan, heat the coconut oil over medium-high heat. When it shimmers, add the frozen butternut squash and cook until it is no longer frozen and the liquid dries, 5 to 8 minutes. 2. In a blender add squash along with the nutritional yeast, tahini, garlic powder, onion powder, paprika, salt, and pepper. Blend until completely smooth. 3. Serve immediately.
Per Serving: Calories 64; Fat 4g; Sodium 689mg; Carbs 7g; Fiber 1g; Sugar 1g; Protein 3g

Keto Mayonnaise

Prep time: 11 minutes | Cook time: 0 minutes | Serves: 16

2 large egg yolks, at room temperature
2 tablespoons freshly squeezed lemon juice

1 tablespoon apple cider vinegar
1 teaspoon salt
1 teaspoon Dijon mustard
1½ cups olive oil or avocado oil

1. Add the egg yolks, lemon juice, vinegar, salt, and mustard in a blender and blend for about 30 seconds or until well combined. 2. With the active blending, pour in the oil in a thin stream until the mixture thickens. 3. Store it in the refrigerator in an airtight jar for up to 1 week.
Per Serving: Calories 187; Fat 21g; Sodium 987mg; Carbs 0g; Fiber 0g; Sugar 0g; Protein 0g

Ranch Dressing

Prep time: 5 minutes | Cook time: 0 minutes | Serves: 12

1 cup Keto Mayonnaise
½ cup sour cream
1½ teaspoons dried chives
1 teaspoon mustard powder
½ teaspoon dried dill

½ teaspoon celery seed
½ teaspoon onion powder
½ teaspoon garlic powder
Salt
Freshly ground black pepper

1. Combine the mayonnaise, sour cream, chives, mustard powder, dill, celery seed, onion powder, and garlic powder. 2. Season with salt and pepper to taste. Stir well to combine, then store in an airtight container in the refrigerator for up to 1 week.
Per Serving (2 tablespoons): Calories 43; Fat 3g; Sodium 478mg; Carbs 3g; Fiber 1g; Sugar 1g; Protein 1g

Avocado-Kale Pesto

Prep time: 16 minutes | Cook time: 0 minutes | Serves: 4

1 avocado, peeled, pitted, and diced
1 cup chopped kale
½ cup fresh basil leaves
½ cup pine nuts
3 garlic cloves, peeled

1 tablespoon freshly squeezed lemon juice
2 teaspoons nutritional yeast
¼ cup extra-virgin olive oil
Sea salt

1. In a food processor, combine the avocado, kale, basil, pine nuts, garlic, lemon juice, and nutritional yeast. Pulse until finely chopped, about 2 minutes. 2. With the food processor working, drizzle the olive oil into the mixture until thick paste forms. Scrape down the sides at least once—season with salt to taste. 3. Store the pesto in an airtight container in the refrigerator for up to 1 week.
Per Serving: Calories 92; Fat 8g; Sodium 546mg; Carbs 3g; Fiber 1g; Sugar 1g; Protein 2g

Tahini Goddess Dressing

Prep time: 5 minutes | Cook time: 0 minutes | Serves: 2

¼ cup water
2 lemon's Juice
3 tablespoons raw tahini
½ teaspoon smoked paprika

⅛ teaspoon ground cayenne pepper (optional)
Sea salt
Freshly ground black pepper

1. Whisk the water, lemon juice, and tahini in a medium bowl until well blended. 2. Add the paprika and cayenne, and season with salt and pepper. Mix until well combined. 3. Store the Tahini dressing in a sealed container in the pantry for up to 6 months.
Per Serving: Calories 40; Fat 3g; Sodium 704mg; Carbs 6g; Fiber 3.6g; Sugar 6g; Protein 18g

Avocado-Herb Butter

Prep time: 25 minutes plus 4 hours to chill | Cook time: 0 minutes | Yields: 2 cups

¼ cup butter, at room temperature
1 avocado, peeled, pitted, and quartered
Juice of ½ lemon
2 teaspoons chopped cilantro

1 teaspoon chopped fresh basil
1 teaspoon minced garlic
Sea salt
Freshly ground black pepper

1. Place the butter, avocado, lemon juice, cilantro, basil, and garlic in a food processor and process until smooth. 2. Season the butter with salt and pepper. Shape it into a log on the parchment paper. Place the parchment butter log in the refrigerator until it is firm, about 4 hours. 3. Slice and serve with fish or chicken. Store unused butter wrapped tightly for up to 1 week.
Per Serving (1 tablespoon): Calories 22; Fat 2g; Sodium 245mg; Carbs 1g; Fiber 0g; Sugar 0g; Protein 0g

Cinnamon Butter

Prep time: 15 minutes | Cook time: 1 hours | Serves: 16

1 cup butter, at room temperature
10 drops of, or another liquid sugar substitute

1 teaspoon pure vanilla extract
1 teaspoon ground cinnamon
¼ teaspoon salt

1. Mix the butter, stevia, vanilla, cinnamon, and salt in a medium bowl
Per Serving: Calories 103; Fat 12g; Sodium 247mg; Carbs 0g; Fiber 0g; Sugar 0g; Protein 0g

Italian Seasoning

Prep time: 5 minutes | Cook time: 0 minutes | Serves: 12

2 tablespoons dried basil
2 tablespoons dried oregano
2 tablespoons dried rosemary

2 tablespoons garlic powder
2 tablespoons dried thyme
2 teaspoons red pepper flakes

1. Combine all the spices. 2. Store the spices in a sealed container at room temperature for up to 6 months.
Per Serving (1 tablespoon): Calories 11; Fat 0g; Sodium 35mg; Carbs 2g; Fiber 1g; Sugar 0g; Protein 0g

Horseradish Butter

Prep time: 7 minutes | Cook time: 0 minutes | Serves: 24

1 cup butter, softened
½ cup coconut oil
1 teaspoon prepared horseradish
1 garlic clove
1 tablespoon fresh chopped basil
1 tablespoon fresh chopped oregano
½ teaspoon freshly ground black pepper
¼ teaspoon sea salt

1. In a blender, pulse the butter, coconut oil, horseradish, garlic, basil, oregano, pepper, and salt until well blended. 2. Scoop the butter mixture onto a double layer of plastic wrap. 3. Fold the wrap over the butter mixture, creating a long tube. Roll in the wrap and twist the ends. 4. Refrigerate or freeze the butter cylinder until it is substantial. Cut off a slice of butter to top vegetables, fish, or steak. 5. Store the butter for up to 1 month.
Per Serving: Calories 108; Fat 12g; Sodium 112mg; Carbs 0g; Fiber 0g; Sugar 0g; Protein 0g

Strawberry Butter

Prep time: 25 minutes | Cook time: 0 minutes | Yields: 3 cups

2 cups shredded unsweetened coconut
1 tablespoon coconut oil
¾ cup fresh strawberries
½ tablespoon freshly squeezed lemon juice
1 teaspoon alcohol-free pure vanilla extract

1. Puree the coconut in a food processor until it is buttery and smooth for about 15 minutes. 2. Add the coconut oil, strawberries, lemon juice, and vanilla to the coconut butter and process until very smooth. 3. Remove strawberry seeds by passing it from the fine sieve. 4. Store the strawberry butter in an airtight container in the refrigerator for up to 2 weeks. 5. Serve chicken or fish with a spoon of this butter on top.
Per Serving: Calories 23; Fat 2g; Sodium 12mg; Carbs 1g; Fiber 0g; Sugar 0g; Protein 0g

Beef Bone Broth

Prep time: 15 minutes | Cook time: 4 hours 40 minutes | Serves: 2

1 pound beef bones
1 tablespoon apple cider vinegar
1 teaspoon sea salt
4 quarts water

1. Preheat the oven to 400°F/200°C. Spread the beef bones on a rimmed baking sheet. 2. Roast uncovered for 40 minutes or until browned. Transfer the bones to a large pot. Pour the oil from the roasting pan and use a fat separator to discard the fat. 3. Transfer the remaining bits to the pot. Add the salt, vinegar, and water to the pot and bring a gentle simmer. 4. Cook partially covered for 4 hours, skimming fat off the surface as it rises.
Per Serving: Calories 45; Fat 1g; Sodium 0mg; Carbs 0g; Fiber 0g; Sugar 0g; Protein 9g

Beef Stock

Prep time: 15 minutes | Cook time: 12 hours | Serves: 8 to 10

2 to 3 pounds of beef bones (beef marrow, knuckle bones, ribs, and any other bones)
8 black peppercorns
5 thyme sprigs
3 garlic cloves, peeled and crushed
2 bay leaves
1 carrot, washed and chopped into 2-inch pieces
1 celery stalk, chopped into big chunks
½ onion, peeled and quartered
1-gallon water
1 teaspoon extra-virgin olive oil

1. Preheat the oven to 350°F/175°C. Place the beef bones in a deep baking pan and roast them in the oven for about 30 minutes. 2. Place the bones to a large pot and add the peppercorns, thyme, garlic, bay leaves, carrot, celery, and onion. 3. Add the water, covering the bones thoroughly, ultimately bring to a boil over high heat, then lower the heat to simmers. 4. Check the stock every hour for the first 3 hours, and skim off any foam from on the top. Simmer for 12 hours in total, and then remove the pot from the heat. Cool the stock for about 30 minutes. 5. Remove any large bones with tongs and strain the stock through a fine-mesh sieve. Discard the leftover vegetables and bones. 6. Pour the stock into containers with tight-fitting lids and cool thoroughly before refrigerating.
Per Serving: Calories 65; Fat 5g; Sodium 25mg; Carbs 1g; Fiber 0g; Sugar 0g; Protein 4g

Chicken Bone Broth

Prep time: 5 minutes | Cook time: 4 hours | Serves: 2 quarts

1 pound chicken bones, preferably roasted
1 tablespoon apple cider vinegar
1 teaspoon sea salt
4 quarts of cold water

1. Place the chicken bones, vinegar, and salt in a large pot. Cover with the water and bring to a simmer over medium heat. 2. Reduce the heat to simmer for about 4 hours, or until reduced to about 2 quarts. 3. Allow the stock to cool thoroughly before refrigerating.
Per Serving: Calories 45; Fat 1g; Sodium 35mg; Carbs 0g; Fiber 0g; Sugar 0g; Protein 9g

Herbed Chicken Stock

Prep time: 15 minutes | Cook time: 12 hours plus 30 minutes to cool | Serves: 8 cups

2 chicken carcasses
6 black peppercorns
4 thyme sprigs
3 bay leaves
2 celery stalks, cut into quarters
1 carrot, washed and chopped roughly
1 sweet onion, peeled and quartered
1 gallon of cold water

1. Place the chicken carcasses in a large stockpot with peppercorns, thyme, bay leaves, celery, carrot, and onion. Add the water, covering them thoroughly, and bring it to a boil over high heat. 2. Lower heat to simmer, stirring every few hours, for 12 hours. When done let the stock cool for 30 minutes. Remove any large bones with tongs and then strain the stock through a fine-mesh sieve. Discard the solid bits. 3. Pour the stock into containers with tight-fitting lids and cool thoroughly. Refrigerate for up to 5 days, or freeze for 3 months.
Per Serving: Calories 73; Fat 5g; Sodium 41mg; Carbs 2g; Fiber 0g; Sugar 0g; Protein 5g

Harissa Oil

Prep time: 15 minutes | Cook time: 5 minutes | Serves: 1 cup

4 to 6 medium-hot dried chiles
2 to 4 hot dried chiles de árbol
2 tablespoons coriander seeds
1 tablespoon cumin seeds
1 teaspoon caraway seeds
4 large garlic cloves, chopped
2 tablespoons tomato paste
2 teaspoons smoked paprika
1 teaspoon salt
1 cup extra-virgin olive oil, divided

1. Remove the stems and tops from the dried chiles and discard any loose seeds. In a bowl place chilies and cover with boiling water. Allow to steep for 30 minutes or until softened. 2. Remove from the water, drain off any excess liquid, and roughly chop, discarding any seeds and membranes. 3. In a large dry pan, toast the coriander, cumin, and caraway seeds over medium-high heat until very fragrant. 4. In a blender, add the chopped chiles, garlic, tomato paste, paprika, and salt and pulse until thick paste forms. 5. With the food processor running, stream in ¾ cup olive oil until well combined. 6. Transfer to a large glass jar and stir in the remaining ¼ cup of olive oil.
Per Serving: Calories 266; Fat 26g; Sodium 341mg; Carbs 6g; Fiber 1g; Sugar 0g; Protein 2g

Buttermilk Ranch Dressing

Prep time: 10 minutes | Cook time: 0 minutes | Yields: 1½ cups

½ cup heavy (whipping) cream
1 teaspoon apple cider vinegar
½ cup mayonnaise
¼ cup sour cream
1 tablespoon freshly squeezed lemon juice
2 tablespoons chopped fresh parsley
2 tablespoons chopped fresh chives
½ teaspoon minced garlic
¼ teaspoon ground cayenne pepper
Sea salt
Freshly ground black pepper

1. Stir the heavy cream and vinegar in a small bowl, and set aside for 10 minutes. 2. In a bowl, whisk the mayonnaise with sour cream, lemon juice, parsley, chives, garlic, cayenne pepper, and the reserved cream mixture until blended. 3. Season with salt and pepper.
Per Serving: Calories 74; Fat 6g; Sodium 24mg; Carbs 3g; Fiber 0g; Sugar 0g; Protein 2g

Lemon-Garlic Dressing

Prep time: 10 minutes | Cook time: 0 minutes | Yields: 1 cup

½ cup sour cream
¼ cup extra-virgin olive oil
1 tablespoon Dijon mustard
¼ cup freshly squeezed lemon juice
2 teaspoons minced garlic

2 teaspoons chopped fresh basil
2 teaspoons chopped fresh parsley
2 teaspoons chopped fresh thyme
Sea salt
Freshly ground black pepper

1. Whisk the sour cream, olive oil, Dijon mustard, lemon juice, garlic, basil, parsley, and thyme in a medium bowl until well blended. 2. Season the dressing with salt and pepper. Refrigerate it for up to 1 week.
Per Serving (2 tablespoons): Calories 98; Fat 10g; Sodium 32mg; Carbs 1g; Fiber 0g; Sugar 0g; Protein 1g

Basil Dressing

Prep time: 10 minutes | Cook time: 0 minutes | Serves: 1 cup

1 avocado, peeled and pitted
¼ cup sour cream
¼ cup extra-virgin olive oil
¼ cup chopped fresh basil
1 tablespoon freshly squeezed

lime juice
1 teaspoon minced garlic
Sea salt
Freshly ground black pepper

1. Place the avocado, sour cream, olive oil, basil, lime juice, and garlic in a food processor and pulse until smooth. 2. Season the dressing with salt and pepper.
Per Serving: Calories 173; Fat 17g; Sodium 321mg; Carbs 1g; Fiber 0g; Sugar 0g; Protein 5g

Grapefruit-Tarragon Dressing

Prep time: 5 minutes | Cook time: 0 minutes | Serves: 4 to 6

½ cup avocado oil mayonnaise
2 tablespoons Dijon mustard
1 teaspoon dried tarragon
Zest and juice of ½ grapefruit
(about 2 tablespoons juice)

½ teaspoon salt
¼ teaspoon freshly ground black pepper
1 to 2 tablespoons water (optional)

1. In a large mason jar or glass measuring cup, shake the mayonnaise, Dijon, tarragon, grapefruit zest and juice, salt, and pepper until smooth and creamy. 2. If a thinner dressing is preferred, thin it out with water.
Per Serving: Calories 86; Fat 7g; Sodium 124mg; Carbs 6g; Fiber 0g; Sugar 0g; Protein 1g

Ranch Seasoning

Prep time: 5 minutes | Cook time: 0 minutes | Serves: 10

6 tablespoons dried dill
1 tablespoon pink Himalayan salt
1 tablespoon freshly ground black

pepper
1 tablespoon onion powder
1 tablespoon garlic powder

1. Combine all the spices. 2. Store the spices in a sealed container at room temperature for up to 6 months.
Per Serving: Calories 12; Fat 0g; Sodium 61mg; Carbs 3g; Fiber 1g; Sugar 1g; Protein 1g

Chimichurri

Prep time: 5 minutes | Cook time: 5 minutes | Serves: 8

1 cup fresh cilantro
2 cups fresh parsley
¼ cup red wine vinegar
3 garlic cloves, halved

½ teaspoon ground cumin
½ teaspoon red pepper flakes
¼ teaspoon pink Himalayan salt
¼ cup extra-virgin olive oil

1. Place the cilantro, parsley, vinegar, garlic, cumin, red pepper flakes, and salt in a blender or food processor. 2. Blend until the ingredients break down, about 20 seconds. 3. Slowly pour in the oil blend until the oil is fully incorporated.
Per Serving: Calories 66; Fat 6g; Sodium 144mg; Carbs 2g; Fiber 1g; Sugar 2g; Protein 1g

Traditional Caesar Dressing

Prep time: 10 minutes plus 10 minutes to cool | Cook time: 5 minutes | Yields: 1½ cups

2 teaspoons minced garlic
4 large egg yolks
¼ cup wine vinegar
½ teaspoon dry mustard
Dash Worcestershire sauce

1 cup extra-virgin olive oil
¼ cup freshly squeezed lemon juice
Sea salt
Freshly ground black pepper

1. In a pan, add the garlic with egg yolks, vinegar, mustard, and Worcestershire sauce and whisk on low heat until bubbly and thicken about 5 minutes. 2. Remove from the heat and let it stand for about 10 minutes to cool. Transfer the yolk mixture to a bowl and whisk in the olive oil in a thin stream. 3. Whisk the lemon juice in a sauce and season the dressing with salt and pepper.
Per Serving (2 tablespoons): Calories 180; Fat 20g; Sodium 121mg; Carbs 1g; Fiber 0g; Sugar 0g; Protein 1g

Ranch Dressing with Buttermilk

Prep time: 10 minutes | Cook time: 60 minutes | Serves: 16

1 cup mayonnaise
1 cup sour cream
¼ cup buttermilk
1 tablespoon onion powder
1 tablespoon dried parsley

2 teaspoons garlic powder
½ teaspoon salt
½ teaspoon dried dill
½ teaspoon mustard powder
¼ teaspoon celery salt

1. Mix the mayonnaise, sour cream, buttermilk, onion powder, parsley, garlic powder, salt, dill, mustard powder, and celery salt in a large bowl. 2. Whisk well to incorporate.
Per Serving: Calories 93; Fat 8g; Sodium 211mg; Carbs 5g; Fiber 0g; Sugar 2g; Protein 1g

Mustard Shallot Vinaigrette

Prep time: 10 minutes | Cook time: 0 minutes | Serves: 8

½ cup olive oil
½ cup apple cider vinegar
3 tablespoons Dijon mustard
1 shallot, minced

½ teaspoon salt
¼ teaspoon freshly ground black pepper

1. Add the olive oil, cider vinegar, mustard, shallot, salt, and pepper in a blender or food processor. 2. Pulse for about 1 minute until combined.
Per Serving: Calories 117; Fat 13g; Sodium 222mg; Carbs 1g; Fiber 0g; Sugar 0g; Protein 0g

Herbed Balsamic Dressing

Prep time: 4minutes | Cook time: 0 minutes | Serves: 8

1 cup extra-virgin olive oil
¼ cup balsamic vinegar
2 tablespoons chopped fresh oregano

1 teaspoon chopped fresh basil
1 teaspoon minced garlic
Sea salt
Freshly ground black pepper

1. Whisk the olive oil with vinegar in a bowl until emulsified, about 3 minutes. Whisk in the oregano, basil, and garlic until well combined, about 1 minute. 2. Season the dressing with salt and pepper.
Per Serving: Calories 83; Fat 9g; Sodium 35mg; Carbs 0g; Fiber 0g; Sugar 0g; Protein 0g

Herbed Infused Olive Oil

Prep time: 5 minutes | Cook time: 45 minutes | Serves: 8

1 cup extra-virgin olive oil
4 large garlic cloves, smashed

4 (4- to 5-inch) sprigs of rosemary

1. Heat the olive oil, garlic, and rosemary sprigs in a medium pan over low heat. Cook until fragrant and garlic is very tender, for 30 to 45 minutes, stirring occasionally. 2. Remove the rosemary and garlic with a slotted spoon and pour the oil into a glass container. 3. Allow cooling thoroughly before covering.
Per Serving: Calories 241; Fat 27g; Sodium 11mg; Carbs 1g; Fiber 0g; Sugar 0g; Protein 0g

Ginger with Lime Dressing

Prep time: 5 minutes | Cook time: 0 minutes | Serves: 8

1 cup extra-virgin olive oil
Juice of 3 limes
2 inches fresh ginger, peeled
1 teaspoon ground cumin

⅓ teaspoon ground cardamom
1 drop of liquid stevia
Sea salt

1. Blend the oil, lime juice, ginger, cumin, cardamom, stevia, and salt in a high-powered blender. 2. Refrigerate the dressing in a covered container for up to 1 week.
Per Serving: Calories 245; Fat 27g; Sodium 321mg; Carbs 0g; Fiber 0g; Sugar 0g; Protein 0g

Garlic and Herb Marinade

Prep time: 15 minutes | Cook time: 0 minutes | Serves: 8

½ cup olive oil
Juice and zest of ½ lemon
Juice and zest of ½ lime
1½ teaspoons minced garlic

2 teaspoons chopped fresh basil
2 teaspoons chopped fresh thyme
1 teaspoon chopped fresh oregano
¼ teaspoon sea salt

1. Whisk the olive oil, lemon and lime juices and zests, garlic, basil, thyme, oregano, and salt in a medium bowl until well combined.
Per Serving: Calories 122; Fat 14g; Sodium 111mg; Carbs 1g; Fiber 0g; Sugar 0g; Protein 0g

Lemon-Tahini Dressing

Prep time: 5 minutes | Cook time: 0 minutes | Serves: 8 to 10

½ cup tahini
¼ cup lemon juice
¼ cup extra-virgin olive oil

1 garlic clove, finely minced or ½ teaspoon of garlic powder
2 teaspoons salt

1. In a jar with a lid, mix tahini, lemon juice, olive oil, garlic, and salt. Cover and shake well until combined and creamy. 2. Refrigerate for up to 2 weeks.
Per Serving: Calories 121; Fat 12g; Sodium 211mg; Carbs 3g; Fiber 1g; Sugar 1g; Protein 2g

Cashew Hummus

Prep time: 10 minutes | Cooking time: 0 minutes | Serves: 8

1 cup raw cashews
2 small cloves garlic, peeled
3 tablespoons tahini
1 tablespoon lemon juice

1 teaspoon salt
½ teaspoon smoked paprika
¼ cup olive oil, extra-virgin

1. Place the cashews in a suitable bowl and cover with cold water. Cover the bowl and soak in the refrigerator overnight or up to 24 hours. 2. Drain the water from the cashews and place them in the bowl of a food processor. Add the garlic and tahini and process until smooth but thick. Add the lemon juice, salt, and paprika and pulse until well combined. 3. With the processor running, stream in the olive oil and process until very smooth and silky but not runny. 4. Serve with raw veggies for dipping, such as celery, cucumber, bell pepper, or broccoli. 5. Leftover hummus can be stored in a sealed container in the refrigerator for up to 4 days.
Per serving: Calories: 59; Total fat 4.3g; Sodium 0mg; Total carbs 5.8g; Fiber 0g; Sugars 5.8g; Protein 0g

Any-Herb Pesto

Prep time: 10 minutes| Cooking time: 0 minutes | Serves: 8

4 cups packed baby arugula leaves
1 cup packed basil leaves
1 cup walnuts, chopped
½ cup shredded parmesan cheese

2 small garlic cloves, peeled and smashed
½ teaspoon salt
¾ cup olive oil

1. In a food processor, pulse the arugula, basil, walnuts, cheese, and garlic until very finely chopped. Add the salt. With the processor running, stream in the olive oil until well blended and smooth. 2. Transfer the prepared mixture to a glass container and store, tightly covered in the refrigerator, for up to 2 weeks.
Per serving: Calories: 102; Total fat 8.5g; Sodium 54mg; Total carbs 6g; Fiber 2.1g; Sugars 2.9g; Protein 2.4g

Keto Peanut Butter Cups

Prep time: 10 minutes | Cooking time: 1 minute | Serves: 16

½ cup cacao butter or coconut oil
¼ cup unsweetened cocoa powder
2 to 4 teaspoons sweetener, sugar-free

½ teaspoon cinnamon
½ teaspoon salt
½ cup unsweetened creamy peanut butter or almond butter

1. Layer a mini muffin tin with 16 liners. 2. Place the cacao butter and cocoa powder into a microwave-safe bowl and microwave on high for almost 30 to 45 seconds or until melted. Stir until creamy. 3. Whisk in the sweetener (if using), cinnamon (if using), and salt. Spoon half of the chocolate mixture into the 16 cups, spreading to cover the bottom of the liner. Reserve the other half of the chocolate mixture. Place this pan in the freezer for almost 10 minutes to set. 4. In a suitable, microwave-safe bowl, microwave the nut butter for almost 30 seconds, until soft, then spread on top of the chocolate in the cups. Freeze for almost 10 minutes. 5. Microwave the cacao butter mixture for an additional 30 seconds, just to soften it. Dollop the remaining chocolate on top of the nut butter. 6. Return this pan to the freezer and freeze until solid. for almost 2 hours. Once frozen, peanut butter cups can be transferred to a zip-top bag and stored in the refrigerator for up to 2 weeks or the freezer for up to 3 months.
Per serving: Calories: 149; Total fat 16.2g; Sodium 116mg; Total carbs 2.2g; Fiber 0.8g; Sugars 0.6g; Protein 1.6g

Basic Marinara

Prep time: 10 minutes | Cooking time: 65 minutes | Serves: 4

2 tablespoons plus ¼ cup olive oil, extra-virgin
2 tablespoons unsalted butter
½ small onion, finely minced
2 ribs celery, finely minced
¼ cup minced carrot (about 1 small carrot)
4 cloves garlic, minced

1 teaspoon salt
¼ teaspoon black pepper
1 (32-ounce) can crushed tomatoes, with juices
2 tablespoons balsamic vinegar
1 teaspoon dried oregano
1 teaspoon dried rosemary
½ to 1 teaspoon red pepper flakes

1. Preheat 2 tablespoons oil and melt the butter in a suitable saucepan over medium heat. 2. Add the onion, celery, and carrot and sauté until just starting to get tender, for almost 5 minutes. Add the garlic, salt, and pepper and sauté for an additional 30 seconds. 3. Whisk in the tomatoes and their juices, vinegar, remaining ¼ cup of olive oil, oregano, rosemary, and red pepper. 4. Cook to a simmer, cover, reduce heat to low, and simmer for almost 30 to 60 minutes to allow the flavors to blend. Serve warm. 5. The sauce will keep, tightly covered in the refrigerator, for up to 1 week. Cooled sauce can be frozen for up to 3 months.
Per serving: Calories: 11; Total fat 0.1g; Sodium 37mg; Total carbs 1.9g; Fiber 0.1g; Sugars 1.4g; Protein 0.5g

Bolognese Sauce

Prep time: 10 minutes | Cooking time: 7 to 8 hours | Serves: 10

3 tablespoons olive oil, extra-virgin
1 pound ground pork
½ pound ground beef
½ pound bacon, chopped
1 sweet onion, chopped

1 tablespoon minced garlic
2 celery stalks, chopped
1 carrot, chopped
2 (28-ounce) cans diced tomatoes
½ cup coconut milk
¼ cup apple cider vinegar

1. Lightly grease the insert of the slow cooker with 1 tablespoon of the olive oil. 2. In a suitable skillet over medium-high heat, heat the remaining 2 tablespoons of the olive oil. Add the pork, beef, and bacon, and sauté until cooked through. for almost 7 minutes. 3. Stir in the onion and garlic and sauté for an additional 2 minutes. 4. Transfer the meat mixture to the insert and add the celery, carrot, tomatoes, coconut milk, and apple cider vinegar. 5. Cover and cook on low for almost 7 to 8 hours. 6. Serve, or cool completely, and store in the refrigerator in a sealed container for up to 4 days or in the freezer for almost 1 month.
Per serving: Calories: 31; Total fat 0.5g; Sodium 2mg; Total carbs 7.5g; Fiber 2.1g; Sugars 4.2g; Protein 0.7g

Bacon Jam

Prep time: 10 minutes | Cooking time: 4 hrs | Serves: 12

3 tablespoons bacon fat, melted and divided
1 pound cooked bacon, chopped into ½-inch pieces
1 sweet onion, diced
½ cup apple cider vinegar
¼ cup granulated erythritol
1 tablespoon minced garlic
1 cup brewed decaffeinated coffee

1. Lightly grease the insert of the slow cooker with 1 tablespoon of the bacon fat. 2. Add the remaining 2 tablespoons of the bacon fat, bacon, onion, apple cider vinegar, erythritol, garlic, and coffee to the insert. Stir to combine. 3. Cook uncovered for almost 3 to 4 hours on high, until the liquid has thickened and reduced. 4. Cool completely. Store the bacon jam in the refrigerator in a sealed container for up to 3 weeks.
Per serving: Calories: 179; Total fat 14.3g; Sodium 493mg; Total Carbs 2.3g; Fiber 2.4g; Sugars 8.7g; Protein 0.9g

Roasted Garlic

Prep time: 10 minutes | Cooking time: 8 hours | Serves: 12

6 heads garlic
¼ cup olive oil
Salt, for seasoning

1. Lay a suitable sheet of foil sheet on your counter. 2. Cut the top off the heads of garlic, exposing the cloves. 3. Place the garlic, cut side up, on the foil and drizzle them with the olive oil. 4. Lightly season the garlic with salt. 5. Loosely fold the foil around the garlic to form a packet. 6. Place the packet in the insert of the slow cooker. 7. Cover and cook on low for almost 8 hours. 8. Let the garlic cool for almost 10 minutes and then squeeze the cloves out of the papery skins. 9. Store the garlic in a sealed container in the refrigerator for up to 1 week.
Per serving: Calories: 47; Total fat 1.7g; Sodium 5mg; Total carbs 8.5g; Fiber 0.5g; Sugars 6.7g; Protein 0.3g

Spinach-Cheese Spread

Prep time: 10 minutes | Cooking time: 6 hrs | Serves: 8

1 tablespoon olive oil, extra-virgin
8 ounces cream cheese
1 cup sour cream
½ cup shredded cheddar cheese
½ cup shredded mozzarella
cheese
½ cup parmesan cheese
½ sweet onion, finely chopped
2 teaspoons minced garlic
12 ounces chopped spinach

1. Grease an 8-by-4-inch loaf pan with the olive oil. 2. In a suitable bowl, stir the cream cheese, sour cream, cheddar, mozzarella, parmesan, onion, garlic, and spinach until well mixed. 3. Transfer the prepared mixture to the loaf pan and place this pan in the insert of the slow cooker. 4. Cover and cook on low for almost 5 to 6 hours. Serve warm.
Per serving: Calories: 40; Total fat 3.1g; Sodium 81mg; Total carbs 2.7g; Fiber 0.5g; Sugars 1.5g; Protein 1g

Marinara Sauce

Prep time: 10 minutes. | Cooking time: 8 hours. | Serves: 12

3 tablespoons olive oil, extra-virgin
2 (28-ounce) cans crushed tomatoes
½ sweet onion, finely chopped
2 teaspoons minced garlic
½ teaspoon salt
1 tablespoon chopped fresh basil
1 tablespoon chopped fresh oregano

1. Lightly grease the insert of the slow cooker with 1 tablespoon of the olive oil. 2. Add the remaining 2 tablespoons of the olive oil, tomatoes, onion, garlic, and salt to the insert, stirring to combine. 3. Cover and cook on low for almost 7 to 8 hours. 4. Remove the cover and stir in the basil and oregano. 5. Store the cooled sauce in a sealed container in the refrigerator for up to 1 week.
Per serving: Calories: 166; Total fat 19g; Sodium 2mg; Total carbs 0.5g; Fiber 0.1g; Sugars 0.1g; Protein 0.2g

Ghee

Prep time: 10 minutes | Cooking time: 6 hours | Serves: 2 cups

1 pound unsalted butter, diced

1. Place the butter in the insert of the slow cooker. 2. Cook on low with the lid set slightly open for almost 6 hours. 3. Pour the melted butter through a fine-mesh cheesecloth into a bowl. 4. Cool the ghee for almost 30 minutes and pour into a jar. 5. Store the ghee in the refrigerator for up to 2 weeks.
Per serving (1 tablespoon): Calories: 70; Total fat 4.1g; Sodium 10mg; Total carbs 8.2g; Fiber 0.7g; Sugars 5.9g; Protein 1.3g

Crab Sauce

Prep time: 10 minutes | Cooking time: 6 hrs | Serves: 24

8 ounces cream cheese
8 ounces goat cheese
1 cup sour cream
½ cup grated asiago cheese
1 sweet onion, finely chopped
1 tablespoon granulated erythritol
2 teaspoons minced garlic
12 ounces crabmeat, flaked
1 scallion, white and green parts, chopped

1. In a suitable bowl, stir the cream cheese, goat cheese, sour cream, asiago cheese, onion, erythritol, garlic, crabmeat, and scallion until well mixed. 2. Transfer the prepared mixture to an 8-by-4-inch loaf pan and place this pan in the insert of the slow cooker. 3. Cover and cook on low for almost 5 to 6 hours. Serve warm.
Per serving: Calories: 93; Total fat 7.1g; Sodium 632mg; Total carbs 7.9g; Fiber 1.9g; Sugars 3.7g; Protein 0.8g

Enchilada Sauce

Prep time: 10 minutes | Cooking time: 7 to 8 hours | Serves: 8

¼ cup olive oil, extra-virgin
2 cups puréed tomatoes
1 cup water
1 sweet onion, chopped
2 jalapeño peppers, chopped
2 teaspoons minced garlic
2 tablespoons chili powder
1 teaspoon ground coriander

1. Lightly grease the insert of the slow cooker with 1 tablespoon of the olive oil. 2. Place the remaining 3 tablespoons of the olive oil, tomatoes, water, onion, jalapeño peppers, garlic, chili powder, and coriander in the insert. 3. Cover and cook on low 7 to 8 hours. 4. Serve over poultry or meat. After cooling, store the sauce in a sealed container in the refrigerator for up to 1 week.
Per serving: Calories: 114; Total fat 0.4g; Sodium 2mg; Total Carbs 9.6g; Fiber 3.7g; Sugars 23.7g; Protein 1.2g

Queso Sauce

Prep time: 10 minutes | Cooking time: 3 to 4 hours | Serves: 8

1 tablespoon olive oil, extra-virgin
12 ounces cream cheese
1 cup sour cream
2 cups salsa verde
1 cup Monterey jack cheese, shredded

1. Lightly grease the insert of the slow cooker with the olive oil. 2. In a suitable bowl, stir the cream cheese, sour cream, salsa verde, and Monterey jack cheese, until blended. 3. Transfer the prepared mixture to the insert. 4. Cover and cook on low for almost 3 to 4 hours. Serve warm.
Per serving: Calories: 79; Total fat 0.3g; Sodium 2mg; Total Carbs 0.1g; Fiber 4.3g; Sugars 12.2g; Protein 0.5g

Golden Caramelized Onions

Prep time: 10 minutes | Cooking time: 10 hours | Serves: 12

6 sweet onions, sliced
¼ cup olive oil, extra-virgin
½ teaspoon salt

1. In a suitable bowl, toss the onions, oil, and salt. Transfer the prepared mixture to the insert of the slow cooker. 2. Cover and cook on low for almost 9 to 10 hours. 3. Serve, or store after cooling in a sealed container in the refrigerator for up to 5 days.
Per serving: Calories: 67; Total fat 6.1g; Sodium 149mg; Total carbs 2.5g; Fiber 1.3g; Sugars 0.4g; Protein 1.9g

Coconut-Curry Simmer Sauce

Prep time: 10 minutes | Cooking time: 5 minutes | Serves: 12

1 (14½-ounce) can full-fat coconut milk
Zest and juice of 1 lime
2 tablespoons curry powder
1 tablespoon soy sauce
1 teaspoon ground ginger
1 teaspoon garlic powder
½ to 1 teaspoon cayenne pepper

1. Whisk all the recipe ingredients in a suitable saucepan over medium-high heat and bring just below a boil. 2. Remove from heat and allow to cool to room temperature. 3. The sauce will keep, tightly covered in the refrigerator, for up to 1 week.
Per serving: Calories: 100; Total fat 7.2g; Sodium 113mg; Total carbs 8.3g; Fiber 1.3g; Sugars 5.4g; Protein 2.3g

Red Wine Vinaigrette

Prep time: 10 minutes | Cooking time: 0 minutes | Serves: 8

½ cup olive oil
½ cup red wine vinegar
1 tablespoon Dijon or stone-ground mustard
½ to 1 teaspoon dried herbs such
as rosemary, basil, thyme, or oregano
½ teaspoon salt
¼ teaspoon black pepper

1. In a suitable bowl or canning jar, mix all the recipe ingredients and whisk or shake until well combined. 2. The dressing will keep, tightly covered in the refrigerator, for up to 2 weeks. 3. Be sure to bring it to room temperature and shake well before serving, as the oil and vinegar will naturally separate.
Per serving: Calories: 204; Total fat 2.5g; Sodium 35mg; Total Carbs 6.4g; Fiber 1g; Sugars 37.3g; Protein 1g

Easiest Creamy Caesar Dressing

Prep time: 10 minutes | Cooking time: 0 minutes | Serves: 8

1 cup mayonnaise
2 small garlic cloves, pressed with a garlic press (or 1 teaspoon garlic powder)
2 tablespoons freshly squeezed lemon juice, from 1 lemon
2 teaspoons Dijon mustard
1 teaspoon anchovy paste
1 teaspoon Worcestershire sauce
½ cup freshly grated parmesan cheese
¼ teaspoon salt
¼ teaspoon black pepper

1. In a canning jar or suitable bowl, mix the mayonnaise, garlic, lemon juice, mustard, anchovy paste, and Worcestershire and whisk well. 2. Add the cheese, salt, and pepper and whisk until well combined and smooth. 3. The dressing will keep, tightly covered in the refrigerator, for up to 1 week. 4. Shake or whisk again before serving.
Per serving: Calories: 192; Total fat 6.6g; Sodium 5mg; Total Carbs 0.7g; Fiber 4.2g; Sugars 16.3g; Protein 3.8g

Tangy Citrus-Poppyseed Dressing

Prep time: 10 minutes | Cooking time: 0 minutes | Serves: 8

½ cup mayonnaise
2 tablespoons buttermilk
2 tablespoons sour cream
Zest and juice of 1 small orange
2 teaspoons sweetener of choice,
sugar-free
1 teaspoon dried tarragon
½ teaspoon salt
¼ teaspoon black pepper
1 tablespoon poppy seeds

1. In a canning jar or suitable bowl, mix the mayonnaise, buttermilk, sour cream, orange zest and juice, sweetener (if using), tarragon, salt, and pepper and whisk well. 2. Add the poppy seeds and shake or whisk until well combined and smooth. 3. The dressing will keep covered tightly in the refrigerator for up to 1 week. 4. Shake or whisk again before serving.
Per serving: Calories: 242; Total fat 17g; Sodium 17mg; Total Carbs 8.8g; Fiber 2.9g; Sugars 14g; Protein 5.4g

Herbed Vegetable Broth

Prep time: 10 minutes | Cooking time: 8 hours | Serves: 8

1 tablespoon olive oil, extra-virgin
4 garlic cloves, crushed
2 celery stalks with greens, chopped
1 sweet onion, quartered
1 carrot, chopped
½ cup chopped parsley
4 thyme sprigs
2 bay leaves
½ teaspoon black peppercorns
½ teaspoon salt
8 cups water

1. Lightly grease the insert of the slow cooker with the olive oil. 2. Place the garlic, celery, onion, carrot, parsley, thyme, bay leaves, peppercorns, and salt in the insert. Add the water. 3. Cover and cook on low for almost 8 hours. 4. Strain the broth through a fine-mesh cheesecloth and throw away the solids. 5. Store the broth in sealed containers in the refrigerator for up to 5 days or in the freezer for up to 1 month.
Per serving: Calories: 41; Total fat 2.1g; Sodium 35mg; Total carbs 5.1g; Fiber 0.1g; Sugars 4g; Protein 0.4g

Herbed Beef Bone Broth

Prep time: 10 minutes | Cooking time: 24 hours | Serves: 8

1 tablespoon olive oil, extra-virgin
2 pounds beef bones with marrow
2 celery stalks with greens, chopped
1 carrot, chopped
1 sweet onion, quartered
4 garlic cloves, crushed
2 tablespoons apple cider vinegar
½ teaspoon whole black peppercorns
½ teaspoon salt
2 bay leaves
5 parsley sprigs
4 thyme sprigs
Water

1. Lightly grease the insert of the slow cooker with the olive oil. 2. Place the beef bones, celery, carrot, onion, garlic, apple cider vinegar, peppercorns, salt, bay leaves, parsley, and thyme in the insert. Add water until the liquid reaches about 1½ inches from the top. 3. Cover and cook on low for almost 24 hours. 4. Strain the broth through a fine-mesh cheesecloth and throw away the solids. 5. Store the broth in sealed containers in the refrigerator for up to 5 days or in the freezer for up to 1 month.
Per serving: Calories: 78; Total fat 8.5g; Sodium 42mg; Total carbs 1.1g; Fiber 0.6g; Sugars 0.1g; Protein 0.4g

Carolina Barbecue Sauce

Prep time: 10 minutes | Cooking time: 3 hours | Serves: 2 cups

3 tablespoons olive oil, extra-virgin
2 (6 ounces) cans tomato paste
½ cup apple cider vinegar
½ cup water
¼ cup granulated erythritol
1 tablespoon smoked paprika
1 teaspoon garlic powder
1 teaspoon onion powder
½ teaspoon chili powder
¼ teaspoon salt

1. Grease the insert of the slow cooker with 1 tablespoon olive oil. 2. In a suitable bowl, beat the tomato paste, remaining olive oil, vinegar, water, erythritol, paprika, garlic powder, onion powder, chili powder, and salt until blended. 3. Pour the prepared mixture into a slow cooker insert. 4. Cover and cook on low for almost 3 hours. 5. After cooling, store the sauce in a container in the refrigerator for up to 2 weeks.
Per serving: Calories: 33; Total fat 3.5g; Sodium 62mg; Total carbs 0.6g; Fiber 0.2g; Sugars 0.1g; Protein 0.2g

Conclusion

If you enjoyed this book or found it helpful, I'd be very grateful if you'd post a short review on Amazon. Your support really does make a difference, and I read all the reviews personally so I can get your feedback and make future books even better.

Thank you for purchasing this book; it was written after much research and experience. I'm delighted to be able to pass on my knowledge to you, the reader. I truly hope that this book will assist you in learning about keto the right way.

The next step is to start implementing the strategies outlined in the Introduction. You have all the necessary information to get started. So, do what needs to be done to start living a healthier, happier life. If you follow a ketogenic diet responsibly, you will not only lose weight but improve your health. Ketogenic meals produce numerous health benefits. So, follow ketogenic, be ketogenic! Thanks again for your support!

Appendix 1 Measurement Conversion Chart

VOLUME EQUIVALENTS (LIQUID)

US STANDARD	US STANDARD (OUNCES)	METRIC (APPROXIMATE)
2 tablespoons	1 fl.oz	30 mL
¼ cup	2 fl.oz	60 mL
½ cup	4 fl.oz	120 mL
1 cup	8 fl.oz	240 mL
1½ cup	12 fl.oz	355 mL
2 cups or 1 pint	16 fl.oz	475 mL
4 cups or 1 quart	32 fl.oz	1 L
1 gallon	128 fl.oz	4 L

VOLUME EQUIVALENTS (DRY)

US STANDARD	METRIC (APPROXIMATE)
⅛ teaspoon	0.5 mL
¼ teaspoon	1 mL
½ teaspoon	2 mL
¾ teaspoon	4 mL
1 teaspoon	5 mL
1 tablespoon	15 mL
¼ cup	59 mL
½ cup	118 mL
¾ cup	177 mL
1 cup	235 mL
2 cups	475 mL
3 cups	700 mL
4 cups	1 L

TEMPERATURES EQUIVALENTS

FAHRENHEIT (F)	CELSIUS (C) (APPROXIMATE)
225 ℉	107℃
250 ℉	120℃
275 ℉	135℃
300 ℉	150℃
325 ℉	160℃
350 ℉	180℃
375 ℉	190℃
400 ℉	205℃
425 ℉	220℃
450 ℉	235℃
475 ℉	245℃
500 ℉	260℃

WEIGHT EQUIVALENTS

US STANDARD	METRIC (APPROXINATE)
1 ounce	28 g
2 ounces	57 g
5 ounces	142 g
10 ounces	284 g
15 ounces	425g
16 ounces (1 pound)	455 g
1.5pounds	680 g
2pounds	907g

Appendix 2 Recipes Index

106 90-Second Bread

A

91 A Go-To Bread!

79 Ahi Tuna Steaks with Bagel Seasoning

46 Alfredo Chicken

93 Alfredo Eggplant Stacks

106 Alfredo Sauce

26 Almond Crackers with Sesame

37 Amazing Cheeseburger Soup

30 Ants On a Log

110 Any-Herb Pesto

98 Apple Crisp

48 Arabic Chicken Shawarma

38 Asian Vegetable Stew

43 Asparagus & Mushroom Nutmeg Stew

42 Autumn Harvest Stew

23 Avocado Breakfast Tacos

49 Avocado Chicken Thigh Chili

30 Avocado Chips

106 Avocado Mayo

17 Avocado Smoothie

107 Avocado-Herb Butter

107 Avocado-Kale Pesto

B

61 Bacon and Blue Cheese Burgers

33 Bacon and Cheese Stuffed Jalapeños

32 Bacon Asparagus

21 Bacon Fritters

36 Bacon It Up Chicken Soup

111 Bacon Jam

55 Bacon Ranch Cheesy Chicken Breasts

90 Bacon-Jalapeño Cheesy "Breadsticks"

31 Bacon-Stuffed Mushrooms

31 Bacon-Wrapped Pickles

30 Bake Kale Chips

85 Baked Haddock

85 Baked Halibut Steak with Herb Sauce

89 Baked Jalapeño and Cheese Cauliflower Mash

86 Baked Keto Halibut

74 Baked Mackerel with Green Veggies

41 Balsamic Beef Stew

48 Balsamic Chicken with Vegetables

43 Balsamic Tofu Stew

49 Barbecued Chicken with Bacon

106 Basic Broth

110 Basic Marinara

109 Basil Dressing

97 Beautiful Chocolate Chip Cookie Cake

59 Beef and Broccoli Foil Packs

108 Beef Bone Broth

108 Beef Stock

39 Beef Veggie Broth

98 Berries Mascarpone

26 Blackened Chicken and Ranch

73 Blackened Salmon

61 Blackened Steak Nuggets

16 Blue Cheese Omelet

21 Blueberry Cake

101 Blueberry Ice Cream

104 Blueberry Smoothie

110 Bolognese Sauce

52 Braised Chicken Thighs

41 Broccoli Cheddar Soup

62 Broiled Lamb Chops with Mint Gremolata and Pan-Fried Zucchini

96 Brown Cookies

97 Brownies

47 Buffalo Chicken Meatballs

39 Buffalo Chicken Soup

32 Buffalo Chicken Thighs

14 Bunless Turkey Burgers

89 Burger Bun for One

46 Butter Chicken

108 Buttermilk Ranch Dressing

107 Butternut Squash "Cheese" Sauce

90 Buttery Mushrooms

101 Buttery Pecan Ice Cream

62 Buttery Pot Roast

72 Buttery Snow Crab Legs

C

64 Cabbage Egg Roll

41 Cabbage Roll Soup

58 Cabbage Rolls

83 Cajun Crab Legs And Veggies

46 Cajun-Crusted Chicken Bites

97 Cake in Olive Oil

99 Candy Almonds

104 Caramel Macchiato

49 Carne Asada Bowls

66 Carnitas

112 Carolina Barbecue Sauce

110 Cashew Hummus

93 Cauliflower Pizza Crust

90 Cauliflower Rice Balls

92 Cauliflower Rice–Stuffed Peppers

104 Cayenne Chocolate Pudding

100 Chai Latte

76 Charred Salmon with Garlic Green Beans

22 Cheddar Breakfast Bake

36 Cheddar Cheesy Soup

30 Cheese Ball

26 Cheese Crackers

46 Cheese Filled Chicken Nuggets

34 Cheeseburgers

60 Cheese-Stuffed Steak Burgers

69 Cheese-Stuffed Tenderloin

36 Cheesy Bacon Keto Soup

22 Cheesy Bacon Quiche

39 Cheesy Bacon Soup

63 Cheesy Bacon Stuffed Pork Chops

89 Cheesy Baked Asparagus

27 Cheesy Broccoli Hot Pockets

93 Cheesy Broccoli Sticks

34 Cheesy Buffalo Chicken Quesadillas

94 Cheesy Cabbage Cribbage

14 Cheesy Cheddar Soufflés

51 Cheesy Chicken Nuggets

49 Cheesy Chicken Tenderloin Packets

16 Cheesy Fat Bombs

85 Cheesy Fried Haddock

32 Cheesy Hangover Homies

15 Cheesy Keto "Hash Browns"

90 Cheesy Loaded Broccoli

81 Cheesy Lobster Tails

16 Cheesy Scrambled Eggs with Greens

59 Cheesy Southwestern Meat Loaf

45 Cheesy Stuffed Chicken

53 Cheesy Turkey Rissoles

28 Cheesy Za'atar Pinwheels

79 Chef's Snapper Veracruz

16 Chia Pudding with Mocha and Coconut

41 Chicken and Cauliflower Rice Soup

36 Chicken and nacho Soup

42 Chicken Bacon Chowder

108 Chicken Bone Broth

53 Chicken Breasts with Mushrooms

55 Chicken Burgers

55 Chicken Cacciatore with Mushroom

39 Chicken Cheese Soup

46 Chicken Cordon Bleu

41 Chicken Cordon Bleu Soup

47 Chicken Curry with Bamboo Shoots

49 Chicken Fajita Stuffed Peppers

47 Chicken Ginger

50 Chicken in Lettuce Cups

25 Chicken Meatballs in Buffalo Sauce

52 Chicken Mole with Black Pepper

38 Chicken Stew with Coconut Cream

51 Chicken Tenders

56 Chicken Thighs with Tangy Lemon Sauce

39 Chicken Veggie Broth

21 Chicken with Waffles

48 Chicken Zucchini "Pasta"

40 Chicken Zucchini Noodle Soup

109 Chimichurri

64 Chipotle Pork Chops

103 Chocolate Almonds

29 Chocolate Coated Apricots

101 Chocolate Coconut Torts

96 Chocolate Doughnut

29 Chocolate Hazelnut Biscotti

17 Chocolate Macadamia Smoothie

103 Chocolate Macaroons

99 Chocolate Peanut Butter Cupcake

99 Chocolate Puddin' Cake

101 Chocolate Pudding

103 Chocolate Tart

101 Chocolate Truffles

101 Chocolaty Cheesecake Bars

15 Chocolaty Chia Pudding

67 Chops with Kalamata Tapenade

37 Cilantro & Lime Soup

107 Cinnamon Butter

80 Citrus-Marinated Tilapia

51 Classical Kung Pao Chicken

78 Classical Salmon Gratin

75 Classical Salmon Poke

32 Classy Crudités with Dip

97 Coconut Cake

100 Coconut Nut Cookies

112 Coconut-Curry Simmer Sauce

84 Cod with Green Pistou

99 Coffee Cake Bites

27 Corn Dog

59 Corn Dogs

111 Crab Sauce

80 Crab-Stuffed Boats

31 Crackers

66 Cranberry Pork Roast

102 Cream Cheese Frosting

89 Creamed Spinach

84 Cream-Poached Trout

49 Creamy Chicken and Spinach Bake

50 Creamy Chicken with Mushrooms

31 Creamy Chipped Artichokes

102 Creamy Coconut Brownies

42 Creamy Enchilada Soup

18 Creamy French Toast

43 Creamy Mixed Vegetable Stew

62 Creamy Mushroom Pot Roast

43 Creamy Mushroom Soup

98 Creamy Shortbread Cookies

54 Creamy Tangy Chicken

40 Creamy Tuscan Soup

99 Crème Brûlée

53 Crispy Bacon-Mushroom Chicken

63 Crispy Baked Pork Chops with Veggie Gravy

25 Crispy Broccoli Salad

94 Crispy Cabbage Steaks

53 Crispy Chicken Thighs

49 Crispy Chicken Thighs with Veggies

80 Crispy Coconut Shrimp

85 Crispy Cod Cakes

92 Crispy Eggplant Rounds

79 Crispy Fish Sticks

82 Crispy Fish with Tartar Sauce

56 Crispy Fried Chicken

84 Crispy Fried Cod Sticks

91 Crispy Green Beans

86 Crispy Haddock

83 Crispy Keto Baked Fish

63 Crispy Pork

28 Crispy Tortilla Chips

29 Crispy Wings

48 Crispy Wrapped Chicken

36 Crunchy Slaw

93 Crustless Spinach and Cheese Frittata

32 Cucumber Salsa

78 Curried Salmon Cakes

D

23 Dark Chocolate Matcha

81 Delicious Cajun Salmon

17 Delicious Carrot Cake Pudding

45 Delicious Chicken Fajita Poppers

46 Delicious Chipotle Drumsticks

32 Delicious Devil Eggs

Delicious Flank Steak with

77 Delicious Glazed Salmon

55 Delicious Jerk Chicken

58 Delicious Mediterranean Meatloaf

97 Delicious Peanut Butter Cookies

64 Delicious Pork Meatballs

81 Delicious Rainbow Salmon Kebabs

36 Delicious Sausage-Sauerkraut Soup

15 Delicious Scotch Eggs

75 Delicious Sesame Salmon

83 Delicious Shrimp Scampi

72 Delicious Shrimp Stir-Fry

98 Delicious Strawberry Shortcake

103 Delicious Swoop Cream

80 Delicious Tuna Cakes

53 Delicious Turkey Meatloaf

15 Deviled Mayo Eggs

65 Dijon Pork Chops

89 Dijon Roast Cabbage

77 Dijon-Ginger Salmon

91 Dinner Rolls

98 Doodles

31 Dragon Tail Poppahs

E

112 Easiest Creamy Caesar Dressing

40 Easy Jalapeño Popper Soup

98 Economical Peanut Butter Pie

22 Egg Casserole

18 Egg Cheese Muffin Sandwiches

15 Egg Cups with Jalapeno

14 Egg Cups with Sausage-Crust

15 Egg Pizza

25 Egg Salad in Avocados

21 Eggs with Avocado Salsa

20 Eggs with Hollandaise Sauce

21 Egg-Stuffed Bell Peppers

14 Egg-Stuffed Meatloaf

111 Enchilada Sauce

100 Energy Booster Drink

F

104 Fast Fudge

90 Faux-Tato" Hash

52 Feta Stuffed Chicken Thighs

73 Fish in Taco Bowls

58 Flank Steak with Chimichurri

91 Flatbread Dippers

18 Flaxseed Piña Colada

73 Foiled Salmon

88 Fried Zuck Patties

G

106 Garlic Aioli

110 Garlic and Herb Marinade

72 Garlic Butter Shrimp with Asparagus

39 Garlic Chicken Soup

89 Garlic Parmesan–Roasted Cauliflower

80 Garlic Scallops

45 Garlicky Dill Wings

75 Garlicky Parmesan Crusted Salmon

46 Garlicky Parmesan Drumsticks

99 German Chocolate Cookie

111 Ghee

75 Ginger Steamed Fish

110 Ginger with Lime Dressing

111 Golden Caramelized Onions

47 Golden Chicken Thighs

74 Golden Coconut Mahi-Mahi

17 Golden Coconut Smoothie

16 Grain-Free Breakfast Cereal

65 Grainy Mustard Sauce

109 Grapefruit-Tarragon Dressing

52 Greek Chicken

40 Greek Egg Soup

25 Green Chicken Meatballs

48 Green Chili Chicken Skewers

17 Green Citrus Smoothie

78 Grilled Salmon Packets

107 Guacamole

H

82 Halibut in a Blanket

86 Halibut with Tangy Basil Sauce

20 Ham Frittata

42 Hamburger Beef Stew

58 Hanger Steak with Herb Cream Sauce

51 Harissa Chicken with Yogurt

108 Harissa Oil

103 Healthy Almond Cookies

15 Healthy Cinnamon Granola

27 Healthy Graham Crackers

37 Healthy Jambalaya Soup

28 Healthy Peanut Butter Cookies

26 Healthy Seedy Crackers

14 Healthy Spinach Omelet

96 Heavenly Chocolate Lava Cakes

93 Herb Cloud Eggs

65 Herb-Braised Pork Chops
65 Herb-Crusted Lamb Chops
109 Herbed Balsamic Dressing
112 Herbed Beef Bone Broth
43 Herbed Broccoli Stew
108 Herbed Chicken Stock
109 Herbed Infused Olive Oil
68 Herbed Lamb Chops
67 Herbed Lamb Racks
112 Herbed Vegetable Broth
45 Herby Chicken Thighs
37 Herby Cucumber Soup
29 Herby Mushroom Galettes
104 Hibiscus Tea
108 Horseradish Butter
79 Hot and Tangy Shrimp
28 Hot Beef Empanadas
54 Hot Chicken Wings
32 Hot Chili-Garlic Wings
100 Hot Cider
25 Hot Jalapeño Poppers

I

86 In Miso Vinaigrette
51 Indian Chicken Tikka Masala
25 Instant Pot Peanuts
82 Instant Shrimp
20 Italian Breakfast
107 Italian Seasoning
39 Italian Soup
65 Italian-Spiced Pork Tenderloin

J

39 Jalapeno & Lime in Shrimp Soup
15 Jalapeño and Bacon Pizza
30 Jalapeño Chips

K

17 Kale Kiwi Smoothie
68 Keto Crusted Lamb Chops
97 Keto Danish
100 Keto Martini
107 Keto Mayonnaise

16 Keto Pancakes
110 Keto Peanut Butter Cups
88 Keto Tater Tots

L

66 Lamb Dogs with Tzatziki
68 Lamb Kebabs with Mint Pesto
67 Lamb Leg with Red Pesto
63 Lamb Sausage
68 Lamb Shanks with Mushrooms
68 Lamb-Vegetable
37 Lasagna Soup
40 Leftover Bone Broth
82 Lemon Butter Cod Steak
92 Lemon Caper Cauliflower Steaks
52 Lemon Chicken and Veggies Stir-Fry
69 Lemon Pork
99 Lemonade Strawberry Shortcake
109 Lemon-Garlic Dressing
48 Lemon-Rosemary Chicken
110 Lemon-Tahini Dressing
55 Lettuce-Wrapped Burger
33 Loaded Chayote Fries
42 Loaded Taco Soup
41 Lobster Bisque
72 Lobster in Mac 'N' Cheese
61 London Broil
18 Low-Carb Pancakes

M

41 Mac & Cheese Stew
74 Macadamia Halibut with Mango Coulis
111 Marinara Sauce
61 Marinated Rib Eye
60 Marinated Steak Kebabs
29 Mascarpone Cheesecakes with Strawberry
20 Mascarpone Pancakes
16 Matcha Smoothie
38 Meat with Vegetable Stew

22 Meatballs
22 Meatballs with Apple Chutney
22 Mexican Breakfast Casserole
61 Mexican-Style Shredded Beef
14 Mini Breakfast Bagels
102 Mini Chocolaty Avocado Tarts
91 Mini Spinach and Sweet Pepper Poppers
103 Minty Chocolate Shake
18 Monkey Bread
19 Morning Doughnuts
48 Moroccan Chicken with Vegetable Tagine
60 Mozzarella-Stuffed Meatloaf
19 Mushroom Cream Crepes
19 Mushroom Quiche
109 Mustard Shallot Vinaigrette
47 Mustard Wings
56 Mustardy Chicken Drumsticks

N

43 No Bean Chili
46 Nut Crusted Chicken Tenders
84 Nut-Crusted Catfish
82 Nut-Crusted Mahi Mahi
77 Nut-Crusted Salmon
102 Nuts Squares
66 Nut-stuffed pork chops
102 Nutty Chocolate Fudge
101 Nutty Chocolate Milkshake
83 Nutty Halibut Curry
73 Nutty Pesto Salmon

O

90 Onion Rings
58 Orange-Herb Pistou
83 Oven-Fried Catfish
89 Oven-Safe Baking Dishes

P

92 Pan Pizza
66 Pancetta-And-Brie–Stuffed Pork Tenderloin

Pan-Fried Salmon and Bok Choy

84 Pan-Fried Shrimp Balls over Garlicky Greens

77 Pan-Seared Garlicky Salmon

88 Parmesan Cauliflower

63 Parmesan Pork Chops

33 Parmesan Zucchini Fries

103 Peanut Butter Bars

96 Peanut Butter Cheesecake

104 Peanut Butter Cheesecake Bites

102 Peanut Butter with Jelly Cookies

106 Peanut Sauce

96 Pecan Cookies

19 Pecan French Toast

76 Pepper-Crusted Salmon

45 Pesto Chicken Pizzas

85 Pesto Flounder with Greens

88 Pesto Pasta

92 Pesto Vegetable Skewers

104 Piña Colada

28 Pizza Muffin

37 Pollo Soup

30 Popcorns

64 Pork Chops in Mushroom Gravy

63 Pork Ribs

66 Pork-and-Sauerkraut Casserole

36 "Potato" Soup

34 Pretzel Bites with Sauce

20 Prosciutto Eggs Benedict

43 Pumpkin Kale Vegetarian Stew

98 Pumpkin Pie Cake

96 Pumpkin Pie with Spiced Pork Rinds

Q

111 Queso Sauce

62 Quick Bratwurst

43 Quick Cream of Asparagus Soup

R

65 Rack of Lamb with Kalamata Tapenade

30 Radish Chips

88 Radish Potatoes

31 Ranch Dorito Crackers

107 Ranch Dressing

109 Ranch Dressing with Buttermilk

109 Ranch Seasoning

29 Raspberry Cookies

40 Red Chili

31 Red Pepper Edamame

112 Red Wine Vinaigrette

74 Redfish with Spicy Crawfish Cream Sauce

100 Refreshing Mint Smoothie

37 Regular Beef Stew

54 Regular Buffalo Chicken

Regular Carrot Cake with

81 Regular Crab Cakes

40 Regular Italian Beef Soup

102 Regular Peanut Butter Cookies

82 Regular Salmon Patties

20 Ricotta Sausage Pie

61 Roast Beef

89 Roasted Asparagus

90 Roasted Broccoli Salad

91 Roasted Brussels Sprouts

54 Roasted Chicken

56 Roasted Chicken Thighs And Zucchini In Wine

84 Roasted Cod with Garlic Butter

111 Roasted Garlic

78 Roasted Herb-Crusted Salmon with Colors

97 Roasted Nut Clusters

Roasted Pork Loin with

77 Roasted Salmon with Olive Salsa

91 Roasted Salsa

75 Roasted Sea Bass

93 Roasted Spaghetti Squash

56 Roasted Whole Chicken with Jicama

55 "Roasted" Duck

67 Rosemary Lamb Chops

62 Rosemary Mint Marinated Lamb Chops

S

72 Salmon Burger

79 Salmon Cakes

77 Salmon in Brown Butter Sauce

75 Salmon in Creamy Sauce

73 Salmon Stuffed Avocado Boats

76 Salmon with Cauliflower Pilaf

77 Salmon with Delicious Tarragon-Dijon Sauce

22 Salmon-Avocado Boats

79 Salmon-Stuffed Mushrooms

104 Salty Pecan Bark

19 Sausage Bread Pudding

17 Sausage Gravy with Biscuits

37 Sausage Soup

21 Sausage Stuffed Peppers

62 Sausage Stuffing with Veggies

26 Savory Cheesy Biscotti

26 Savory Snack

90 Savory Zucchini Boats

85 Seared Cod with Coconut-Mushroom Sauce

74 Seared Mackerel

78 Seared Salmon

52 Sesame Chicken Thighs

76 Sheet Pan Salmon with Beans

38 Shellfish Stock

59 Shepherd's Pie

67 Shepherd's Pie with Cauliflower Mash

83 Shrimp Alfredo and Zoodles

73 Shrimp with Cauliflower Rice

72 Silky Buttered Scallops

96 Silky Chocolate Soufflés

97 Simple Cinnamon Pretzels

59 Slow Cooker Herb-and-Garlic Short Rib Stew

60 Slow Cooker Swedish Meatballs

88 Smashed Cauliflower

54 Smoked Paprika Drumsticks
76 Smoked Salmon Sushi Roll
103 Snicker Bites
81 Southern-Style Catfish Steak
50 Spaghetti Chicken Bowls
53 Spice -Infused Turkey Breast
68 Spiced Curried Lamb
17 Spiced Pear Bars
64 Spiced Pork Loin
81 Spiced Snow Crab Legs
45 Spiced Wings
42 Spicy Bacon Cheeseburger Soup
47 Spicy Blackened Chicken Tenders
61 Spicy Brisket
45 Spicy Chicken with Pork Rind
47 Spicy Chipotle Aioli Wings
38 Spicy Chipotle Chicken Chili
38 Spicy Cilantro Soup
73 Spicy Creamy Shrimp
81 Spicy Fish Bowl
47 Spicy Jerk Chicken Kebabs
52 Spicy Paprika Chicken
92 Spinach and Artichoke–Stuffed Peppers
61 Spinach and Provolone Steak Rolls
21 Spinach Mushroom Quiche
50 Spinach Stuffed Chicken Thighs
111 Spinach-Cheese Spread
106 Sriracha Mayo
33 Steak Bites with Pepper Sauce
60 Steak with Blue Cheese Butter
58 Steak with Broccoli Noodles
94 Steamed Cauliflower
101 Strawberries Coconut Whip
108 Strawberry Butter
100 Strawberry Cheesecakes
103 Strawberry Milkshake
96 Strawberry Pie
34 Stuffed Mushrooms with Burrata
92 Stuffed Portobello Mushrooms
64 Sweet and Spicy Ribs

81 Sweet Buttery Salmon
104 Sweet Iced Tea
91 Sweet Pepper Nachos
26 Sweet Snack
69 Sweet-and-Sour Pork Chops

T

107 Taco Seasoning
107 Tahini Goddess Dressing
51 Tandoori Chicken Vegetable Skewers
72 Tangy Buttery Lobster Tail
50 Tangy Chicken Zoodle Bowls
112 Tangy Citrus-Poppyseed Dressing
74 Tangy Cod
73 Tangy Dill Salmon
45 Tangy Fried Chicken
98 Tangy Lime Bars
64 Tangy Pulled Pork
77 Tangy Salmon and Asparagus
30 Taquitos
27 Tasty Pretzel Bites
67 Tender Lamb Roast
86 Teriyaki Halibut
75 Teriyaki Salmon with Spicy Mayo and Vegetables
38 Texas Chili
86 Thai-Inspired Seafood Chowder
100 Three-Layered Chocolate Cream Cake
31 Tofu Fries
109 Traditional Caesar Dressing
50 Traditional Chicken Teriyaki
25 Traditional Deviled Eggs
32 Traditional El Presidente Guac
79 Traditional Fish Tacos
54 Traditional Hungarian Chicken
56 Traditional Jamaican Jerk Chicken
80 Traditional Lobster Tails
14 Traditional Pancake with Keto Twist

16 Traditional Pumpkin Muffins
78 Traditional Salmon Cakes
22 Traditional Spice Muffins
34 Traditional Spinach-Artichoke Dip
76 Traditional Sushi
53 Tropical Chicken
18 Tropical Coconut Smoothie
78 Tropical Ginger Salmon Burgers
27 Tropical Macaroons
33 Tropical Shrimp Dippers
54 Tropical-Chicken Curry
25 Tuna Filled Deviled Eggs
82 Tuna Tomatoes
68 Tunisian Lamb Ragout
55 Turkey Ragout with Pumpkin
36 Turkey Soup
41 Turkey, Onion & Sage Stew
43 Turmeric Stew
106 Tzatziki

V

92 Vegetable Burgers

W

60 Weeknight Chili
18 Whey Waffles
93 White Cheddar and Mushroom Soufflés
42 White Chicken Chili
63 Wrapped Pork Tenderloin
80 Wrapped Scallops
80 Yummy Italian Baked Cod

Z

38 Zesty Chicken Soup
88 Zucchini Boats
33 Zucchini Chips
21 Zucchini Egg Bake
88 Zucchini Fries
14 Zucchini Frittata
93 Zucchini Fritters

Made in the USA
Las Vegas, NV
27 November 2023